THE STATEHOOD OF PALESTINE

Palestine as a territorial entity has experienced a curious history. Until World War I, Palestine was part of the sprawling Ottoman Empire. After the war, Palestine came under the administration of Great Britain by an arrangement with the League of Nations. In 1948, Israel established itself in part of Palestine's territory, and Egypt and Jordan assumed administration of the remainder. By 1967, Israel took control of the sectors administered by Egypt and Jordan, and by 1988, Palestine reasserted itself as a state. Recent years have seen the international community acknowledging Palestinian statehood as it promotes the goal of two independent states, Israel and Palestine, coexisting peacefully. This book draws on the League of Nations arrangements to show that Palestine was constituted as a state by 1924. Palestine remained a state after 1948, even as its territory underwent permutation. This book provides a detailed account of contemporary international interaction with Palestine to show that Palestine is recognized as a state today.

John Quigley is the President's Club Professor in Law at the Moritz College of Law at The Ohio State University. After earning his A.B., LL.B., and M.A. degrees at Harvard University, he was a research associate at Harvard Law School. He has written extensively in international law, in particular, on the Arab-Israeli conflict.

The Statehood of Palestine

INTERNATIONAL LAW IN THE MIDDLE EAST CONFLICT

John Quigley

Moritz College of Law
The Ohio State University

CAMBRIDGE
UNIVERSITY PRESS

CAMBRIDGE UNIVERSITY PRESS
Cambridge, New York, Melbourne, Madrid, Cape Town,
Singapore, São Paulo, Delhi, Tokyo, Mexico City

Cambridge University Press
32 Avenue of the Americas, New York, NY 10013-2473, USA

www.cambridge.org
Information on this title: www.cambridge.org/9780521151658

First published 2010
Reprinted 2011

A catalog record for this publication is available from the British Library.

Library of Congress Cataloging in Publication Data

Quigley, John B.
  The statehood of Palestine : international law in the Middle East conflict /
  John Quigley.
    p. cm.
  Includes bibliographical references and index.
  ISBN 978-0-521-76811-5 (hardback) – ISBN 978-0-521-15165-8 (pbk.)
  1. Palestine–International status.   2. Palestinian Arabs–Legal status, laws,
  etc. I. Title.
  KZ4282.Q54 2010
  341.26–dc22   2010024606

ISBN 978-0-521-76811-5 Hardback
ISBN 978-0-521-15165-8 Paperback

This book is dedicated to
Ian Brownlie
(1932–2010)
In appreciation for his encouragement of my work
In respect for his contributions to international law
In sadness over his untimely passing

Contents

Preface

Two states living peacefully side by side is said to be the appropriate solution for the Israeli-Palestinian conflict. The major powers repeat this formula to the point that it has become a mantra. As regards Palestine, the meaning of this formula varies according to the speaker. Some assume that Palestine is not yet a state but should become one, when and if agreement is reached with Israel. Others assume that Palestine is already a state. For them, "two states side by side" is shorthand for a call on Israel to leave the Palestine territory it has occupied since 1967.

The identity and character of Palestine have long been an enigma. After World War I, Palestine became one of a number of experimental international entities. A generation later it was rent by conflict as two separate communities fought over it. Then Palestine came apart under three separate foci of control. As the twentieth century neared its end, an effort was made to put some of Palestine back together.

What Palestine was through these permutations is far from obvious. The ambiguity over Palestine's status, in light of its less than ordinary creation and its less than felicitous history, is what prompts the inquiry undertaken in this book. The solution to the puzzle of Palestine's identity and status holds implications for resolving the intractable conflict between Israelis and Palestinians.

Not every reader will be persuaded by the book's conclusion, which is that Palestine became, and remains, a state. At a minimum, it is the author's hope that his examination of Palestine statehood will contribute to clarifying the analysis of the territorial component of the Israeli-Palestinian conundrum.

Columbus, Ohio
August 2010

ix

Note on translations. Passages quoted in the text from sources published in languages other than English have been translated into English by the author.

Acknowledgments

The author's work on this book was facilitated by a research grant at the Moritz College of Law of The Ohio State University and by the supportive research environment provided by the College. Three colleagues in particular at the College provided invaluable counsel. Professor Stanley K. Laughlin advised on microstates, Professor Amy Cohen provided direction to sources on colonialism, and Professor Annecoos Wiersema reviewed a draft of an article that preceded the book manuscript.

The author's inquiry into Palestine's status has required close examination of historical material that was not always readily available. A diligent contingent of research librarians at the College – Linda Poe, Melanie Oberlin, Katherine Hall, and Thomas Sneed – facilitated access to far-flung documents and, importantly, to unpublished documents recently digitized at the National Archives in London.

In a seminar course at the College on the Middle East Conflict, the author's students helped him think through a number of issues. In particular, J.D. candidates Reem Aly and Nikki Swift produced thoughtful research papers on the status of Palestine. Critical assistance with Arabic-language sources was kindly provided by Lina Mounayer, B.A. in Law, Damascus, and an LL.M. candidate at the College. Expertise on computing software was ably provided by Jenny Pursell, Kyle Shutt, and Sharron Tucker of the College staff, and on graphics by Andrea Reinaker.

Attorney Anis F. Kassim, former Editor-in-Chief of the *Palestine Yearbook of International Law*, kindly consulted on the status of Palestine. Professor Stefan Talmon gave guidance on a number of legal issues, and Professor Susan Akram assisted on Arab League sources. The author is grateful for the opportunity to have presented a paper on the topic of this book at a United Nations conference in Geneva,

Switzerland, in July 2009, and for feedback provided by participants in that conference.

The author appreciates the permission granted by the United Nations Cartographic Section to reprint three United Nations maps.

An intellectual debt must be acknowledged to the author's three erstwhile roommates – Robert N. Cable, Daniel R. Pascale, and W. Haywood Burns, who – each in a different way – provided encouragement and inspiration to pursue issues that led eventually to the writing of this book. And a special acknowledgment is due to C. Robert Wells, instructor in English at the St. Louis Country Day School, who is always in my mind as I endeavor to commit my thoughts to writing by the standards of clarity that he demanded.

Table of Cases Cited

Cases are cited in the style used by the particular institution. Abbreviations appearing in the citations are explained on the Abbreviations page.

Abbreviations

The following abbreviations are used in citations.

A	Assembly. See GA (used in documents of General Assembly)
A/CN	a commission of the General Assembly (United Nations)
A/PV	Provisional Verbatim Record of a meeting of the General Assembly (United Nations)
C	Committee (used in documents of committees of the General Assembly of the United Nations)
c.	chapter, preceding number of statute book chapter, Acts of Parliament (United Kingdom)
CAB	Cabinet (United Kingdom National Archives code for documents of the British Cabinet)
Cir.	Circuit Court of Appeals (federal courts of the United States)
Cmd.	Command Paper (United Kingdom, Parliamentary Paper)
CN	Commission (of an organ of the United Nations)
C.P.	Cabinet Paper, used in numbering of documents of the British Cabinet. In the numbers that follow "C.P.", an enclosed two digit number is a year in the twentieth century. A non-enclosed number is the sequential number for the particular year.
Dist.Ct.	District Court (first instance federal court in the United States)
E	Economic. See ECOSOC (used in documents of ECOSOC)
ECOSOC	Economic and Social Council (United Nations)

ECWA	Economic Commission for Western Asia (United Nations)
E.D.	Eastern District (first instance federal court of the United States, located in a state that has more than one federal court district, where one such district is designated as "eastern")
ES	Emergency Special Session (of the General Assembly of the United Nations)
ESCWA	Economic and Social Commission for Western Asia (United Nations)
EWCA	Court of Appeal of England and Wales
F.	Federal Reporter (reports of decisions of Court of Appeals, United States)
FAO	Food and Agriculture Organization (United Nations)
FCA	Federal Court of Australia
FCAFC	Federal Court of Australia Full Court
F.C.R.	Federal Courts Reports (Canada)
F.Supp.	Federal Supplement (reports of decisions of first instance federal courts, United States)
GA	General Assembly (United Nations)
Geo. 5	George V, King, United Kingdom (used in citation to Acts of Parliament during his reign)
H.C.	High Court (Israel)
ICJ	International Court of Justice
K.B.	King's Bench (United Kingdom)
PCIJ	Permanent Court of International Justice
P.D.	Piskei Din (Hebrew "rulings of law" – reports of decisions of the Supreme Court of Israel)
PV	Provisional Verbatim Record of a meeting (United Nations)
LNTS	League of Nations Treaty Series
S	Security. See SC (used in documents of the Security Council)
SC	Security Council (United Nations)
S.D.	Southern District (first instance federal court of the United States, located in a state that has more than one federal court district, where one such district is designated as "southern")

SPC	Special Political Committee of the General Assembly (United Nations)
S/PV	Provisional Verbatim Record of a meeting of the Security Council (United Nations)
SR	Summary Record (of a meeting of a United Nations organ)
ST	Secretariat (used in documents of the Secretariat of the United Nations)
TIAS	Treaties and Other International Acts Series (United States)
UNESCO	United Nations Economic, Social and Cultural Organization
UNIDO	United Nations Industrial Development Organization
UNTS	United Nations Treaty Series
U.S.	United States Supreme Court (in reports of decisions)
U.S.C.	United States Code (legislative acts of US Congress)
WHA	World Health Assembly (policy-making body of WHO)
WHO	World Health Organization (United Nations)

PART ONE

A NEW TYPE OF STATE

I

Why Palestine and Statehood?

In 1996, Yassir Arafat said he planned to declare Palestine a state. Israeli Prime Minister Benjamin Netanyahu threatened that if he did, Israel would reoccupy sectors of the West Bank of the Jordan River that it took in 1967 but turned over to a Palestinian administration under a 1993 agreement. Netanyahu said that a declaration of Palestine statehood would nullify the Israeli-Palestinian agreement.

The strong Israeli reaction underscored the explosive character of the statehood issue in the Israeli-Palestinian relationship. As far as the Israeli government was concerned, Palestine statehood might come at the end of a process of negotiation but not before. If statehood were to materialize for Palestine, it would be on terms negotiated with Israel, which might involve significant constraints on Palestine's freedom of action. Statehood was to be the reward for an agreement in which Israel might gain major concessions in return for recognizing Palestine as a state.

In early 2009, the explosive character of the Palestine statehood issue surfaced in another way. Israel had just invaded the Gaza Strip, incurring criticism for overreaching in its tactics. Television viewers watched as bombs fell on urban communities in densely populated Gaza City. A United Nations storage depot was hit, destroying supplies that were much needed by the civilian population. In the Hague, the International Criminal Court was deluged with missives from human rights organizations suggesting that the bombing might be criminal in nature, as war crimes.

The Court's jurisdiction to investigate war crimes is limited, however. Palestinian officials invoked a clause in the Court's statute that provides for jurisdiction if the state in whose territory the crimes occur files its consent. In the name of Palestine, they gave their consent. It would be valid if Palestine were a state.

3

Suddenly the issue of Palestine statehood loomed large. Statehood for Palestine had been asserted in a 1988 declaration that led to recognition by some states but not by others. The Palestinians were recognized as enjoying a right of self-determination, but it was not clear what that meant. Palestine had been admitted to observer status at the United Nations but not to membership in the organization. Palestinian institutions exercised administrative authority in the territory Palestine claimed, but the Israeli army did as well. In light of these contradictory circumstances, could Palestine be considered a state?

THE CONTEXT OF PALESTINE'S EMERGENCE

Modern Palestine appeared on the international landscape in an unusual manner. Palestine's status was defined by decisions made by the organized international community, decisions that included not only Palestine but also other territories whose fate was at issue during the Great War that would come to be called World War I.

The decisions were made around a conference table outside Paris at the end of that war. The major powers conferred to resolve the status of territories they were wresting from a defeated foe. Palestine was one of those territories.

As will be seen, a decision was made to eschew colonial acquisition in favor of a solution that fell in between colonial rule on the one hand and independence on the other. The status devised for these territories would confound an entire generation of lawyers, who would strain to fit it into the categories known to the law for analyzing territorial arrangements.

STATEHOOD

Beyond the story of how Palestine emerged, any analysis of Palestine's status raises the question of statehood and what it entails. Answering the question of whether Palestine is a state requires an understanding of what it takes to be a state. That exercise draws one into a realm informed in part by legal norms, but also by history and circumstance. Must a putative state have total control over its affairs? Must it be independent? Must it be recognized as a state by the community of nations? Answers to these background questions are not obvious. Strange as it may seem, the international community has not developed hard and fast rules about statehood.

Nonetheless, the law is far from irrelevant. While issues of fact are important, the facts remain to be assessed under rules of law. James Crawford, a student of statehood, calls the creation of a state "a mixed question of law and fact."[1] David Raič, another student of the subject, refers to states as "legal persons."[2] If a state is a "legal person," there must be some way in which a state becomes constituted as such. One finds, in fact, a set of criteria that are said to be the requirements for statehood. These criteria, which will be examined in Chapter 16, contemplate control over a defined population in a defined territory by a government capable of entering into relations with other governments.

Analysts of statehood have raised penetrating questions, however, about whether such a definition comports with reality. Stephen Krasner, for example, deconstructs the sovereign-state model with a blistering attack on its premises. International practice of accepting various entities as states, he avers, does not conform to the idea of a territory ruled by an administration that is universally regarded as representing a state.[3]

If one asks whether Italy is a state, the answer seems obvious. But the international landscape is also dotted with so-called microstates. Some of these, as will be seen in Chapter 19, have little control over their own affairs. A larger, outside state may play a major role in the microstate's affairs. Nonetheless, such entities seem to be states. One finds states in which a government once existed but has ceased to function, leading to anarchy. One also finds states whose territory is occupied by a foreign army.

Even for what one may regard as "obvious" states, the requirements for their statehood often escape ready definition. European states do not control their own affairs in many important spheres of activity. Supranational institutions routinely order the states of Europe to change their policies regarding economic affairs or the observance of human rights.

RECOGNITION

One especially murky concept that invades discussions of statehood is recognition. An entity purporting to be a state must, it is said, be recognized by entities already regarded as states. Some measure of acceptance may be required if an entity is to function effectively as a state. Yet some entities manage with minimal contact with other states. Rhodesia functioned largely on its own from 1965 to 1980, after the major powers decided that the style of rule in Rhodesia violated international standards. If an entity appears to possess the attributes normally associated with statehood, it is, arguably, a state even if other states refuse to deal with it.

If recognition is required, the question arises about how it must be expressed. Must a putative state produce a pack of letters from other states in which they say that they recognize it? Can recognition be presumed from the conduct of states? If states interact with an entity in ways that one finds interaction only among states, can that be taken as recognition? This book will not seek to resolve the many difficult issues surrounding recognition. Yet they cannot be avoided. They will be examined in Chapter 18.

SOVEREIGNTY IN RELATION TO STATEHOOD

A term that causes unease in analyzing statehood is "sovereignty." Diplomats and scholars often use it to mean a condition that inevitably accompanies statehood. It is often taken to express the essence of statehood, after Jean Bodin, who analyzed the concept in the sixteenth century. Bodin wrote that "Sovereignty is the absolute, perpetual power of the state, superior to the laws."[4] Sovereignty is said to be an attribute of the state. A state is said to "enjoy" sovereignty.

The term "sovereignty" is, however, sometimes used to refer to the rights of a people rather than the rights of a state. Thus, a given people is said to enjoy sovereignty within a particular territory. Even as applied to states, the term may have multiple meanings. Krasner identifies four distinct usages. One relates to recognition. Is the entity recognized by other states? If it is, then it is sovereign. A second usage implies that no outside actor controls decision making for the entity purporting to be a state. Only a state that controls its own affairs is sovereign. A third usage Krasner identifies relates to the domestic realm. Does the entity have control over what occurs there, or does one find a general situation of control by various local factions to the exclusion of control by a central authority? The term in this meaning often appears as an adjective modifying the word "control." One speaks of whether a central authority has "sovereign control" over all the territory it claims or, indeed, over any of the territory it claims.

A fourth usage that Krasner identifies is one he calls "interdependence" sovereignty. Does the entity control the flow of persons, goods, and information across its borders? States are sometimes said to have lost "sovereignty" if they cannot control the knowledge flow that comes in digital form. They cannot control public health because of the ease with which persons can move from one place to another. They cannot control their economies because of international capital flows.

These various meanings of the term "sovereignty" might seem to imply that it is held by some single entity with respect to a given territory. Yet one finds suggestions that sovereignty in certain situations may be divisible. In later chapters, certain analysts of the situation of Palestine in the years following World War I will be seen to speak of Palestine's sovereignty as being split.

Krasner cites as an example of ambiguity in the use of the term "sovereignty" the so-called exclusive economic zone. This is an offshore area of ocean space in which a coastal state has the right to control fisheries but not foreign shipping, which it must allow unimpeded.[5] The authoritative international statement on maritime law, the United Nations Convention on the Law of the Sea, recites that the coastal state has

> sovereign rights for the purpose of exploring and exploiting, conserving and managing the natural resources, whether living or non-living, of the waters superjacent to the seabed and of the seabed and its subsoil.[6]

Given that other states have rights of passage for their shipping, the use of the term "sovereign" in regard to natural resources suggests that a state may have sovereignty for some purposes but not for others. One analyst calls this "functional sovereignty."[7] The matter is even murkier when one realizes that even with regard to natural resources, the coastal state's rights, according to maritime law, are not exclusive, even though the UN Convention calls them "sovereign" rights. The Convention makes clear that a coastal state must allow other states to fish in the exclusive economic zone to the extent that the coastal state does not exploit a particular species to the maximum sustainable yield.[8] Hence, the coastal state's "sovereign " right over fisheries is subject to obligations to other states. If a "sovereign" right confers only partial rights, the implication is that sovereignty does not give total control.

In any event, the term "sovereignty" need not be the focus of attention in assessing whether an entity, such as Palestine, is a state. Sovereignty may be a way of describing an entity regarded as a state, but it is not a criterion for statehood.[9] Despite the ambiguities involved in defining "statehood" and "sovereignty," and over whether such recognition is required and what it may mean, it will be suggested that the concept of statehood is not without significance for Palestine. The issue of whether Palestine is a state is more than an exercise in definition and categorization. If Palestine is a state, it may involve itself in the life of the international community in ways that may materially enhance the situation of its people. If Palestine is a state, it may be better positioned to achieve independence. In the early 1990s, when negotiations for a final status with Israel appeared to be close to resolution, the matter was less pressing because it was widely thought that independence would come soon. But nearly two decades on, that independence remains elusive.

While statehood and what it entails form a background for analyzing the status of Palestine, such an analysis of Palestine may in turn help clarify the very meaning of statehood. In particular, the status created for Palestine after World War I involved control by an outside state, yet with attributes for Palestine that arguably were those of a state. If one can speak of statehood in such a situation, then the commonly understood concept of statehood may need revision.

WHAT THIS BOOK IS NOT

The issue of Palestine statehood is separate from the question of what ultimate status Palestine may have. Even if Palestine is not presently a state, it could become one. Moreover, a people, in their exercise of self-determination, may choose to constitute themselves as an independent state if they have the requisite right in a particular territory. Or they may decide on some other arrangement. They may merge with a neighboring state if that is their choice. If Palestine desires to merge with Jordan, or with Israel, or with anyone else, that is a choice it has a right to make, assuming consent on the other side. Palestine statehood need not inevitably lead to an independent Palestine state.

For purposes of this book, the very terminology reflected in the title is problematic. If one refers to "Palestine," is one thereby prejudging the issue of statehood? The United Nations refers to the issue on its agenda as the "Question of Palestine." It calls the observer organization to which it has accorded status "Palestine." In this book, the term "Palestine" is used without meaning to prejudge status.

A reader will find little in this book on the Israeli-Palestinian conflict as such. Was the project of bringing Jews to settle in Palestine a brilliant blow for self-determination or a violation of that very principle? To whom does the territory of Palestine rightfully belong? The story of the conflict between Jew and Arab under British rule and the establishment of Israel in the territory of Palestine has been told by others, and even by this author in his previous books, *Palestine and Israel: A Challenge to Justice* [10] and *The Case for Palestine: An International Law Perspective.*[11] This book restricts itself to the question of statehood as one piece of the larger Israeli-Palestinian puzzle, while hopefully providing enough of the context to make the analysis understandable. Of necessity, the story begins with the Great War that remade the landscape of much of the contemporary world, including the region in which Palestine was to emerge.

2

A Land in Flux

Palestine has long been a territorial designation on the eastern shore of the Mediterranean Ocean. The ancient territory mirrors the expanse that carried the designation Palestine into modern times. In terms of its population, Palestine is one of the most stable areas on the planet. The culture of Palestine's ancient people was impacted by an Arab invasion from the East in the seventh century, which brought to them the Arabic language and the religion of Islam. From 1517, Palestine pertained to the sprawling empire of the Turks, called Ottoman after Othman I, a fourteenth-century Turkish ruler. Under Ottoman administration in Palestine, central governance was weak, leaving the people in the main under their own local rule.[1]

STATEHOOD IN BRITISH ASSURANCES

World War I brought Great Britain and France into conflict with the Ottoman Empire. Britain shared a common objective with Arabs throughout Ottoman territories – the overthrow of Ottoman rule. The British wanted military help from Arabs. The Arabs wanted an assurance of independence once the Ottomans were defeated. Sir Henry McMahon, the British high commissioner in Egypt, communicated about this mutual assistance with a leader of the Arab nationalist movement, Hussein Ibn Ali, Sherif of Mecca. To seal this marriage of convenience, McMahon made a commitment to Arab independence in a letter dated October 24, 1915:

> The two districts of Mersin and Alexandretta, and portions of Syria lying to the west of the districts of Damascus, Homs, Hama and Aleppo, cannot be said to be purely Arab, and should be excluded from the limits demanded. With the above modification, and without prejudice to our

existing treaties with Arab chiefs, we accept those limits. As for those regions lying within the proposed frontiers wherein Great Britain is free to act without detriment to the interests of her ally, France, I am empowered in the name of the Government of Great Britain to give the following assurances and make the following reply to your letter: (1) Subject to the above modifications, Great Britain is prepared to recognise and support the independence of the Arabs in all the regions within the limits demanded by the Sherif of Mecca.[2]

In other words, the British were promising Arab independence after what they anticipated would be a successful military campaign against the Ottomans. But it would be debated whether the assurance of independence expressed in McMahon's letter covered Palestine. Mersina and Alexandretta were excluded because they were seen, appropriately, as belonging to Turkey. McMahon's reference in the letter to the interests of France was related to Lebanon. As would later be said by a Palestine representative, "The portions excluded [from McMahon's commitment] fell within the then French sphere of interest and claims."[3] France had a long-standing connection in Lebanon with a Roman Catholic population called the Maronites, who in the twelfth century had sided with French Crusaders against the Muslims, and for whom France had intervened militarily during civil strife in 1860. France anticipated that the Maronite territory would become a Christian-majority state after the demise of the Ottoman Empire, hence its exclusion from the state that was to be under the Sherif of Mecca.

The term "district" in the letter probably meant the areas immediately surrounding Damascus, Homs, Hama, and Aleppo. All four are located considerably north of Palestine, Damascus being the most southerly. An area "lying to the west" of the surroundings of Damascus would be southern Lebanon, but not Palestine.[4]

Arab leaders understood the letter in this way: They regarded it as a commitment that Palestine would be part of a single large Arab-majority state or one of a group of Arab-majority states. A few years later, the McMahon letter was read to mean precisely that by the Political Intelligence Department of the British Foreign Office. The Department prepared a memorandum on the point for the British delegation at the Versailles peace conference that followed the war. The memorandum, referring to Palestine, read:

H.M.G. [His Majesty's Government] are committed by Sir Henry McMahon's letter to the Sherif on October 24, 1915, to its inclusion in the boundaries of Arab independence.[5]

The same reading was given to the McMahon letter by the Middle East Department of Britain's Colonial Office in a confidential memorandum to the Cabinet dated February 12, 1924:

> The natural meaning of the phrase "west of the district of Damascus," has to be strained in order to cover an area lying considerably to the south as well as to the west of Damascus city.[6]

Notwithstanding the evident understanding within the British government as to the letter's meaning, Britain insisted publicly that the reference to portions of Syria lying west of the Damascus district included the Jerusalem sanjak (district) and hence, that Palestine was outside the area in which McMahon had promised Arab statehood.[7] The disagreement related not to statehood but to whether the state would be an Arab state. As will be seen shortly, Britain soon began to characterize Palestine as a state. The disagreement as to the meaning of the McMahon letter related to the character of the state once Britain began, as it did, to promote a Jewish "national home" in Palestine.[8]

STATEHOOD IN THE SYKES-PICOT TREATY

The Sherif of Mecca, having received Britain's commitments, led an armed revolt against the Ottomans beginning in June 1916.[9] Under the Sherif, Arab forces made serious inroads against Turkish forces.[10] During the war, Britain made still another commitment, this one to France. Britain and France were part of the Entente, the powers allied against the Ottoman Empire. Britain and France agreed, between themselves, to promote an Arab state, or a confederation of states, in the territory to be taken from the Ottoman Empire but reserved a major role for themselves. This understanding came in the agreement of May 16, 1916 called the Sykes-Picot Agreement, named for the British and French representatives who had struck the deal. The arrangement was kept secret at the time because the role Britain and France hoped to reserve for themselves would have angered the Arabs and jeopardized their collaboration. The Sykes-Picot Agreement contemplated statehood for the Ottoman territories, but it was a statehood combined with significant rights for France and Britain. The agreement, which included a map designating different sectors by color, read in part:

> 1. That France and Great Britain are prepared to recognize and protect an independent Arab state or a confederation of Arab states (a) and

(b) marked on the annexed map, under the suzerainty of an Arab chief. That in area (a) France, and in area (b) Great Britain, shall have priority of right of enterprise and local loans. That in area (a) France, and in area (b) Great Britain, shall alone supply advisers or foreign functionaries at the request of the Arab state or confederation of Arab states.

2. That in the blue area France, and in the red area Great Britain, shall be allowed to establish such direct or indirect administration or control as they desire and as they may think fit to arrange with the Arab state or confederation of Arab states.

3. That in the brown area there shall be established an international administration, the form of which is to be decided upon after consultation with Russia, and subsequently in consultation with the other allies, and the representatives of the sheriff of Mecca.[11]

The blue French area was Syria and Lebanon, while the red British area was Jordan and Mesopotamia. The brown area was Palestine. Russia had been consulted and had agreed to the Sykes-Picot text.[12]

The thrust of the Sykes-Picot Agreement would be described years later in a United Nations study, which said that it provided for statehood, with sovereignty in the local populations:

Although the European Powers sought to establish spheres of influence, they recognized that sovereignty would rest with the rulers and people of the Arab territories, and the Sykes-Picot agreement specified recognition of an "independent Arab State" or "confederation of Arab States."[13]

BRITAIN'S ASSURANCES REGARDING WORLD JEWRY

By 1917, the military collaboration with the Arabs had dealt major blows to the Ottoman Empire. But the war was far from over in the Near East or in Europe against the Ottoman ally, Imperial Germany. Britain, while wooing Arab leaders, also saw advantage in courting the World Zionist Organization, a Europe-based Jewish group that had its eye on Palestine as a site for a state for world Jewry. Britain was keen to keep Russia as an ally in the war against Germany. Jews in Russia were on the liberal side of the political spectrum, and many tended toward pacifism. Britain feared that if resistance to Germany waned in the east, Germany might be able to commit more troops in the west.

The Foreign Office made inquiries of Russia's foreign minister whether a declaration by Britain of sympathy for Zionist national aspirations might encourage Russia's Jews to fight for the Entente.[14] Just at that time, April 1917, A.J. Balfour, the foreign secretary, made a visit to the United States. Balfour thought that a move by Britain in support of Zionism might have resonance in the United States as well. According to a note prepared a few years later by the Foreign Office,

> during this visit the policy of the declaration as a war measure seems to have taken more definite shape. It was supposed that American opinion might be favourably influenced if His Majesty's Government gave an assurance that the return of the Jews to Palestine had become a purpose of British policy.[15]

On November 2, 1917, the British cabinet issued a declaration of support for Zionism, conveyed in a letter signed by Balfour. The letter read:

> His Majesty's government view with favour the establishment in Palestine of a national home for the Jewish people, and will use their best endeavours to facilitate the achievement of this object, it being clearly understood that nothing shall be done which may prejudice the civil and religious rights of the existing non-Jewish communities in Palestine, or the rights and political status enjoyed by Jews in any other country.

"The Balfour Declaration," explained Secretary of State for the Colonies Victor Cavendish in 1923, "was a war measure ... designed to secure tangible benefits which it was hoped could contribute to the ultimate victory of the Allies."[16] As described in an internal British government memorandum in 1924, the Balfour Declaration

> had a definite war object. It was designed to enlist on behalf of the Allies the sympathy of influential Jews and Jewish organizations all over the world. The Declaration was published at a time when the military situation was exceedingly critical. Russia had dropped out of the Alliance. Italy appeared to be at her last gasp; and the Germans, freed from anxiety in the East, were massing hugh (sic) forces on the Western front in preparation for the great offensive of 1918. The promise to the Jews was in fact made at a time of acute national danger.[17]

The British government was quick to exploit the Balfour Declaration against Germany. British planes airdropped copies of it over German and Austrian territory, aimed at Jewish soldiers in the armies of the Central Powers. Pamphlets written in Yiddish urged Jewish soldiers to switch sides: "Stop fighting the Allies, who are fighting for you, for all the Jews." "An Allied victory means the Jewish people's return to Zion."[18] A few days after the issuance of the Balfour Declaration, British troops advancing into Palestine from the south took Gaza in heavy fighting. On December 9, 1917, Jerusalem surrendered.[19]

As fighting against the Ottoman Empire, however, continued into 1918, France and Britain were intent on forcing Turkey to give up its territories permanently, in line with Sykes-Picot. But at the same time, they came under pressure to accord some international status to these territories, rather than to absorb them as colonies. Pressure was brought to bear from Russia, from the United States, from within Europe, and from the territories themselves.

LENIN, TROTSKY, AND SELF-DETERMINATION

By 1918, Russia was in the control of the Bolshevik party, which championed the cause of colonial peoples. Vladimir Lenin's new socialist Russia castigated the European powers for exploiting the peoples of Africa and Asia. Anti-imperialism was central to the Bolshevik credo.

Making the issue even more challenging to the European powers, Lenin viewed an end to colonialism as a step toward an end to the capitalist mode of production. In "Imperialism, the Highest Stage of Capitalism," published in early 1917, Lenin analyzed colonialism as a logical extension of capitalism.[20] The peoples of the colonies were victimized, he wrote, as their resources and labor were exploited by the imperialists. The world thus was divided between oppressed nations and oppressor nations.[21] One of the Bolsheviks' first decrees upon assuming power in Russia in November 1917 was a call "to all struggling people and their governments to begin immediate negotiations for a just democratic world."[22] The Bolshevik campaign against capitalism necessarily involved a campaign against colonialism.

Since Imperial Russia had been consulted on Sykes-Picot, the files of the Russian Foreign Office contained a copy of this secret document. The Bolsheviks found it and realized the impact that disclosure could have, since it showed that France and Britain intended a role for themselves in the Ottoman territories. Along with a whole packet of secret wartime treaties, Leon Trotsky, as commissar for foreign affairs, made the Sykes-Picot treaty public and used it to denounce the European powers. Trotsky said that the secret treaties revealed the Entente's "dark plans of conquest."[23]

The impact of the disclosure proved even greater than the Bolsheviks had anticipated. France and Britain attempted damage control. On January 5, 1918, British Prime Minister David Lloyd George said that

Britain was reassessing its plans for a postwar disposition in the Ottoman territories. He said:

> Mesopotamia, Syria and Palestine are in our judgment entitled to a rec-
> ognition of their separate national conditions.... Much has been said
> about the arrangements we have entered into with our Allies on this
> and other subjects. I can only say that as new circumstances like the
> Russian collapse and the separate Russian negotiations [with Germany]
> have changed the conditions under which those arrangements were made,
> we are, and always have been, perfectly ready to discuss them with our
> Allies.[24]

WOODROW WILSON AND SELF-DETERMINATION

Pressure on Britain and France over how they would treat the Ottoman territories came not only from the East, but from across the Atlantic.[25] In a speech to a joint session of the U.S. Congress on January 18, 1918, President Woodrow Wilson declared principles that should guide a post-war settlement. Wilson railed against the Europe-dominated order that he saw as a cause of the Great War. And he denounced secret agreements among the European powers, which included, though he did not name it, Sykes-Picot. As a counterweight to that approach to diplomacy, Wilson demanded, as follows, that the postwar agreements be above board:

> It will be our wish and purpose that the processes of peace, when they
> are begun, shall be absolutely open and that they shall involve and permit
> henceforth no secret understandings of any kind.

In the same breath, Wilson denounced control of foreign territories:

> The day of conquest and aggrandizement is gone by; so is also the day
> of secret covenants entered into in the interest of particular governments
> and likely at some unlooked-for moment to upset the peace of the world.

Then Wilson listed fourteen propositions, which became known as his "fourteen points" for a just postwar order. The first was "Open covenants of peace, openly arrived at, after which there shall be no private international understandings of any kind but diplomacy shall proceed always frankly and in the public view." Wilson's fifth point focused on colonialism. Wilson said:

> A free, open-minded, and absolutely impartial adjustment of all colonial
> claims, based upon a strict observance of the principle that in determining

all such questions of sovereignty the interests of the populations concerned must have equal weight with the equitable claims of the government whose title is to be determined.

In his twelfth point, Wilson dealt specifically with the Ottoman territories, as follows:

The Turkish portions of the present Ottoman Empire should be assured
a secure sovereignty, but the other nationalities which are now under
Turkish rule should be assured an undoubted security of life and an abso-
lutely unmolested opportunity of autonomous development.[26]

Thus, Soviet Russia and America, unlikely allies, combined to pressure Britain and France over the status of territories being wrested from
Turkey.

THE PALESTINE ARAB QUEST FOR INDEPENDENCE

The European powers were accustomed to gaining territory by warfare,
even territory far from their borders. It might have seemed to be the
natural order of things for France and Britain to take Ottoman territories as colonies. Britain and France were under domestic pressure to
extract financial advantage to compensate for the losses they had suffered in the war. Mesopotamia, which would shortly be referred to as
Iraq, was known to hold deposits of oil, a commodity whose utility was
just becoming apparent. In Britain, the idea of taking oil to compensate
for the costs of the war enjoyed a certain popularity.[27]

Internal opposition to the acquisition of colonies was showing itself as
well. In 1902, the British economist J.A. Hobson published his influential
book *Imperialism: A Study* in which he analyzed colonialism as a search
for markets and resources that resulted in domination to the detriment of
local populations.[28] Hobson's ideas would shortly gain currency among
revolutionaries elsewhere in Europe, including the Bolsheviks, who were
intent on overturning the established order. As the Great War drew to a
close, the question was raised in European public opinion as to whether
territorial spoils would go the victors or whether territories being taken,
in particular from the Ottoman Empire, should be set free.

Pressure in the same direction came from inside the Ottoman territories themselves. The populations of these territories expected to be independent once Turkey was defeated. Colonialism was being challenged
everywhere by the peoples living under it.[29] The nationalism that had

swept Europe in the nineteenth century was impacting the areas that
Europe had colonized. The Arabs had helped the Entente, and independence was to be the outcome.

For Palestine, the independence question was complicated by Britain's
support for Zionism. News of the Balfour Declaration filtered through
the region and caused concern as a threat to the Arab majority. If Britain
planned to turn Palestine into something akin to a state for world Jewry,
the promise of Arab independence rang hollow. To make matters worse
from the Arab viewpoint, in April 1918, Britain organized a Zionist
commission to visit Jerusalem. Palestine's Arabs saw that what Britain
had put on paper it intended to implement on the ground. The commission reported to the British government that the Arabs of Palestine
regarded the Zionists as outsiders who were coming to rob them of their
country.[30] To allay Arab concerns, Britain issued a statement in June
1918, declaring,

> [i]n regard to the areas occupied by Allied forces … [i]t is the wish
> and desire of His Majesty's Government that the future government of
> these regions should be based upon the principle of the consent of the
> governed.[31]

An armistice was signed between the Entente and Turkey on October
31, 1918. Sentiment in the region remained strong in favor of an early
withdrawal by the French and British. Faisal, son of Hussein, established
a government in Damascus that soon controlled much of Syria. But the
French and British did not plan to depart. In a statement they circulated in Syria on November 9, 1918, they tried again to assuage local
feelings:

> The object aimed at by France and Great Britain in prosecuting in the
> East the War let loose by the ambition of Germany is the complete and
> definite emancipation of the peoples so long oppressed by the Turks and
> the establishment of national governments and administrations deriv-
> ing their authority from the initiative and free choice of the indigenous
> populations.[32]

At the same time, Britain continued to promote the Jewish aspirations
for Palestine.

In December 1918, Lloyd George gained the private agreement of
French Prime Minister Georges Clemenceau to modify the terms of
Sykes-Picot to put Palestine under British rather than international
administration.[33] At this stage, no definitive decisions were reached, but

it was this private agreement that would set the path toward Britain assuming control in Palestine.

Reflecting concern over Britain's apparent intent to implement the Balfour Declaration in Palestine, a Palestine Arab Congress convened in Jerusalem in January 1919. The major towns of Palestine sent delegations. As protection against Zionism, some delegates wanted Palestine to unite with Syria. Others favored seeking a separate Palestine state and asking for British guarantees against Zionist immigration.[34]

Pressure thus was being exerted on Britain and France from multiple directions to give play to self-determination in the Ottoman territories. In the end, the two allies set a course toward a postwar disposition that would see the Ottoman territories as entities enjoying an international status and protection against exploitation of their resources.

3

A League of Nations

Jan Smuts was a prominent South African political and military figure, and a member of Britain's imperial war cabinet. In December 1918, Smuts penned an outline for an international organization of states. The document came to be called the Smuts Plan for a League of Nations. As Smuts saw it, the projected League would, as one of its functions, deal with the administration of the territories that were being taken from the defeated Central Powers. Smuts saw the Allies' desire for economic reparation as a threat to an appropriate postwar settlement. Referring to the "statesmen of Europe," he said that they

> will be greatly tempted to use their unique opportunity for the aggrandizement of their own peoples and countries. Have they not fought and suffered on an unparalleled scale? And must they quixotically throw away the fruits of victory now that the great opportunity has come?[1]

Smuts saw a countervailing factor at work because the Entente had purported to fight in the name of principle. Smuts wrote:

> [I]f the peace really comes, not in the settlement of universal human principles and the dawning of a better order, but in a return of the old policy of grab and greed and partitions, then the bitterness of the disillusion would indeed be complete.[2]

The new international organization, Smuts said, should ensure that the territories of the defeated powers not be taken as colonies:

> What are these fundamental principles which must guide the league in its territorial policy as the general heir or successor of the defunct empires? They have been summed up for the last two years in the general formula of "No annexations, and the self-determination of nations."[3]

Some of these territories – here Smuts named Finland, Poland, Czechoslovakia, and Yugoslavia – "will probably be found sufficiently capable of statehood to be recognized as independent states of the usual type from the beginning."[4] Others – and here Smuts named Iraq, Syria, and Lebanon – "are as yet deficient in the qualities of statehood" and will "require the guiding hand of some external authority to steady their administration" but would be capable of local autonomy. Still a third group – and here Smuts included Palestine – "owing chiefly to the heterogeneous character of the population" would require administration "to a very large extent by some external authority" to the exclusion of local autonomy. Smuts averted to the circumstance that in Palestine, in his estimation, "the administrative co-operation of the Jewish minority and Arab majority would not be forthcoming."[5]

As to how these territories should be administered, Smuts first considered but discarded the possibility of international administration. Instead, the League should

> nominat[e] a particular state to act for and on behalf of it in the matter, so that, subject to the supervision and ultimate control of the league, the appointment of the necessary officials and the carrying on of the necessary administration should be done by this mandatary state.[6]

The "mandatary" state – a term new to international parlance – would not have "general powers of interference over the affairs of the territory affected" but would be given by the league a "charter, clearly setting forth the policy which the mandatary will have to follow."[7] The "mandatary state," Smuts wrote,

> shall in no case adopt an economic or military policy which will lead to its special national advantage. In fact for all territories which are not completely independent states the policy of the open door, or equal economic opportunity for all, must be laid down.[8]

Smuts drew upon ideas being circulated during the war, prominently a proposal by J.A. Hobson.[9] Building on his 1902 *Imperialism: A Study*, Hobson argued for an "open door," meaning open access to economic activity, as among the European powers. In Hobson's view, an "open door" would reduce conflict among the European powers, since they would not need to contest the right of economic access. To protect indigenous populations from economic exploitation, Hobson advocated international action, either in the form of a "joint international protectorate" to be exercised by an international authority yet to be established, or via "delegation of this duty of protection by this international authority to the Government of some single nation."[10] Smuts opted for the latter.

In 1922 at the University of Vienna, Hersch Lauterpacht wrote a dissertation on the mandate system as it would develop out of Smuts' plan. Lauterpacht analyzed mandates from the legal standpoint but also explained that criticism of colonialism provided much of the inspiration. Lauterpacht wrote that the negative effects of colonialism were obvious by the time of the Great War, and that what he called the "radical attempt" to solve that situation "with guarantees and safeguards, thus lay not only in the passing political circumstances of the Peace Conference, and in the conceptions of Wilson, Smuts and others, but also in the spirit of the time and its demands."[11]

Smuts referred to the territories that would be entrusted to a "mandatary" as "not completely independent states." They would be states, but only partially independent. Others of these territories would be states, and independent. Smuts wrote:

> Many of the states which arise from the break-up of the empires will be able to look after their own affairs as new independent states, and will not require administrative assistance or control.[12]

Thus, Smuts' approach, grounded in skepticism about colonialism, was that all the territories being formed from the breakup of the empires of the Central Powers would be "states," but that some would become independent immediately, whereas others would require oversight.

STATEHOOD IN A BRITISH DRAFT CONVENTION ON MANDATES

The British government was already drafting language to characterize the relationships that would come about. Its thinking about statehood mirrored Smuts'. On January 24, 1919, Britain circulated a Draft Convention Regarding Mandates, which it conceived as a multilateral treaty to cover all the territories being separated from the Central Powers. The Draft Convention introduced the idea that not all the mandate territories would enjoy the same status. The Draft Convention divided the territories into two categories. One category was labeled "vested territories." In these, "the States placed in charge" would be invested with "all powers and rights of a sovereign government" but would report annually to the League of Nations. They would hold the territory "upon trust to afford to their inhabitants peace, order and good government," with no expectation of eventual independence.

A second category was labeled "assisted states," which were conceived as entities to be brought to independence. According to the Draft Convention,

> 2. The High Contracting Parties further agree that all the territories named in the protocol hereto as "assisted States" which in consequence of the late war are to attain their independence, shall be entitled to such assistance as they may desire for the purpose of securing peace, order and good government for the population of those states and may for the purpose of obtaining such assistance select in concert with the Council of the League of Nations some state member of the League as assisting power unless under any convention in connection with the Peace Treaty an assisting power has already been assigned to them.

The Draft Convention further provided that the prerogatives of the "assisting States" would be determined by agreement with the "assisted State." Thus,

> 6. In respect of assisted States the assisting States shall be invested with such powers, rights, duties, and responsibilities as shall be given to them by any agreements with the Assisted States, and they shall report the terms of such agreements to the League of Nations and shall also make a report every year to the League showing the steps taken to carry out those terms.[13]

The Draft Convention characterized the territories that were to become "assisted states" as those that "in consequence of the late war are to attain their independence."[14] The Draft Convention's reference to "assisted States" was a reference to the Ottoman territories, even though the Draft Convention made no mention of specific geographic entities. The Draft Convention conceived of the Ottoman territories as states immediately upon the anticipated establishment of mandates over them.

The British formulation about mandates was revised at a meeting on January 30, 1919 of the Council of Ten, a grouping of major powers at the Versailles conference. It was in that revision that language was written to deal with mandates over the territories of the Central Powers as an article of the League of Nations founding document, then in draft stage, rather than in a separate treaty.[15] In the revision of January 30, 1919 the two categories of mandate territory were expanded to three. What in the Draft Convention Regarding Mandates had been characterized as "assisted states," namely, those that "are to attain their independence," were referred to in the January 30, 1919 revision as "certain communities formerly belonging to the Turkish Empire that have reached a stage of development where their existence as independent nations can be provisionally recognized."[16] This language would be carried over into the final draft of the League's founding document.

STATEHOOD IN THE LEAGUE OF NATIONS COVENANT

The finalizing of the founding document, which would be called a covenant, took place against a backdrop of events in Europe that even further inclined the assembled leaders toward an anticolonial position in regard to the territories being taken from the Central Powers. In spring 1919, additional pressure was building on the European powers to promote the interests of local populations. Leftist elements in Europe were spreading Bolshevism westward, challenging the prevailing capitalist-oriented governments. Worker riots in Berlin were followed by a briefly successful communist coup in Bavaria. The government of Hungary fell in a Bolshevik-inspired revolt. The threat of Bolshevism made the challenge of the calls by Lenin and Trotsky for the rights of working people all the more compelling.

In response, the European leaders at Versailles took action on two fronts. One was to create an International Labor Organization to promote worker rights. The leaders hoped to blunt worker movements in central and western Europe and thereby avert more anticapitalist revolts. A treaty, denominated the Constitution of the International Labor Organization, was adopted on June 28, 1919, as part of the Treaty of Peace with Germany.[17]

A second response was finalization of the plans for the territories of the Central Powers. Again as part of the Treaty of Peace with Germany, on June 28, 1919, the text was adopted of a Covenant for the League of Nations.[18] Article 22 of the Covenant followed the Council of Ten draft. Its fourth paragraph reproduced, practically verbatim, the language of the Council of Ten draft. Article 22 read:

1. To those colonies and territories which as a consequence of the late war have ceased to be under the sovereignty of the States which formerly governed them and which are inhabited by peoples not yet able to stand by themselves under the strenuous conditions of the modern world, there should be applied the principle that the well-being and development of such peoples form a sacred trust of civilisation and that securities for the performance of this trust should be embodied in this Covenant.

2. The best method of giving practical effect to this principle is that the tutelage of such peoples should be entrusted to advanced nations who

by reason of their resources, their experience or their geographical position can best undertake this responsibility, and who are willing to accept it, and that this tutelage should be exercised by them as Mandatories on behalf of the League.

3. The character of the mandate must differ according to the stage of the development of the people, the geographical situation of the territory, its economic conditions and other similar circumstances.

4. Certain communities formerly belonging to the Turkish Empire have reached a stage of development where their existence as independent nations can be provisionally recognized subject to the rendering of administrative advice and assistance by a Mandatory until such time as they are able to stand alone. The wishes of these communities must be a principal consideration in the selection of the Mandatory.

5. Other peoples, especially those of Central Africa, are at such a stage that the Mandatory must be responsible for the administration of the territory under conditions which will guarantee freedom of conscience and religion, subject only to the maintenance of public order and morals, the prohibition of abuses such as the slave trade, the arms traffic and the liquor traffic, and the prevention of the establishment of fortifications or military and naval bases and of military training of the natives for other than police purposes and the defence of territory, and will also secure equal opportunities for the trade and commerce of other Members of the League.

6. There are territories, such as South-West Africa and certain of the South Pacific Islands, which, owing to the sparseness of their population, or their small size, or their remoteness from the centres of civilisation, or their geographical contiguity to the territory of the Mandatory, and other circumstances, can be best administered under the laws of the Mandatory as integral portions of its territory, subject to the safeguards above mentioned in the interests of the indigenous population.

7. In every case of mandate, the Mandatory shall render to the Council an annual report in reference to the territory committed to its charge.

8. The degree of authority, control, or administration to be exercised by the Mandatory shall, if not previously agreed upon by the Members of the League, be explicitly defined in each case by the Council.

9. A permanent Commission shall be constituted to receive and examine the annual reports of the Mandatories and to advise the Council on all matters relating to the observance of the mandates.

The English spelling "mandatary" was replaced with "mandatory." The three categories of mandate territory were defined in paragraphs 4, 5, and 6. At a meeting of experts from the Allied powers in London in July

1919, chaired by Alfred Milner, the British colonial secretary, the three categories were, for convenience sake, designated by letters: mandates of Class A, Class B, and Class C.[19] The Class A territories were those regarded as closest to independence, hence "provisionally recognized" as such. These were the territories being detached from Turkey (paragraph 4), which included Palestine.[20] The Class C territories were the farthest from independence and were to be administered under the law of the mandatory power (paragraph 6). The Class B territories, all in "Central Africa" (paragraph 5), fell in between in terms of their status. Six territories would be constituted as Class B mandates – British Togo, British Cameroons, Tanganyika, Belgian East Africa, French Togo, French Cameroons.[21]

The paragraph 4 text on Class A mandates defined them in terminology that differed from that of Britain's Draft Convention Regarding Mandates. Whereas the Draft Convention had characterized the territories closest to independence as "assisted States," paragraph 4 referred to "communities" being provisionally recognized as "independent nations." Some lawyers would take this terminology to mean that it was the populations, rather than the territories, that were being provisionally recognized as independent.[22]

However, the reference to "communities" and to "independent nations" was understood by the Allies who set up the mandate system to mean the territories, not the peoples. Balfour read "independent nations" in this way: quoting Covenant Article 22(4) in an August 11, 1919 memorandum to George Curzon, who would soon replace him as foreign secretary, Balfour referred to "the 'independent nation' of Palestine, and the 'independent nation' of Syria."[23]

This reading of Covenant Article 22(4) did no damage to the text. The Class A mandate territories were being recognized, provisionally, as "independent nations." "Nation" is commonly used in the sense of "state," and that is how it was used in Covenant Article 22(4). That usage of the term "nation" was reflected, not incidentally, in the title of the organization being established by the Covenant. The title was "League of Nations." The League was an association of states. In the title of the organization, "nations" meant "nation states." The same is true for the use of "nations" in Covenant Article 22(4).

The phrase "independent nations" in Covenant Article 22(4) has been widely understood in this fashion, namely, to mean that the territorial entities were being recognized. "Underlying Article 22," wrote H. Duncan Hall, a League Secretariat official who dealt with mandates, "was the assumption of independent national sovereignty for mandates.... The assumption of sovereignty was immediate for 'A' territories (as the terms of Article 22, paragraph 4, indicated)."[24] D.P. O'Connell, a leading legal analyst, wrote that "[t]he Class 'A' mandates ... were described in the Covenant of the League of Nations as 'independent nations.'"[25] In a UN Security Council debate in 1948, Egypt construed Covenant Article 22(4) as meaning that "Palestine was provisionally recognized as an independent nation."[26] Shabtai Rosenne was legal adviser to the Foreign Ministry of Israel in the early years of the Israeli state. In 1950, Rosenne wrote, "The statehood of the territories formerly part of Asiatic Turkey was provisionally recognized, but not their independence."[27]

An Egyptian court, in a 1927 case, read Article 22(4) to mean that it was the territories that were recognized as provisionally independent and that they were, under the mandate system, states. The case concerned inhabitants of Syria and Lebanon, and what nationality they held. Referring to the Covenant as a source of law on the issue, the court stated that

> Syria and the Lebanon, being countries placed under an "A" Mandate, are, in accordance with the Covenant of the League of Nations [an apparent reference to Article 22(4)], to be deemed to be independent States and persons of public international law and the inhabitants have acquired the nationality of those States.[28]

In a case involving the status of Palestine, a U.S. court in 2005 read Covenant Article 22(4) the same way, stating that

> Palestine was among those territories deemed to "have reached a stage of development where their existence as independent nations [could] be provisionally recognized."[29]

Covenant Article 22(4) meant that the Class A mandate territories were states. These states were not yet independent, but their independence was being recognized provisionally during the period of tutelage. Independence would follow at the termination of the mandate. By treating the mandate territories as states, Covenant Article 22(4) was employing a concept of "state" that did not require present independence.

LOCAL REACTION TO MANDATE STATEHOOD

Covenant Article 22(4) set up statehood, but because it did not contemplate immediate independence, the prospect of a mandate over Palestine found little favor with its Arab population. Aware of Britain's intention to back Zionism, the Arabs of Palestine feared that they might never achieve independence, particularly if Britain got the mandate over Palestine.

As noted, substantial sentiment was expressed in Palestine in favor of uniting with Syria on the rationale that a single larger, stronger state might be better positioned to resist Zionism. On July 2, 1919, the General Syrian Congress, meeting in Damascus, adopted a resolution demanding immediate independence for a Syria that was to include Palestine. Covenant Article 22, the resolution declared, "relegates us to the standing of insufficiently developed races requiring the tutelage of a mandatory power."[30]

In the wake of the adoption of the Covenant, President Wilson sent a U.S. fact-finding commission to Palestine to ascertain popular sentiment. When it returned in August 1919, the King-Crane Commission recommended a mandate for a Syrian state, to include both Lebanon and Palestine. The commissioners said that the mandate should go to the United States, which they found the Palestine Arabs to prefer over Britain, but in the event the United States declined, they said, then the mandate could go to Britain. The commissioners recommended against what they termed the "extreme Zionist program" because they found that Palestine Arab concern over Zionist aims was so deep that military force might be required to implement them.[31]

On March 8, 1920, the General Syrian Congress proclaimed Syria, including Lebanon and Palestine, to be a sovereign independent state. Faisal, who was highly regarded for having led the successful Arab military effort against Turkey, was elected King.[32]

STATEHOOD IN THE ALLIES' SAN REMO RESOLUTION

Before the mandate system could be implemented, particular outside states had to be assigned as mandatories. The League of Nations left that task to the Allies. In the spring of 1920, the Allies made plans for a conference for that purpose. Britain was eying Palestine, and even before the conference began, the British government had drafted language for the mandate that it hoped to gain over Palestine. It considered using the term "commonwealth" to describe the entity that would eventually emerge after Zionist immigration. Eric Graham Forbes Adam, who would shortly represent Britain at the Allied conference, penned a memorandum on March 18, 1920 to Curzon in which he explained,

The use of the phrase [commonwealth] did not, to our mind, imply any acceptance in the mandate of the Jewish idea that the Palestinian state set up by the mandate would ever become a Jewish state.[33]

The term "commonwealth" would not survive the drafting process, but what is telling in Adam's wording is his reference to "the Palestinian state set up by the mandate." That phrase reflected his understanding that the mandate entity, on being created, would immediately be a state.

On April 2, 1920, Herbert Samuel, who would shortly assume the post of high commissioner for Britain in Palestine, similarly indicated that Palestine would be a state when the mandate went into effect. Samuel wrote a proposal to Curzon for a territorial disposition in the former Ottoman territories. Samuel anticipated "[f]ive states to be constituted." Palestine, as one of the five, would, in Samuel's contemplation, be "administered by Great Britain under a mandate and subject to the general supervision of the League of Nations."[34]

The Supreme Council of the Allied and Associated Powers (Britain, France, Italy, Japan) held its meeting in San Remo, Italy. On 25 April 1920, the Council approved mandates for Britain in Iraq and Palestine (including Transjordan), and for France in Syria (including Lebanon). In their resolution, the Allies agreed

(a) To accept the terms of the mandates article as given below with reference to Palestine, on the understanding that there was inserted in the *procès-verbal* an undertaking by the mandatory Power that this would not involve the surrender of the rights hitherto enjoyed by the non-Jewish communities in Palestine; ...

(b) That the terms of the mandates article should be as follows:
The High Contracting Parties agree that Syria and Mesopotamia shall, in accordance with the fourth paragraph of Article 22, Part I (Covenant of the League of Nations), be provisionally recognised as independent States, subject to the rendering of administrative advice and assistance by a mandatory until such time as they are able to stand alone. The boundaries of the said States will be determined, and the selection of the Mandatories made, by the Principal Allied Powers.

The High Contracting Parties agree to entrust, by application of the provisions of Article 22, the administration of Palestine, within such boundaries as may be determined by the Principal Allied Powers, to a mandatory, to be selected by the said Powers. The mandatory will be responsible for putting into effect the declaration originally made on the 8th [2nd] November, 1917, by the British Government, and adopted by the other Allied Powers, in favour of the establishment in Palestine

of a national home for the Jewish people, it being clearly understood
that nothing shall be done which may prejudice the civil and religious
rights of existing non-Jewish communities in Palestine, or the rights
and political status enjoyed by Jews in any other country: ...

   The terms of the mandates in respect of the above territories will
be formulated by the Principal Allied Powers and submitted to the
Council of the League of Nations for approval....

(c) The mandatories selected by the Principal Allied Powers are: France
for Syria, and Great Britain for Mesopotamia, and Palestine.[35]

The provision on Palestine thus read differently from the provision
on Syria and Mesopotamia and omitted reference to any provisional
recognition of Palestine as an independent state. The provision on
Palestine read differently for the apparent reason that the mandatory
would administer, hence the thrust of the provision was to make that
point clear. In any event, the understanding of the resolution was that
all the Class A mandates were states. Before leaving San Remo, Curzon
telegraphed a memorandum to the Foreign Office in London to explain
the San Remo decisions. In explaining to the Foreign Office how the
boundaries between the mandate territories would be fixed, Curzon
wrote that "[t]he boundaries of these States will not be included in the
Peace Treaty [with Turkey] but are also to be determined by the principal
Allied Powers."[36] Curzon thus referred to the Class A mandate territories
as states.

   A few weeks later, Britain's King George reflected the same understanding of Palestine as a state in a message, dated July 7, 1920, "to the
people of Palestine." He said,

   The Allied Powers whose Arms were victorious in the late War have
   entrusted to My Country a Mandate to watch over the interests of
   Palestine and to ensure to your Country that peace and prosperous development which has so long been denied to you.[37]

King George used "country," a more evocative if less precise a term
than "state," but what he clearly meant to convey to the population was
that he regarded Palestine as a state.

   Palestine would be a state, as Herbert Samuel said, even though its
administration was entrusted to Great Britain. In preparation for the
anticipated mandate, Britain sent Samuel as high commissioner to
Palestine, in July 1920, to replace Britain's military administration with
a civilian administration.[38] Formally, Britain was still a belligerent occupant, but it would govern through civilians.[39] The Arabs of Palestine

continued to protest Britain's sponsorship of the Zionist project. The Faisal government in Damascus sought to help them. Undeterred by the Allies' allocation of Palestine to Britain at San Remo, the Faisal government adopted a constitution on July 3, 1920 for a Syria that was to encompass Lebanon, Transjordan, and Palestine. Faisal's government was short-lived, however. France demanded that he acknowledge France as mandatory in Syria. When Faisal refused, French troops occupied Damascus and displaced him.[40]

4

A State Detached

What was lacking in the summer of 1920 before the mandate system could actually be implemented was a peace treaty with Turkey. Although it had been driven out of its territories, Turkey had yet to give them up in a formal sense. In August 1920, the Allies signed with Turkey what they hoped would be a peace treaty, a document by which Turkey relinquished its territories outside Turkey itself. The Treaty of Sèvres of August 10, 1920 tracked Covenant Article 22 and the San Remo decisions on the future status of these territories. France was to be a mandatory in Syria, Britain in Palestine and Mesopotamia. The treaty included a section headed "Syria, Mesopotamia, Palestine," which read, in part:

> Article 94. The High Contracting Parties agree that Syria and Mesopotamia shall, in accordance with the fourth paragraph of Article 22, Part I (Covenant of the League of Nations), be provisionally recognised as independent States subject to the rendering of administrative advice and assistance by a Mandatory until such time as they are able to stand alone.
>
> A Commission shall be constituted within fifteen days from the coming into force of the present Treaty to trace on the spot the frontier line described in Article 27, II (2) and (3). This Commission will be composed of three members nominated by France, Great Britain and Italy respectively, and one member nominated by Turkey; it will be assisted by a representative of Syria for the Syrian frontier, and by a representative of Mesopotamia for the Mesopotamian frontier. The determination of the other frontiers of the said States, and the selection of the Mandatories, will be made by the Principal Allied Powers.
>
> Article 95. The High Contracting Parties agree to entrust, by application of the provisions of Article 22, the administration of Palestine, within

such boundaries as may be determined by the Principal Allied Powers, to a Mandatory to be selected by the said Powers. The Mandatory will be responsible for putting into effect the declaration originally made on November 2, 1917, by the British Government, and adopted by the other Allied Powers, in favour of the establishment in Palestine of a national home for the Jewish people, it being clearly understood that nothing shall be done which may prejudice the civil and religious rights of existing non-Jewish communities in Palestine, or the rights and political status enjoyed by Jews in any other country.

The Mandatory undertakes to appoint as soon as possible a special Commission to study and regulate all questions and claims relating to the different religious communities. In the composition of this Commission the religious interests concerned will be taken into account. The Chairman of the Commission will be appointed by the Council of the League of Nations.

Article 96. The terms of the mandates in respect of the above territories will be formulated by the Principal Allied Powers and submitted to the Council of the League of Nations for approval.[1]

Thus, by Article 94, reference is made to the fact that Syria and Mesopotamia, under Covenant Article 22(4), were provisionally being recognized as independent states. Where Covenant Article 22(4) reads that "communities" are being provisionally recognized, Article 94 substitutes the names of the states (Syria and Mesopotamia). Where Covenant Article 22(4) reads "independent nations," Article 94 substitutes "independent states." This wording indicated that the Allies understood Covenant Article 22(4) to say that the Class A mandate territories, as opposed to their peoples, were being provisionally recognized, and that they were being provisionally recognized as independent states.

The provision on Palestine (Article 95) did not, to be sure, use the term "state." However, the usage in Article 94 is an interpretation of Covenant Article 22(4), which applied to Palestine as a Class A mandate. Moreover, in other provisions, the Treaty of Sèvres referred to all the territories detached from Turkey as states, thus including Palestine.[2] In its provisions on the nationality of inhabitants, for example, the Treaty of Sèvres referred to the territories being detached as states. Ottoman nationals would become nationals of the "states" that were formed from Ottoman territory:

Article 123. Turkish subjects habitually resident in territory which in accordance with the provisions of the present Treaty is detached from

Turkey will become ipso facto, in the conditions laid down by the local law, nationals of the State to which such territory is transferred.

Under the Turkish Nationality Law of 1869, inhabitants of Palestine were "Ottoman nationals."[3] An article in the Treaty of Sèvres on Ottoman property similarly provided for its transfer to "states." It read:

> Article 240. States in whose favour territory is detached from Turkey shall acquire without payment all property and possessions situated therein registered in the name of the Turkish Empire or of the Civil List.

An article on assumption of the Ottoman public debt also referred to "states." That article read:

> Article 241. States in whose favour territory has been detached from Turkey ... under the present Treaty, shall participate in the annual charge for the service of the Ottoman Public Debt contracted before November 1, 1914.... The Governments of the States of the Balkan Peninsula and the newly-created States in Asia in favour of whom such territory has been or is detached from Turkey shall give adequate guarantees for the payment of the share of the above annual charge allotted to them respectively.

As will be seen shortly, the Treaty of Sèvres would not be ratified, hence never came into force. Nonetheless, the fact that these provisions were drafted by the Allies reflected their position that the Class A mandates, including Palestine, were states.

STATEHOOD IN THE PALESTINE MANDATE INSTRUMENT

Even though instruments for the mandates had yet to be approved, the League of Nations made preparations for its supervisory role. On November 29, 1920, the Council of the League of Nations approved a constitution for a Permanent Mandates Commission, which was to monitor the conduct of the mandatory powers.[4] The mandatory powers were to report to the Commission on their progress in fulfilling their obligations. France and Britain, in anticipation of commencing administration, concluded a treaty delineating the borders of Palestine, Syria, Lebanon, and Iraq.[5]

Even as the Treaty of Sèvres awaited ratification, Britain went ahead with the drafting of a mandate instrument. The Foreign Office took the lead, with input from the Inter-Departmental Conference, Board of Trade, War Office, and India Office. The Zionist leaders who had lobbied for the Balfour Declaration were consulted. They made proposals for specific language to be included. Britain shared early drafts with the

Allies. On November 30, 1920, Curzon alerted the Cabinet that France and Italy had complained in regard to an early draft that Arab rights were being ignored. France and Italy objected to a draft preamble clause that read:

> Recognising the historical connection of the Jewish people with Palestine and the claim which this gives them to reconstitute Palestine as their National Home.

This formulation, which Britain never made public, would have altered the Balfour Declaration phrasing about a national home in Palestine to read that the whole of Palestine was to become the national home. The draft was changed to reflect the Balfour Declaration phrasing.[6]

Herbert Samuel, from his post as high commissioner in Jerusalem, proposed language about the finances of Palestine. Curzon duly informed the Cabinet that

> During the last few hours a telegram has been received from Sir H. Samuel, urging that, in order to facilitate the raising of loans by the Palestine Administration, which will otherwise be impossible, words should be added to Article 27, providing that on the termination of the Mandate, the future Government of Palestine shall fully honour the financial obligations incurred by the Palestinian Administration during the period of the Mandate. This appears to be a quite reasonable demand, and I have accordingly added words (italicised at the end of Article 27) in order to meet it.[7]

Samuel was concerned that Palestine would be hard pressed to borrow funds if lenders worried that upon termination of the mandate the loans might not be repaid. His proposal was incorporated in what eventually became, not Article 27, but Article 28. This provision reflected the separate status of Palestine over and against Britain, hence reinforcing its separate statehood. Upon termination of the mandate, the Government of Palestine, not the Government of Great Britain, would be obligated to Palestine's creditors. The finances of Palestine were being established on the basis of Palestine being a state separate from Britain and solely responsible on its financial obligations.[8]

Britain submitted a draft of the mandate instrument to the League of Nations on December 7, 1920 and used the following formulation for the basic powers it would enjoy as mandatory in Palestine:

> Article 1. His Britannic Majesty shall have the right to exercise as Mandatory all the powers inherent in the government of a Sovereign State, save as they may be limited by the terms of the present Mandate.[9]

This formulation would be dropped in the final text of the mandate instrument, but Jacob Stoyanovsky at the University of Paris, who had just written his dissertation on the mandate system, read it as confirming that Britain would not hold sovereignty in Palestine, since limitations would be imposed.[10] The concept of the role of a mandatory power – a concept that would be reflected in the final text – was that it was to enjoy only such powers as were specified.

While Britain drafted, sentiment continued to build in Palestine against Britain as a potential mandatory power. When Winston Churchill, as Secretary of State for the Colonies, visited Palestine in March 1921, the Palestine Arab Congress gave him a memorandum titled *Report on the State of Palestine* to express their concerns. They sent a copy to the President of the League of Nations. "It is the idea of transforming Palestine into a home for the Jews," they wrote, "that Arabs resent and fight against."[11] In reply, Churchill defended Britain's policy of promoting Zionism and Zionist immigration to Palestine. Palestine Arabs were not convinced. When Samuel, as high commissioner, visited the Jordan Valley the following month, he was greeted by banners proclaiming, "Palestine is our country" and "Down with Zionism."[12]

The City of Jaffa was the port of entry for Jews migrating to Palestine. On May 1, 1921, a group of Arabs attacked Jews in the streets there, in an "explosion of popular sentiment," as the Palestine administration reported to London. Churchill's visit, and his dismissal of Arab concerns, a British intelligence officer wrote, "put the final touch to the picture."[13] Churchill, too, got the message. On August 11, 1921, in a confidential memorandum, he reported to the Cabinet that

> [t]he Zionist policy is profoundly unpopular with all except the Zionists. Both Arabs and Jews are armed and arming, ready to spring at each other's throats.[14]

That same month, a delegation from the Palestine Arab Congress traveled to London and asked for repeal of the Balfour Declaration and for the convening of a national assembly in Palestine.[15] On August 18, 1921, the British Cabinet discussed those possibilities but decided against them. Foreign Office officials told the Arab delegation that Britain would not change course.[16]

In September 1921, the Palestine Arab Congress delegation proceeded from London to Geneva, where the Council of the League was meeting. There it met with Balfour.[17] The delegation told League officials that the Arabs of Palestine opposed the terms of the draft Palestine Mandate, in particular an article that called for implementation of the Balfour Declaration.[18] When it became clear that the draft instrument would not be altered, the delegation asked the League not to confirm the mandate for Britain.[19]

The Council of the League went ahead, however, with allocation of the mandates as they had been determined by the Allies at San Remo. In anticipation of an eventual peace treaty with Turkey, the Council approved the Palestine Mandate on July 24, 1922, as an agreement between the League and Britain. Like the other mandate instruments approved by the League, the Palestine Mandate was a treaty. "The contracting parties" were "on one side, the League of Nations represented by its Council, and, on the other side, the mandatory powers."[20] The preamble and the key provisions relevant to Palestine's status read as follows:

> The Council of the League of Nations: Whereas the Principal Allied Powers have agreed, for the purpose of giving effect to the provisions of Article 22 of the Covenant of the League of Nations, to entrust to a Mandatory selected by the said Powers the administration of the territory of Palestine, which formerly belonged to the Turkish Empire, within such boundaries as may be fixed by them; and

> Whereas the Principal Allied Powers have also agreed that the Mandatory should be responsible for putting into effect the declaration originally made on November 2nd, 1917, by the Government of His Britannic Majesty, and adopted by the said Powers, in favor of the establishment in Palestine of a national home for the Jewish people, it being clearly understood that nothing should be done which might prejudice the civil and religious rights of existing non-Jewish communities in Palestine, or the rights and political status enjoyed by Jews in any other country; and

> Whereas recognition has thereby been given to the historical connection of the Jewish people with Palestine and to the grounds for reconstituting their national home in that country; and

> Whereas the Principal Allied Powers have selected His Britannic Majesty as the Mandatory for Palestine; and

> Whereas the mandate in respect of Palestine has been formulated in the following terms and submitted to the Council of the League for approval; and

> Whereas His Britannic Majesty has accepted the mandate in respect of Palestine and undertaken to exercise it on behalf of the League of Nations in conformity with the following provisions; and

Whereas by the afore-mentioned Article 22 (paragraph 8), it is provided that the degree of authority, control or administration to be exercised by the Mandatory, not having been previously agreed upon by the Members of the League, shall be explicitly defined by the Council of the League of Nations; confirming the said Mandate, defines its terms as follows:

Article 1. The Mandatory shall have full powers of legislation and of administration, save as they may be limited by the terms of this mandate.

Article 2. The Mandatory shall be responsible for placing the country under such political, administrative and economic conditions as will secure the establishment of the Jewish national home, as laid down in the preamble, and the development of self-governing institutions, and also for safeguarding the civil and religious rights of all the inhabitants of Palestine, irrespective of race and religion.

Article 3. The Mandatory shall, so far as circumstances permit, encourage local autonomy....

Article 17. The Administration of Palestine may organize on a voluntary basis the forces necessary for the preservation of peace and order, and also for the defence of the country, subject, however, to the supervision of the Mandatory, but shall not use them for purposes other than those above specified save with the consent of the Mandatory. Except for such purposes, no military, naval or air forces shall be raised or maintained by the Administration of Palestine....

Article 24. The Mandatory shall make to the Council of the League of Nations an annual report to the satisfaction of the Council as to the measures taken during the year to carry out the provisions of the mandate. Copies of all laws and regulations promulgated or issued during the year shall be communicated with the report....

Article 28. In the event of the termination of the mandate hereby conferred upon the Mandatory, the Council of the League of Nations ... shall use its influence for securing, under the guarantee of the League, that the Government of Palestine will fully honour the financial obligations legitimately incurred by the Administration of Palestine during the period of the mandate, including the rights of public servants to pensions or gratuities.[21]

Article 1 differed from Britain's August 1921 draft, in that it did not characterize Britain's role by reference to the concept of sovereignty. Instead of saying that Britain had "powers inherent in the Government of a Sovereign State" but subject to limitations, it said that Britain had "full powers of legislation and administration." Those powers were qualified, to be sure, by the terms of the Mandate. The Palestine Mandate also referred, in the preamble, to Covenant Article 22, which imposed obligations on the mandatories. In either of the two formulations of Article 1, the powers given to Britain were broad but not unlimited. Although the Palestine Mandate did not characterize the status of Palestine, the instrument was adopted in implementation of Covenant Article 22, which, as indicated, contemplated statehood for the Class A mandate territories.

The separate identity of Palestine is reflected in particular in Article 17, addressing military matters. The "Administration of Palestine" was permitted to use military forces for purposes other than those specified only with the consent of Britain. That formulation makes no sense unless Palestine was regarded as a juridical entity separate from Britain. Article 28, dealing with financial obligations after the mandate's anticipated termination, followed Samuel's proposal in imposing those obligations on the "Government of Palestine." That formulation assumed Palestine's statehood status under the mandate. It also anticipated that in the post-mandate period the only difference would be the replacement of the "Administration of Palestine" by a "Government of Palestine."

STATEHOOD IN THE TREATY OF LAUSANNE

For reasons not relating to the Ottoman territories, the Treaty of Sèvres was replaced by a new peace treaty, signed at Lausanne on July 24, 1923. This new peace treaty did gain ratification and entered into force for Britain on August 6, 1924.[22] Thus, the Treaty of Lausanne was the instrument whereby Turkey relinquished its territories. The Treaty of Lausanne omitted the detailed treatment of these territories seen in Article 94 and 95 of the Treaty of Sèvres, because by 1923, the issues of the allocation of the mandates had been resolved by the extension of mandates to particular mandatory powers. In the Treaty of Lausanne, Article 16 was the only provision relating to the Ottoman territories. It provided as follows:

> Turkey hereby renounces all rights and title whatsoever over or respecting the territories situated outside the frontiers laid down in the present Treaty and the islands other than those over which her sovereignty is recognised by the said Treaty, the future of these territories and islands being settled or to be settled by the parties concerned.

The Palestine Mandate is sometimes said to have entered into force on September 29, 1923, the date Turkey signed the Treaty of Lausanne, because of this renunciation.[23] The Treaty of Lausanne did not enter into force, however, until August 6, 1924, which made Turkey's renunciation of rights effective only then.

Like the failed Treaty of Sèvres before it, the Treaty of Lausanne referred to the territories being detached from Turkey as states.[24] A provision in the Treaty of Lausanne on the Ottoman public debt was one of them. It read:

> Article 46. The Ottoman Public Debt ... shall be distributed under the conditions laid down in the present Section between Turkey, the States in favour of which territory has been detached from the Ottoman Empire after the Balkan wars of 1912–13 [and certain other states].

The Treaty of Lausanne included a number of protocols. In Protocol XII, relating to continuity of obligations under concessions granted by the Ottoman Empire, reference was made in the following terms to the "state" that "acquires" the territory:

> Article 9. In territories detached from Turkey under the Treaty of Peace signed this day, the State which acquires the territory is fully subrogated as regards the rights and obligations of Turkey towards the nationals of the other Contracting Powers, and companies in which the capital of the nationals of the said Powers is preponderant, who are beneficiaries under concessionary contracts entered into before the 29th October, 1914, with the Ottoman Government or any local Ottoman authority.

The Treaty of Lausanne's provision on nationality referred to the territories that had been detached from Turkey as "states." It read:

> Article 30. Turkish subjects habitually resident in territory which in accordance with the provisions of the present Treaty is detached from Turkey will become ipso facto, in the conditions laid down by the local law, nationals of the State to which such territory is transferred.

These provisions indicated that the Allies, and Turkey as well, regarded the Class A mandate territories, including Palestine, as states. The phrase "State to which such territory is transferred" meant, wrote Stoyanovsky, "the newly constituted States," rather than the mandatories.[25]

Albert Millot, like Stoyanovsky, wrote a dissertation on the mandate system at the University of Paris. Millot too read Article 30 as reflecting the statehood of the Class A mandates. He wrote that, with the ratification of the Treaty of Lausanne, the former Ottoman territories "were set up as states, that is to say, as international moral persons, subjects of international law, hence capable of rights and bearing obligations."[26] The Egyptian court that, as indicated in Chapter 3, construed Covenant Article 22(4) as making the Class A mandates states, also viewed statehood for the Class A mandates as flowing from the Treaty of Lausanne. The court referred to "the Treaty of Lausanne in virtue of which ... Syria and the Lebanon were constituted as States detached from the Turkish Empire."[27]

Article 30 of the Treaty of Lausanne was read by a British court in a 1940 case as having made Palestine a state. The case of *King v. Ketter* centered on the nationality status of a man who was a resident of Palestine. Ketter asserted that, by virtue of being an inhabitant of Palestine, he was a national of Great Britain. His lawyer argued that, as applied to the Palestine Mandate, the phrase "State to which such territory is transferred" in Article 30 of the Treaty of Lausanne meant Britain, and therefore that residents of Palestine became British nationals. On appeal, the lawyer's argument was rejected. The Court of Criminal Appeal ruled that:

> [t]here was no provision in art. 30 for the transfer of territory to Great Britain. If there had been, there would have been no need for the mandate.[28]

The court thus read Article 30 to mean that Palestine was the "state" to which territory was transferred.[29]

The Treaty of Lausanne, in particular by its Articles 30 and 46, contemplated that all the Class A mandate territories were states. The Treaty of Lausanne was, following the failure of ratification of the Treaty of Sèvres, the definitive treaty providing the territorial disposition coming out of World War I. The courts that had occasion to deal with territorial status in the former Ottoman territories referred to it as authority, and there was no question but that these territories were states.

5

The Class A Mandates

Even though Palestine, Iraq, and Syria were all Class A mandates, the instruments establishing their status used varying terminology, and the arrangements for governance differed.[1] The local population played a greater role in governance in Iraq and Syria than in Palestine. Iraq's status was set by a treaty between Iraq and Britain, whereas the status of Syria, like that of Palestine, was set by an instrument agreed between the mandatory power and the League of Nations.

These differences in the form and substance of the Class A mandates, plus the differing references in the San Remo Resolution and the Treaty of Sèvres, might lead one to conclude that while Iraq, and perhaps Syria, were states while under mandate, Palestine was not. As will be seen in this chapter, however, these differences bespoke no difference as to statehood.

THE IRAQ MANDATE

The terms of the relationship with the mandatory were highly contentious in all the Class A mandate territories. The populations opposed the mandate system and sought immediate independence. The Arab population of Iraq was more successful than that of Palestine in wresting concessions from Britain. In summer 1920, serious disorders in Iraq threatened the administration that Britain had established at the war's end. Britain was obliged to bring in troops, and by mid-autumn 1920 they had restored order. The British commissioner put in place an Iraqi-based administration and invited Faisal, who had been removed by the French in Syria, to participate in Iraq's governance. Faisal was elected King of Iraq and was crowned in August 1921.[2]

For Iraq, Britain drafted and submitted to the League of Nations for approval an instrument that would have defined the terms of the Britain-Iraq relationship. But, with Iraqi opposition still strong, Britain withdrew the draft in favor of concluding a treaty with Iraq to define the relationship.[3] In 1922, Britain and Iraq signed the Treaty of Alliance, which would be ratified in 1924.[4] The Treaty of Alliance contemplated that the administration of Iraq would be in the hands of Faisal as King, and Britain would perform an advisory role. Article 1 was the key provision. It read:

> At the request of His Majesty the King of Irak, His Britannic Majesty undertakes subject to the provisions of this treaty to provide the State of Irak with such advice and assistance as may be required during the period of the present treaty, without prejudice to her national sovereignty. His Britannic Majesty shall be represented in Irak by a High Commissioner and Consul-General assisted by the necessary staff.[5]

Thus, Britain referred to Iraq as a state and recognized its sovereignty. Like other treaties of the era between states, the Treaty of Alliance was published in the League of Nations Treaty Series. Hence, Iraq was a state, even as it remained under mandate.

Norman Bentwich was a British barrister who became legal secretary to Britain's military administration in Palestine in 1918 and attorney-general of Palestine once the mandate went into effect. An accomplished international lawyer, he would later teach law at the Hebrew University in Jerusalem. Bentwich wrote legal analyses of the mandate system as implemented in Palestine and other Class A mandates. In his analysis of Iraq, Bentwich referred to it as an "infant state."[6]

Iraq was regarded as a state despite the fact that the Treaty of Alliance subjected it to substantial oversight by Britain. The high commissioner was given a far-reaching role. Article 4 of the Treaty of Alliance provided:

> His Majesty the King of Irak agrees to be guided by the advice of His Britannic Majesty rendered through the High Commissioner on all important matters affecting the international and financial obligations and interests of His Britannic Majesty for the whole period of this treaty.

Article 4 coexisted with Article 1. Thus, subjection to British advice was not regarded as inconsistent with Iraq's status as a state. Covenant Article 22 referred to mandate territories as being under tutelage. Iraq was subject to significant tutelage.

In May 1923, Britain informed the League Council that the Treaty of Alliance would be the vehicle whereby it would carry out the mandate. After the Treaty's ratification in 1924, the Council adopted a resolution (September 27, 1924) in which it recited that "the purpose of the said Treaty of Alliance is to ensure the complete observance and execution in Iraq of the principles which the acceptance of the Mandate was intended to secure." The resolution called for an annual report by Britain to the Council, to include copies of laws and regulations. The resolution specified that any modification of the terms of the treaty would require the Council's consent.[7]

Iraq functioned on this basis under mandate.[8] Britain submitted reports to the League. Iraq's status as a state was not regarded as inconsistent with its status as a mandate territory under tutelage. The Iraq mandate and its implementation reflected the compatibility of statehood with mandate status.

THE SYRIA MANDATE

Although Syria, like Iraq, had been expressly denominated a state in the San Remo Resolution and the Treaty of Sèvres, no treaty was concluded with the mandatory, in this case France. Instead, a mandate instrument was confirmed by a resolution of the League Council on July 24, 1922, the same day the League confirmed the Palestine Mandate. The text of the Syria Mandate mentioned statehood, but in terms that were less explicit than those of the Iraq-Britain Treaty of Alliance. The Syria Mandate recited:

> The Mandatory shall frame, within a period of three years from the coming into force of this mandate, an organic law for Syria and the Lebanon.

> This organic law shall be framed in agreement with the native authorities and shall take into account the rights, interests, and wishes of all the population inhabiting the said territory. The Mandatory shall further enact measures to facilitate the progressive development of Syria and the Lebanon as independent States. Pending the coming into effect of the organic law, the government of Syria and the Lebanon shall be conducted in accordance with the spirit of this mandate.[9]

In keeping with this provision, France dealt separately with Lebanon and Syria. A constitution was adopted for Lebanon in 1926 under which it began to function with a minimum of oversight. The president of Lebanon was authorized by the constitution to negotiate and ratify treaties, although they were subject to Article 3 of the Syria Mandate, which gave control of foreign relations to France.[10] The 1926 constitution referred to Lebanon as "the State of the Lebanon."[11]

In Syria, the anticipated constitution was adopted only in 1930. During the 1920s, executive departments in government were headed by Syrians, but with French advisers attached to them and with French nationals holding the high-level posts.[12] The 1930 constitution recited that "Syria is an independent and sovereign State."[13]

Lebanon and Syria thus were both regarded as states, even as they remained mandate territories. Even after the Lebanon constitution of 1926 and the Syria constitution of 1930, France continued to report to the Permanent Mandates Commission, as required of a mandatory power. Syria's status became an issue in a number of formal proceedings, and its statehood was uniformly recognized. One such proceeding was the 1927 Egyptian court case that is related in Chapters 3 and 4, but there were others.

In a 1929 French administrative-law case, a French postal employee had been working in Beirut under France's high commissioner for Lebanon. The high commissioner had denied the employee's request for a salary increase. The employee appealed to the Conseil d'Etat, France's highest administrative-law court. The Conseil had jurisdiction only over the French administration, however. The Conseil ruled that a decision by the high commissioner for Lebanon was not an act of a French administrative authority. The employee, the Conseil said, worked for "a service belonging to the mandated States,"[14] and since Lebanon was a state separate from France, the Conseil found that it had no jurisdiction.

Both Lebanon and Syria were treated as states in a 1940 arbitration proceeding. Each, as a state, was party to an important multilateral treaty, the International Telecommunication Convention.[15] When Lebanon and Syria found themselves in a dispute with Egypt, also a state party to the Convention, over the transmission of telegrams, they invoked an arbitration clause, leading to an arbitration by a panel of three arbitrators (Dutch, Norwegian, Danish). As they resolved the dispute, the arbitrators characterized Lebanon and Syria as "states of the Levant under French mandate."[16]

In a 1947 extradition case, Syria was treated as a state by the Supreme Court of Palestine. Palestine had extradited a fugitive from Lebanon under a 1921 extradition treaty that had been concluded between Palestine on the one hand and Syria and Lebanon on the other. The individual being extradited challenged the proceedings by arguing that the treaty had lapsed because Lebanon became independent in 1943, a fact that he took to mean that it was a different entity from the one that had concluded the extradition treaty. The Supreme Court of Palestine, however, viewed Lebanon's emergence to independence as effecting no change as to its statehood. It said that changes in government "have as such no effect upon the continued validity of the state's international obligations."[17] The Supreme Court of Palestine thus regarded Syria as having been a state while under France's mandate.

The mode of implementation of the Syria mandate involved, as it had with Palestine, an agreement between the mandatory and the League of Nations, but, unlike Palestine, the mode of governance was a constitution – actually two constitutions, one for Syria and one for Lebanon. Under those constitutions, Syria and Lebanon were clearly states. Thus the Syria mandate, like the Iraq mandate, demonstrated the compatibility of mandate status and statehood.

TRANSJORDAN IN THE PALESTINE MANDATE

Transjordan exhibited still a different arrangement between mandatory and mandate territory, both in regard to actual administration and in regard to the legal instruments used. Transjordan was included in the Palestine Mandate, but with the proviso that Britain might administer it separately and that the clause in the Palestine mandate about a Jewish national home would not apply to Transjordan. Article 25 of the Palestine Mandate provided that

> [i]n the territories lying between the Jordan and the eastern boundary of Palestine as ultimately determined, the Mandatory shall be entitled, with the consent of the Council of the League of Nations, to postpone or withhold application of such provisions of this mandate as he may consider inapplicable to the existing local conditions, and to make such provision for the administration of the territories as he may consider suitable to those conditions, provided that no action shall be taken which is inconsistent with the provisions of Articles 15, 16 and 18.[18]

Exercising this option, Britain determined not to apply to Transjordan the provisions of the Palestine Mandate respecting the Jewish national home, and the League Council, on September 16, 1922, approved.[19]

Britain arranged for local councils to be set up in the three districts into which Transjordan was divided administratively. The councils were to be assisted by a small number of British officers sent from Palestine. An arrangement was made with Abdullah, brother of Faisal and Emir in Transjordan, that Abdullah would administer Transjordan. In April 1923, Herbert Samuel, as high commissioner in Palestine, announced in Amman, capital of Transjordan that

> [s]ubject to the approval of the League of Nations, His Majesty's Government will recognize the existence of an independent government in Trans-Jordan under the rule of His Highness the Emir Abdullah, provided that such government is constitutional and places His Britannic Majesty's Government in a position to fulfill its international obligations in respect of the territory by means of an agreement to be concluded between the two Governments.[20]

The arrangement for Transjordan thus involved local administration, subject to providing enough of a role for Britain that it could fulfill its obligations as mandatory. Samuel would continue to be responsible for Transjordan, but as a representative of Britain in its role as mandatory, rather than in his role as high commissioner of Palestine.[21] Henri A. Rolin, who as a member of Belgium's delegation participated in the elaboration of the League Covenant, found Transjordan's status to be akin to that of Iraq, by which he meant statehood.[22]

The contemplated agreement between Britain and Transjordan was concluded only five years later, on February 20, 1928.[23] It gave Emir Abdullah the powers of legislation and administration.[24] The Emir agreed, however, to be guided by British advice on specified issues.[25] The Agreement contained no provision specifically characterizing Transjordan's status. However, it was concluded in the form of an international treaty between the British Crown and the Emir, hence appearing to be premised on Transjordan statehood. One provision referred to Transjordan, and to Palestine as well, as "countries."[26] Another provision expressed Britain's lack of objection to any "association" that Transjordan might form with "neighbouring Arab states."[27]

The League Council then considered whether this arrangement was consistent with Britain's obligations under the Palestine Mandate. The British representative affirmed to the Council

> that my Government regards itself as responsible to the Council for the proper application in Transjordan of all the provisions of the Palestine mandate, except those which have been excluded under Article 25.[28]

The Council then adopted a resolution approving the arrangement. It read:

> As regards the Agreement of February 20th, 1928, between Great Britain and Transjordan, the Council takes note of the declaration of the representative of Great Britain according to which his Government regards itself as responsible to the council of the League of Nations for the application in Transjordan of the Palestine mandate, with the exception of the articles which, based on Article 25, are not applicable,
>
> And acknowledge that this Agreement is in conformity with the principles of the mandate, which remains fully in force.[29]

Thus, Britain and the Permanent Mandates Commission understood that the mandate continued in force.[30] Abdullah continued administering until the mandate was terminated with Britain's withdrawal in 1946, after which the name "Transjordan" was changed to "Jordan."

Transjordan represented a method of implementing mandate status that, as with the other mandates, was unique to itself. Transjordan's status was set by the Palestine Mandate, but then as well by a treaty between Transjordan and Britain. Transjordan was treated as a state, and its arrangement with Britain was regarded by the League of Nations as being compatible with the obligations of a mandatory power.

THE PALESTINE MANDATE AS POTENTIALLY DIFFERENT

The implementation of mandate status in the Class A mandates was thus far from uniform. Because of the aim of establishing a Jewish national home, the Palestine Mandate differed from the others by giving the mandatory power a greater role in administration. As Max Laserson, an international law practitioner and analyst of the era, described the difference,

> [t]he mandate for Palestine is much less a charter of Arab rights, for instance, than the Mandates for Iraq and Syria. In the other "A" Mandates, while safeguarding the rights of minorities, the principal concern of the Mandate is for the welfare of the majority element in the population, aiming at eventual political self-determination. The Palestine Mandate, however, has embodied another *clausula*, which is not provided by Art. 22 of the Covenant, viz. the encouragement and facilitation of Jewish immigration, and the establishment of the Jewish National Home, notwithstanding the fact that the Jews are numerically a minority of the population.[31]

Stoyanovsky also attributed the difference in the arrangement for Palestine to the aim of implementing the Jewish national home provision.[32] Jews could be brought into Palestine only by an outside power. A majority-rule administration, which would have been predominantly Arab, would hardly have been willing to do so. Jan Smuts justified a central role for the mandatory power in Palestine on the basis of the population division. Stoyanovsky said that "the administrative co-operation of the Jewish minority and Arab majority would not be forthcoming."[33]

Rolin expressed the same understanding of why Palestine's administration differed from Iraq's, namely, the diversity of its population, but found the limitations on its "capacity to act" to mean that while Iraq was, presently, a state, Palestine was not. He did, however, regard the communities under mandate as possessing legal personality, as demonstrated, he said, by the fact that the mandatory powers concluded treaties on behalf of the mandate territories.[34]

Rolin did not distinguish between Palestine and Syria (which he likewise thought was not a state) and the Class B and Class C mandates in arriving at this conclusion. But that distinction was key. All the Turkish territories fell under the same regime as regards their status. They were all Class A mandates. The reference in Covenant Article 22(4) to "certain communities formerly belonging to the Turkish Empire" included all the non-Turkish Ottoman territories that became mandates.[35] The League Council, when it adopted the mandate instrument for Palestine, did so under the agenda item, "A Mandates."[36] That designation was not questioned by the states concerned. The U.S. Department of State referred to Palestine as a Class A mandate in a 1927 publication,[37] and again in a legal opinion in 1948.[38] Green Hackworth, in his digest of U.S. practice in international law, classified Palestine as a Class A mandate.[39] Analysts did not question the designation.[40]

In 1937, William Ormsby-Gore, Britain's Colonial Secretary, represented Britain before the Permanent Mandates Commission. In discussion in the Commission, Ormsby-Gore referred to Palestine as a Class A mandate.

His Majesty's Government conceived it as of the essence of such a mandate as the Palestine mandate, an A mandate, and of Article 22 of the Covenant, that Palestine should be developed, not as a British colony permanently under British rule, but as a self-governing State or States with the right of autonomous evolution.[41]

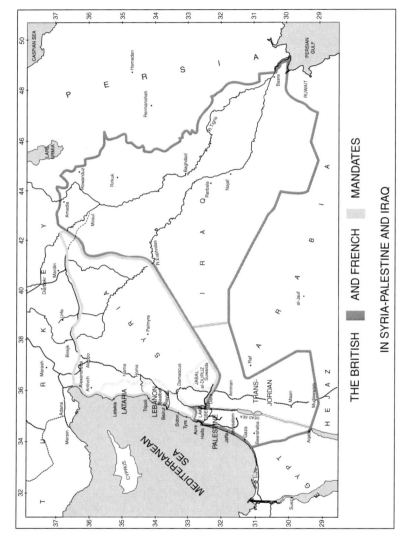

MAP 1. The British and French Mandates in Syria-Palestine and Iraq originally from George Antonius, *The Arab Awakening*, Khayats, Beirut, 1938, redrawn from a map by Tom Wrigley.

Ormsby-Gore's reference to "State or States" apparently related to the fact that Transjordan was included in the Palestine Mandate. The difference in mode of administration, which was key for Rolin, is of less import than the wording of Covenant Article 22(4) and of the Treaty of Lausanne. Moreover, Rolin's view would repeatedly be tested in the real world, when issues arose requiring a determination about Palestine's status. It is to those issues that we now turn.

6

Palestine in Operation

In conformity with Palestine's status as a Class A mandate, Great Britain carried out its administration of the country based on Palestine's status as a state. The statehood status of Palestine was, moreover, understood and acknowledged by the states of the international community as particular issues arose. With regard to the law in force, Britain recognized Palestine as having its own law, namely, the law that was in force when Britain assumed control. As stipulated by Article 46 of an Order-in-Council adopted in 1922 to provide for the governance of Palestine,

> [t]he jurisdiction of the Civil Courts shall be exercised in conformity with the Ottoman Law in force in Palestine on November 1st, 1914, and such later Ottoman Laws as have been or may be declared to be in force by Public Notice ...[1]

English law, as Article 46 further provided, could be used to the extent that no applicable Ottoman law could be found.[2]

Over the course of the mandate, significant elements of English law were in fact introduced, displacing Ottoman law on many topics.[3] Ottoman law, however, continued as the basic law of Palestine, most prominently the Ottoman Civil Code and Ottoman Land Code.[4] As well, an Ottoman practice was carried over whereby religious courts representing the various religious communities handled matters of personal status, including family law.[5] The courts of the Islamic community were particularly firmly rooted. The files of the Jerusalem Islamic court contain cases dating from the sixteenth century.[6]

It was in the external aspects of administration, however, that the statehood of Palestine showed most clearly: Palestine had to deal with the outside world. Palestine had relations with other states that required the conclusion of treaties. Palestine's citizens had connections with other states and required for that purpose a nationality. Palestine's status came up as an issue in a variety of ways during the time of Britain's administration. In all these interactions, the states of the international community dealt with Palestine as a state.

PALESTINE'S TREATIES

The statehood of Palestine was reflected in the conclusion of treaties in the name of Palestine. Under Palestine Mandate Article 12, Britain was responsible for Palestine's foreign relations, which included treaty-making authority. It read:

> Article 12. The Mandatory shall be entrusted with the control of the foreign relations of Palestine and the right to issue exequaturs to consuls appointed by foreign Powers. He shall also be entitled to afford diplomatic and consular protection to citizens of Palestine when outside its territorial limits.

Britain extended to Palestine a number of its own multilateral and bilateral treaties.[7] As well, the Palestine administration executed treaties in the name of Palestine,[8] and these treaties, like the treaties of other states, were published in the League of Nations Treaty Series. Palestine was party, for example, to a multilateral treaty that established an international agency to deal with locust plagues, the International Agreement for the Establishment of an International Bureau of Intelligence on Locusts, concluded at Damascus in 1926. That treaty referred in its text to the parties as the "contracting states."[9] The five parties were Turkey, Transjordan, Iraq, Syria, and Palestine. The fact that Turkey concluded a treaty with four of the Class A mandates shows that it regarded them as states.

Palestine was party to bilateral treaties on the exchange of postal parcels with the United States,[10] and with four European states: Switzerland,[11] Italy,[12] Greece,[13] and France.[14] Palestine was also party to bilateral treaties on various topics with states in the immediate region. One was the Agreement with Egypt Regarding the Reciprocal Enforcement of Judgments.[15] This Agreement ensured that judgments issued in the courts of either state would be enforced in the courts of the other. Another bilateral treaty with Egypt dealt with extradition,[16] and still another concerned commercial relations.[17] Treaties entered into by the Palestine administration were "concluded directly between Palestine and certain foreign countries"[18] and reflected Palestine's sovereign capacity.

Palestine's treaties were, to be sure, concluded under Britain's authority as mandatory. However, the capacity to conclude them was that of the Palestine state. Arnold McNair in his classic treatise on the law of treaties draws a distinction, in regard to states not fully independent, between the *power* to conclude treaties and the *capacity* to do so.[19] McNair gives the example of a protectorate. A protected state may have the capacity to conclude treaties, even if the power to do so on its behalf rests with the protecting state.[20] Thus, a state may have capacity to conclude treaties even if the power to do so rests with another state. Here Britain had the power, while Palestine had the capacity. The conclusion of treaties in the name of Palestine indicated that Palestine was regarded as a state by Britain and by Palestine's treaty partners.

Most telling in regard to Palestine's status was a 1922 bilateral treaty concluded between Palestine and Great Britain. The Agreement between the Post Office of the United Kingdom of Great Britain and Ireland and the Post Office of Palestine for the Exchange of Money Orders, signed in London, January 10, 1922, and in Jerusalem, January 23, 1922, provided for a regular exchange of money orders. This treaty, like Palestine's other treaties, was registered with the League of Nations and published in the League of Nations Treaty Series.[21] Had Britain understood Palestine and itself to constitute a single state, the matter could have been handled by domestic law. By concluding a treaty with Palestine, Britain was indicating that it regarded Palestine as a state.

PALESTINE NATIONALITY

The statehood of Palestine was reflected in the regulation of nationality. Nationality is an aspect of statehood. The Class A mandates each had their own nationality, whereas the Class B and Class C mandates did not.[22] Palestine Mandate Article 7 required Britain to enact legislation to provide for Palestine nationality. It read:

> Article 7. The Administration of Palestine shall be responsible for enacting a nationality law. There shall be included in this law provisions framed so as to facilitate the acquisition of Palestinian citizenship by Jews who take up their permanent residence in Palestine.

As was explained in Chapter 4, the nationality of Ottoman nationals resident in Palestine was transferred from Turkey to Palestine by Article 30 of the Treaty of Lausanne. Article 7 of the Palestine Mandate required Britain to enact a "nationality" law to provide for the acquisition of "citizenship." Article 7 thus used two different terms – "nationality" and "citizenship." The terminology relating to an individual's connection to a state is often a source of confusion. "Nationality" is the proper term for the connection between an individual and a state, a connection that leads to obligations for the state and rights for the individual at the international level. In this context, "nationality" has nothing to do with race or ethnicity. "Citizenship" is the term commonly used in domestic legislation to identify individuals enjoying certain rights under the law of a particular state.[23] Article 7, in any event, required Britain to make provision on this issue for Palestine.

Following through on its obligation under Article 7, Britain enacted the Palestinian Citizenship Order on July 24, 1925, as an order in council.[24] The Palestine administration then adopted a Passport Ordinance, under which passports were issued with the designation "British Passport. Palestine."[25] The Palestine administration extended citizenship to its inhabitants, granted naturalization to immigrants, and issued passports for travel.[26]

Pierre Orts, Chair of the Permanent Mandates Commission, took Article 7 of the Palestine Mandate to be a reflection of Palestine statehood. At a Commission meeting in 1937, Orts said that

[t]he mandate, in Article 7, obliged the Mandatory to enact a nationality law, which again showed that the Palestinians formed a nation, and that Palestine was a State, though provisionally under guardianship.[27]

Orts was not only the chair of the Permanent Mandates Commission but its senior member, having served from the Commission's inception in 1921. Orts had heard each and every report by Britain as mandatory. He had as much information as anyone about the nature of the mandates system. A lawyer by training, with an orientation toward public law, Orts understood what he was saying when he called Palestine a state.

Palestine statehood was reflected in the availability of naturalization, which was provided for in the Citizenship Order. Naturalization was made available, in particular, to accommodate Jews who might migrate to Palestine in connection with the "national home" project. Nearly all persons who became naturalized in Palestine during the years of the mandate were Jews.[28] Naturalization was open to persons who had resided in Palestine for at least two of the immediately preceding three years and who intended to stay, provided they were of good character and knew either English, Arabic, or Hebrew.[29]

Palestine statehood was assumed in the oath administered to a person who applied for Palestine naturalization. The oath, to be taken upon being naturalized, ran: "I swear that I will be faithful and loyal to the Government of Palestine."[30] By this oath, an individual swore loyalty to Palestine, obviously on the assumption that Palestine was a state. Naturalization is a procedure whereby an individual becomes attached to a state. Through naturalization, "an alien by birth acquires the nationality of the naturalising State."[31] Application for Palestine naturalization was made not to the British government, but to the high commissioner of Palestine.[32] An alien who became naturalized in Palestine became attached, not to Britain, but to Palestine.

One important aspect of nationality is that nationals are entitled to representation abroad by diplomatic and consular officials. Under Palestine Mandate Article 12, Palestine citizens were to be represented abroad by Britain. They were to be represented not by their own state, but by another. Consular and diplomatic representation is normally provided by the state of nationality, but representation by some other state is not unknown in international practice. Nationals of small states are sometimes provided consular protection by other states. (Examples will be seen in Chapter 19.) Consular protection may also be provided by another state when a national's state has no government. During the period from 1948 to 1950, for example, when Germany had no government, the United States provided consular services for German nationals in U.S. territory.[33]

It was seen above that with respect to treaties, Britain had the power while Palestine had the capacity. The same was true with respect to representation of Palestine citizens abroad. Britain had the power, but the capacity rested with Palestine.

Quincy Wright, a University of Chicago political scientist and international-law theorist who would author a major treatise on the mandates,[34] cited a citizenship decision of the Supreme Court of Palestine as reflecting the separate status and separate citizenship of Palestine. The case involved an Anglo-Italian extradition treaty of 1873. In 1925, Italy was seeking the extradition of certain Palestine residents who had been Ottoman nationals. The Anglo-Italian treaty had been made applicable to Palestine. Like some other extradition treaties, this one did not require a state to extradite its own nationals, referring in that regard to "subjects of the United Kingdom." The court held that the individuals, as Palestine residents, were not British subjects because Britain did not have sovereignty in Palestine. The court said:

[T]o hold that the petitioners are British subjects would involve holding that the crown, having accepted the responsibility of governing Palestine as a mandatory, has thereby acquired sovereignty, a view for which no authority has been cited.[35]

The individuals were not British subjects, in the Court's view, because Britain was not sovereign in Palestine. This case accurately reflected the arrangements that had been made for citizenship in Palestine. The inhabitants of Palestine lost their Ottoman nationality but gained a new nationality, that of Palestine. That new nationality had to be that of a state.

Third states regarded Palestine citizenship as they did the citizenship of any state, except that a third state would deal with a British consulate on issues requiring consular assistance. Palestine citizenship was recognized by the courts of other states when issues of personal status arose.[36] A court in Egypt found there to be a Palestine nationality in a 1925 case. A Palestine resident sued an Egyptian in an Egyptian "mixed court," which had jurisdiction in the case only if the plaintiff were a foreigner. In Ottoman times, Palestinians and Egyptians were Ottoman nationals, and Palestinians would not have been considered foreigners. The mixed court held in the plaintiff's favor, saying:

[F]ormer Ottoman territories placed under a Mandate have the character of regular States, and their inhabitants possess the nationality of those States in accordance with Article 30 of the Treaty of Lausanne. The plaintiff, therefore, has Palestinian nationality, and is a foreign subject in Egypt.[37]

In a 1928 case involving a Palestine inhabitant of Egypt who was similarly seeking to sue an Egyptian in a mixed court, the court again found that the plaintiff was entitled to sue on the basis that the Palestine inhabitant was a foreigner.[38]

The separate nationality of the citizens of Palestine was also reflected in Britain's practice in dealing with Palestine inhabitants when they were in the territory of Britain.[39] As was seen in *King v. Ketter*, the British Court of Criminal Appeal case cited in Chapter 4, Palestine citizens were considered aliens when in Britain. In that case, a Jerusalemite holding a "British Passport. Palestine" was convicted in Britain of the criminal offense of failing to depart from Britain after being ordered deported. Ketter appealed, arguing that, as a Palestine resident, he was a British subject. The court dismissed his appeal, saying that "there has been no annexation of Palestine. It follows that he is not a British subject, but an alien."[40] The court understood that Palestine nationality was self-standing, that it was the nationality of Palestine.[41]

PALESTINE IN PROCEEDINGS ABOUT THE
OTTOMAN PUBLIC DEBT

Palestine was found to be a state in two international proceedings that called for interpretation of the status of Class A mandate territories under the Treaty of Lausanne. One was an international arbitration, which resulted in a decision in 1925. The Treaty of Lausanne's provisions on the Ottoman debt provided the underlying law. As indicated in Chapter 4, Article 46 of the Treaty of Lausanne called for the Ottoman debt to be borne by Turkey and the states formed out of the Ottoman Empire. In case of dispute about allocation of the debt, Article 47 of the Treaty of Lausanne provided that the Council of the League of Nations would appoint an arbitrator. A dispute did arise, and the Council appointed Eugène Borel, a professor at the University of Geneva who, as a member of the prestigious Institute of International Law, would later participate in its deliberations about the mandate system.[42] Statehood emerged as an issue after Borel completed the arbitration, when he came to apportioning the expenses of the arbitration. Under Article 47, the expenses of such an arbitration were to "be borne by the parties concerned." Borel decided in that regard that

> [t]he only proper procedure is to divide the expenses in an equal fashion among the states as such. This presents a problem of how to regard the countries in Asia under British mandate and under French mandate. Iraq is a Kingdom with respect to which Great Britain has assumed responsibilities equivalent to those of a mandatory Power. Under British mandate, Palestine and Transjordan each have an organization quite distinct. One thus has three states sufficiently separated to be considered here as distinct parties.

> France has received a single mandate from the Council of the League of Nations but, in the countries in question there are two distinct states: Syria and Lebanon, states each with its own constitution, and with a nationality clearly separated one from the other. With regard to the matter to resolve here, the Arbitrator believes that five states of Asia have appeared before him, three under British mandate and two under mandate of France.

> The conclusion that follows is that the expenses of arbitration, including the honorarium of the Arbitrator, are to be divided into nine parts,

assessed to: the states under British mandate for three parts; the states under French mandate for two parts; Bulgaria, Greece, Italy and Turkey each for one part.[43]

To Borel, the differences in administration between Iraq, Syria, and Palestine were irrelevant to their status. He found that each was a state.

PALESTINE IN THE PERMANENT COURT
OF INTERNATIONAL JUSTICE

Palestine statehood was also seen in a second 1925 case, this one decided by the Permanent Court of International Justice, the court that had been established in concert with the League of Nations. The *Mavrommatis Palestine Concessions* case involved Palestine's responsibility for a public works concession that had been granted in Ottoman times by the Ottoman authorities. The individual to whom the concession had been granted was a national of Greece. When the Government of Palestine acted in a way that Greece viewed as violating the rights of its national, Greece sued Britain in the Permanent Court of International Justice, alleging that the Government of Palestine had failed to live up to the concession agreement.

Greece framed its claim carefully, alleging a violation on the part of the "Government of Palestine and consequently on the part of His Britannic Majesty's Government, in its capacity as Mandatory Power for Palestine."[44] Greece sued Britain, rather than Palestine, because the Permanent Court was a court of limited jurisdiction. Article 26 of the Palestine Mandate required "the Mandatory" to submit to the Court's jurisdiction in the event that another member of the League questioned its performance under the Palestine Mandate. Had it not been for this provision, Greece would not have had a basis for jurisdiction over Palestine.

The Permanent Court of International Justice, in analyzing Greece's claim, referred to Palestine in a way that indicated that the Court regarded Palestine as a state. The Court viewed the case as raising the responsibility of a successor state to the treaty obligations of a state that it has replaced. The Court posed to itself a question as to the obligations of the "successor state," meaning the successor to the Ottoman Empire in the territory of Palestine.[45] In that connection, the Court identified Palestine as the successor state, saying, "Palestine is subrogated as regards the rights and obligations of Turkey."[46] Protocol XII, Article 9, of the Lausanne Treaty specified that "the State which acquires the territory" is "fully subrogated as regards the rights and obligations of Turkey." By saying that Palestine was thus subrogated, the Court made clear that it regarded Palestine as the state that had acquired the territory. In other words, the state acquiring the territory was the mandate state. The Court read Article 9 as referring to Palestine as a state.

Earlier in the same case, the Permanent Court averted to the separate status of Palestine in discussing Palestine Mandate Article 11, which provided, in part, that

> [t]he Administration of Palestine shall take all necessary measures to safeguard the interests of the community in connexion with the development of the country and, subject to any international obligations accepted by the Mandatory, shall have full power to provide for public ownership or control of any of the natural resources of the country or of the public works, services and utilities established or to be established therein.

The Court said that the Britain's international obligations as mandatory differed from those of Palestine: "the international obligations of the Mandatory," it said, "are not, *ipso facto*, international obligations of Palestine."[47] This statement of the Permanent Court, along with similar statements of other courts, led Quincy Wright to say that "courts, both national and international, have assumed that the mandatory is not sovereign."[48]

The Court also found Palestine statehood in the Treaty of Lausanne's provision on the Ottoman debt, just as Borel did in the Ottoman Debt Arbitration. The Court said that Article 46, the provision of the Treaty of Lausanne on the Ottoman debt, "lays down rules for the subrogation of the successor states as regards the rights and obligations of the Turkish authorities."[49] The Court's reference to "successor State" was to Palestine.

Judge Bustamante, who wrote separately in the *Mavrommatis* case, referred to Britain's limited status in regard to Palestine as he analyzed the issue of whether the Permanent Court had jurisdiction over the case filed by Greece. He said:

> Great Britain is not the sovereign of Palestine but simply the Mandatory of the League of Nations and she has accepted the Permanent Court's jurisdiction for any dispute arising between her, as Mandatory, and any Member of the League from which she holds the mandate.[50]

Palestine was a state, even though Britain bore responsibility for Palestine's foreign relations and for domestic administration.

PALESTINE AS A STATE IN
MOST-FAVORED-NATION TREATIES

In 1932, Palestine statehood was graphically demonstrated by an international controversy, albeit a controversy that came to public knowledge only years later. In that year, Britain enacted new tariffs for goods entering Britain from foreign countries, generally imposing a duty of 10 percent.[51] But "foreign countries" was not to include territories of the British Empire. Under the Import Duties Act, 1932, a "colonial preference" would be given to goods entering Britain "from any part of the British Empire." The Import Duties Act authorized the government to accord this "colonial preference" to, among others, "any territory in respect of which a mandate of the League of Nations is being exercised by the Government of the United Kingdom."[52] Parliament did not want to disadvantage its mandate territories by imposing the new duty on their exports to Britain.

The British government promptly issued an order granting a preference to three territories that Britain held as Class B mandates: Tanganyika, Cameroons, and Togoland.[53] The British government hesitated, however, on Palestine. If it accorded its Class A Mandate a preference, other countries with which Britain had a bilateral most-favored-nation treaty might claim that goods entering from their own territories were entitled to the same preference. Under such treaties, each state agrees to admit goods of the other at a tariff rate no higher than it charges on like goods entering from any other state.

The British cabinet discussed whether it could find a way to extend a preference to Palestine without having to reduce tariffs on products it imported from Palestine when they entered from states with which it had most-favored-nation treaties. Those states might raise objections if Britain showed a preference for Palestine, the Cabinet concluded, "due to its [Britain's] Mandatory status."[54] The Cabinet appointed a Committee on Imperial Preference for Palestine to study the matter and report back.

The Cabinet also decided to ask the states with which it had most-favored-nation treaties whether they would invoke these provisions if Britain extended a preference to Palestine. If the answers were affirmative, the Cabinet agreed, then Britain would seek the consent of these countries to submit the matter to the Permanent Court of International Justice for adjudication.[55] But the government would say nothing publicly about its intent to take the matter to the Court, fearing that "the negotiations with foreign countries would be prejudiced."[56]

The issue of a colonial preference for Palestine was expected to be raised in Parliament, and the Cabinet agreed that "the less said the better," deciding that "the proper course" was "in Parliament to play for time." If Parliament did bring it up, the government would not mention the most-favored-nation treaties and its concern that they might be invoked to Britain's detriment, but would say only "that very difficult legal and other complications were involved and that the whole question was being considered carefully in all aspects."[57] The government shortly was in fact asked in the House of Commons about a preference for Palestine and replied vaguely.[58]

Like the members of Parliament, the Permanent Mandates Commission pressed the British government to extend the same preference to Palestine that it had extended to Tanganyika, Cameroons, and Togoland, in order to avoid harm to Palestine's economy. The Commission was aware that the British government had stated in the House of Commons that the reason it had not yet done so related to unspecified legal difficulties.[59]

In keeping with the Cabinet's decision about seeking the inclination of Britain's most-favored-nation treaty partners, the British government did quietly approach Brazil, the United States, France, Italy, and Spain. With the United States, the most-favored-nation provision was found in a commercial treaty dating from 1815. It provided:

> No higher or other duties shall be imposed on the importation into the territories of his Britannick majesty in Europe of any articles, the growth, produce, or manufacture of the United States, than are or shall be payable on the like articles being the growth, produce, or manufacture of any other foreign country.[60]

The Import Duties Act applied to a wide range of goods exported by the United States to Britain.[61] Its economic impact on the United States was substantial.[62] In a confidential note to Henry Stimson, the U.S. Secretary of State, Britain's ambassador in Washington referred to the 1815 treaty and indicated that his government was contemplating "a preference to Palestinian produce imported into the United Kingdom." He inquired "whether the United States Government feel any objection to this proposal."[63] Stimson did object. In a reply note addressed to the British government, he wrote:

> The Government of the United States considers that Palestine is a "foreign country" within the meaning of the term as used in Article 2 of

the Convention, and therefore holds that any tariff privileges accorded to Palestine should also accrue to the United States.

In the same note, Stimson also objected to the preferences that Britain had already extended to the three Class B mandates. Stimson did not characterize them as "foreign countries," but said that he failed to perceive "any ground" on which they should "be treated as if they were possessions of the mandatory power."[64]

Italy replied that it, too, would invoke its commercial treaty with Britain, which dated from June 15, 1893, and similarly called for most-favored-nation treatment. "This results," explained the Italian Ministry for Foreign Affairs,

> from the fact that Palestinian territory, judging by the standard of the other territories under mandate, is to be considered as a foreign country *vis-à-vis* the mandatory nation, and therefore not as forming part of the British Empire.[65]

Spain replied

> that, in accordance with the terms of Article 22 of the Covenant of the League of Nations, ... the territory in question can in no way be considered as Imperial territory, but only as a foreign country dependent on the League of Nations, which from an economic point of view, is in a similar position as regards the Mandatory Power as it is in regard to other countries and Sovereign States.[66]

Brazil replied that it did not object, so long as the preference did not apply to oranges, "so that the similar product of Brazil exported to Great Britain would not be unfavourably affected."[67] France replied that it did not object.[68]

The Secretary of State for the Colonies reported the five replies to the Cabinet.[69] The Foreign Office told the Cabinet that its assessment of the replies was that Britain's partners in the commercial treaties regarded Palestine as a "foreign country" and "would claim for their goods imported into the United Kingdom any preferential rate which might be accorded to goods from Palestine. This attitude," the Foreign Office explained to the Cabinet, "is in accordance with the view of the situation which the Law Officers have taken in the past."[70] The "law officers" were the Attorney General and Solicitor General, the officials who advised the British government on legal matters.

The law officers had been consulted as to whether the most-favored-nation treaties could be invoked by Britain's treaty partners if Britain were to grant a preference to Palestine. As the Secretary related to the Cabinet:

> The question of possible damages was referred to the Law Officers in connexion with the Palestine question, and they then took the view that if preferences were granted in a case where His Majesty's Government's treaty obligations did not permit the grant of preference, the risk of a claim for damages for breach of treaty would be a serious one.[71]

The Secretary was saying that it was the view of the British government's legal advisors that Palestine was a "foreign country," meaning a state. The law officers, according to the Foreign Office, had advised that the Class B mandates, to which preferences had already been extended, were not "foreign countries," but that the Class A mandates were.[72]

Addressing the Cabinet's plan to take the matter to the Permanent Court of International Justice, the Foreign Office advised caution. It said

> that the case of His Majesty's Government in this matter must (in view of the series of adverse opinions by successive law officers) be regarded as a weak one and that His Majesty's Government in the United Kingdom would be running a serious risk of losing it if it were referred to a court for a legal decision.[73]

The following week, the Committee on Imperial Preference for Palestine, citing the negative replies from other governments, reported to the Cabinet "that the proposal to extend Imperial Preference to Palestine must be abandoned."[74]

In the event, Britain did not take the matter to the Permanent Court of International Justice and issued no preference order for Palestine.[75] Its own legal advisors regarded Palestine as a state and thought that, if presented with the question, the Permanent Court of International Justice would so decide.

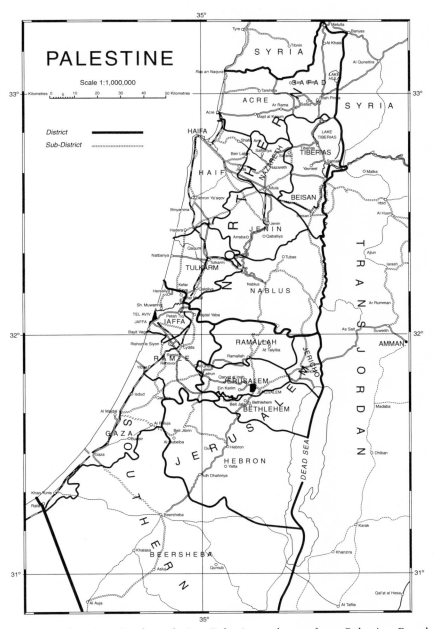

MAP 2. Administrative boundaries, Palestine redrawn from Palestine Royal Commission, Report, July 1937, Cmd. 5479

7

A State Awaiting Independence

Writing in 1948, H. Duncan Hall bemoaned "twenty years of inconclusive speculation among international lawyers as to where sovereignty was really lodged."[1] "Sovereignty" was not the only legal category by which to examine Palestine's status, but it was the term that lawyers invoked most frequently – more frequently than "statehood." To some lawyers, it seemed that the League of Nations had assumed sovereignty.[2] It was, after all, the League that had set up the mandate system, and the League that monitored the activity of the mandatory powers. Hersch Lauterpacht inclined to this analysis, concluding, as he did in his dissertation, that "sovereignty lies with the League of Nations and is derived from it."[3] Lauterpacht's view on this point attracted little following, however. Although the League had created and supervised the system, it had not selected the mandatory powers and did not itself provide administration.

Some lawyers thought that sovereignty rested, collectively, with the Allied and Associated Powers.[4] Frederick Pollock, the historian of English law, said that "ultimate sovereignty" passed to the Allies under the peace treaty.[5] As regarded the Ottoman territories, it was the Allies who had occupied them, forced Turkey to relinquish them, and then parceled them out to mandatories. One writer called this the "joint sovereignty" of the Allies.[6] The weakness of this approach was that although the Allies had set the mandate system in motion, as a group, they played no ongoing role and were expected to have none.

SOVEREIGNTY IN SEARCH OF A HOME

The mandatory powers may have seemed logical candidates to be the sovereignty holders, despite the "no annexations" principle. It was they, after all, who controlled the mandate territories. However, the view that sovereignty rested with the mandatory powers attracted few adherents. Rolin, who had surveyed the literature for his 1927 lectures on the mandate system at the Hague Academy of International Law, had not found any writers who espoused the view that sovereignty rested with the mandatory powers.[7] The possibility that sovereignty rested with the mandatory powers was examined by J.L. Brierly, professor of international law at Oxford University who served on the Committee of Experts for the Progressive Codification of International Law that had been established by the League of Nations. Brierly analyzed the mandate system in the first edition of his classic international law monograph, *The Law of Nations*. Brierly noted factors that seemed to negate mandatory sovereignty. He pointed out that the mandatories "must account for their actions, the territories are not annexed to their dominions, and the populations do not take their nationality."[8]

Lauterpacht, in his edition of Oppenheim's international law treatise, added more reasons to Brierly's, namely,

> [t]hat Germany and Turkey divested themselves of all rights of ownership in the mandated areas was clear. That the mandatories had not acquired all of those rights was equally clear; for (i) by the terms of the mandates they agreed to exercise their mandates on behalf of the League, and the mandates, at any rate, contained no cession of the territory to the mandatory.... (ii) the mandatory had no power without the consent of the Council of the League to annex, cede, or otherwise to dispose of the mandated territory; (iii) he was subject to varying restrictions as to the recruiting and training of the inhabitants ...; (iv) the inhabitants did not *ipso facto* acquire the nationality of the mandatory; (v) economically, he was under an obligation, at any rate in the case of the "A" and "B" mandates, to adopt the policy of the "open door," that is, he was bound to ensure to the nationals of all States members of the League the same rights in respect of commerce and trade as were open to the nationals of the mandatory. Secondly, the dominant element was that of trusteeship for the inhabitants of the mandated areas.[9]

Brierly and Lauterpacht made a persuasive case against mandatory sovereignty. The International Court of Justice came to the same conclusion in a case involving a Class C mandate.[10] The territory of the mandates was not territory of the mandatory. A mandatory power was forbidden to claim title. The operative principle for the mandates, as others have pointed out, was "no annexation."[11] The "no annexation" principle distinguished the mandate system from colonialism. "The administrating power in any mandate territory is not there by any right of possession," wrote Aaron Margalith, a Jerusalem-born political scientist, "but as a Mandatory with specifically delegated powers."[12]

Britain did not hold sovereignty in Palestine, even though it held legislative and administrative authority. Norman Bentwich explained the relationship as follows: "[A]mong the leading doctrines of international law in its extended sphere, is the right of nationalities, great and small, in the East as in the West, to live their national life, and the duty of the greater States to train them to that end."[13]

Consistent with the "no annexation" principle, Britain never claimed sovereignty in Palestine. The issue of Britain's legal status in its mandate territories came up in litigation in the High Court of Justice of Uruguay. Britain and Uruguay had a bilateral extradition treaty dating from 1884 that covered Britain's "Colonies and foreign possessions."[14] Britain asked Uruguay to apply this clause to nationals of Britain's mandate territories. Britain acknowledged, however, that the clause could not properly apply to such nationals, since the mandate territories were neither colonies nor possessions. So it asked the Uruguayan court to apply the treaty provision by analogy to include nationals of mandate territories. The court declined, saying that the treaty must be applied by its terms. The position taken by Britain showed that it understood that its mandate territories were not under its sovereignty.[15]

The mandate system was erected as a corrective to the colonial system that had prevailed in relations between the European powers and territories in Africa and Asia. The mandatory power exercised only those prerogatives accorded to it.[16] Great Britain as mandatory power in Palestine was subject to international scrutiny to ensure that it served the "beneficiaries," rather than its own interests.[17] The Permanent Mandates Commission required Britain to justify its practices of administration by submitting written reports and subjecting itself to questioning.[18] The citizenry of Palestine was able to petition the Commission to make complaints. The Jewish Agency for Palestine represented the interests of the Jewish community. The Arab Higher Committee represented the Arab community. During the Arab revolt of 1936, for example, the Arab Higher Committee protested to the Commission over the use of tear gas by British personnel against rebels.[19]

SOVEREIGNTY ANALYSIS QUESTIONED

Some lawyers found even the effort to locate sovereignty in regard to mandate territories to be inappropriate. Rolin said that most of the lawyers who made up the Institute of International Law were of this view.[20] Arnold McNair, sitting as a judge on the International Court of Justice in a case involving a Class C mandate, said that the "doctrine of sovereignty" had "no application." To McNair, the mandate system created "a new relationship between territory and its inhabitants on the one hand and the government which represents them internationally on the other." McNair said that this system "does not fit into the old conception of sovereignty and is alien to it." "Sovereignty over a Mandated Territory," McNair declared, "is in abeyance."[21]

Quincy Wright found sovereignty to be an applicable concept in analysis of the mandate territories, but he could not identify a single actor that held it. Wright devised the idea that sovereignty might be shared by several entities. He wrote:

> [S]overeignty of the areas is vested in the League acting through the Covenant amending process, and is exercised by the mandatory with consent of the Council for eventual transfer to the mandated communities themselves. In the case of Iraq and possibly other A communities, it appears that the native community already shares in the sovereignty. With this interpretation, sovereignty is in some cases held jointly by the League and the mandated community, the exercise of sovereignty being in those cases divided between them and the mandatory in proportions which vary according to the terms of the particular mandate.[22]

SOVEREIGNTY IN THE POPULATION

Still another viewpoint was that sovereignty rested with the peoples of the mandate territories. This view grew from the self-determination concept that was said to underpin the concept of the mandates. Judge Fouad Ammoun, a judge in the International Court of Justice, addressing not Palestine in particular but the mandates in general, viewed their populations as sovereign. Surveying the various opinions about sovereignty in the mandates, Ammoun found the view that the population held sovereignty to be the "more accurate view."[23] Paul Pic, professor at the University of Lyons and one of the earliest analysts of the mandate system, also found sovereignty in the "people under mandate."[24] "These territories belong virtually to the native populations or communities," he wrote, "for whom the League of Nations is set up as the defender, and in regard to whom it plays a role something like that of a family advisor."[25]

Henry Cattan found sovereignty in the population to be the correct analysis on the basis of Turkey's renunciation of sovereignty. In the

Treaty of Lausanne, Turkey had renounced sovereignty. Cattan, who lectured at the Jerusalem Law School during the mandate years, and who would later represent the Arab Higher Committee at the United Nations, reasoned that since the mandate system involved "no annexation," sovereignty must have been renounced by Turkey in favor of the populations of the various territories.[26]

Judge Ammoun, arguing that sovereignty rested with the populations, rejected Wright's view that sovereignty was shared. "[A]ll that is conceivable," Ammoun wrote, "is a distinction between the possession of sovereignty and its exercise."[27] That phrase captured the essence of the legal character of the mandate territories, particularly the Class A mandates. Sovereignty was held by the people, even if they were temporarily unable to exercise it. Cattan shared Ammoun's analysis about a split between sovereignty and its exercise. The people of Palestine, said Cattan, held sovereignty, but the exercise of that sovereignty was limited by the powers accorded to the mandatory.[28]

As applied to Palestine, a theory of sovereignty resting in the people raised the question, "which people," given the inclusion of the Balfour Declaration in the Palestine Mandate. In a recent book, lawyer Howard Grief, focusing on the Balfour Declaration, suggested that the "people" for whom sovereignty was intended in Palestine were not "the Arab inhabitants of the country at that time," but rather "World Jewry – including the approximately 80,000 Jews already living in Palestine, and those Jews expected to immigrate there in the future – clearly the national beneficiary of the Mandate for Palestine." Grief said that sovereignty "was held in abeyance for the Jewish People until Palestine could be fully developed as an independent Jewish State."[29] Grief's exclusion of the Arabs is difficult to sustain, however, because the Balfour Declaration specifically references the rights of Palestine's population in its entirety. Nathan Feinberg, professor of international law at Hebrew University, also focused on the Balfour Declaration in defining the circle of people who might be included in those enjoying sovereignty and included Jews not then present in Palestine but who might immigrate. Unlike Grief, Feinberg did not exclude the Arabs of Palestine.[30]

MANDATES AS COMPARABLE TO PROTECTORATES

Analysts who said that the mandate territories were not states, and that their populations did not hold sovereignty, typically did not distinguish the three classes of mandate. Nor did they examine the practice of the exercise of the Class A mandates or the documents executed by the major powers in regard to the Class A mandates.[31] McNair, cited above, was analyzing South West Africa, which was a Class C mandate. McNair made no distinction between a Class C mandate and a Class A mandate; rather, he spoke about mandates in general.

Paul Fauchille, author of the leading French treatise in international law of the mandate era, did distinguish among the three categories of mandates. Fauchille considered that the Class A mandates had been established in such a fashion that the population shared in sovereignty, but he did not find that to be the case in the Class B or Class C mandates. Stating a view similar to Wright's about shared sovereignty, Fauchille wrote that

> in the Class B and Class C mandates full sovereignty is the mandatory's, but that in the Class A mandates, one finds, as in protectorates properly so called, a sharing of sovereignty between the "communities" or "independent nations" and the mandatory.[32]

Lawyers who did not regard the Class A mandates, Palestine in particular, as states focused on the mandatory powers' control; their assumption was that administration by an outside power negated statehood. That assumption was not a necessary one and was not borne out by the state practice of the era. In the early twentieth century, a split between statehood on the one hand and the power of administration on the other was seen in the law relating to protectorates. An example was Morocco, in its relation with France. The Sultan of Morocco, by the 1912 Treaty of Fez with France, placed Morocco under France's protection. The treaty gave France extensive authority over Morocco: France could station military forces there at its discretion and take police action in Morocco. It could require the Sultan to carry out legislative reforms. A French commissioner was to act as intermediary for Morocco's contact with representatives of foreign governments. Any decrees the Sultan might issue required France's consent. France had control of Morocco's foreign relations.[33] Despite France's powers of administration, when the issue of Morocco's status arose before the International Court of Justice, as it did in a 1952 case, the Court held that Morocco was a state. Parsing the Treaty of Fez, the Court said that Morocco "has retained its personality as a State in international law."[34]

Even less control by a state over its territory was reflected in another early twentieth-century situation, the arrangement between Panama and the United States for the Canal Zone. A 1903 treaty between the

United States and Panama gave the United States the right to construct a canal through Panama, granting the United States nearly total control of a strip of land in the center of Panama for that purpose. Article 2 of the Treaty identified the territory constituting the "zone." Article 3 then provided:

> The Republic of Panama grants to the United States all the rights, power and authority within the zone ... which the United States would possess and exercise if it were the sovereign of the territory ... to the entire exclusion of the exercise by the Republic of Panama of any such sovereign rights, power or authority.[35]

Despite this grant of rights to the United States, the Canal Zone remained the territory of Panama, as would be later recognized by the two states when, in a 1977 treaty, they abrogated the 1903 treaty.[36]

Thus, sovereignty in the absence of administrative control was familiar ground in the international practice of the early twentieth century. An analogy with protectorates recommended itself to many analysts as they strived to classify the novel institution of mandates, in particular the Class A mandates. Hersch Lauterpacht, writing in 1922, found "almost complete unanimity on the point that the areas in this category [Class A mandates] are to be described as protectorates under international law.[37] Lauterpacht said that "the qualities of the protectorate"

> correspond with the circumstances in the Mandated territories of the A group; for they are after all States, which "in certain international relationships are represented by another State" and which "are not members of the international community with full rights."[38]

Class A mandate territories, like protected states, lacked "full rights" in the sense that they were not independent. Lauterpacht was able to conclude that the Class A mandates were states even though, as indicated above, he found sovereignty to lie with the League of Nations. By his analysis, statehood did not depend on locating sovereignty in the people of the territory.

Brierly called the Class A mandates "countries." Like Lauterpacht, he considered their status to be similar to that of a protected state. Brierly characterized the relationship as that of a "responsible" protectorate because of the mandatory's obligations:

> The mandatory state, unlike a protecting state, is in theory disinterested, and it assumes obligations, as well as rights, both to the population under mandate and to the League.[39]

A protecting state was free to seek its own advantage from the relationship; it had no obligation to promote independence and was not accountable to any international organization. By contrast and this is why Brierly used the term "responsible" protectorate a mandatory power holding a Class A mandate was precluded from gaining advantage from its relationship to the mandate territory, was required to move the territory toward independence, and was accountable to the League of Nations. Thus, a territory under a Class A mandate appeared to enjoy an even higher status than a protected state.

Mandates were also described as protectorates by Henri Rolin, professor at the University of Brussels and a specialist in colonial law. This Henri Rolin, whose dates are 1874–1946, is not the Henri A. Rolin cited above and in previous chapters, whose dates are 1891–1973. (Both Rolins were Belgian, and both analyzed the mandate system.) The elder Rolin wrote in 1920 that Covenant Article 22(4) contemplated eventual independence but that up until the time of independence, the "communities"

> will have a part of sovereignty: that is the meaning that is evidently to be attributed to their provisional existence "as independent nations." But this sovereignty will not be complete, because the mandatory will have the right and the power to "guide their administration." Only the name is lacking in the Treaty [Covenant Article 22(4)] to complete the identification of this regime, well known in international law and in colonial law. It is a protectorate.[40]

The elder Rolin continued,

> Paragraph 4 [of Covenant Article 22], concerning the first category of mandates (Asian Turkey) readily allows one to see to whom sovereignty is attributed. It will be shared, as in any protectorate properly so called, between the "communities" or "independent nations" and the mandatory.[41]

He regarded what he called the "protected communities" as possessing an international status and holding an "exclusive right to enjoyment of the patrimony of the territory."[42] The younger Rolin disputed the elder Rolin on this point, saying that his elder placed too much weight on the difference between the Class A mandates on the one hand and the Class B and C mandates on the other.[43]

Giulio Diena, professor of international law at Turin, and later at Pavia, served, like Brierly, as a member of the League's Committee of

Experts for the Progressive Codification of International Law. Like the elder Henri Rolin, Diena likened mandates to protectorates. Lecturing on the mandate system at the Hague Academy of International Law in 1924, Diena said,

> Given that these communities, while destined to become, after a more or less extended period of time, completely independent, are presently guided in their internal administration by the mandatory; that in their external relations they are under the control of the mandatory, which also has the task of diplomatic and consular protection of the citizens of the communities themselves and the right to issue exequaturs to consuls of foreign powers, it is beyond doubt that one has here an international protectorate.[44]

Diena addressed a counterargument that had been made to the analogy. The counterargument was that protectorates are established by a treaty between the two states involved, whereas mandates were established by the League of Nations. A protected state by an act of will concedes power to a protecting state, whereas mandate territories were placed in the mandate relationship by the League. Diena replied that treaties for protectorates may be concluded on the side of the protected state by one that lacks "full juridical capacity." He explained,

> In substance, there does not seem to be any essential difference between an international protectorate and the legal situation in which the communities that are the object of Class A mandates *presently* [Diena's emphasis] find themselves vis-à-vis the mandatory and vis-à-vis third parties.[45]

Diena then responded to a writer who had termed mandates "colonial protectorates." Diena distinguished a "colonial protectorate" from an "international protectorate," saying that a colonial protectorate

> differs from an international protectorate in that it has as its object populations that have no state organization and territories that, at the time this type of protectorate is established, are from the international law point of view *res nullius*, whereas the latter takes place between two states. The communities at issue in paragraph 4 of Article 22 for Class A mandates are not savage tribes, but, to the contrary, are capable of taking on organization as states, and to the end of establishing a protectorate on the part of the mandatory, they are already considered as states, even without possessing full sovereignty. From this point of view one can explain why in paragraph 4 where it is declared that these communities can be recognized as independent nations, the adverb *provisionally* has been added,

which ... would be questionable if the term *independent nations* were used in the sense of fully sovereign states.[46]

Like Balfour, Diena took the phrase "independent nations" to refer to the mandate territory, not to the population, and found Class A mandates to be states. Diena distinguished "state" from "fully sovereign state," finding the former to be the condition of a Class A mandate during the pendency of the mandate, and the latter to be the objective upon the mandate's eventual termination. Diena considered that the Class A mandates were states even if they lacked "full sovereignty."

LEGALITY OF THE MANDATES

One other issue commanded attention in regard to the Palestine mandate, namely, whether its call for a Jewish national home violated the self-determination notion contained in Covenant Article 22, and, arguably, in the general international law of the era. Balfour acknowledged the conflict between self-determination for the Palestine population and the espousal of a Jewish national home. In correspondence with Prime Minister Lloyd George on February 19, 1919, Balfour wrote, "The weak point of our position of course is that in the case of Palestine we deliberately and rightly decline to accept the principle of self-determination." Balfour justified the espousal of a Jewish national home on the basis that "we consider the question of the Jews outside Palestine as one of world importance" and that "we conceive Jews to have a historic claim to a home in their ancient land."[47]

By summer 1919, the League Covenant had been adopted. In a memorandum to Curzon on August 11, 1919, Balfour acknowledged an inconsistency between what the Allies were doing by promoting Zionism and the wording of the Covenant, presumably Article 22. He said:

> The contradiction between the letters of the Covenant and the policy of the Allies is even more flagrant in the case of the "independent nation" of Palestine than in that of the "independent nation" of Syria. For in Palestine we do not propose even to go through the form of consulting the wishes of the present inhabitants of the country, ...[48]

The question of the legality of the mandate is of secondary importance in the question of Palestine statehood. On the statehood issue, what matters is what the international community established, how it conceived Palestine as an entity, and how the states of the international community regarded Palestine. Palestine could have been created as a state even if it was done in a way that violated the rights of the inhabitants.

PALESTINE AS A STATE

A United States court, in a 2005 case, was faced with the question of whether Palestine was a state and would thus be entitled to immunity from a civil lawsuit. Addressing the question of Palestine's status under the British mandate, the court said that Palestine was not a state at that time, reasoning that

> [d]uring the currency of the mandate, the United Kingdom exercised suzerainty over the administration and laws of the defined territory.[49]

In taking that position, the court misread the state practice of the period. The Class A mandates were conceived as states, and Palestine especially so, despite the fact that Britain was to administer.

When Iraq was admitted as a member of the League in 1932, Japan's delegate to the League, Harukazu Nagaoka, in a statement of welcome to Iraq, reflected the understanding that the mandates were states that upon termination of the mandate would become independent. He characterized Iraq as a state that was becoming independent. Referring to Covenant Article 22, Nagaoka expressed his "sincere hope that this state, now independent and sovereign, may continue to prosper as a member of the League."[50]

Stoyanovsky, who viewed sovereignty as resting with the population, regarded Palestine as a state. While acknowledging that Palestine was different from Syria and from Iraq in terms of administration, he called statehood the "juridical position" of Palestine. Using terminology from the law of family relations, Stoyanovsky characterized Palestine as an

> infant state, under the guardianship of the Mandatory. It is represented by the Administration of Palestine, whatever the composition of that body from time to time may be – as distinguished from but under the effective control of, the Mandatory."[51]

Just as Palestine was a state separate from Britain, said Stoyanovsky, so too did it have a separate government. The Administration of Palestine was not the Government of Britain.

Cattan, eschewing creative adjectives like "infant," simply found Mandate Palestine, along with the other Class A mandates, to be states. He said:

[T]he various Arab countries, including Palestine, which were subjected to mandates under Article 22 of the covenant became states under international law, even though their powers of self-government were restricted and were exercised by a Mandatory.[52]

The apparent consequence for those analysts who said that a Class A mandate was not a state was that there would be no state at all. These analysts would have been the first to agree that the territory was not *terra nullius*, that is, some third state could not have entered and planted its flag to claim sovereignty. Whether there can be territory that is not *terra nullius* but not attributable to some state is, however, questionable. The system of international relations that came out of the Peace of Westphalia of 1648 was premised on the existence of states. Quincy Wright, analyzing sovereignty in the mandates in 1923, said, "The tendency of modern international law is to conceive of all the land territory of the world as under the sovereignty of some state."[53]

When France challenged British sovereignty over the Ecrehos islands in the English Channel, "it did not itself claim sovereignty but continued to treat the Ecrehos as res nullius."[54] The assumption was that the Ecrehos islands were either part of a state (Britain) or *res nullius*. Could the mandate system have introduced a concept that there may be territory that is neither *res nullius* nor part of a state? There is no reason to think that it did.

Crawford points out that "it was not argued" with respect to the Class A mandates, "that the status of the territories concerned was that of independent states."[55] It was argued, however, and quite persuasively, that they were "states," even if not independent. While, as H. Duncan Hall complained, there was endless disagreement among legal analysts over sovereignty as the concept applied to the Class A mandates, there was less disagreement over whether they were states.

Sir Humphrey Waldock recognized the statehood status of mandate territories during his work in 1970 as special rapporteur in the International Law Commission on Succession of States in Respect of Treaties. Waldock used the term "new state" to identify an independent state that had previously formed part of an existing state. This definition, as he explained, applied to the emergence into independence of a colony, since a colony was previously part of an existing state. But Waldock said that the term "new state"

excludes a union of States, a federation with an existing State and the emergence to independence of a trusteeship territory or mandated territory or a protected State.[56]

Mandate territories were excluded, apparently because of Waldock's understanding that they had never been "part of" the mandatory power. Like protected states, their status was separate from that of the administering state. If a former mandate territory was not a "new state," then Waldock's implication was that it had been a state while under the mandate.

The two highest officials of the Palestine administration both conceived that what they were administering was a state. Herbert Samuel, who as high commissioner of Palestine was the official primarily responsible for promoting a Jewish homeland in Palestine, called the mandates "states," as was seen in Chapter 3. Norman Bentwich, Attorney-General of Palestine, used the term "infant state" to characterize Iraq under its mandate, as seen in Chapter 5. He used the same term to characterize all the Class A mandates, writing:

> Article 22 of the Covenant of the League distinguishes between the Mandates for the countries detached from Turkey and the Mandates for the German Colonies; and ... provides for the treatment of the former as infant or minor States.[57]

As will be discussed in Chapter 18, a key element in determining whether a particular entity is a state is the attitude of the states of the international community. For determining Palestine's international status, the view of the states of the era is most relevant, and first and foremost those states immediately involved. The Principal Allied Powers in World War I conceived the mandate system and distributed the mandates among themselves. The Allies viewed the Class A mandates as states. Britain was the key actor, and it, as indicated, regarded Palestine as a state. The other Allies shared in this view, as seen in Covenant Article 22(4) and in the Treaty of Lausanne.

Even states that were not members of the League of Nations accepted what the Allies and the League had brought into being. The United States had been heavily involved in the mandate concept. As seen in Chapter 2, President Woodrow Wilson's promotion of self-determination provided part of the impetus for it. Although the United States did not become a member of the League, it concluded a bilateral treaty with Britain in which it acknowledged the mandate system established in the League Covenant. This bilateral treaty, after first reproducing the text of the Palestine Mandate, provided that "the United States consents to the administration of Palestine by His Britannic Majesty, pursuant to the mandate recited above."[58]

The states of the international community dealt with the Class A mandates on the basis on which the Allies and the League had formed them. The younger Henri Rolin, as rapporteur on the topic of mandates for the Institute of International Law, wrote that the arrangement fashioned by the League for the mandate territories

> has gained the acceptance not only of the states signatory to the various treaties of peace and of other states that have become members of the League of Nations, but the United States of America itself has, either expressly or tacitly, approved the text of the mandate instruments, so that one can say that it is a matter not of a spontaneous creation of the colonial policy of certain states, or even of a private character devised in a treaty binding a small number of states, but rather a true institution of general international law that most states of the world recognize and accept.[59]

The statehood of the Class A mandates was accepted by the international community. Palestine's citizenship and treaties were recognized. The question of the status of the mandate territories was raised in the form of a draft resolution before a meeting of the Institute of International Law in 1931, but no vote was taken.[60] When practical issues arose that required consideration of Palestine's status, the consistent verdict was that Palestine was a state. That was the outcome in the arbitration over the Ottoman public debt. That was the outcome as courts construed the Treaty of Lausanne in citizenship cases. That was the outcome when Great Britain contemplated a tariff preference for Palestine. Britain's own government lawyers agreed with Spain, Italy, and the United States that Palestine was a state.

Opinions of analysts can be found supporting every conceivable position on sovereignty and on the statehood of the Class A mandates. What analysts say is of less import than what states did. International law rules are made and implemented by states in their interactions. The Class A mandates, including Palestine, were states because that is how they were erected and that is how they were considered as they operated in the international arena. The states of the era had no difficulty separating the concept of statehood from that of independence. They did not regard an absence of independence in relation to Palestine as a negation of its statehood.

PART TWO

STATEHOOD IN TURMOIL

8

A Post-Mandate State

With the exception of Palestine, the Class A mandates gained independence by arrangement with the particular mandatory. Iraq was the first, becoming independent in 1932. Lebanon followed in 1941, and Syria in 1943. Transjordan's independence came in a treaty with Britain in 1946. As for Palestine, Britain in 1937 considered the possibility of splitting Palestine but in 1939 issued a White Paper that projected in the following terms a withdrawal leading to independence for Palestine as a single territorial unit:

> The objective of His Majesty's Government is the establishment within ten years of an independent Palestine state in such treaty relations with the United Kingdom as will provide satisfactorily for the commercial and strategic interests of both countries in the future. [1]

Independence for Palestine as a single unit would require an accommodation between Arabs and Jews. These two communities, the White Paper projected, would "share authority in government in such a way that the essential interests of the each are secured."[2]

ARAB LEAGUE ON PALESTINE STATEHOOD

The Arab states, having themselves only recently emerged into independence, pressed Britain on the issue of Palestine. They formed the League of Arab States, whose aims included Palestine independence. In a document titled the Alexandria Protocol, adopted in Alexandria, Egypt, in October 1944, they recited that the League would be composed of the "independent Arab States": Iraq, Egypt, Syria, Transjordan, and Lebanon. Palestine was not to be a member, being still under the mandate and therefore not independent. However, the Alexandria Protocol included a section on Palestine, which stated that the committee forming the organization was

> of the opinion that the pledges binding the British Government and pro-
> viding for ... the achievement of independence for Palestine are permanent
> Arab rights whose prompt implementation would constitute a step toward
> the desired goal and toward the stabilization of peace and security.

The committee declared "its support of the cause of the Arabs of Palestine and its willingness to work for the achievement of their legitimate aim and the safeguarding of their just rights."[3]

A charter was adopted on March 22, 1945 as the League's founding document. By then, Yemen and Saudi Arabia were participating. In an annex to the Charter, Palestine was identified as a state, and provision was made, as follows, for its representation in the League:

Annex on Palestine

At the end of the last Great War, Palestine, together with the other Arab States, was separated from the Ottoman Empire. She became independent, not belonging to any other State.

The Treaty of Lausanne proclaimed that her fate should be decided by the parties concerned in Palestine.

Even though Palestine was not able to control her own destiny, it was on the basis of the recognition of her independence that the Covenant of the League of Nations determined a system of government for her.

Her existence and her independence among the nations can, therefore, no more be questioned *de jure* than the independence of any of the other Arab States.

Even though the outward signs of this independence have remained veiled as a result of *force majeure*, it is not fitting that this should be an obstacle to the participation of Palestine in the work of the League.

Therefore, the States signatory to the Pact of the Arab League consider that in view of Palestine's special circumstances, the Council of the League should designate an Arab delegate from Palestine to participate in its work until this country enjoys actual independence.[4]

On December 4, 1945, the Arab League provided for Palestine's partici-
pation in its deliberations, giving it a vote on matters relating to Palestine. The League set up a procedure for choosing Palestine delegates that was to involve their nomination by the Arab Higher Committee and appointment by the Council of the Arab League.[5]

On June 12, 1946, the Arab League, looking toward a Palestine that was under majority rule, approved the appointment of four Palestine delegates to the League and designated them as constituting the Arab Higher Committee, "which the Arab League had decided to establish in Palestine." The League characterized the Arab Higher Committee, which, as indicated in Chapter 7, spoke for the Palestine Arabs in the League of Nations, as "representing all of the Arabs of Palestine and speaking in their name and uniting all their efforts and endeavours for the sake of Palestine."[6] Appointing Palestine delegates and indicating its concern for Palestine's situation, the Arab League assumed a responsibility for assuring that Palestine would come to independence within the mandate borders.[7]

UNITED NATIONS CHARTER AND PALESTINE STATEHOOD

While the Arab League was acting to preserve Palestine's statehood, the major powers were forging a new organization to replace the League of Nations. In October 1945, the Charter of the United Nations was adopted, and it contained provisions that were relevant to Palestine's status. The Charter contemplated the possibility that League mandates that had not ended in independence might be converted to a supervisory arrangement to be called a "trusteeship." The United Nations would monitor the trusteeships, much in the way the League, through the Permanent Mandates Commission, had monitored the mandates. This contemplated conversion appeared in Chapter XII, Article 77, of the Charter, which read:

1. The trusteeship system shall apply to such territories in the following categories as may be placed thereunder by means of trusteeship agreements: a. territories now held under mandate; b. territories which may be detached from enemy states as a result of the Second World War; and c. territories voluntarily placed under the system by states responsible for their administration.
2. It will be a matter for subsequent agreement as to which territories in the foregoing categories will be brought under the trusteeship system and upon what terms.

Article 80 was a default provision, preserving mandate rights:

1. Except as may be agreed upon in individual trusteeship agreements, made under Articles 77, 79, and 81, placing each territory under the trusteeship system, and until such agreements have been concluded,

nothing in this Chapter shall be construed in or of itself to alter in any manner the rights whatsoever of any states or any peoples or the terms of existing international instruments to which Members of the United Nations may respectively be parties.

2. Paragraph 1 of this Article shall not be interpreted as giving grounds for delay or postponement of the negotiations and conclusion of agreements for placing mandated and other territories under the trusteeship system as provided for in Article 77.

On April 18, 1946, the League of Nations dissolved itself.[8] With that act, one party to the Palestine Mandate went out of existence. UN Charter Article 77(2) left it to subsequent agreement as to which territories would go under trusteeship. The League's Assembly, at its final session, adopted a resolution on mandates, in which it said that it

1. Expresses its satisfaction with the manner in which the organs of the League have performed the functions entrusted to them with respect to the mandates system and in particular pays tribute to the work accomplished by the Permanent Mandates Commission;

2. Recalls the role of the League in assisting Iraq to progress from its status under an 'A' Mandate to a condition of complete independence, welcomes the termination of the mandated status of Syria, the Lebanon and Transjordan, which have, since the last session of the Assembly, become independent members of the world community;

3. Recognizes that, on the termination of the League's existence, its functions with respect to the mandated territories will come to an end, but notes that Chapters XI, XII and XIII of the Charter of the United Nations embody principles corresponding to those declared in Article 22 of the Covenant of the League;

4. Takes note of the expressed intentions of the Members of the League now administering territories under mandate to continue to administer them for the well-being and development of the peoples concerned in accordance with the obligations contained in the respective Mandates, until other arrangements have been agreed between the United Nations and the respective mandatory Powers.[9]

Egypt, a member state of the League, abstained on the vote on this resolution because it objected to paragraph 4. Egypt said that Palestine should be brought to independence, rather than being placed under trusteeship. Egypt's delegate relied on Covenant Article 22. He said:

The terms of Article 22 of the Covenant of the League of Nations, referred to in the preamble of the resolution under consideration, provide that the system of mandates was meant for peoples not yet able to stand alone in the strenuous conditions of the modern world. Palestine, after the last war, was considered to be a territory coming under this provision. The opinion of my Government is that Palestine has intellectually, economically, and politically reached a stage where it should no longer continued under mandate or trusteeship or whatever other arrangements may be considered. Palestine is not behind the countries the independence of which has lately been admitted, and to which reference is made in the resolution; she is not behind Iraq, Syria, the Lebanon or Transjordan. I therefore feel that I have to make all reservations in the Assembly, as I did in the committee, with regard to the fourth paragraph of the resolution, ...

It is the view of my Government that mandates have terminated with the dissolution of the League of Nations, and that, in so far as Palestine is concerned, there should be no question of putting that country under trusteeship. I have not chosen the procedure of submitting a formal resolution whereby the Assembly expresses the wish that the independence of Palestine shall be declared; I chose in the committee, and I intend here, simply to abstain from voting on this resolution.[10]

Earlier in the meeting, Britain had declared its intent not to conclude a trusteeship agreement with the UN for Palestine. Speaking generally about its role as a mandatory power, Britain told the League's final Assembly meeting that

[t]he mandates administered by the United Kingdom were originally those for Iraq, Palestine, Transjordan, Tanganyika, part of the Cameroons, and part of Togoland. Two of these territories have already become independent sovereign States, Iraq in 1923,[11] and Transjordan just the other day in 1946. As for Tanganyika and Togoland under their mandate, and the Cameroons under their mandate, His Majesty's Government in the United Kingdom have already announced their intention of placing them under the trusteeship system of the United Nations, subject to negotiations on satisfactory terms of trusteeship.

The future of Palestine cannot be decided until the Anglo-American Committee of Enquiry have rendered their report, but until the three African territories have actually been placed under trusteeship and until fresh arrangements have been reached in regard to Palestine – whatever those arrangements may be – it is the intention of His Majesty's Government in the United Kingdom to continue to administer these territories in accordance with the general principles of the existing mandates.[12]

In 1950, the International Court of Justice would rule in regard to another mandate territory, South-West Africa, that a mandate was not terminated by the dissolution of the League of Nations. Referring to UN Charter Article 80(1), the Court said that this provision applied to mandate territories and that the rights of states and peoples survived the demise of the League.[13]

Article 80(1) preserved to the population of Palestine its rights under the mandate. When David Ben Gurion testified on behalf of the Jewish Agency for Palestine before a UN Special Committee on Palestine in 1947, he invoked Article 80 as preserving Jewish rights under the Palestine Mandate.[14] Article 80 encompassed whatever rights had been obtained under mandate arrangements, including the statehood that Palestine enjoyed. By saying that it would continue to administer Palestine on the basis of the Palestine Mandate after the League disbanded, Britain was acknowledging that the rights of Palestine and its population under Covenant Article 22(4) did not terminate with the demise of the League. Britain was acknowledging that Palestine's statehood subsisted.

PLANS FOR PALESTINE INDEPENDENCE

UN Charter Article 77 did not require Britain to place Palestine under a trusteeship, but Britain was obligated by Covenant Article 22(4) to bring Palestine to independence. Its obligation upon the demise of the League thus would seem to have been either to bring Palestine to independence itself, or, if unable to do so, to place it under a UN trusteeship that would bring it to independence. The Anglo-American Committee of Inquiry, to which Britain referred in its statement to the League Assembly, called for a trusteeship. The Committee of Inquiry had been set up by the U.S. and British governments to find solutions to Britain's inability to devise a solution for ending the mandate. On May 1, 1946, the Committee issued its report. The Committee recommended that "Palestine shall be neither a Jewish State nor an Arab State" and said that the best way to bring about a nonsectarian state was that "the Government of Palestine be continued as at present under mandate pending the execution of a Trusteeship Agreement under the United Nations."[15]

To implement this approach, British and U.S. officials in July 1946 devised what became known as the Morrison Plan, which called for a central government for Palestine with, at least initially, a British high commissioner in charge. An Arab province and a Jewish province would be created under the central government.[16] Each province would have administrative and legislative power, and each would determine its own immigration levels, consistent with absorptive capacity.[17]

The Arab states responded negatively to the Morrison Plan. They proposed instead a route to early independence for Palestine. A constituent assembly would be elected, and it in turn would draft a constitution. After adoption of a constitution, parliamentary elections would be held, whereupon Britain would withdraw and recognize Palestine's independence.[18]

The Jewish Agency also reacted negatively to the Morrison Plan. Seeing the plan rejected by both Arabs and Jews, the British government next proposed a five-year British trusteeship under a British high commissioner. This new approach, which came to be called the Bevin Plan after the British foreign secretary Ernest Bevin, anticipated a constituent assembly to be elected in four years. With the consent of the constituent assembly, the high commissioner would then take steps "to establish the institutions of the independent State." The British government explained, "Throughout the period of the mandatory rule in Palestine, it has been the object of His Majesty's Government to lay the foundations for an independent Palestinian State in which Arabs and Jews would enjoy equal rights."[19]

The Bevin Plan, like the Morrison Plan before it, was greeted negatively, leading the British government to give notice to terminate the mandate unilaterally, even if no governing mechanism could be put in place. On April 2, 1947, Britain asked that a special session of the UN General Assembly be convened on "the Question of Palestine." Britain indicated that it would "submit to the Assembly an account of their administration of the League of Nations mandate" and would "ask the Assembly to make recommendations, under Article 10 of the Charter, concerning the future government of Palestine."[20]

UNITED NATIONS EFFORTS

The matter was taken up by the UN General Assembly's First Committee, which was responsible for political and security matters. The Committee, and then the General Assembly itself, invited the Arab Higher Committee to participate in discussion of Palestine.[21] On May 9, 1947, Henry Cattan, as the representative of the Arab Higher Committee, requested independence for Palestine. "It is high time," Cattan told the First Committee, "that

Palestine's right to independence should be recognized, and that this tor-
mented country should enjoy the blessing of a democratic government."
Cattan advised against linking the issue of the Palestine Mandate with
that of the Jewish refugees in Europe. He referred to the situation with the
refugees as "a humanitarian problem," and said it was "the duty and concern of the civilized world to treat it as such." But, he said, "The linking
of the refugee problem with Palestine has made and will continue to make
the solution of both problems infinitely more difficult, if not impossible."
Cattan said, "We are asking nothing more than what each of you would
wish for his own country; nothing more than what is consecrated by the
lofty principles and purposes of your very Charter."[22]

In line with Cattan's request, five Arab states asked to add as an
agenda item "the termination of the Mandate over Palestine and the
declaration of its independence."[23] The request was based on the premise
that, under Covenant Article 22, the Palestine state was not yet independent and that, upon Britain's withdrawal as the mandatory, the mandate would terminate, and the state should become independent.

The General Assembly's General Committee, which was in charge
of the agenda, declined that request, however.[24] In determining how
best to proceed, the First Committee consulted both the Jewish Agency
for Palestine and the Arab Higher Committee as organizations that
"represented a considerable element of the population of Palestine."[25]
A special session of the General Assembly was called, at which the
Assembly appointed an eleven-nation Special Committee on Palestine to
report "on the question of Palestine."[26] It did so on August 31, 1947, but
the eleven nations could not agree on an approach. They split into two
camps, each advocating a route to independence but in differing ways.
Seven of the eleven nations recommended that Palestine be divided into
two states, with an economic union between them. Three recommended
that Palestine should be a federal state composed of a Jewish entity and
an Arab entity. One state abstained.[27]

The majority states explained that their proposal for partition with
economic union was prompted in significant measure by the atrocities
against Jews perpetrated by the Nazi government in Germany. They
wrote:

> It is not without significance that only since the rise of Nazism to power
> in Germany, with the resultant mass movement of Jews to Palestine, has
> the Palestine question become sufficiently acute to require the devising
> of solutions outside the framework of the normal evolution of an "A"

Mandate. Thus, all of the significant solutions devised for Palestine are of comparatively recent origin.[28]

This statement seemed to justify Cattan's concern that the issue of the Jewish refugees in Europe was leading the United Nations toward an approach in Palestine that might deviate from the legal requirements involved in terminating a Class A mandate.

The British government did not commit itself to any particular plan. In a top-secret memorandum dated September 18, 1947, written for the information of the Cabinet, however, Bevin as foreign secretary expressed horror at the Special Committee's majority proposal for partition. Bevin told the Cabinet that the Special Committee proposal was

> so manifestly unjust to the Arabs that it is difficult to see how, in Sir Alexander Cadogan's words "we could reconcile it with our conscience". There are also strong reasons of expediency for declining the responsibility for giving effect to this proposal. The attempt to do so would precipitate an Arab rising in Palestine which would have the moral approval of the entire Moslem world and would be more or less actively supported by the neighbouring Arab States.[29]

Cadogan, to whom Bevin referred, was Britain's representative at the United Nations. To demonstrate the unjust nature of the majority proposal, Bevin recited as follows:

> The frontiers drawn by the authors of this plan are more favourable to the Jews and more unfavourable to the Arabs than those drawn in any partition plan which has at any time been contemplated by His Majesty's Government. The present population in the area allocated to the Jewish State consists of approximately 500,000 Jews and 500,000 non-Jews, mainly Arab.[30]

Cadogan did not express his reservations at the United Nations, however. The General Assembly proceeded to organize an Ad Hoc Committee on Palestine, composed of all of the UN member states, to make a final proposal. On November 25, 1947, the Ad Hoc Committee approved the Special Committee majority plan for partition with economic union. The vote was 25 in favor, 13 against, with 17 abstentions.[31] This sufficed for Committee approval, since only a majority vote was required. It would not suffice for the General Assembly, however, which needed a two-thirds vote. But on November 29, 1947, the UN General Assembly, at which the same fifty-seven states were represented, adopted the plan for partition with economic union as Resolution 181, in a vote that was 33 in favor, 13 against, with 10 abstentions.[32] This vote met the two-thirds majority requirement. As adopted, the central clause of Resolution 181 read as follows:

> Independent Arab and Jewish States ... shall come into existence in Palestine two months after the evacuation of the armed forces of the mandatory Power has been completed but in any case not later than 1 October 1948.

The economic union, as provided by Part I(D) of the Resolution 181 partition plan, was to involve a customs union, a joint currency system with a single foreign exchange rate; joint operation of railways, highways, postal, telephone and telegraph services, and ports and airports; and joint operation of irrigation, land reclamation, and soil conservation. Overseeing all these activities would be a nine-member Joint Economic Board, composed of three representatives of each state and three appointed by the UN Economic and Social Council (ECOSOC). Thus, considerable substance was contemplated for the economic union, maintaining Palestine as a single unit in important aspects of state administration.

RESOLUTION 181 AND PALESTINE STATEHOOD

Resolution 181 did not contain language expressly characterizing the status of Palestine as it existed under mandate. The call in Resolution 181 for two "independent" states, however, was consistent with the Covenant Article 22(4) characterization of the Class A mandates as states. The Palestine state would be converted into two states linked together in an economic union and would become independent. Moreover, various provisions of Resolution 181 were written on the assumption that Palestine, under mandate, was a state.

Palestine's status as a state under the mandate was reflected in Part I(C) of Resolution 181's partition plan, which required the two projected states to make certain declarations to the United Nations prior to attaining independence. Chapter 3 of the declaration section addressed the obligations of the two projected states as successors to the Palestine state. Each state would make a declaration involving obligations regarding citizenship, treaties, and the public debt.

Chapter 3(1) of the declaration section recited that citizens of Palestine, at least those living outside Jerusalem, for which there was to be a special regime, would become citizens of the Jewish or Arab state respectively. Thus, the General Assembly recognized that there was a Palestine citizenship under the mandate and dealt with it as an issue of succession of states. Palestine citizens would become citizens of one or the other of the two projected states. Chapter 3(1) required each projected successor state to recognize the inhabitants of its territory as citizens. This disposition was in accord with international practice for the succession of states and followed what had been done, as recounted in Chapter 4, when Palestine succeeded to the Ottoman Empire.

Chapter 3(2) of the declaration section called for Palestine treaties to be honored by both the Arab state and the Jewish state. Referring to each as "the state," Chapter 3(2) provided that

> [t]he State shall be bound by all the international agreements and conventions, both general [multilateral] and special [bilateral], to which Palestine has become a party. Subject to any right of denunciation provided for therein, such agreements and conventions shall be respected by the State throughout the period for which they were concluded.

Successor states are normally required to honor the treaties of predecessor states.[33] This provision acknowledged that treaties that had been concluded in the name of Palestine were treaties of the state of Palestine, and that Palestine's obligations under those treaties would devolve onto each of the two successor states.

Chapter 3(3) of the declaration section was based on Palestine Mandate Article 28, which, it will be recalled, provided that "the Government of Palestine," upon termination of the mandate, would be responsible for debts incurred by Palestine. Chapter 3(3) required the two projected states to honor Palestine's debts. Referring to each of the two projected states, Chapter 3(3) specified that

(a) The State shall respect and fulfil all financial obligations of whatever nature assumed on behalf of Palestine by the mandatory Power during the exercise of the Mandate and recognized by the State. This provision includes the right of public servants to pensions, compensation or gratuities.

(b) These obligations shall be fulfilled through participation in the Joint Economic Board in respect of those obligations applicable to Palestine as a whole, and individually in respect of those applicable to, and fairly apportionable between, the states.

This provision complied not only with the stipulation contained in Palestine Mandate Article 28 but also with the general proposition that a successor state succeeds to the debt of a predecessor state.[34]

Chapter 4 of the declaration section of Resolution 181 provided that if any dispute were to arise relating to the obligations undertaken by declaration, the International Court of Justice would have jurisdiction to hear and decide the matter. Thus, enforcement was provided to ensure compliance.

Palestine's statehood was also reflected in Resolution 181 in a provision on Palestine's assets. A counterpart to the debt provision was written into Resolution 181 as Part I(E) of the partition plan, providing for the disposition of Palestine's assets. Part I(E) called for allocation of Palestine's assets between the two projected states. Thus, both the debts and assets of Palestine were to be assumed by the two states. This disposition too followed international practice upon state succession, whereby successor states assume the assets of predecessor states, along with their debts.

The Resolution 181 provisions on all these matters – the assumption of debts and assets, the continuity of treaties, and the continuity of citizenship – followed international practice on the succession of states and were premised on Palestine being an existing state as of the date of the anticipated termination of the mandate.

NON-IMPLEMENTATION OF RESOLUTION 181

Resolution 181 contained provisions aimed at ensuring implementation. In Part I(B) of the partition plan, Resolution 181 set up a five-nation commission to administer Palestine as Britain withdrew. Resolution 181 also requested the Security Council to act if armed force were used to thwart implementation. At the same time, however, Resolution 181 was framed as a recommendation. It did not purport to "divide" Palestine of its own force. It urged the Arab and Jewish communities to set up states but did not purport to require them to do so. The key provision in this regard read that the General Assembly:

> Recommends to the United Kingdom, as the mandatory Power for Palestine, and to all other Members of the United Nations the adoption and implementation, with regard to the future government of Palestine, of the Plan of Partition with Economic Union set out below.

The General Assembly thus referred to its call for partition with economic union as recommendatory. Canada expressed the general understanding of Resolution 181 the following year during a discussion in the UN Security Council when it said, "we regard the resolution of the General Assembly [Resolution 181] as having the force of a recommendation."[35]

This recommendation was not regarded as just by the Arab states that had recently come to independence or by the Arab Higher Committee, which represented the Palestine Arabs at the United Nations. To the Arabs, Resolution 181 seemed a continuation of the policy of the Balfour Declaration. Just as World War I had given the major powers a reason to take up the idea of a Jewish state in Palestine, so World War II gave them a reason to continue the project. Reluctant to accept large numbers of displaced Jews into their own territories, the major powers conflated the issue of Palestine with the issue of Jewish resettlement.

In one critical respect Resolution 181 was even more threatening to the Palestine Arabs than the Balfour Declaration had been. Resolution 181 envisaged not the amorphous concept of a "national home" but a territorial state configured to account for future migration, taking more than half of Palestine's territory. In keeping with the UN Special Committee's concept that European Jews would need to be accommodated, Resolution 181 proceeded on the assumption that the Jewish state required more territory than the numbers of Jews then in Palestine would merit.

Within a short time, it became clear that a division of Palestine with economic union could not be implemented. The Arab community of Palestine viewed a split of the territory between it and the Jewish minority as unfair, in particular because of the specifics of the proposed division. The Palestine Arabs were not alone in viewing Resolution 181 as an inappropriate approach to resolving the status of Palestine upon termination of the mandate. A U.S. diplomat commented that he found "no necessary connection between the humanitarian problem of succoring the displaced persons of Europe and the political problem of creating a new nationalist state in Palestine."[36] The British historian Arnold Toynbee found "neither merit nor justice" in "compensating victims [the Jews of Europe] at the expense of innocent third parties [the Palestine Arabs]".[37] Many of those Jews seeking to leave their home areas would, moreover, have preferred resettlement in the West. A 1945 U.S. government report concluded on the basis of survey data that European Jews expressing a desire to go to Palestine did so "because they realize that their opportunity to be admitted into the United States or into other countries in the Western Hemisphere [is] limited, if not impossible."[38] Thus, even if one took as a given the need to accommodate these Jews, as the UN Special Committee on Palestine did, territory in Palestine was not the only possible solution.

A POSSIBLE TRUSTEESHIP

In February 1948, the Palestine Commission that had been set up by Resolution 181 reported to the Security Council that implementation of Resolution 181 was not feasible – unless the United Nations used armed force. The Commission's chair told the Security Council that because of "chaotic conditions of violence and lawlessness" in Palestine, "the only way of implementing the plan of partition as it has been envisaged by the General Assembly, consists in providing for assistance by non-Palestinian military forces available not in some symbolical form but in effective, adequate strength."[39] The various UN organs switched to focusing on possibilities for Palestine that, at least in the short term, would not involve dividing its territory.

On March 19, 1948, the United States asked the Security Council to request that the General Assembly set up a temporary trusteeship in Palestine until the two parties could reach a settlement.[40] On April 1, 1948, at the urging of the United States, the Security Council asked the Secretary-General to call a special session of the General Assembly to "consider further the question of the future government of Palestine," in other words, to work towards a trusteeship.[41] The Secretary-General complied with the request, and the General Assembly began a special session on April 16, 1948, attempting to find a solution along these lines.[42]

The next day, April 17, 1948, the Security Council called for a cessation of violence. In the hope of gaining cooperation between the two communities toward a political settlement, the Council asked them to

> [r]efrain, pending further consideration of the future government of Palestine by the General Assembly, from any political activity which might prejudice the rights, claims, or positions of either community.[43]

That request constituted a call to refrain from assertions of sovereignty or statehood by one community or the other while the General Assembly devised an arrangement for Palestine. The posing of the issue as that of "the future government of Palestine" reflected an assumption of Palestine statehood. Palestine was a state. All that it lacked was a government. The United States explained its trusteeship plan by arguing

> that the Assembly should consider the establishment of a temporary trusteeship which would provide a Government and essential public services in Palestine pending further negotiations. If the Mandatory Power actively co-operated, the General Assembly would thus be able to establish United Nations governmental authority in the country.[44]

The United States took it upon itself to draft a full-blown trusteeship agreement that set the terms for a trusteeship. The U.S. draft trusteeship agreement called for the United Nations itself, rather than any individual state, to serve as trustee.[45] Palestine citizens would continue to be citizens of Palestine.[46] Palestine treaties, both bilateral and multilateral, would continue to be binding on Palestine.[47] Agreement was to be sought between the Jewish and Arab communities on a plan of government, so that the trusteeship could terminate "as soon as possible."[48] The U.S. draft trusteeship agreement reflected continuity between Palestine under British mandate and Palestine under the proposed short-term UN trusteeship. The call for continuity in regard to both citizenship and treaty obligations reflected an assumption that Palestine under the mandate was a state and that it would continue to be one. The same assumption was reflected in the proposal to seek a plan of government.

The Jewish Agency for Palestine denounced the trusteeship proposal. It wanted a state of its own and said it was prepared to declare one.[49] The Arab Higher Committee took the following view:

> The British Government is morally and legally bound to hand over the administration only to one Palestinian Government representing the lawful citizens of Palestine. This handing over must comprise the whole of Palestine as one unit.[50]

The Arab Higher Committee told the First Committee of the General Assembly that it would accept the trusteeship proposal, so long as it were short-term, and so long as it would lead to "the independence of Palestine as a single democratic State in which the legitimate rights of the different sections of the citizens would be safeguarded."[51] Jamal Bey Husseini, speaking for the Arab Higher Committee, explained in the following terms the Committee's plans if the trusteeship proposal were to be rejected:

> Failing agreement on this question, I am authorized to inform your august body that the Arabs of Palestine are determined to proceed on the following lines, at the termination of the mandate. Article 22 of the Covenant of the League of Nations and Article 28 of the Palestine mandate explicitly and implicitly impose that there should emerge, at that date, an independent Palestinian Government. Now that the mandatory has failed to fulfill this duty, the overwhelming majority of the people of the country have decided to carry it out themselves, in expression of their inalienable right of self-determination. This action on their part is in complete harmony with the United Nations Charter and is a principal

requirement of the Covenant of the League of Nations under which the
mandate was given.[52]

The Arab Higher Committee thus regarded the emergence of Palestine to
independence as being required to fulfill the Palestine Mandate's Article
28 stipulation for a "Government of Palestine" to be formed upon termination of the mandate, and to follow through on the League Covenant
Article 22(4) provisional recognition of Palestine.

On May 4, 1948, in keeping with the aim of providing for a temporary
trusteeship, the First Committee of the General Assembly appointed a
subcommittee to draft a resolution on a provisional regime for Palestine.[53]
The violence to which the Security Council had referred on April 17,
1948 involved hostilities for which the Council held both the Jewish
Agency for Palestine and the Arab Higher Committee responsible. The
preponderance of the violence came from military units acting under the
auspices of the Jewish Agency, which was implementing a plan to take
Palestine militarily.[54] As these units captured the Arab-populated cities
and villages of Palestine, they drove out Arab civilians, precipitating
what quickly became a mass exodus.[55] By mid-May 1948, several hundred
thousand Palestine Arabs had fled in fear or had been physically forced
out of their home areas. By June 1, 1948, the Intelligence Branch of the
military organization that by then was called the Israel Defense Force
estimated the number of Arabs who had fled at 391,000.[56] A more recent
study estimates that 441,961 had fled by May 15, 1948.[57] With Britain
doing little to preserve order, public pressure built in the Arab states for
military action by the Arab League to counter what the Egyptian press
began calling a "catastrophe" befalling the Palestine Arabs.[58]

Henri Rolin (the younger) had written that it would violate the obligations of the League's Council were the Council to authorize a mandatory to "evacuate" the territory under "conditions that would leave
it exposed to anarchy."[59] He was probably correct on this point, since
a population under mandate was entitled to see its interests protected
by a mandatory power. Under UN Charter Article 80, that entitlement
carried over after the demise of the League. But Britain had made no
provision for the governance of Palestine upon its departure, which was
then planned for May 15. Conditions in the spring of 1948 approached
anarchy as Britain prepared to withdraw. The only steps Britain took
in preparation for departure were of a legal character. The British government repealed a number of statutory provisions, including the 1922
Order in Council that had served as a constitution for Palestine.[60]

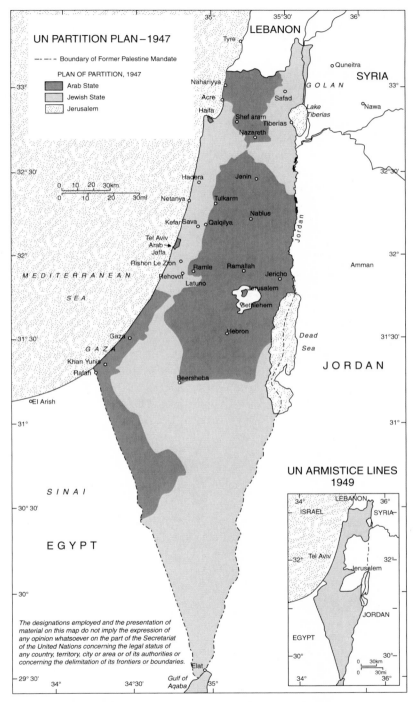

MAP 3. UN partition plan – 1947, No. 3067 rev.1, April 1, 1983.
Source: Courtesy UN Cartographic Section.

On 13 May 1948, the U.S. Department of State issued a memorandum on the U.S. position in regard to the legal situation in Palestine upon the anticipated, and imminent, British withdrawal. The State Department did not know what administration or administrations might seek to preserve order. The memorandum was titled Recognition of Successor States in Palestine.[61] A "successor" state, as already indicated, is one that follows upon another. The memorandum thus assumed that the state or states that might emerge upon Britain's withdrawal would be successors to the Palestine state as it was under the mandate.

9

The State Comes Apart

It was in this set of circumstances that, on May 14, 1948, a People's Council, working with the Jewish Agency, declared statehood for a Jewish state to be called Israel. The declaration read:

> On the 29th November, 1947, the United Nations General Assembly passed a resolution calling for the establishment of a Jewish State in Eretz-Israel; the General Assembly required the inhabitants of Eretz-Israel to take such steps as were necessary on their part for the implementation of that resolution. This recognition by the United Nations of the right of the Jewish people to establish their State is irrevocable.

> This right is the natural right of the Jewish people to be masters of their own fate, like all other nations, in their own sovereign State.

> Accordingly we, members of the People's Council,[1] representatives of the Jewish community of Eretz-Israel and of the Zionist movement, are here assembled on the day of the termination of the British mandate over Eretz-Israel and, by virtue of our natural and historic right and on the strength of the resolution of the United Nations General Assembly, hereby declare the establishment of a Jewish state in Eretz-Israel, to be known as the State of Israel.

> We declare that, with effect from the moment of the termination of the Mandate being tonight, the eve of Sabbath, the 6th Iyar, 5708 (15th May, 1948), until the establishment of the elected, regular authorities of the State in accordance with the Constitution which shall be adopted by the Elected Constituent Assembly not later than the 1st October 1948, the People's Council shall act as a Provisional Council of State, and its executive organ, the People's Administration, shall be the Provisional Government of the Jewish State, to be called "Israel"....

> The State of Israel is prepared to cooperate with the agencies and rep-
> resentatives of the United Nations in implementing the resolution of the
> General Assembly of the 29th November, 1947, and will take steps to
> bring about the economic union of the whole of Eretz-Israel.

The term "Eretz-Israel" means "Land of Israel." The Jewish Agency did
not specify the borders of the state it was declaring. The declaration's
reference to General Assembly Resolution 181 suggested that the resolution's recommended dividing line might provide the border.

On the day of this declaration, May 14, 1948, the UN General
Assembly was in session discussing the trusteeship proposal for Palestine.
The U.S. delegates were speaking in favor of the proposal, and their
expectation was that the General Assembly would approve it. However,
President Harry Truman, on behalf of the United States, immediately
endorsed the Jewish Agency's action by giving de facto recognition to
Israel. Truman apparently acted without consulting his diplomats who
were dealing with the Palestine issue.[2] Dean Rusk, a U.S. delegate to
the General Assembly, relates that he was informed that afternoon of
President Truman's decision, in a telephone call from Clark Clifford,
Special Counsel to Truman. Rusk reports that he objected, saying, "But
this cuts across what our Delegation has been trying to accomplish in the
General Assembly under instructions and we already have a large majority for that approach." Word of the U.S. recognition of Israel reached
the General Assembly from news sources, causing "pandemonium" in
the General Assembly, according to Rusk, because the U.S. move had
undermined the trusteeship plan.[3] Philip Jessup, who was a U.S. delegate
at the General Assembly, read aloud the statement from President Harry
Truman:

> This Government has been informed that a Jewish State has been pro-
> claimed in Palestine, and recognition has been requested by the Provisional
> Government thereof. The United States recognizes the Provisional
> Government as the *de facto* authority of the new State of Israel.[4]

Jessup, who had been urging other governments to accept the U.S. trusteeship proposal, reported later that Truman took the decision to recognize Israel without informing his own Department of State beforehand,
and that "all of the friendly delegations who were working with us to
bring about a peaceful solution of the Palestine crisis were taken completely by surprise."[5]

The same day, the General Assembly relieved the Palestine Commission
of its functions, since implementation of Resolution 181 was by then
out of the question. In its place, the General Assembly provided for

the appointment of a mediator, to "promote a peaceful adjustment of the future situation of Palestine" by contacts with the parties.[6] The formulation "future situation of Palestine" suggested that the General Assembly continued to regard Palestine as a state, even as its domestic situation was in turmoil.

PALESTINE STATEHOOD IN UN SECURITY COUNCIL DISCUSSIONS

On May 15, 1948, military forces of the Arab League states entered Palestine, saying that they were doing so to protect the population from atrocities. The UN Security Council met to deal with the situation. At that session of the Security Council, the Jewish Agency for Palestine questioned the motivation of the Arab League states and charged them with aggression. But China challenged the Jewish Agency, blaming it for a breakdown of order in Palestine. In a reference to the ongoing efforts towards establishing a trusteeship, China criticized the declaration of a Jewish state, saying: "The prompt proclamation of the Jewish state last evening reduced considerably the prospects of peace in Palestine."[7]

The Arab Higher Committee spoke for the Palestine Arabs at that session of the Security Council. The Committee regarded itself as entitled to govern Palestine. It questioned the legal capacity of the Jewish Agency to raise the issue of who might, or might not, be committing aggression in Palestine. Speaking for the Committee, Isa Nakhleh, a British-trained barrister and member of the Palestine bar, referred to the League Covenant as determining what should occur upon Britain's withdrawal:

> By the provisions of Article 22 of the Covenant of the League of Nations, the people of Palestine were recognized provisionally as an independent nation. Now that the Mandate has ended, the people of Palestine consider themselves to be an independent nation. The majority of the population of Palestine, the 1,300,000 Arabs, considers that the Jewish minority – whether the 300,000 Palestinian citizens or the 400,000 foreigners[8] – is a rebellious minority which has revolted against the sovereignty of the majority of the population of the country. We, the Arab Higher Committee, representing the majority of the people of Palestine, consider that any attempt to create any foreign government in Palestine is nothing but an act of rebellion which will be put down by force.[9]

The Arab Higher Committee viewed Palestine as a state threatened by internal rebellion.

At the same Security Council meeting, the Jewish Agency for Palestine announced the declaration of a state: "The State of Israel has now been established within Palestine."[10] That verbal formulation differed from what the People's Council had used in the declaration. The declaration recited that Israel was being establishing within "Eretz-Israel," and on the basis of Resolution 181. By saying that Israel was being established "within Palestine," the Jewish Agency for Palestine acknowledged that territory of Palestine was being claimed. Thus, consistent with the view of the Arab Higher Committee, the Jewish Agency for Palestine regarded the declaration of May 14 as an effort to create a state within an existing state. The two bodies differed on the propriety of that action, but they agreed that it represented an attempted secession.

The formation of Israel as a state has appropriately been analyzed in this way.[11] Israel was not "created" by the United Nations. Crawford writes that Israel did not confine itself to the borders proposed in Resolution 181, and Israel "did not comply with the prescribed conditions [in Resolution 181] for protection of minorities."[12] Additionally, Resolution 181 could not be a basis of statehood in the legal sense, because Resolution 181 was, as indicated in the previous chapter, recommendatory only. It did not purport, of its own force, to establish either a Jewish or an Arab state.

Secession involves separation "from a State."[13] "Revolt followed by secession is a mode of losing territory."[14] Secession has been defined as "the creation of a State by the use or threat of force without the consent of the former sovereign."[15] The establishment of Israel within the territory of Palestine satisfies this definition. The "former sovereign" was Palestine.

ARAB LEAGUE EFFORTS AT ESTABLISHING A PALESTINE GOVERNMENT

As of May 15, 1948, most of Palestine's territory was beyond the control of the military forces loyal to the People's Council. Both the United Nations and the Arab League began to focus on solutions in the new situation, on the assumption that Palestine continued as a state. The Arab League said that it was trying to preserve the territorial integrity of Palestine, and that by entering Palestine militarily, it sought to restore governmental authority there. In a cablegram to Trygve Lie, the UN Secretary-General, Abdul Rahman Azzam Pasha, the Arab League Secretary-General, explained that the Arab League states were acting

> by virtue of their responsibility as members of the Arab League which is a regional organization within the meaning of Chapter VIII of the Charter of the United Nations.[16]

Chapter VIII of the UN Charter provides for the possibility that regions may establish their own agencies to keep the international peace. Azzam Pasha said that the circumstances in Palestine involved a threat to the peace and presaged a lack of governance:

> The recent disturbances in Palestine further constitute a serious and direct threat to peace and security within the territories of the Arab States themselves. For these reasons, and considering that the security of Palestine is a sacred trust for them, and out of anxiousness to check the further deterioration of the prevailing conditions and to prevent the spread of disorder and lawlessness into the neighbouring Arab lands, and in order to fill the vacuum created by the termination of the Mandate and the failure to replace it by any legally constituted authority, the Arab Governments find themselves compelled to intervene for the sole purpose of restoring peace and security and establishing law and order in Palestine.[17]

Next, Azzam Pasha affirmed the League's aim of facilitating the establishment of a government in Palestine:

> The Arab States recognize that the independence and sovereignty of Palestine which was so far subject to the British Mandate has now, with the termination of the Mandate, become established in fact, and maintain that the lawful inhabitants of Palestine are alone competent and entitled to set up an administration in Palestine for the discharge of all governmental functions without any external interference. As soon as that stage is reached the intervention of the Arab States, which is confined to the restoration of peace and establishment of law and order, shall be put an end to, and the sovereign State of Palestine will be competent in co-operation with the other States members of the Arab League, to take every step for the promotion of the welfare and security of its peoples and territory.[18]

Finally, Azzam Pasha declared that "the sovereign State of Palestine" would ensure equality for all of Palestine's inhabitants:

> The Governments of the Arab States hereby confirm at this stage the view that had been repeatedly declared by them on previous occasions, such as the London Conference[19] and before the United Nations mainly, the only fair and just solution to the problem of Palestine is the creation of United State of Palestine based upon the democratic principles which will enable all its inhabitants to enjoy equality before the law, and which would guarantee to all minorities the safeguards provided for in all democratic constitutional States affording at the same time full protection and free access to Holy Places. The Arab States emphatically and repeatedly declare that their intervention in Palestine has been prompted solely

by the considerations and for the aims set out above and that they are not inspired by any other motive whatsoever. They are, therefore, confident that their action will receive the support of the United Nations as tending to further the aims and ideals of the United Nations as set out in its Charter.[20]

The reference by Azzam Pasha to the "vacuum created by the termination of the mandate and the failure to replace it by any legally constituted authority" was taken by Crawford as an assertion by the League that Palestine, far from being a state, was, upon Britain's withdrawal, *terra nullius*, meaning territory belonging to no state.[21] The Arab League position, writes Crawford, was "that British abandonment of Palestine, and the termination of the Mandate, left Palestine as *terra nullius* and hence open to occupation by any state, existing or to be created," and that, "This was one justification given for the Arab invasion after 15 May 1948."[22]

Crawford took Azzam Pasha's mention of a "vacuum" as a vacuum of sovereignty. However, as is clear from the cablegram, the Arab League was not asserting a vacuum of sovereignty in Palestine. The League regarded Palestine as a state, but one that was suffering a vacuum in governance, since Britain was departing with no administrative structure in place. The Arab League position, as Azzam Pasha would explain to Lie a few weeks later, was that, upon Britain's withdrawal, "there was no legal Government in the country."[23] The League's justification for intervening was not that Palestine belonged to no one, but that the Palestine Arabs required protection. Elsewhere in the cablegram of May 15, 1948, Azzam Pasha explained:

> Peace and order have been completely upset in Palestine, and, in consequence of Jewish aggression, approximately over a quarter of a million of the Arab population have been compelled to leave their homes and emigrate to neighbouring Arab countries.[24]

That figure, as seen in the previous chapter, was a fair, if conservative, estimate of the numbers of Arabs who by May 15, 1948 had fled Palestine.

When Count Folke Bernadotte, who had been appointed UN mediator, asked the Arab states in July 1948 to extend a truce with Israeli forces, the Arab League reiterated that its purpose was to restore order. It said

> that the Arab States have not intervened militarily in Palestine except when compelled [to do so] and in response to the repeated appeals addressed to

them by the Arab inhabitants who constitute the overwhelming majority in Palestine. These [appeals purported to ask us] to put an end to the
massacres that had been committed by the criminal Zionist gangs, and to
work for the restoration of the security and peace that had been disturbed
by these gangs. In fact, the Arab armies have succeeded in saving a large
number of the Arab inhabitants and restoring security, order and tran-
quility to the areas occupied by them.[25]

The Arab League sought to set up governing institutions in Palestine. On
July 10, 1948, the League declared that it was establishing a "provisional
civil administration" to be called an "All-Palestine Government," that
would "manage the public civil affairs," but "on condition that it shall
not have competence at present over the higher political affairs," which,
for the time, the Arab League was reserving to itself. The Arab League's
declaration called for basic institutions of governance, including a judiciary and departments for health services, a treasury, agriculture, post
and telegraph, and economic affairs.[26]

Fighting continued, however, and on July 15, 1948, the UN Security
Council, in calling for a truce, made a finding "that the situation in
Palestine constitutes a threat to the peace."[27] The wording "situation
in Palestine" was based on an assumption that Palestine continued
as a state.

Organizing an administration for Palestine in opposition to the
recently declared Israel proved more than the Arab League could manage. There were few Arabs left in the areas taken by the forces loyal
to the Provisional Council. Both the rural areas and the cities were
depopulated. And just at the time the Arab League called for a civil
administration – mid-July 1948 – the Arabs lost the only major urban
center that until then had escaped depopulation. The Provisional Council
forces, by then reorganized as the Israel Defense Force (IDF), entered
the adjoining towns of Lydda and Ramleh in the center of Palestine
and forced nearly the entire population to walk eastward towards the
Jordanian-held sector of Palestine.[28]

A GOVERNMENT FOR "ALL PALESTINE"

By late summer 1948, the IDF occupied nearly 80% of Palestine's territory. Egypt held Gaza. Jordan held the area then known as Central
Palestine, or sometimes as Eastern Palestine, but which Jordan was
beginning to call the West Bank of the Jordan River. The United Nations
did not appear disposed to reverse the territorial gains of the IDF.

A report by Bernadotte issued on September 16, 1948 called for boundaries to be negotiated, but with Israel to hold territory amounting to
more than had been contemplated for a Jewish state in Resolution 181.
With regard to the remainder of Palestine's territory, Bernadotte advised
as follows:

> The disposition of the territory of Palestine not included within the
> boundaries of the Jewish State should be left to the Governments of the
> Arab States in full consultation with the Arab inhabitants of Palestine,
> with the recommendation, however, that in view of the historical connex-
> ion and common interest of Transjordan and Palestine, there would be
> compelling reasons for merging the Arab territory of Palestine with the
> territory of Transjordan, subject to such frontier rectifications regarding
> other Arab States as may be found practicable and desirable.[29]

On September 22, 1948, the Arab Higher Committee organized a provisional assembly and a provisional government cabinet in Gaza. On
October 1, 1948, the assembly, called the Palestinian National Council,
proclaimed Palestine's independence, within the mandate boundaries.
The Proclamation of the Independence of Palestine recited:

> Acting on the basis of the natural and historic right of the Arab peo-
> ple of Palestine to freedom and independence ... We, members of the
> Palestinian National Council, meeting in the city of Gaza, proclaim on
> this day ... October 1st, 1948, the full independence of the whole of
> Palestine as bounded by Syria and Lebanon from the north, by Syria and
> Transjordan from the east, by the Mediterranean from the west, and by
> Egypt form the south, as well as the establishment of a free and demo-
> cratic sovereign State.[30]

The All-Palestine Government cabled Trygve Lie to explain that "the
Arabs of Palestine" were declaring

> Palestine in its entirety and within its boundaries as established before
> the termination of the British Mandate an independent State.[31]

The All-Palestine Government aspired to serve as a government for
Palestine in as much territory as it might be able to control, and in the
hope of eventually controlling the entirety of Palestine. The aim, as
explained by the foreign minister of the All-Palestine Government in a
telegram to the U.S. vice-consul in Jerusalem, was "that Palestine Arabs
would have a legal position vis-à-vis Arab League and as evidence [of]
determination to continue [to] fight against Jews."[32] The establishment
of the All-Palestine Government was described in one periodical at the

time as "an attempt by the Arabs of Palestine to develop momentum," in the face of loss of territory.[33]

A provisional constitution for Palestine was adopted, along with a Palestine flag. Passports were issued.[34] The All-Palestine Government was accorded diplomatic recognition by most Arab League states: Egypt, Syria, Lebanon, Iraq, Saudi Arabia, Yemen, and Afghanistan.[35]

Jordan, however, did not accord recognition. Abdullah, by then King of Jordan, sought to incorporate Central Palestine into Jordan. He argued, as had Bernadotte, that this action was better calculated to protect those Palestine Arabs whose territory had not fallen to the IDF.[36] The other Arab League states were concerned that Abdullah might be motivated by a desire to expand his realm, and beyond that, that his incorporation of a portion of Palestine might appear to be a tacit recognition of Israel.[37]

In mid-October 1948, the IDF pushed Egyptian forces out of sectors of the northern Negev they had held, confining them to a narrow strip of the Mediterranean coast around Gaza city. The All-Palestine Government relocated to the safety of Cairo.[38] Egypt feared that the presence of the All-Palestine Government in Gaza might provoke Israel to invade Gaza to drive it out.[39]

CENTRAL PALESTINE

In October 1948, the same month in which the All-Palestine Government was declared, King Abdullah organized a meeting in Amman, Jordan, of Arabs from Central Palestine. The purpose was to show that these Palestine Arabs favored an affiliation with Jordan. Another meeting, with the same aim, followed in Jericho on December 1, 1948.[40] At that meeting a resolution was adopted proposing the merger of Central Palestine with Jordan, and explaining it in the following terms:

> [T]he people of Palestine now see through political and military developments in Palestine that the time has come when active steps should be taken with the cooperation of the neighboring Arab States to safeguard their future and decide their ultimate fate of living a life of independence and freedom.[41]

Central Palestine Arabs feared that their territory would be overrun and that they would be driven out, like the Palestine Arabs in sectors of Palestine that the IDF had occupied. At the same time, they pressed Jordan to ensure that affiliation with Jordan would not prejudice the status of their territory as part of Palestine.[42] On December 7, 1948, the Jordanian government approved the merger, and on December 13, 1948, the Jordanian Parliament did as well.[43]

The fear of being overrun was based in reality. Just at that period, the provisional government of Israel was contemplating a military offensive to occupy Central Palestine.[44] In the event, it did not do so. Israel was anxious to apply for membership in the United Nations and was under pressure to repatriate the Palestine Arabs who had fled the country, and who overwhelmingly desired to return to their homes.[45] Britain was a close ally of Jordan. The Jordanian Legion was still under British officers. Had the IDF tried to take Central Palestine, Britain might well have intervened on Jordan's side.[46]

ADMISSION OF ISRAEL TO THE UNITED NATIONS

On November 29, 1948, the provisional government of Israel asked the United Nations to admit Israel as a member state. A letter signed by Moshe Shertok (Sharett), as Foreign Minister, recited:

> On May 14 1948, the independence of the State of Israel was proclaimed by the National Council of the Jewish people in Palestine by virtue of the natural and historic right of the Jewish people to independence in its own sovereign State and in pursuance of the General Assembly resolution of November 29, 1947. Since that date Israel has been consolidated administratively and defended itself successfully against the aggression of neighbouring States. It has so far achieved recognition by nineteen Powers.

> On behalf of the Provisional Government of Israel, I have now the honour to request the admission of Israel as a Member of the United Nations in accordance with Article 4 of the Charter. [47]

Henry Cattan, speaking to the UN General Assembly on behalf of the Arab Higher Committee, objected (paraphrase):

> He could not agree that the United Nations could admit to membership the Government of a State which had come into being through the expulsion of the majority of the rightful inhabitants of the territory which it claimed ...[48]

The Security Council decided not to act on Israel's application.[49]

On December 11, 1948, the General Assembly, by Resolution 194, set up a three-nation Conciliation Commission to carry forward the work of the Mediator on Palestine. In the same resolution, the General Assembly called for protection of religious sites, referring in several paragraphs to sites "in Palestine."[50] The member states thus continued to refer to Palestine as a state, even though by this time the IDF controlled most of its territory. Also in Resolution 194, by paragraph 11, the General Assembly called on Israel to repatriate "the refugees wishing to return to their homes and live at peace with their neighbours."

The Arab Higher Committee and the Arab League states were confident of their legal position that Palestine, coming out of the mandate, was a state that should become independent under a government that would control Palestine in its entirety. On December 17, 1948, Syria suggested in the Security Council that the admission of Israel to the United Nations might violate international law. In that regard, Syria raised the question of the status of Palestine. It asked the Security Council to seek from the International Court of Justice an advisory opinion on the following questions:

1. Do the recommendations of the General Assembly in the resolution of 29 November 1947 for a partition plan with economic union, which was rejected by the Arabs of Palestine, create right to the Jewish minority to proclaim their separate state at the termination of the Mandate on the area assigned to them by that resolution?
2. What is the international status of Palestine at the termination of the Mandate on 15 May 1948?
3. Under the present circumstances would the Security Council be acting in conformity with the United Nations Charter and the international law if it recommended the admission of the State of Israel to membership in the United Nations?
4. Is the General Assembly empowered to partition Palestine between Arabs and Jews without consulting the lawful inhabitants of the country in securing their consent?[51]

Only Belgium voted with Syria to seek such an advisory opinion. No state voted against, but all the rest abstained, hence the Syrian proposal failed.[52] The International Court of Justice was not asked for its opinion about the status of Palestine. In 1932, as related in Chapter 6, Britain's law officers had advised that the Permanent Court of International Justice, predecessor to the International Court of Justice, would likely have found Palestine to be a state.

Despite the likelihood of major power opposition, the provisional government of Israel made military moves in November–December 1948 against Egypt in an effort to occupy Gaza and the Sinai Peninsula.

The Royal Air Force flew reconnaissance missions over this theater. On January 7, 1949, five RAF aircraft were shot down by Israeli forces near the Egypt-Palestine border.[53] Britain threatened to intervene against Israel if it persisted.[54] The United States threatened to withdraw its support for UN membership for Israel and warned Israel against further offensives.[55] The provisional government canceled its invasion plan.[56]

In the winter and spring of 1949, armistice agreements that would define areas of control in Palestine were concluded between Israel and Egypt (February 24, 1949), and between Israel and Jordan (April 3, 1949). Those agreements reflected an assumption of continuing Palestine statehood in various of their provisions. The Israel-Egypt General Armistice Agreement referred to the "Egypt-Palestine" frontier.[57] The Agreement spoke of Palestine as being in need of restoration of its peace:

> The establishment of an armistice between the armed forces of the two Parties is accepted as an indispensable step towards the liquidation of armed conflict and the restoration of peace in Palestine.[58]

The Israel-Jordan General Armistice Agreement contained a comparable provision.[59] In defining the armistice line, the Israel-Jordan agreement referred to the line extending to "the southernmost tip of Palestine."[60] The agreement made Jordan responsible for "all Iraqi forces in Palestine."[61]

The conclusion of the armistice agreements was taken by a number of states as reason to act favourably on Israel's application for membership in the United Nations. Membership has two basic requirements. The applicant entity must be a state. And it must be "peace-loving." By spring of 1949, most member states were prepared to say that Israel qualified on both counts.

The Arab states objected, along the lines of Cattan's plea to the General Assembly, arguing that Israel was not "peace-loving," because it took Palestine territory by force of arms, and because it was refusing to repatriate the Arabs it had forced out. Admission to UN membership requires action by both the Security Council and the General Assembly. On March 4, 1949, the Security Council voted to admit Israel. Britain abstained on the vote. The President of the Security Council ruled that the resolution was adopted.[62] Arab states argued that the UN Charter requires the affirmative vote of each member of the Security Council, hence that the resolution had failed. UN Charter Article 27 does require the "concurring vote" of the five permanent members on non-procedural matters. But a practice had developed to regard resolutions as

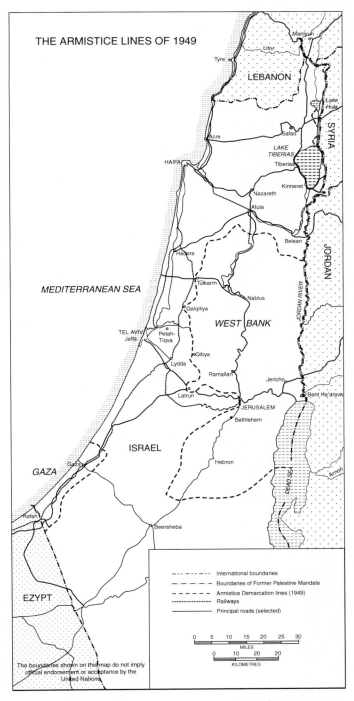

THE ARMISTICE LINES OF 1949

Manfrun
Litnr
Tyre
LEBANON
Lake Hula
Acre
Safad
SYRIA
LAKE TIBERIAS
HAIFA
Tiberias
Nazareth
Kinneret
Afula
Beisan
JORDAN
Hadera
MEDITERRANEAN SEA
Tulkarm
Nablus
JORDAN RIVER
Qalqiliya
WEST BANK
TEL AVIV
Jaffa
Petah-Tiqva
Qibya
Lydda
Ramallah
Jericho
Latrun
Beni Ha'arava
JERUSALEM
Bethlehem
ISRAEL
Hebron
GAZA
Gaza
DEAD SEA
Arnon
Rafah
Beersheba

EZYPT

International boundaries
Boundaries of Former Palestine Mandate
Armistice Demarcation lines (1949)
Railways
Principal roads (selected)

0   5   10   15   20   25   30
MILES
0   10   20   20
KILOMETRES

The boundaries shown on this map do not imply
official endorsement or acceptance by the
United Nations

MAP 4. Armistice lines of 1949, No. 547.1, October 31, 1953
Source: Courtesy UN Cartographic Section

adopted even if a permanent member abstained. Whether that practice was consistent with Article 27 was never resolved in a formal way. The General Assembly, however, viewed the action of the Security Council as an adopted resolution. On May 11, 1949, the General Assembly adopted its own resolution to admit Israel, thereby bringing it into the world body.[63]

Palestine in Three Pieces

Even after admitting Israel as a member, the United Nations continued to refer to Palestine using terminology that reflected its statehood. The General Assembly called the commission it set up in its December 11, 1948 resolution to pursue peacemaking the "Conciliation Commission for Palestine."[1] "Palestine" or "The Question of Palestine" would remain the issue on the UN agenda.

The Arab Higher Committee felt that the Conciliation Commission was too timid in its approach to securing the territorial integrity of Palestine. In a June 17, 1949 memorandum to the Conciliation Commission signed by Isa Nakhleh as its representative, the Arab Higher Committee complained that the Conciliation Commission was disregarding the views of Palestine Arabs and that it was allowing the Jewish population to "enjoy their plunders of Arab wealth and property."[2] Nonetheless, the Conciliation Commission strove for a negotiated settlement between the two communities. Those efforts could have potentially led to a single state that would encompass the Palestine mandate territory. Or, they could have led to a federated state or to two separate states, with a variety of possible divisions of territory.

The IDF-controlled sectors of Palestine continued to be areas of conflict. The IDF confined thousands of Arab males in prison camps and required them to do forced labor as "civilian war internees."[3] The Arab League complained to the UN that the IDF was "compelling Arabs to do forced labour."[4] Israel's government imposed martial law in localities where Arabs predominated.

The Conciliation Commission pressed Israel to repatriate the displaced Palestine Arabs. But when Palestine Arabs from rural areas tried to return to their home villages, as many did, they were detained by the IDF as "infiltrators." In the locations to which Palestine Arabs had been displaced – Gaza, the West Bank, and neighboring Arab states – the Red Cross and the American Friends Service Committee (Quakers) began to provide relief services, a task soon assumed by the United Nations, which established for the purpose the UN Relief and Works Agency for Palestine Refugees in the Near East (UNRWA).[5]

GAZA

Gaza underwent a major demographic transformation. Thousands of Arabs who had been displaced from Jaffa, Palestine's main port city, and from southern Palestine fled by boat or on foot southward to Gaza as Jewish Agency forces shelled those areas in early 1948. Within a short time, the population of Gaza more than trebled – from 80,000 to 280,000.[6] Gaza came under the control of the Egyptian army upon its entry into Palestine on May 15, 1948. As the titles of some of its later enactments on Gaza would indicate, Egypt regarded itself as a belligerent occupant.[7] Belligerency occupancy, as will be explained in Chapter 17, is a status that does not involve a claim of sovereignty.

On May 26, 1948, the Minister of Defense issued Order No. 153 of 1948, formalizing Egypt's military control. Gaza was described by the Government of Egypt at the time as the "areas subject to the supervision of the Egyptian forces in Palestine."[8] Egypt gradually regularized its administration of Gaza. An administrative governor appointed by Egypt issued Order No. 6 on June 1, 1948, providing that the courts of Gaza should continue to apply the law that had been in force up until May 15, 1948.[9] By Order No. 274, issued August 8, 1948 by the Minister of War and Navy, the administrative governor was granted whatever powers had been held by Britain's high commissioner.[10] The British Order in Council of 1922, which provided a basis for governance of Palestine, was to continue in force.

The administrative governor, called the governor-general, continued the publication of the *Palestine Gazette*, which had been issued during the mandate for new enactments.[11] Law No. 621 of December 12, 1953, titled, On the Organic Status of the Region under Egyptian Military Occupation in Palestine, provided for the continuing validity of Palestine laws in force. This provision was repeated in Law No. 255 of May 11, 1955, an amended version of Law No. 621 issued under the same title.[12] Palestine law was preserved, administered by the courts of Palestine, and located in Gaza.[13] Court judgments were issued in the name of Palestine. A few provisions of Egyptian law were made applicable to Gaza, but apart from these exceptions, the law in force remained what it had been before 1948.[14]

By protecting Palestine, Egypt was exposing itself to attack from Israel, even after it moved the All-Palestine Government to Cairo.[15] The Government of Israel, as indicated in Chapter 9, had been convinced in early 1949 to forego occupying Gaza. In 1951, however, David Ben Gurion, as Prime Minister of Israel, inquired of the British government how it might react if Israel took Gaza. The British government reacted negatively, and Ben Gurion did not pursue the project.[16] During the early 1950s, Palestine Arab guerrillas raided into Israel from time to time, and Israel retaliated. In a 1955 raid into Gaza, the IDF killed thirty-nine Egyptian soldiers.[17] The UN Security Council condemned the attack as a violation of Israel's 1949 armistice agreement with Egypt.[18]

In October 1956, Britain and France, concerned over Egypt's nationalization of the Suez Canal in July of that year,[19] collaborated with Israel on a plan that called for Israel to invade Gaza, whereupon Britain and France would intervene as apparent peacemakers and occupy the Canal.[20] Implementing the plan, Israel invaded and occupied Gaza, and Britain and France intervened. Israeli Foreign Minister Golda Meir claimed Gaza as an "integral part" of Israel, and said that Israel would not return to the 1949 armistice line.[21] Israel proposed to UN Secretary-General Dag Hammarskjold that Israel assume administration of Gaza from Egypt, but Hammarskjold refused to promote the idea.[22] The United States pressured Israel to withdraw, which it did in March 1957.[23] Egypt resumed control of Gaza.

The All-Palestine Government continued as the titular administration of Gaza, operating from Cairo. In 1959, however, Egypt promoted in its place a Gaza-based congress of Palestinians, resulting in the creation in December 1959 of a Palestine National Union as a transitional entity that was to lead to the establishment of a Palestine government.[24] As explained by the governor-general, the goal of the Palestine National Union was "to engender cooperation among all Palestinians to liberate the rest of their homeland."[25] The Arab Higher Committee, which had initiated the All-Palestine Government, relocated from Cairo to Beirut and from there continued to promote independence for Palestine.[26]

Egypt claimed no sovereignty over Gaza. In keeping with the Arab League's position, Egypt regarded Gaza as part of Palestine.[27] A constitution was adopted for Gaza by Egypt in 1962, replacing the Order in Council of 1922.[28] The constitution proclaimed, "The Gaza Strip is an indivisible part of the land of Palestine."[29] Palestine courts in Gaza continued to issue decrees "in the name of the people of Palestine."[30] As before, a governor-general appointed by the president of Egypt governed Gaza.[31] A legislative council of limited competence was set up.[32] Control remained in the hands of the governor-general.[33] In 1964, amendments were introduced to increase the representative nature of the legislative council.[34]

Egypt's role in Gaza during this period has been described as that of a "placeholder" for Palestine.[35] The term "trustee" was employed by Arab governments to refer to Egypt's status in regard to Gaza.[36] The 1962 constitution reflected this role for Egypt in a provision that read, "This constitution shall continue to be observed in the Gaza Strip until a permanent constitution for the state of Palestine is issued."[37] The premise of Egypt's tenure in Gaza was that Palestine continued to exist as a state, one that Egypt was protecting and administering pending the establishment of an administration for Palestine.

WEST BANK OF THE JORDAN RIVER

Central Palestine was denominated by Jordan as the West Bank of the Jordan River, to indicate its geographic relation to Jordan, which was located on the eastern side of the Jordan River. A military governor assumed control and on May 24, 1948 issued an order proclaiming the continuing validity of the law in force as of May 15, 1948.[38] Then, as indicated, in December 1948 Jordan and the West Bank were merged. On October 20, 1949, King Abdullah announced that the two sectors constituted a single country.[39] On November 2, 1949, military rule was declared to be at an end by promulgation of the Law Amending Public Administration Law in Palestine. Under this law, King Abdullah assumed for Jordan the powers previously exercised by Britain as mandatory, and the laws of Palestine were declared to remain applicable.[40] Thus, in the West Bank Jordan viewed itself as playing a role similar to that being assumed by Egypt in Gaza.

In April 1950, elections were held for a Jordan parliament that would include the West Bank.[41] Once the West Bank was represented, giving a merger resolution more weight, the issue was taken again to the parliament. On April 24, 1950, the parliament, the product of the 1950 election, adopted a resolution of merger that read:

> [I]in accordance with the right of self-determination ... the Jordan Parliament, representing both banks, decides ...

1. Approval is granted to complete unity between the two banks of the Jordan, the Eastern and the Western, and their amalgamation in one single State ...
2. Arab rights in Palestine shall be protected. These rights shall be defended with all possible legal means and this unity shall in no way be connected with the final settlement of Palestine's just case within the limits of national hopes, Arab cooperation and international justice.[42]

This language has been interpreted as placing the Palestinians "only *provisionally*" under Jordanian sovereignty.[43] "[I]f the West Bank Palestinians invited Jordanian intervention," writes Allan Gerson,

it is doubtful that they ever formally ceded their rights to control of the region, either by virtue of the 1948 Jericho Convention or through their subsequent participation in the 1950 general elections for a joint Parliament. What seems most probable is that the intent was to cede sovereignty temporarily to Jordan until such time as the indigenous population might find it opportune to reassert control.[44]

The British government, in a statement recognizing the merger, referred to the West Bank as "the part of Palestine which is now united to the Kingdom of Jordan."[45] Thus, Britain appeared to regard the West Bank as part of Palestine even as it merged with Jordan. Of the states of the world, only Britain and Pakistan formally recognized the merger.[46] However, a merger is not the kind of action that necessarily leads to formal recognition by other states.

The other Arab states initially regarded the merger as unlawful. In a 1950 judicial proceeding in Egypt, an Egyptian court was asked to enforce the judgment of a court in Nablus, West Bank, on the basis of the 1929 Egypt–Palestine treaty on the enforcement of court judgments. The Egyptian court declined, saying that "the judgement was rendered in the name of His Majesty King Abdullah Ibn El Hussain," and "that the authority that this sovereign exercises on this piece of territory is illegitimate." The court said that the treaty had lost force because

Palestine, in the sense contemplated by the Convention of 1929, no longer exists. The party with whom Egypt concluded the Convention on reciprocity concerning the reciprocal enforcement of judgments no longer exercises any authority over Sichem [Nablus] and has been replaced by another State.[47]

The court's reluctance to enforce the treaty seemed to be based on the fact that Palestine was no longer exercising administration in Nablus, and not that Palestine was no longer a state. Within a short time, in any event, Arab League states concluded a variety of regional treaties, in which Jordan participated, that applied to Jordan's territory as defined by Jordan. A 1952 treaty on reciprocal enforcement of court judgments required the courts of the participating states to enforce judgments "made by the competent legal authorities in any of the member States of the Arab League."[48] The states of the international community began dealing with Jordan in a fashion that acknowledged its control of the West Bank.[49] Since Jordan had stipulated that its control was without prejudice to the resolution of the situation in Palestine, this acknowledgment did not amount to viewing the West Bank as being excluded from Palestine.

Palestine law continued in force in the West Bank, even after the merger.[50] A law adopted on September 16, 1950. provided:

> Even though the two Banks (the East and the West) of the Hashemite Kingdom of Jordan were united, the laws and regulations that are in force in each of them shall remain in effect until new unified and universal laws for both Banks are issued, . . .[51]

Much new legislation was adopted in Jordan after 1950 that replaced Palestine legislation in the West Bank.[52] Nonetheless, Palestine law was not entirely displaced. In particular, real property continued to be governed by the Ottoman Land Code of 1858.[53] Jordan offered its own citizenship to the Palestine Arabs of the West Bank. It offered its citizenship, in fact, even to Palestine Arabs located elsewhere, as a way of providing them citizenship when there was no effective Palestine government that could do so.[54] Jordan administered the West Bank in keeping with the Arab League consensus that Palestine continued as a state. Like Egypt in Gaza, Jordan characterized itself as a caretaker or trustee in the West Bank.[55]

ISRAEL

The establishment of Israel within the territory of Palestine was a transforming event for Palestine. As already seen, the 1948 declaration of Israeli statehood was regarded by many states as an act that foiled any efforts to achieve an orderly transfer of power from the mandatory to the population of Palestine. That act, and the military activity aimed at taking territory in Palestine, also ran up against the self-determination right of the Palestine population.[56] Israel was, however, admitted into

UN membership in 1949. The act of admitting Israel involved a judg-ment that Israel was a state, since statehood is a prerequisite of UN membership.

One may question the legality of that judgment, as, indeed, it was questioned at the time, given the obligation under UN Charter Article 80 to respect the rights of peoples who had been under mandates. The people of Palestine had, in the main, been driven by force or the threat of force out of their territory by this entity that the UN member states were now accepting as a "peace-loving state." Israel, moreover, took the position that it would not readmit the displaced Palestine Arabs until full peace was achieved between itself and the Arab states.[57]

When the UN was considering membership for Israel, it pressed Israel's representatives to make commitments to respect the rights of the Palestine Arabs. Abba Eban, the chief interlocutor on Israel's behalf, adroitly avoided making firm commitments, but the colloquies with him showed that the UN delegates understood that they were accepting an entity that was not respecting the rights of the Palestine Arabs.[58]

Whatever criticisms can be made of the decision to admit Israel as a member state, the decision was made, and since then the international community has dealt with Israel as a state. However, the admission of Israel to UN membership did not negate the statehood of Palestine.

It was understood by the new parliament of Israel (Knesset) that Israel was establishing itself out of the territory of the Palestine state. This understanding was reflected in a 1948 statute it adopted about the law in force in Israel. The Knesset said, as follows, that the law of Palestine would continue in force:

> The law which existed in Palestine on the 5th Iyar, 5708 (14th May, 1948) shall remain in force, insofar as there is nothing therein repugnant to this Ordinance of to the other laws which may be enacted by or on behalf of the Provisional Council of State, and subject to such modifications as may result from the establishment of the State and its authorities.[59]

This reference to "Palestine" and this assumption of Palestine law by Israel constituted a recognition by the Knesset that Palestine under the mandate was a state. Israel was not establishing itself in the way a state might assert authority over an uninhabited island. Palestine was a state with a body of law. Israel was succeeding to that state and to its law.

Israel, to be sure, declined to follow one requirement of a successor state, namely, that it honor the treaties of the predecessor state. As indi-cated in Chapter 8, the UN General Assembly's Resolution 181 called on the two projected states to honor Palestine treaties. Israel took the position, however, that it was entitled to operate on a "clean slate" as regards treaties of the prior sovereign.[60]

CONTINUITY OF PALESTINE

In a 2005 court case in the United States, the U.S. Court of Appeals took a separate assumption, that control in Palestine by Egypt, Jordan, and Israel was a negation of Palestine statehood. The issue of Palestine statehood had arisen because the Palestine Liberation Organization, upon being sued for acts of violence, had asserted immunity based on being the representative of a state. The U.S. Court of Appeals rejected that contention, saying:

> Following the United Kingdom's relinquishment of the mandate and the onset of the 1967 Arab-Israeli war, the Israelis occupied much of the land designated for a future Arab state, and the Egyptians and Jordanians seized the rest. The net result is that, at all times, other states had control over the defined territory.[61]

The Court said that the control by these other states negated Palestine statehood. The court, however, misread the position of the international community on Palestine statehood. Not only the Arab League, but the international community as a whole, continued to deal with Palestine as a state after 1948. UN Charter Article 80, quoted in Chapter 8, called for preservation of rights of states and people under mandate arrangements. A Palestine state had been provisionally recognized as independent by League Covenant Article 22(4), hence it held rights.

For Palestine, Article 80 meant the preservation of its statehood. The League's provisional recognition of Palestine as a state remained valid. The United Nations discussion from 1948 onward in regard to Palestine reflected the assumption that Palestine remained a state. The member states referred to the entity as "Palestine," whether in reference to the refugees as "Palestine" refugees, or in reference to their agenda item: "Question of Palestine." These states were not using the term "Palestine" to refer to a state that had gone out of existence or that did not exist but might come into existence in the future. They were referring to it as a state then existing, even if it had yet to come to independence.

When the United States asked the UN Security Council to admit Israel as a member state in 1948, it was careful to put that proposal within the context of the overall Palestine situation. The United States suggested that Israel's admission, far from eliminating Palestine, would aid "in reaching that final adjustment of a peaceful situation of the Palestine question." It referred to the fact that the General Assembly's First Committee was, at that very time, "in the midst of its consideration of the future situation of Palestine."[62]

Palestine was not, to be sure, represented as such at the United Nations. Egypt and Jordan, in the capacities they assumed in Gaza and the West Bank, oversaw the interests of Palestine at the UN. The Arab Higher Committee continued to operate at the United Nations under the name "Palestine Arab Delegation." It was not regarded as an official representative of the Palestine state, but it nonetheless participated in UN proceedings to speak in defense of the Palestine Arabs. At times at the request of Arab states,[63] and at times at its own request,[64] the Palestine Arab Delegation made representations to the Special Political Committee of the UN General Assembly when the Committee deliberated on reports filed by the UNRWA.[65] The Committee decided "to authorize the persons constituting the said delegation to speak in this Committee and to make such statements as they may deem necessary, without such authorization implying recognition of the above-mentioned organization."[66]

In 1952, the United States asked the UN Secretary-General to record the 1944 parcel post treaty it had concluded with Palestine, and the treaty was duly published in the United Nations Treaty Series. Had the United States thought that Palestine had ceased to exist, there would have been little point to submitting the treaty.[67]

Through the 1950s, efforts to reconstitute a Palestine government continued at the international level. In 1955, British Prime Minister Anthony Eden proposed a variant of Resolution 181 that would have involved a Palestine government that gained control not only of Gaza and the West Bank but also of Galilee and the Negev.[68] Israel rejected the idea of ceding control of the Palestine territory it had taken in 1948.[69] Although Eden's effort failed, it showed that Palestine was still regarded as a territorial entity whose situation was seen as needing to be resolved.

The 1955 episode also showed that the international community had made no judgment about Israel's borders. The 1949 armistice agreements explicitly stated that the lines they drew were not international borders. Some have suggested that the Resolution 181 line is the only appropriate border for Israel. Thus, Professor Anthony D'Amato, who views Resolution 181 as a lawful disposition of territory, argues that the Resolution 181 line is the only border the international community has recognized for Israel.[70] As recently as 2006, a Canadian court ruled that the western sector of Jerusalem cannot not be regarded as territory under Israel's sovereignty even though Israel has held it since 1948. The court, accepting the position of the Canadian government on the matter, said that sovereignty in Jerusalem is unresolved.[71] Whatever may be said about Israel's borders within the Palestine from which it seceded, they remain undefined.

PALESTINE WITHOUT A GOVERNMENT OF ITS OWN

Over and above the roles assumed by Egypt and Jordan, the Arab League regarded itself as a protector of the interests of Palestine. Through the 1950s and into the 1960s, the League actively explored the establishment of a Palestine government or government-in-exile that might eventually be able to govern what the League called the "Palestine entity."[72] These efforts reflected the League's view that Palestine continued as a state.[73]

Britain and Israel dealt with Palestine's assets and liabilities on the basis of Israel as a successor state in a portion of the territory of Palestine. Britain reached a financial settlement with Israel that applied to the portions of Palestine over which Israel had established control. Israel took the assets of the Palestine Government located in that territory and assumed financial liability on certain of the Palestine Government's obligations.[74]

The secession by Israel left the remainder of Palestine in an odd position administratively, namely, the assumption of the responsibility for administration by two neighboring states. A state can exist in such circumstances, however. Krystyna Marek, a student of state continuity in international law, writes, "A State, temporarily deprived of its organs, can be conceived."[75] Marek's view, as will be seen in Chapter 19, is reaffirmed by current international practice. The fact that Palestine had no effective government did not mean that Palestine had ceased to exist as a state. States whose territory is occupied, even annexed, may continue in existence as states for long periods of time. The issue arose with regard to the Baltic states – Estonia, Latvia, and Lithuania – when they asserted statehood in 1991 on the rationale that their statehood had not ceased upon their incorporation by the USSR in 1940.[76] The European Community concurred. It issued a statement, saying,

> The Community and its member States warmly welcome the restoration of the sovereignty and independence of the Baltic States which they lost in 1940. They have consistently regarded the democratically elected

parliaments and governments of these states as the legitimate representatives of the Baltic peoples.[77]

Governmental control had been lost, but not statehood. Crawford cites a number of states – not only the Baltic states, but also Ethiopia, Austria, Czechoslovakia, and Poland – that were annexed in a fashion deemed unlawful but continued to be regarded as states even though they were not "effective."[78] The fact that Palestine had no national administration exercising powers in its territory did not signify its extinction as a state.

That Palestine statehood continued was implicitly affirmed by an Israeli court in 1951 when an Israeli judge had to consider the question of whether a person who had held Palestine citizenship during the mandate and who, as of 1951, resided in Israel, was a citizen of Israel. Israel to that date had adopted no statute on citizenship; hence, it had no citizenship. The judge answered the question in the affirmative based on general legal concepts of state succession.

> [I]n the case of transfer of a portion of the territory of a State to another State, every inhabitant of the ceding State becomes automatically a national of the receiving State .... If that is the case, is it possible to say that the inhabitants of part of a State which is transformed into an independent State are not *ipso facto* transformed into the nationals of that State?[79]

The judge's reference to "part of a State" was to Israel as a part of Palestine. The judge was assuming Palestine to be a state, out of which a new state had been formed in part of its territory.

PALESTINE NATIONALITY AFTER 1948

The citizenship status of Palestine Arabs became problematic, in the absence of a governmental authority for Palestine. Some Palestine Arabs remained in territory controlled by Israel. Some remained in, or went to, Gaza, hence were under Egypt. Some remained in, or went to, the West Bank, hence were under Jordan. Some went to other countries.

According to one view, Palestine citizenship ceased with the end of the mandate, rendering those who held it stateless.[80] The displaced Palestine Arabs were characterized as stateless in a 1952 UN report authored by Manley Hudson, professor of international law at Harvard University. Hudson concluded:

> Out of the large number of Arab refugees from Palestine, some have been naturalized (particularly those in Jordan), but the majority must be considered as stateless.[81]

Hudson did not elaborate or explain this conclusion. The term "state-less" conceals a certain ambiguity. A distinction had been drawn in a 1949 United Nations study on the subject of statelessness between state-lessness *de jure* and statelessness *de facto*. According to the study:

1. *Stateless persons de jure* are persons who are not nationals of any State, either because at birth or subsequently they were not given any nationality, or because during their lifetime they lost their own nationality and did not acquire a new one.
2. *Stateless persons de facto* are persons who, having left the country of which they were nationals, no longer enjoy the protection and assistance of their national authorities, either because these authorities refuse to grant them assistance and protection, or because they themselves renounce the assistance and protection of the countries of which they are nationals.[82]

The Palestine Arabs, after Britain's withdrawal from Palestine, fit nei-ther the de jure nor the de facto category of statelessness. They no longer enjoyed the protection or assistance of their national authorities because there was no functioning national authority. Following Hudson's view, some analysts have characterized Palestine Arabs, at least those out-side the territory that became Israel, as stateless.[83] However, Egypt and Jordan, each in its own way, provided them with protection, Egypt con-sidering them to be Palestine nationals, Jordan considering them to be Jordan nationals with the potential of again being considered Palestine nationals if a Palestine administration should emerge.

One can perhaps speak of the displaced Palestine Arabs as "stateless" in the sense that their state did not have an administration to protect them domestically or abroad. But this was not statelessness in what the UN study called the de jure sense, that is, having the nationality of no state. To use a contemporary example, Somalia since the early 1990s has lacked an administration capable of protecting Somali nationals domestically or abroad. Yet Somalis remain nationals of Somalia. Lex Takkenberg and Christoph Bierwirth take the lack of restoration of an effective Palestine government from 1948 to mean that Palestine nation-ality lapsed, because, they say, there is no nationality without a state.[84] What was lacking, however, was not a state. What was lacking was an effective government.

Tevfik Erim, a Turkish lawyer who served as legal advisor to the UN Conciliation Commission for Palestine and was therefore close to the situation in which the Palestine Arabs found themselves, assumed that

Palestine nationality survived the events of 1948, despite the absence of a Palestine administration. Erim's analysis appeared in a document issued by the Commission in 1951, when it set about identifying which persons qualified as those Palestine "refugees" whom the General Assembly had called on Israel to repatriate in its Resolution 194 of December 11, 1948. The General Assembly had tasked the Commission with achieving the implementation of this repatriation. Resolution 194 specified that

> the refugees wishing to return to their homes and live at peace with their neighbours should be permitted to do so at the earliest practical date.[85]

The Commission identified such refugees by reference to Palestine nationality under the Palestine Citizenship Order of 1925, and the groups so identified included persons who were neither Arabs nor Jews. Predominantly, they were Greeks, Turks, and Armenians. The Commission said that these groups had not fled Palestine, as, indeed, in the main they had not. "As regards refugees from Palestine," the Commission said, "they were obliged to leave their homes because they were of Arab origin."[86]

The issue addressed by Erim was the status of these minority persons who held Palestine nationality. Some of these, Erim said,

> had acquired another nationality after 29 November 1947, either by resuming their former nationality or by becoming naturalized citizens of a country in which they have racial ties with the majority of the population.

Such persons, Erim said, were now nationals of that other country. Some, however, had not acquired such a nationality. These persons would be entitled, he said, to rights of residency and to protection for their property by Israel. What is instructive for present purposes is the manner in which Erim referred to these minority persons who had not acquired another nationality. The legal advisor referred to them as "those who have retained their Palestinian citizenship."[87] Erim thus was of the view that Palestine citizens who had not acquired a new nationality continued to be nationals of Palestine. While Erim was only required to address the situation of the minority persons, he was also saying that Palestine nationality had not been extinguished by the events of 1948.

Guy Goodwin-Gill and Jane McAdam conclude that Palestine nationality lapsed as a matter of domestic law because it was based on the authority of Britain as the mandatory power. They note, however, that Britain had provided for a continuation of Palestine nationality. Although Britain repealed certain pieces of legislation upon its withdrawal from

Palestine, it did not repeal the Palestine Citizenship Order 1925.[88] As was explained to the British Parliament by the Attorney-General, the law of Palestine was, in general, being left in place upon Britain's withdrawal.[89] That included the law relating to nationality. Palestine nationality was part of the law of Palestine that was carried over in all three of the sectors into which Palestine had been divided. It remained relevant as well for the Palestine Arabs who went to other countries, since they, too, were Palestine nationals under the 1925 order. Goodwin-Gill and McAdam write:

> With the termination of the British mandate on 14/15 May 1948, their nationality status may have become uncertain from a *municipal law* perspective, although from an international law perspective, their 'link' to the territory remained.

Goodwin-Gill and McAdam cite General Assembly Resolution 194, paragraph 11, on repatriation, as recognizing the "link" of Palestine Arabs to the territory of Palestine. They call it the "'international status' of Palestinians as mandate citizens."[90] Indeed, that status was preserved by UN Charter Article 80. Mandate citizenship did not die when the last British soldier left Palestine.

Goodwin-Gill and McAdam note that the goals of paragraph 11 of Resolution 194 could not realistically be accomplished without some international protection function.[91] Repatriation, and the related property compensation for which paragraph 11 also called, could be handled only with international oversight. The General Assembly was recognizing the attachment of the Palestine Arabs to the territory of Palestine.

Thus Palestine nationality attached to the Palestine state, which had not gone out of existence upon Britain's withdrawal. In Gaza, Palestine nationality was acknowledged by Egypt in its role as administrator. In 1950, Egypt adopted a nationality law defining Egyptian nationality.[92] Like Egyptian legislation generally, this law did not apply to Gaza. It did not mention Gaza or Gazans and thus did not extend Egyptian nationality to Gazans. Andreas Zimmermann has taken this to mean that Gazans were stateless.[93] That view, however, is not consistent with the status of Gaza and its inhabitants. Egypt honored Palestine nationality both for indigenous Gazans and for persons in Gaza who had been displaced from other parts of Palestine.[94] Both groups continued to regard themselves as citizens of Palestine.[95] Passports were issued from Cairo by the All-Palestine Government.[96]

As for the West Bank, the Palestine Arabs who remained, or went, there were accorded Jordan nationality.[97] However, because the entire arrangement for Jordan's control of the West Bank was provisional in nature, Jordan's grant of nationality was subject to the resolution of Palestine's situation.

Israel did not deal with the nationality question until 1952, when it adopted legislation on Israeli nationality for the first time. Palestine Arabs who remained in the sectors of Palestine occupied by Israel were accorded Israeli nationality, so long as they had remained in place after the events of 1948. However, this legislation excluded the Palestine Arab refugees from Israeli nationality.[98]

Under international law, as the Israeli judge correctly determined in the 1951 case just cited, it is the new sovereign who must offer nationality to the population of the territory over which it assumes control. This applies to persons who were properly nationals of the former sovereign, regardless of their physical location. One hundred or more Palestine Arabs were studying at universities in the United States when the mandate ended.[99] When their short-term student visas expired, the U.S. Department of Justice took the position that Israel was obliged to allow them entry, on the rationale that Israel was required to regard them as its nationals.[100] Israel refused. The U.S. position on this matter reflected an assumption that Israel was a successor to the former sovereign. Israel was in default of its obligations as a successor state by refusing to repatriate Palestine Arabs who, for whatever reason, were outside the country.

The nationality status of Palestine Arabs has needed to be determined by administrative officials and courts in many countries when Palestine Arabs have had dealings there. Germany, like Egypt, regarded Palestine nationality to have survived the events of 1948. On December 12, 1984, Germany's Interior Minister, referring to an explanation given by the German Foreign Ministry, said that, "on legal and political grounds," a "Palestinian nationality endures."[101]

The Arab states acknowledged the Palestine nationality of Palestine Arabs who were displaced into their territories. The Arab states soon began to issue travel documents to Palestine Arabs that were premised on their continuing Palestine nationality. The precise nature of these documents varied from one Arab state to another.[102] In Syria, under a 1963 law, the document was valid for a period of six years and could be renewed at Syrian consulates abroad.[103] In 1965, the League of Arab States agreed collectively that Palestine nationals were entitled to travel documents to be issued by the state into whose territory they had been displaced. The agreement referred to the fact that Palestine nationality was retained.[104]

In the United States, the matter has come before various courts. While some of them have referred to Palestinians who did not acquire the nationality of another state as stateless,[105] others have acknowledged Palestinians as holding Palestine nationality, even when their travel documents were issued by another state. These cases have typically involved a Palestine Arab's request for asylum. In a 2001 case, a U.S. court acknowledged the Palestine nationality of a Palestine Arab born in Gaza in 1965 who had resided in Saudi Arabia. The court characterized the man's nationality status by saying that

> Abdelwahed also claims that he was easily identified as a Palestinian because his identification card was so marked. Abdelwahed is Palestinian. Just as the passport of an American residing in another country says "United States of America" on the front, or the passport of an alien residing in the United States has the name of his or her country on the front, the identification of a Palestinian residing in Saudi Arabia would logically state that he or she is a Palestinian.[106]

Australian and British courts have given similar characterizations. An Australian federal court referred to an asylum seeker from a village in the West Bank as a "citizen of Palestine."[107] Another panel of the same court referred to an asylum seeker born in 1977 and a resident of Jenin, West Bank, as a "citizen of Palestine."[108] A British court struck the same note. In a 2009 case, the British Court of Appeal referred to an asylum seeker born in Hebron, West Bank, circa 1974, as a "Palestinian national."[109]

It may seem odd, to be sure, that a citizenship can continue in the absence of a government of the relevant state. However, a variety of nationality arrangements are found in international practice that vary from the normal situation. Governments-in-exile may administer the citizenship of the states they represent, even though they exercise no control in their territory. Niue is a state whose features will be described in Chapter 19. Niue accords citizenship to no one. Inhabitants of Niue are citizens of New Zealand. So Niue is a state with no citizenship. For Palestine Arabs, Palestine citizenship, but with protection in the form of travel documents supplied by an Arab state, represented an unusual situation, but not a legally impossible one.

PART THREE

PALESTINE IN THE WORLD COMMUNITY

11

An Organization for Palestine

Eighteen years after Britain's withdrawal, a new effort was made toward implementing independence for Palestine. In May 1964, a convention was held in Jerusalem, with the backing of the Arab League, of representatives of Palestine Arab communities and social and professional groups. A Palestine National Council (PNC) was formed, to represent Palestine Arabs, whether living in the territory of Palestine or elsewhere. The PNC, which was intended as a policy-making body, organized the Palestine Liberation Army (PLA), whose function was to protect and extend territory in Palestine.[1] The PNC also set up the Palestine Liberation Organization (PLO) as the nascent government for the "Palestine entity."[2] A cablegram was sent to the UN Secretary-General announcing and explaining the action.[3]

As its founding document, the PNC adopted the Palestine National Covenant, which focused on establishing governance over Palestine. The Covenant contained the following opening articles:

Article 1. Palestine is an Arab homeland bound by strong national ties to the rest of the Arab Countries and which together form the large Arab homeland.

Article 2. Palestine with its boundaries at the time of the British Mandate is a regional indivisible unit.

Article 3. The Palestinian Arab people has the legitimate right to its homeland and is an inseparable part of the Arab Nation. It shares the sufferings and aspirations of the Arab Nation and its struggle for freedom, sovereignty, progress and unity.

Article 4. The people of Palestine determines its destiny when it completes the liberation of its homeland in accordance with its own wishes and free will and choice.

Article 5. The Palestinian personality is a permanent and genuine characteristic that does not disappear. It is transferred from fathers to sons.

Article 6. The Palestinians are those Arab citizens who were living normally in Palestine up to 1947, whether they remained or were expelled. Every child who was born to a Palestinian parent after this date whether in Palestine or outside is a Palestinian.

Article 7. Jews of Palestinian origin are considered Palestinians if they are willing to live peacefully and loyally in Palestine.[4]

The Covenant thus reaffirmed Palestine as a state within the mandate boundaries and provided a definition of Palestine nationality.[5]

The PNC's claim that it represented Palestine Arabs wherever they might reside met with resistance from Jordan, which still viewed itself as representing the Palestine Arabs in their quest for territorial independence.[6] Jordan, however, joined with other Arab states in seeking a voice for the PLO at the United Nations. Jordan signed joint Arab-state letters asking the General Assembly's Special Political Committee to hear representatives of the PLO at Committee sessions.[7] The Special Political Committee did accept the participation of PLO representatives[8] while continuing to receive the Palestine Arab Delegation.[9] Internationally, various states began to recognize the PLO as the representative of the Palestine Arabs. PLO offices opened within a short time in over sixty states, some of which accorded diplomatic immunities to the Palestine functionaries.[10]

OCCUPATION OF GAZA AND THE WEST BANK

Just as these efforts toward Palestine independence were beginning, a new territorial shift set them back. On June 5, 1967, Israel invaded and occupied Gaza, over the resistance of both the Egyptian army and the PLA.[11] Egypt charged Israel with aggression, but Israel countercharged, telling the UN Security Council that Egypt had attacked three villages in southern Israel and had launched fighter jets in Israel's direction.[12] Jordan came to Egypt's defense, whereupon Israel invaded and occupied the West Bank, overcoming the resistance of both the Jordanian army and the PLA.[13]

Israel's claim in the Security Council that there had been an Egyptian attack was apparently an invention, and Israel soon abandoned it.[14] In a second attempt at justification, Israel said that Egypt had been on the verge of attacking and that Israel had merely acted to preempt it.[15] The facts did not substantiate that justification either.[16] Israel's cabinet, which had adopted a formal decision to initiate military action against Egypt the day before the invasion, knew that Egypt was not about to attack.[17] In any event, within a few days Israel had occupied both Gaza and the West Bank, the two sectors of Palestine that had escaped its reach in 1948. The latter sector included the old city of Jerusalem, which fell on the Jordanian side of the 1949 armistice line.

Unlike what it had done in 1956, the United States did not pressure Israel to withdraw, and the IDF settled in to govern the two sectors. Israel's occupation put it in the position of a belligerent occupant. The Israeli government extended the application of Israeli law to the sections of Jerusalem that it had just occupied, raising concern that it planned to retain them permanently. The UN General Assembly condemned this measure as a violation of the obligations of a belligerent occupant, which is prohibited from annexing territory it occupies.[18] Except in Jerusalem, however, Israel did not attempt to displace the law in force in the West Bank. A military governor appointed to head a military administration for the West Bank issued a proclamation reciting that

> the law in existence in the Region on June 7, 1967, shall remain in force in so far as it does not in any way conflict with the provisions of this Proclamation or any Proclamation or Order which may be issued by me, and subject to modifications resulting from the establishment of government by the Israel Defense Forces in the Region.[19]

Another military governor was appointed for Gaza, and a similar proclamation was issued to continue the law in force there.[20] Thus, with the exception of Jerusalem, Israel did not move toward attempting to annex Gaza or the West Bank.

Thousands of Arabs were forced out of Gaza and the West Bank by the IDF during the 1967 hostilities, and the IDF prevented the return of thousands more who had happened to be out of the country at the time of the invasion. The UN Security Council called on Israel to allow their repatriation.[21]

The Security Council made no finding about who bore the responsibility for the initiation of the June 1967 hostilities. Its formal response came in November 1967, when it adopted Resolution 242, which declared that the acquisition of territory by force is "inadmissible" and called for the normalization of relations between Israel and the Arab states.[22] The following year, the UN General Assembly became concerned over Israel's continuing refusal to repatriate the Palestine Arabs displaced by the 1967 hostilities and set up the three-nation Special Committee to Investigate Israeli Practices Affecting the Human Rights of the Population of the Occupied Territories.[23] Israel shortly began to insert its own civilians into the West Bank as settlers, a measure that violated the law of belligerent occupation and potentially threatened the implementation of Palestine statehood. The UN Security Council would later condemn the settlement policy as unlawful and as "a serious obstruction to achieving a comprehensive, just and lasting peace in the Middle East."[24]

Israel took over many executive functions of government in Gaza and the West Bank but did not completely displace existing institutions. In the West Bank, Jordan continued to pay the salaries of thousands of civil servants working in schools and in other public service institutions.

The IDF decreed regulations in Gaza and the West Bank, violations of which were handled in tribunals it established. At the same time, the IDF let the Palestinian courts function. Israel also ended the subordination of the West Bank courts to the Jordanian Court of Cassation in Amman.[25] However, as result of extending its own laws to east Jerusalem, Israel closed the Palestinian courts there.

An Israeli officer was designated as being in charge of the judiciary and took over administration of the courts and oversight of the practicing bar in Gaza and the West Bank. Although the Palestinian courts continued to be staffed by Palestinian judges, this officer became responsible for their appointment.[26] The Gaza and West Bank magistrate and district courts dealt with general civil and criminal matters, applying the same law as before June 1967.[27]

Other legal and quasi-legal institutions functioned as before.[28] Islamic courts continued to exercise jurisdiction in domestic-relations law and matters of personal status. This jurisdiction extended as well to inheritance matters, which gave the Islamic courts cases involving the real property of decedents.[29] The judgments of the Islamic courts were implemented by the execution department of the civil courts.[30] For many commercial or family-related disputes, individuals respected in the community were sought out to promote a settlement. Even for homicides, a traditional practice involving community involvement was used to provide compensation in situations that might otherwise involve a criminal prosecution.[31] In 1976, elections for seats on municipal councils were held throughout both Gaza and the West Bank, a development that enhanced local governance.[32] Israel's tenure in Gaza and the West Bank thus involved a significant dose of administration by existing institutions.

PALESTINE IN THE UNITED NATIONS GENERAL ASSEMBLY

International organizations of states began accepting the PLO into their ranks, acknowledging the PLO as the representative of the people of Palestine and, by implication, as the representative of Palestine. In 1969, the PLO was admitted as a member state of the Organization of the Islamic Conference, an interstate organization.[33] That same year the UN General Assembly, in calling on Israel to repatriate the Arabs that it was excluding from Gaza and the West Bank, affirmed "the inalienable rights of the people of Palestine."[34] In 1970, the General Assembly resolved "that the people of Palestine are entitled to equal rights and self-determination" and declared "that full respect for the inalienable rights of the people of Palestine is an indispensable element in the establishment of a just and lasting peace in the Middle East."[35] In 1971, in a resolution on liberation movements, the Assembly

> confirm[ed] the legality of the peoples' struggle for self-determination and liberation from colonial and foreign domination and alien subjugation, notably in southern Africa ... as well as of the Palestinian people.[36]

In the same resolution, the Assembly affirmed the "legitimacy" of the Palestinian people's "struggle" to "restore" its right to "freedom, equality and self-determination." That right was clearly to be exercised in the territory to which Palestinian self-determination applied. The Assembly did not characterize Palestine or its status, but by framing the issue as one of "restoring" a right to territory, the Assembly implied a continuing statehood status. The resolution condoned armed force, which was then being employed by the PLO and PLA, as a legitimate means of achieving this end.[37]

In 1971, the General Assembly called for implementation of Security Council Resolution 242 and declared that "the territory of a State shall not be the object of occupation or acquisition by another State resulting from the threat or use of force."[38] The General Assembly did not identify the "state" as Palestine. With regard to the West Bank, there might have been ambiguity because of the merger with Jordan. With regard to Gaza, however, the "state" had to be Palestine, since Gaza was in no sense the territory of Egypt.

The PLO's acceptance at the United Nations was facilitated by the fact that it was modifying its territorial objective and was asserting Palestine statehood in a way that was consistent with Israeli statehood. Fatah, by then the principal constituent group of the PLO, from 1969 called for a "democratic secular state" in the territory of mandate Palestine, to be inhabited by all then residing there plus those Arab refugees who would choose to return.[39] Fatah's espousal of a "democratic secular state" signified a willingness to accommodate to the Zionist presence.[40] The PNC made a further concession in June 1974, when it stated that it would endeavor to "liberate Palestinian soil and to set up on any part of it which is liberated by the militant national authority of the people."[41] This call represented a move in the direction of exercising statehood in Gaza and the West Bank. While it was left unclear whether this would be a first step toward taking additional territory, the aspiration to control a part of Palestine's territory was a step toward recognizing Israel.[42]

On October 10, 1974, the UN General Assembly invited the PLO to participate in plenary sessions of the Assembly when "the Question of Palestine" was being discussed. The rationale the Assembly gave for the invitation was that the PLO was the representative of the Palestinian people and that "the Palestinian people is the principal party to the question of Palestine."[43] Such participation is normally open only to member states.[44] The United States issued visas for PLO representatives to enter the United States. PLO participation at the United Nations was seen as promoting a peaceful settlement. A U.S. court upheld the issuance of visas to the PLO representatives, saying that "a primary goal of the United Nations is to provide a forum where peaceful discussion may replace violence as a means of resolving disputed issues."[45]

Also in October 1974, the Arab heads of state, at a conference in Rabat, Morocco, declared the PLO to be the sole legitimate representative of the Palestinian people and affirmed their right to statehood in any sector of Palestine that Israel might evacuate.[46] This action led Jordan to alter its position on the PNC and PLO.[47] If those bodies represented the Palestine Arabs, the underpinnings for the attachment of the West Bank to Jordan were in doubt, and in particular, the participation of the West Bank population in Jordan's parliament. On the rationale that the PNC and PLO were assuming responsibility for the West Bank, King Hussein of Jordan suspended the Jordanian parliament.[48] The change in Jordan's position confirmed the provisional nature of the 1950 incorporation of the West Bank into Jordan. As well, by this time the PLO was beginning to undertake a variety of social-service projects in Gaza and the West Bank, setting the stage for a role in governance.[49]

The UN General Assembly invited Yassir Arafat, in his capacity as Chairman of the PLO, to address it in plenary session in New York. In UN practice, only heads of state were asked to address plenary sessions.[50] No other representative of an entity representing a people and claiming statehood had been so invited.[51] Saying that he bore both a freedom fighter's gun and an olive branch, Arafat asked in his speech that the General Assembly not let the olive branch fall from his hand and that it "enable our people to establish national independent sovereignty over its own land."[52] This invitation to Arafat would be the first of a series of actions at the UN in which it treated the PLO less in the way it traditionally treated liberation organizations and more in the way it treated governments of states.

On November 22, 1974, the UN General Assembly adopted a resolution that called for extraordinary measures in support of Palestine. First, it affirmed

> the inalienable rights of the Palestinian people in Palestine, including: (*a*) The right to self-determination without external interference; (*b*) The right to national independence and sovereignty.

The mention of "independence" was clearly a reference to Palestine as a state. Then the General Assembly called for a series of measures to bring about independence for Palestine. It asked the Secretary-General to "establish contacts with the Palestine Liberation Organization on all matters relating to the question of Palestine," thereby requiring the Secretariat to work actively on the matter. It also

> recognize[d] the right of the Palestinian people to regain its rights by all means in accordance with the purposes and principles of the Charter of the United Nations.

Perhaps even more significant was the next clause in which the General Assembly

> appeal[ed] to all States and international organizations to extend their support to the Palestinian people in its struggle to restore its right, in accordance with the Charter.[53]

The General Assembly was asking the entire international community to help the Palestinian people implement Palestine statehood.

On the same day, the General Assembly adopted a resolution on Palestine's status at the United Nations. The resolution began by mentioning the acceptance of the PLO by various international institutions:

> Noting that the Diplomatic Conference on the Reaffirmation and Development of International Humanitarian Law Applicable in Armed Conflicts, the World Population Conference and the World Food

Conference have in effect invited the Palestine Liberation Organization to participate in their respective deliberations,

Noting also that the third United Nations Conference on the Law of the Sea has invited the Palestine Liberation Organization to participate in its deliberations as an observer.

The resolution then opened a whole range of international activity for the PLO. It said that the General Assembly

1. Invites the Palestine Liberation Organization to participate in the sessions and the work of the General Assembly in the capacity of observer;
2. Invites the Palestine Liberation Organization to participate in the sessions and the work of all international conferences convened under the auspices of the General Assembly in the capacity of observer;
3. Considers that the Palestine Liberation Organization is entitled to participate as an observer in the sessions and the work of all international conferences convened under the auspices of other organs of the United Nations; . . .[54]

This invitation to participate in all conferences that were convened under the auspices of the General Assembly, whatever the subject matter, represented extraordinary access for an entity that was not a member state. Erik Suy, a former UN legal counsel, said that the rationale was that the PLO had a legitimate interest in the full range of topics that might be considered at UN conferences. He said that the broad invitation was based on the assumption that Palestine would become a state.[55] Whether the assumption was of statehood in, presumably, the near future, or of statehood already existing but lacking independence involves a fine reading of the intent of the member states of the General Assembly. It would be just as reasonable to regard these statements and privileges as reflecting an assumption of Palestine's present status as a state. Suy elsewhere used the term "proto-state" to characterize Palestine as the UN was treating it.[56] Suy acknowledged that "it is extremely difficult to formulate a clear picture" of what is implied by observer status and related privileges.[57]

Like the General Assembly, the Economic and Social Council (ECOSOC) is one of the main organs of the United Nations. The PLO was given a role there as well. ECOSOC had established five regional commissions, made up of states, to deal with economic and social issues affecting particular regions of the world.[58] One was the Economic Commission for

Western Asia. On May 9, 1975, the Economic Commission for Western Asia granted the PLO observer status in the Commission.[59]

On November 10, 1975, the General Assembly asked the Security Council "to consider and adopt the necessary resolutions and measures in order to enable the Palestinian people to exercise its inalienable national rights" and called for

> the invitation of the Palestine Liberation Organization, the representative of the Palestinian people, to participate in all efforts, deliberations and conferences on the Middle East which are held under the auspices of the United Nations, on an equal footing with other parties.[60]

The General Assembly resolution of the previous year had invited PLO participation in such conferences, but the "equal footing" language accorded the PLO the same status as governments.

At the same time, the General Assembly went so far as to create a permanent committee to work toward implementing independence for the Palestinians in the territory of Palestine. This was the twenty-nation Committee on the Exercise of the Inalienable Rights of the Palestinian People, established in a resolution in which the General Assembly deplored the nonfulfilment of "the exercise by the Palestinian people of its inalienable rights in Palestine, including the right to self-determination without external interference and the right to national independence and sovereignty." The General Assembly's reference to rights "in Palestine" was a reference to Palestine as a state. In the same resolution, the Assembly characterized the nonfulfillment to date of Palestinian rights as a threat to international peace.[61]

PALESTINE IN THE UNITED NATIONS SECURITY COUNCIL

At the United Nations, it is the Security Council that is responsible for the international peace. Responding to the General Assembly's request, the Security Council decided to hold Council discussions to seek ways to implement Palestine statehood. On November 30, 1975, the Security Council scheduled a discussion on the Middle East, to be held on January 12, 1976. The Council's president read out a statement indicating that a majority of its members had agreed that the PLO would be invited to participate.[62]

On December 4, 1975, another session of the Security Council was held in which the Middle East was discussed, and several member states proposed that the PLO be invited to participate in the day's debate. The Council has two mechanisms for inviting entities other than Member States to its meetings. Under the Security Council Rules of Procedure, any person may be invited to supply information. Thus, Rule 39 provides:

> The Security Council may invite members of the Secretariat or other persons, whom it considers competent for the purpose, to supply it with information or to give other assistance in examining matters within its competence.

A Rule 39 invitation does not give a right to participate in the Council debate, however.

The other mechanism falls under Security Council Rule 37, which is reserved for UN member states and which affords a right to participate in Council debate. Rule 37 provides, in part, that

> [a]ny Member of the United Nations which is not a member of the Security Council may be invited, as the result of a decision of the Security Council, to participate, without vote, in the discussion of any question brought before the Security Council when the Security Council considers that the interests of that Member are specially affected ...,

Although the proponents of the proposal to invite the PLO did not link the invitation to either rule, the Council president explained:

> If [the proposal] is adopted by the Council, the invitation to the PLO to participate in the debate will confer on it the same rights of participation as are conferred when a Member State is invited to participate under rule 37.[63]

Iraq and Belorussia argued for inviting the PLO on the basis that it had been accorded permanent observer status by the General Assembly and that it was a central actor in resolving Middle East issues.[64] The United Kingdom objected that participation under Rule 37 is open only to member states, that the PLO did not represent a member state, and that it did not "claim to be a State at all, nor to be the Government of a State."[65] The UK wanted the invitation to be issued under Rule 39.

The UK's characterization of the PLO was questionable. The PLO did claim to represent a state. The PLO was formed with the aim of achieving the "liberation," in its terminology, of "Palestine," and it represented Palestine in that endeavor. Even before the PLO, both the Palestine Arab Delegation and the All-Palestine Government had argued for independence for "Palestine." They aspired to represent Palestine. They considered Palestine to be a state. So, too, did the Arab League states, specifically Jordan and Egypt, which had assumed the administration of sectors of Palestine.

The Security Council did not find the UK objection persuasive. The Council voted to invite a PLO representative on the basis of the Council president's explanation.[66] A PLO representative was immediately seated and participated in the debate.[67] Leo Gross, professor at the Fletcher School of Law and Diplomacy at Tufts University in the United States and a former consultant to the UN Legal Department, found this action extraordinary. Gross wrote:

> Clearly what was involved was not merely a procedural issue and respect for precedent. What was involved was a constitutional issue of the first magnitude.[68]

Granting the rights accorded by Rule 37, as the Security Council did, meant that the Council was treating the PLO as the government of a state.

At the January 12, 1976 meeting, the issue surfaced again. The president referred to the understanding from the meeting of November 30, 1975, that a PLO representative should participate in the debate. The president reiterated that the proposal was

> not being put forward under rule 37 or rule 39 of the provisional rules of procedure of the Security Council, but, if it is adopted by the Council, the invitation to the PLO to participate in this debate will confer on it the same rights of participation as are conferred when a Member State is invited to participate under rule 37.[69]

Mirroring the previous objection by the United Kingdom, the United States opposed an invitation on this basis since it involved treating the PLO representative as a representative of a state. The U.S. delegate argued that

> [t]he PLO is not a State. It does not administer a defined territory. It does not have the attributes of a Government of a State. It does not claim to be a State.[70]

The Soviet delegate, referring to the PLO as representative of "the Arab people of Palestine," responded that during World War II, governments in exile spoke "on behalf of their countries and peoples."[71] Whether the exile entities like the Free French were in fact governments-in-exile may be less than entirely clear,[72] but the Soviet delegate's point was that whatever recognition they had was based on their representing a state. The USSR, for example, on August 25, 1943, recognized the Comité Français de la Libération Nationale "as representing the State interests of the French Republic."⁷³ Hence, the Soviet argument equated Palestine with a state. In the face of the U.S. objection, the Security Council reaffirmed its invitation to the PLO.⁷⁴ A PLO representative then participated in the debate.⁷⁵

The Security Council's acceptance here of the PLO stood in sharp contrast to Security Council practice in regard to other entities that promoted self-determination. The representatives of a number of self-determination movements were invited on various occasions to Security Council sessions when matters relating to decolonization were on the table, but always under Rule 39.⁷⁶ The Liberation Front of Mozambique (FRELIMO), the African Independence Party of Guinea and Cape Verde (PAIGC), and the Popular Movement for the Liberation of Angola (MPLA) were all invited under Rule 39.⁷⁷ The South-West Africa People's Organization (SWAPO) was invited under Rule 39.⁷⁸ Even the United Nations Council for Namibia, an entity established by the UN itself to oversee Namibia's progression to independence, was invited under Rule 39.⁷⁹ The distinction the Security Council made here indicated that the PLO was more than the embodiment of a self-determination movement. It represented a state.

ACCEPTANCE BY INTERNATIONAL ORGANIZATIONS

In 1976 and 1977, Palestine received additional acknowledgment as a state. In August 1976, Palestine was accepted as a member state by the Non-Aligned Movement, an organization of states that sided with neither the USSR nor the West on Cold War issues.⁸⁰ In September 1976, the Arab League accepted Palestine, as represented by the PLO, as a full member.⁸¹ The League indicated its view that Palestine was a state "even though the outward signs of [its] independence have remained veiled as a result of *force majeure*."⁸² The reference to *force majeure* was obviously to Israel's occupation of the territory of Palestine.

David Raič, a leading analyst of statehood in international law, did not regard the Arab League decision as appropriate, since at that juncture he did not regard Palestine as a state, on two counts. First, Raič said that no state had been declared. Second, he said, there was no government. But Raič ignored the fact that Palestine was not in need of being declared. It was not a new state. The PLO had declared its aim of forming a government for Palestine, a state it assumed to exist. The PLO aspired to be the government of Palestine.

In March 1977, the PNC, meeting in Cairo, did clarify that the "national authority" of which it had been speaking since 1974 was to be the government of a state.[83] While the PNC did not disavow the notion of a democratic secular state in the entirety of the Palestine mandate territory as an ultimate aim, it now took the position that a government might be set up for the West Bank and Gaza only.[84]

PALESTINE IN THE UNITED NATIONS ECONOMIC AND SOCIAL COUNCIL

These steps by the PLO toward implementing statehood found resonance at the United Nations. In July 1977, ECOSOC considered admitting the PLO to membership in the Economic Commission for Western Asia. As already mentioned, the Commission, which functions under the auspices of ECOSOC, had admitted the PLO as an observer in 1975. Several member states of ECOSOC objected on the basis that the Commission was open only to states and that Palestine was not a state.[85] Disregarding these objections, ECOSOC adopted a resolution admitting the PLO.[86] As the objecting states had correctly argued, because the Economic Commission for Western Asia is an organization of states,[87] the only basis on which the PLO could have been admitted was that it represented a state. Thus ECOSOC's action was premised on Palestine statehood. This action was particularly significant because ECOSOC is one of the principal organs of the United Nations.[88] Once it was admitted to the Economic Commission for Western Asia as a member state, the PLO participated actively in its work.[89]

THE GENERAL ASSEMBLY AND THE RIGHT OF REPLY

Like the Security Council, the UN General Assembly treated Palestine as a state in the manner in which it allowed participation by the PLO. On October 10, 1977, Moshe Dayan made a statement as a representative of Israel in a plenary meeting of the General Assembly.[90] The following day, when the Assembly again met in plenary session, the Assembly president called on Farouk Kaddoumi, a representative of the PLO, to reply to Dayan's statement. Under Rule 73 of the General Assembly Rules of Procedure, the Assembly president may

> accord the right of reply to any member if a speech delivered after he has declared the list closed makes this desirable.[91]

146   Palestine in the World Community

"Member" here means a UN member state. When the president announced that he would call on Kaddoumi to speak, the U.S. delegate objected "that only representatives of Member States are qualified to participate in the general debate." The Israeli delegate also objected, citing Rule 73 as limiting the right of reply to "members." He also referred to the conditions for membership in the United Nations: "Articles 3 and 4 of the Charter lay down that only States – I repeat 'States' – can be Members of the Organization." Overriding these considerations, the president called on Kaddoumi, who then replied to Dayan.[92] Neither Israel nor the United States objected formally, so no vote was taken on a point of order.[93] Rather, the Assembly acquiesced in the ruling of the president. The United States and Israel were correct in arguing that this right of reply for the PLO was premised on the PLO representing a state. The General Assembly was treating Palestine as a state.

PALESTINE IN UN PEACE EFFORTS

Peace initiatives at the United Nations also showed that Palestine was being regarded as a state by the international community. On December 2, 1977, the UN General Assembly, repeating language it had used when setting up the Committee on the Exercise of the Inalienable Rights of the Palestinian People, resolved that peace in the Middle East could be achieved only if the Palestinian people were accorded their "right to independence and national sovereignty in Palestine."[94]

The United States at the time was promoting talks between Israel and Egypt that were to deal not only with Israel-Egypt issues but also with the Palestine question. Cyrus Vance, who served as Secretary of State in the United States under President Jimmy Carter, described the U.S. perspective on Palestine sovereignty: "Our view," Vance later wrote, "was that sovereignty ultimately resided in the people of the West Bank and Gaza."[95] Language suggesting that a territorial resolution should be based on the legal entitlements of the Palestinian people was included in the 1978 Camp David accords (Israel-Egypt) brokered by Vance and Carter. One of the Camp David accords described anticipated negotiations relating to Gaza and the West Bank as follows:

> The solution from the negotiations must also recognize the legitimate right of the Palestinian people and their just requirements. In this way, the Palestinians will participate in the determination of their own future ...[96]

Despite its merger with the West Bank, Jordan continued to proclaim Palestinian sovereignty. Jordan's UN representative said in 1979 that the Palestinian people were the bearers of sovereignty in the West Bank. He referred to its 1950 incorporation as an act that would not "prejudice the ultimate solution of the Palestine problem."[97]

Affirmation of Palestine statehood in ever more explicit terms came from the UN General Assembly as it too promoted peace efforts. In 1980, the General Assembly held an emergency special session on the Question of Palestine. In Resolution ES/7–2, the General Assembly reiterated prior language on Palestinian rights but added the specific mention of a "state," affirming

> the inalienable rights in Palestine of the Palestinian people, including: (*a*) The right to self-determination without external interference, and to national independence and sovereignty; (*b*) The right to establish its own independent sovereign State.[98]

The following year the General Assembly took new action aimed at implementing independence for Palestine. It decided

> [t]o convene, under the auspices of the United Nations, an International Conference on the Question of Palestine not later than 1984, on the basis of General Assembly resolution ES-7/2.[99]

That conference was held in Geneva two years later, from August 29 to September 7, 1983. Following upon the conference, the General Assembly adopted Resolution 38/58C in which it called for a conference that would be aimed specifically at a territorial settlement. The Assembly envisaged "an International Peace Conference on the Middle East in conformity with the following guidelines":

(a) The attainment by the Palestinian people of its legitimate inalienable rights, including the right to return, the right to self-determination and the right to establish its own independent State in Palestine;
(b) The right of the Palestine Liberation Organization, the representative of the Palestinian people, to participate on an equal footing with other parties in all efforts, deliberations and conferences on the Middle East;
(c) The need to put an end to Israel's occupation of Arab territories, in accordance with the principle of the inadmissibility of the acquisition of territory by force, and, consequently, the need to secure Israeli withdrawal from the territories occupied since 1967, including Jerusalem....

(f) The right of all States in the region to existence within secure and internationally recognized boundaries, with justice and security for all the people, the *sine qua non* of which is the recognition and attainment of the legitimate, inalienable rights of the Palestinian people as stated in subparagraph (*a*) above.[100]

The General Assembly invited all the parties to the conflict, other concerned states, and, specifically, the United States and USSR to participate. By the following year, however, Israel and the United States had indicated they would not participate, prompting the General Assembly to adopt the following resolution:

The General Assembly,

Recalling its resolution 38/58 C of 13 December 1983, in which it, *inter alia*, endorsed the convening of the International Peace Conference on the Middle East, ...

Having considered the reports of the Secretary-General of 13 March and 13 September 1984, in which he stated that, *inter alia*, "it is clear from the replies of the Governments of Israel and the United States of America that they are not prepared to participate in the proposed Conference",

Reiterating its conviction that the convening of the Conference would constitute a major contribution by the United Nations toward the achievement of a comprehensive, just and lasting solution to the Arab-Israeli conflict,

1. *Takes note* of the reports of the Secretary-General;

2. *Reaffirms* its endorsement of the call for convening the International Peace Conference on the Middle East in conformity with the provisions of General Assembly resolution 38/58 C;

3. *Expresses its regret* at the negative response of the two Governments and calls upon them to reconsider their position toward the Conference; ...[101]

The General Assembly continued efforts in this direction, but little came of them, as Israel and the United States held to their position, particularly their refusal to deal with the PLO.

MAP 5. Territories occupied by Israel since June 1967, No. 3243 rev.4, June 11, 1997.
Source: Courtesy UN Cartographic Section.

12

A Government for Palestine

The states of the international community were dealing with Palestine as a state not only through their participation in UN organs but as well in their individual relations with the PLO. In Chapter 11, it was indicated that when the PLO declared itself, states began receiving its representatives as they do diplomats. By the early 1980s, PLO officials were able to say that the PLO maintained more diplomatic missions than did Israel, even if the precise status of the PLO missions varied.[1] Exact figures were elusive. By one count, about sixty states recognized the PLO and accorded diplomatic status to PLO missions, while another fifty or so gave recognition but did not accord diplomatic status.[2] By another count, the PLO was recognized by 131 states. Compilers of this latter list found diplomatic relations with forty-seven states and sub-diplomatic relations with eighteen. For sixty-six states, the compilers were unable to determine the exact nature of the relationship.[3]

The ambiguities were reflected in Italy's approach to relations with the PLO. A PLO office opened in Rome in 1974. When a question of diplomatic immunity arose in a court case in Italy, the Italian Foreign Ministry informed the court that the PLO office

> has not been recognized as having a diplomatic status in the strict sense but, in practice, it has been arranged in such a way that the directors of the office have been allowed to enjoy such status, allowing them to be accredited by one of the Arab embassies located in the capital among the members of its own staff.[4]

One source of ambiguity was whether recognition of the PLO implied recognition of Palestine as a state or only recognition of the PLO as the representative of the Palestinian people.[5] The Italian Foreign Ministry gave a highly nuanced explanation to the Italian court about Italy's view of Palestine. It said that the PLO,

> although it is an entity which largely represents the aspirations of the Palestinian people, [it] does not have (at least at the present stage) the typical characteristics of a State organization: characteristics that are generally required for formal recognition.[6]

By saying that the PLO lacked the "typical characteristics of a State organization," the Foreign Ministry was leaving it unclear whether it viewed Palestine as a state. The Foreign Ministry confined itself to addressing the status of the PLO, which obviously could not be a state, only the representative of a state.

Determining the actual content of any one of the 100-plus recognitions requires scrutiny of the relevant documents and analysis of the recognizing state's conduct toward the PLO.[7] Austria, on December 13, 1978, by concurrent action of the parliament and the government, conferred full diplomatic status on the PLO representative in Vienna.[8] Chancellor Bruno Kreisky explained Austria's action as "a new form of diplomatic recognition," given that the PLO was not fully in control of territory.[9]

Senegal accepted a PLO mission at the ambassadorial level on December 1, 1981. That status implied full diplomatic privileges and immunities.[10] Greece, Cyprus, Turkey, and Malta all accorded diplomatic status to the PLO missions they had admitted, including diplomatic immunity for personnel.[11]

On August 14, 1986, Spain accorded diplomatic status to the PLO mission that had functioned in Madrid since 1977. A Spanish Foreign Ministry spokesman explained that the PLO mission was granted the right to use a diplomatic pouch, official honors, and the protection normally afforded to embassies. The mission would be included on Spain's diplomatic list, but under "other representations" rather than as an "embassy." The mission's personnel would not enjoy immunity.[12]

Diplomatic status is an institution whereby states accept the representatives of other states. They accord them diplomatic privileges and immunities, including immunity from arrest, so that they may carry out the work of the home state without interference.[13] The PLO was, at a minimum, being recognized as the representative of a Palestinian people that was seen as enjoying a right of self-determination in territory that had, since the time of the mandate, been regarded as that of

Palestine. The states that accorded status to the PLO were, of course, the same states that, as members of the UN Security Council, UN General Assembly, or UN Economic and Social Council, were taking the view that Palestine was a state. When these states gave recognition to the PLO on any basis, they were implicitly recognizing it as the governing body for the Palestine state.

A DECLARATION

What remained at the level of international formalities was to make it more evident that the PNC and the PLO were akin to a government that was structured to administer Palestine if the political situation could be resolved. In December 1987, protests began in Gaza and the West Bank, continuing into 1988, aimed at Israel's occupation. That action led to proposals for a declaration about Palestine's status. In early 1988, prominent international lawyers were consulted. A memorandum was prepared that recounted the basis of Palestine statehood, including, prominently, the status of Palestine under Britain's mandate and the preservation of Palestinian rights under UN Charter Article 80.[14]

On July 31, 1988, in response to these steps, Jordan renounced its provisional 1950 claim to the territory of the West Bank.[15] Jordan's King Hussein explained that

> Jordan is not Palestine.... The independent Palestinian state will be established on the occupied Palestinian land after its liberation, God willing.... In addition to the Palestine Liberation Organization's ambition to embody the Palestinian identity on Palestinian national soil, there should be the separation of the West Bank from the Hashemite kingdom of Jordan.... We have responded to the wish of the representatives of the Palestinian people for unity with Jordan in 1950. We respect the wish of the P.L.O. for an independent Palestinian state.... We had never imagined that the preservation of the legal and administrative links between the two banks could constitute an obstacle to the liberation of the occupied Palestinian land.[16] Yet lately it has transpired that there is a general Palestinian and Arab orientation toward highlighting the Palestinian identity in a complete manner, in every effort or activity related to the Palestinian question and its developments. Liberating the occupied Palestinian land could be enhanced by dismantling the legal and administrative links.

One immediate consequence of this renunciation was that Jordan no longer considered West Bank residents to be nationals of Jordan. By an order issued by the Jordanian government on August 20, 1988, "every person residing in the West Bank prior to 31.7.1988 is a Palestinian and not a Jordanian citizen."[17] As both an accommodation and a transitional measure, Jordan decided to allow passports issued to West Bank residents to remain valid until their expiration date, and to issue new passports that would be valid for a period of two years.[18]

On November 15, 1988, the PNC, meeting in Algiers, adopted a Declaration of Independence. In a series of preamble paragraphs, the document recounted Palestine's history and explained why Palestine was a state. Referring to the events that followed World War I, the Declaration's preamble noted the recognition given to Palestine by the Covenant of the League of Nations and the Treaty of Lausanne, as follows:

> At a time when the modern world was fashioning its new system of values, the prevailing balance of power in the local and international arenas excluded the Palestinians from the common destiny, and it was shown once more that it was not justice alone that turned the wheels of history.

> The deep injury already done the Palestinian people was therefore aggravated when a painful differentiation was made: a people deprived of independence, and one whose homeland was subjected to a new kind of foreign occupation, was exposed to an attempt to give general currency to the falsehood that Palestine was "a land without a people." Despite this falsification of history, the international community, in article 22 of the Covenant of the League of Nations of 1919 and in the Lausanne Treaty of 1923, recognized that the Palestinian Arab people was no different from the other Arab peoples detached from the Ottoman State and was a free and independent people.

Continuing, the Declaration described in the following terms how the events of 1948 and 1967 affected the Palestinian people:

> Despite the historical injustice done to the Palestinian Arab people in its displacement and in being deprived of the right to self-determination following the adoption of General Assembly resolution 181 (II) of 1947, which partitioned Palestine into an Arab and a Jewish State, that resolution nevertheless continues to attach conditions to international legitimacy that guarantee the Palestinian Arab people the right to sovereignty and national independence.

> The occupation of Palestinian territory and parts of other Arab territory by Israeli forces, the uprooting of the majority of Palestinians and their displacement from their homes by means of organized intimidation, and the subjection of the remainder to occupation, oppression and

the destruction of the distinctive features of their national life, are a
flagrant violation of the principles of legitimacy and of the Charter of
the United Nations and its resolutions recognizing the national rights
of the Palestinian people, including the right to return and the right to
self-determination, independence and sovereignty over the territory of its
homeland....

Next, the Declaration referred to Palestine as the state of its people and
proclaimed the following:

By virtue of the Palestinian Arab people's natural, historic and legal right
to their Homeland Palestine, and of the sacrifices of their successive gen-
erations in defense of the liberty and independence of their homeland;

Pursuant to the resolutions of the Arab Summit conferences;

By the authority of the international legitimacy, as embodied in the resolutions of the United Nations since 1947;

In implementation of the Palestinian Arab people's right to self-determination, political independence, and sovereignty on their soil;

The National Council proclaims, in the name of God and the Palestinian
Arab people, the establishment of the State of Palestine on our Palestinian
land, with the Holy City of Jerusalem as its capital.[19]

In a companion document, the PNC stated its intentions "in the
political field," indirectly addressing the issue of territory. The statement
called for

(a) The need to convene an effective international conference on the
    subject of the Middle East problem and its essence, the question of
    Palestine, under the auspices of the United Nations and with the par-
    ticipation of the permanent members of the Security Council and all
    parties to the conflict in the region, including the Palestine Liberation
    Organization, the sole legitimate representative of the Palestinian
    people, on an equal footing, with the provision that the said interna-
    tional conference shall be convened on the basis of Security Council
    resolutions 242 (1967) and 338 (1973) and shall guarantee the legiti-
    mate national rights of the Palestinian people, first and foremost
    among which is the right to self-determination, in accordance with
    the principles and provisions of the Charter of the United Nations
    concerning the right to self-determination of peoples, the inadmis-
    sibility of seizure of land belonging to others by means of force or
    military invasion, and in accordance with United Nations resolutions
    concerning the question of Palestine;
(b) Israel's withdrawal from all the Palestinian and Arab territories which
    it has occupied since 1967, including Arab Jerusalem;

(c) Cancellation of all measures of attachment and annexation and removal of the settlements established by Israel in the Palestinian and Arab territories since the year 1967;

(d) An endeavour to place the occupied Palestinian territories, including Arab Jerusalem, under United Nations supervision for a limited period, in order to protect our people and to provide an atmosphere conducive to a successful outcome for the international conference, the attainment of a comprehensive political settlement and the establishment of security and peace for all through mutual acceptance and satisfaction, and in order to enable the Palestinian State to exercise its effective authority over those territories;

(e) Solution of the Palestine refugee problem in accordance with United Nations resolutions on that subject;

(f) Assurance of freedom of worship and the practice of religious rites at the holy places in Palestine for adherents of all religions;

(g) The Security Council's establishment and assurance of arrangements for security and peace among all the concerned States in the region, including the Palestinian State.

The statement also addressed Palestine's relation to Jordan, as follows:

The Palestine National Council confirms its previous resolutions with regard to the privileged relationship between the two fraternal peoples of Jordan and Palestine, together with the fact that the future relationship between the States of Jordan and Palestine will be established on the basis of a confederacy and of free and voluntary choice by the two fraternal peoples, in corroboration of the historical ties and vital common interests which link them.[20]

The call in subparagraph (b) for Israel's withdrawal from Gaza and the West Bank, along with the proposal in subparagraph (a) for a conference based on Security Council Resolution 242, suggested that the territory contemplated for implementation of Palestine statehood was Gaza and the West Bank.

In a separate document, perhaps the most significant one for institutional purposes, the PNC asked the PLO to form a provisional government for Palestine. The document recited:

1. A provisional Government shall be formed for the State of Palestine as soon as possible, in accordance with circumstances and the evolution of events.

2. The Central Council[21] and the Executive Committee[22] of the Palestine Liberation Organization shall be empowered to appoint a time for the formation of the provisional Government, the Executive Committee shall be entrusted with its formation, and it shall be presented to the

Central Council for a motion of confidence. The Central Council shall adopt the provisional system of government until such time as the Palestinian people exercises full sovereignty over the land of Palestine.

3. The provisional Government shall be composed of Palestinian leaders, notables and skilled human resources within the occupied homeland and outside, on the basis of political pluralism and in such a manner as to embody national unity.

4. The provisional Government shall draw up its programme on the basis of the instrument of independence, the political programme of the Palestine Liberation Organization and the resolutions of the national councils.

5. The Palestine National Council hereby entrusts the Executive Committee of the Palestine Liberation Organization with the powers and responsibilities of the provisional Government until such time as the formation of the Government is declared.[23]

LEGAL BASIS OF THE DECLARATION

The Declaration of Independence cited two sources of legitimacy: It referred to the Palestinian people's "inalienable rights in the land of its patrimony" and to General Assembly Resolution 181 as providing "the conditions for international legitimacy that guarantees the right of the Palestinian Arab people to sovereignty on their homeland."

The reference to Resolution 181, which had been relied upon as well by the Jewish National Council when it declared statehood in 1948, reflected the change in territorial aspirations indicated above. This reference amounted to recognition of a Jewish state in a portion of the territory of Palestine. The accompanying political statement referred to Israel in a fashion that questioned its legitimacy while at the same time acknowledging Israel to be a state. The statement called Israel "a fascist, racist, colonialist state based on the usurpation of the Palestinian land and on the annihilation of the Palestinian people." A colonialist state would not enjoy international legitimacy. Nonetheless, the reference to Resolution 181, together with the political statement's reference to Gaza and the West Bank, bespoke an acceptance of Israel.

The reference in the preamble to the "new system of values" of the "modern world" recalled the promotion of self-determination at the Versailles conference. The preamble recited that the Palestinian people had been "excluded" from self-determination – a reference to the Balfour Declaration – yet had been recognized as a "free and independent people" in the League of Nations Covenant and the Treaty of Lausanne. The Declaration thus was harkening back to the Palestine statehood of the Covenant and to the Covenant's recognition of Palestine statehood and of provisional independence. The Declaration was not proclaiming a new state, but reaffirming an existing state, and setting up a provisional government for it.

The PLO had been pressed by the United States to aim for an affiliation with Jordan.[24] Arafat said that once Palestine was independent, a confederative relationship with Jordan might be a possibility.[25] Jordan's renunciation had the effect of shifting more responsibilities in the West Bank onto Palestinian institutions. Jordan stopped paying the salaries of thousands of West Bank civil servants and teachers. The PLO began to pay the salaries of many. Some administrative and judicial functions in the West Bank were assumed by newly constituted neighborhood committees.[26] These committees, which operated under PLO auspices, organized food distribution and schools.[27] Actual control by the PLO increased both in the West Bank and in Gaza.

13

The World Reacts

The Palestine Declaration elicited immediate approbation. States that had previously acknowledged or recognized the PLO made statements directed more clearly to their attitude toward a Palestine state. The USSR issued the following statement:

> Faithful to the fundamental principle of freedom of choice, the Soviet Union recognizes the proclamation of the Palestinian state, being guided by the realization that comprehensive settlement will also lead to the practical conclusion of the historic process of creating this state.[1]

By early 1989, approximately 100 states, which meant a majority of the states of the world, had expressed their recognition of Palestine.[2] As with the pre-1988 recognitions, the new expressions were not uniform in content. More states now established diplomatic or quasi-diplomatic relations with Palestine. Some states that recognized Palestine as a state on the basis of the Declaration elevated the status of an existing PLO office in their territory to the status of an embassy.[3] The USSR, for example, allowed the PLO to "reorganize" its Moscow mission as "the embassy of the state of Palestine in the Soviet Union." The USSR representative at PLO headquarters in Tunis was elevated to the status of "ambassador."[4]

Many states were explicit in their recognitions in referring to Palestine as a state. The Gulf Cooperation Council members – Kuwait, Saudi Arabia, Qatar, Bahrain, United Arab Emirates, and Oman – quickly recognized Palestine as a state. Oman, for example, announced that it was granting "official and legal recognition to the Palestinian state proclaimed at the PNC session held in Algiers from 12th-15th November."[5] Oman explained the Palestine Declaration as follows:

> The desire to establish the state of Palestine has been declared, but the state itself has not yet been established. Hence, what has actually taken

place was the decision to establish this state .... The Palestinian brothers have explained to us the nature of recognition which has moral dimensions, so we immediately announced our recognition.[6]

This text has been interpreted as an expression of moral support, rather than as the recognition of a state.[7] However, in saying that Palestine "has not yet been established," Oman was probably referring to Israel's occupation of Palestine territory, which in Oman's view did not derogate from Palestine's status as a state. Oman's reference to "moral dimensions" did not mean that Oman was not recognizing in a legal sense.

A number of European states declined to extend diplomatic recognition, but their caution was not necessarily based a view that Palestine was less than a state. French President François Mitterand devoted considerable attention to the Palestine Declaration. Mitterand characterized the European reaction, including France's, in a nuanced way,

> Many European countries are not ready to recognize a Palestine state. Others think that between recognition and non-recognition there are significant degrees; I am among these.[8]

So while France was not recognizing, neither was it not recognizing. Mitterand announced that France would receive a "general delegation" of Palestine in Paris, conferring a status that was one step short of diplomatic status.[9] The term "delegation," or "general delegation" is used in contradistinction to "embassy," to indicate a level of relations short of diplomatic relations.[10] However, personnel of a "general delegation" may be accorded diplomatic status by some host states. Mitterand said as well that

> [t]he recognition of a Palestinian State poses no problems of principle for France. France has taken note of the Algiers proclamation and recognizes the right of the Palestinians to live on a territory constituted as an independent state.

He went on to say that

> I cannot embark on a legal analysis here. But you know that our country has always based its decisions to recognize states on the principle of effectiveness, which implies the existence of responsible, independent power exercised over a territory and a people.[11]

By putting the matter this way, Mitterand was suggesting that France's disinclination to recognize Palestine did not mean that it did not regard Palestine as a state. It is not unknown, as will be seen in Chapter 18, for a state to withhold recognition from an entity that it regards as a state. Mitterand hailed what he termed "the rebirth of the Palestinian nation."[12] In using the term "rebirth," Mitterand was viewing the Palestine Declaration not as the proclamation of a new state, but as the affirmance of a state with historical roots.

France's designation of Palestine's mission as a "general delegation" did not yield diplomatic immunity for its personnel, but the French Government would say some years later that the Palestine "General Delegate" in Paris enjoyed diplomatic immunity in France because she held diplomatic credentials from another state.[13] In 2010 France agreed that the Palestine representative be designated as "ambassador" instead of "general delegate."

THE DECLARATION ACKNOWLEDGED

Expressions of approbation over the Palestine Declaration came not only from individual states, but from the organized international community. UN Secretary-General Javier Perez de Cuellar said that the Declaration opened opportunities for peace by virtue of its acceptance of Israel.[14] The UN General Assembly invited PLO Chairman Yasser Arafat to address it.[15] Significantly, the General Assembly adopted Resolution 43/177 in which it characterized the Declaration as promoting UN aims. Resolution 43/177 recited that

The General Assembly ...

Recalling its resolution 181 (II) of 29 November 1947, in which, *inter alia*, it called for the establishment of an Arab State and a Jewish State in Palestine,

Mindful of the special responsibility of the United Nations to achieve a just solution to the question of Palestine,

Aware of the proclamation of the State of Palestine by the Palestine National Council in line with General Assembly resolution 181 (II) and in exercise of the inalienable rights of the Palestinian people,

Affirming the urgent need to achieve a just and comprehensive settlement in the Middle East which, *inter alia*, provides for peaceful coexistence for all States in the region,

Recalling its resolution 3237 (XXIX) of 22 November 1974 on the observer status for the Palestine Liberation Organization and subsequent relevant resolutions,

1. Acknowledges the proclamation of the State of Palestine by the Palestine National Council on 15 November 1988;
2. Affirms the need to enable the Palestinian people to exercise their sovereignty over their territory occupied since 1967;
3. Decides that, effective as of 15 December 1988, the designation "Palestine" should be used in place of the designation "Palestine Liberation Organization" in the United Nations system, without prejudice to the observer status and functions of the Palestine Liberation Organization within the United Nations system, in conformity with relevant United Nations resolutions and practice;
4. Requests the Secretary-General to take the necessary action to implement the present resolution.[16]

One hundred and four states voted in favor of Resolution 43/177, thirty-six abstained; only the United States and Israel voted against it.

Frederic Kirgis found that the resolution did not demonstrate Palestine statehood because, he said, the General Assembly

did not recognize a Palestinian state; nor did it call the PLO a provisional government. Instead, it acknowledged that the Palestine National Council had proclaimed the State of Palestine, affirmed the need to enable the Palestinian people to exercise sovereignty over the occupied territories, and changed the PLO's designation to "Palestine" in the UN system.[17]

Crawford addressed the resolution from the standpoint of recognition and said that the General Assembly has no authority to recognize states.[18] John Dugard has argued that the General Assembly, by admitting states to membership, performs a role of recognizing states in a collective fashion.[19] Since UN membership requires statehood, a favorable General Assembly vote for an entity's admission would seem to be a statement about its status as a state. In Resolution 43/177 the Assembly did not, to be sure, call for Palestine's admission as a member state. By acknowledging as a positive development a document that affirmed Palestine's statehood, however, the Assembly seemed to be accepting the fact of Palestine statehood.

Moreover, the change of name to "Palestine" in Resolution 43/177 reinforced the resolution's acceptance of Palestine as a state. "Palestine" is the title of a territorial entity. If "Palestine" was to be represented, albeit as an observer, at the United Nations, it could be nothing other than a state. In referring to a "need to enable the Palestinian people to exercise their sovereignty," these states were saying that the Palestinian people held sovereignty and that what remained was to find a way for them to exercise it on the ground. Resolution 43/177 read in a fashion that assumed that the state being declared presently existed, even if it was not able to function independently.

THE DECLARATION AS A PRECURSOR TO INDEPENDENCE

In an action that indicated even more strongly the international community's favourable reaction to the Palestine Declaration, the General Assembly, in a companion resolution, outlined a procedure for bringing the Palestine state to independence. This was General Assembly Resolution 43/176, in which the Assembly noted Arafat's speech to the Assembly, which he had given on December 13, 1988, and recited, in the following terms, how the Palestine Declaration was expected to contribute to peace:

> The General Assembly, Having considered the reports of the Secretary-General,
>
> Having noted with appreciation the statement made on 13 December 1988 by the Chairman of the Palestine Liberation Organization,
>
> Stressing that achieving peace in the Middle East would constitute a significant contribution to international peace and security,
>
> Aware of the overwhelming support for the convening of the International Peace Conference on the Middle East,
>
> Noting with appreciation the endeavours of the Secretary-General to achieve the convening of the Conference,
>
> Welcoming the outcome of the nineteenth Extraordinary Session of the Palestine National Council as a positive contribution towards a peaceful settlement of the conflict in the region,
>
> Aware of the ongoing uprising (intifadah) of the Palestinian people since 9 December 1987, aimed at ending Israeli occupation of Palestinian territory occupied since 1967,
>
> 1. Affirms the urgent need to achieve a just and comprehensive settlement of the Arab-Israeli conflict, the core of which is the question of Palestine;
> 2. Calls for the convening of the International Peace Conference on the Middle East, under the auspices of the United Nations, with the participation of all parties to the conflict, including the Palestine Liberation Organization, on an equal footing, and the five permanent members of the Security Council, based on Security Council resolutions 242 (1967) of 22 November 1967 and 338 (1973) of 22 October 1973[20] and

the legitimate national rights of the Palestinian people, primarily the right to self-determination;

3. Affirms the following principles for the achievement of comprehensive peace:
   (a) The withdrawal of Israel from the Palestinian territory occupied since 1967, including Jerusalem, and from the other occupied Arab territories;
   (b) Guaranteeing arrangements for security of all States in the region, including those named in resolution 181 (II) of 29 November 1947, within secure and internationally recognized boundaries;
   (c) Resolving the problem of the Palestine refugees in conformity with General Assembly resolution 194 (III) of 11 December 1948, and subsequent relevant resolutions;
   (d) Dismantling the Israeli settlements in the territories occupied since 1967;
   (e) Guaranteeing freedom of access to Holy Places, religious buildings and sites;
4. Notes the expressed desire and endeavours to place the Palestinian territory occupied since 1967, including Jerusalem, under the supervision of the United Nations for a limited period, as part of the peace process;
5. Requests the Security Council to consider measures needed to convene the International Peace Conference on the Middle East, including the establishment of a preparatory committee, and to consider guarantees for security measures agreed upon by the Conference for all States in the region;
6. Requests the Secretary-General to continue his efforts with the parties concerned, and in consultation with the Security Council, to facilitate the convening of the Conference, and to submit progress reports on developments in this matter.[21]

Resolution 43/176 was adopted by a vote of 138 to two (again Israel and the United States), with only two abstentions. The fact that nearly all the states that abstained on Resolution 43/177 voted in favor of Resolution 43/176 indicated their view that, despite their caution on recognition, they regarded Palestine as a state that needed to be brought to independence. The reference in paragraph 4 to an "expressed desire" for UN supervision was to paragraph (1)(f) of the Palestine National Council political statement that read:

(f) To invite the United Nations to place the occupied Palestinian territories under international supervision, in order to protect our masses and to terminate the Israeli occupation;

The Palestine National Council thus was calling for something akin to the temporary trusteeship that the United States had proposed in 1948.

The United Nations' reaction to the Palestine Declaration is significant not only for what the organization did, but for what it did not do. Had the General Assembly viewed Palestine statehood as unlawful, or had it viewed the assertion of Palestine sovereignty to violate the rights of some other state, it would have said so. One may compare in this regard the UN reaction five years earlier to a declaration of statehood for a Turkish Republic of Northern Cyprus. The international community found this declaration invalid, on the ground that Turkey had occupied territory belonging to Cyprus and that the putative state was therefore an infringement on Cypriot sovereignty. The UN Security Council took action, pronouncing that independence declaration illegal.

"Concerned at the declaration by the Turkish Cypriot authorities issued on 15 November 1983 which purports to create an independent State in northern Cyprus, ... [c]onsidering ... that the attempt to create a 'Turkish Republic of Northern Cyprus' is invalid," the Security Council said that it "[c]onsiders the declaration referred to above as legally invalid and calls for its withdrawal."[22]

The Security Council regarded an assertion of authority over territory that it considered to be Cypriot as a threat to the peace. When the Palestine Declaration was issued, the Security Council took no similar action. The Palestine Declaration did not involve an assertion of sovereignty over territory of any other state.

The UN Security Council, moreover, shortly took a step that indicated a highly favorable reaction to Palestine's assertion of statehood. Building on the 1975–76 practice recounted above, the Security Council began to let Palestine participate routinely in Security Council sessions when relevant issues appeared on its agenda.[23] Under Security Council rules, only a "state" is entitled to participate.[24] No longer would Palestine require an invitation from the Council when issues of relevance to Palestine were to be debated.

PALESTINE AND THE WORLD HEALTH ORGANIZATION

On April 3, 1989, the PLO Central Council strengthened the Palestine governmental structure by naming a president. The Council selected

Yassir Arafat as "President of the State of Palestine."[25] In a series of moves, the PLO began to act like the government of a state by seeking to bring Palestine into membership in inter-state organizations and by ratifying major treaties. The PLO shortly applied for Palestine membership in two specialized agencies of the United Nations – the World Health Organization (WHO), and the UN Economic, Social and Cultural Organization (UNESCO).[26]

On April 6, 1989, Arafat, signing as Chairman of the PLO and President of the State of Palestine, sent the WHO a letter applying for membership for Palestine.[27] Membership in the WHO is open only to states.[28] The United States, which at the time contributed one fourth of the WHO budget, reacted negatively to the application.[29] It informed the organization that if Palestine were admitted as a member state, the U.S. would withhold its dues.[30] Arafat called the U.S. threat "blackmail."[31] WHO Director General Hiroshi Nakajima, fearing for the financial viability of the organization, travelled to Tunis to ask the PLO to withdraw its application.[32] Nakajima next visited Washington for discussion about the U.S. threats. He came away from Washington telling the press that U.S. officials had made clear that the United States would end its contributions to the organization "immediately and entirely."

Nakajima said, "Such a move would seriously affect our operations since it would deprive WHO of $US100 million, out of a total of $US130 million earmarked for this year, and hit voluntary US contributions on health programmes such as those against Aids and tropical diseases."[33] He said that without U.S. funds, "We would have to stop most of the activity (for the rest) of this year."[34] "It would mean," he said, "the complete destruction of WHO."[35]

In a statement that did not mention Palestine as a putative state but focused on the PLO, U.S. Secretary of State James Baker explained:

> The United States vigorously opposes the admission of the P.L.O. to membership in the World Health Organization or any other U.N. agencies. We have worked, and will continue to work, to convince others of the harm that the P.L.O.'s admission would cause to the Middle East peace process and to the U.N. system.

"To emphasize the depth of our concern," Baker said, "I will recommend to the President that the United States make no further contributions, voluntary or assessed, to any international organization which makes any change in the P.L.O.'s present status as an observer organization." Continuing, Baker said, "Political questions such as this should not be raised in specialized agencies" of the United Nations because "such politicization detracts from the important technical work of these organizations."[36] Baker's position thus related more to his assessment of the impact of Palestine's admission, than to the merits of its application.

When Nakajima was unable to convince the PLO to withdraw the application, or to convince the U.S. to withdraw its threat, he asked the World Health Assembly, the WHO governing body, to put the matter off, telling it that he hoped that "we do nothing to jeopardize the future of our Organization."[37] The World Health Assembly, voting 83 to 47, decided to postpone action on the Palestine application.[38] States that supported the application voted against the Assembly's resolution to postpone, which recited that "the legal and other issues related to the application of Palestine for membership of the World Health Organization require further detailed study."[39] The resolution asked the Director General to report back the following year, expressing at the same time "the hope that the Palestinian people will be fully represented within the World Health Organization by their legitimate representatives."[40] The resolution also called for increased health-related work in Gaza and the West Bank.[41]

A number of member states in the World Health Assembly averted to Palestine's status as they explained their positions on the 1989 resolution. Sweden, which voted to postpone, said that it hoped "that the Palestinians will soon have their own State on their own territory," but that Sweden did not "recognize the declared State of Palestine" because "the international criterion of effective control of territory is not met."[42] Cuba responded on this point, asserting that Palestine did meet the criteria for statehood.[43] Supporting Cuba, Algeria rejected what it termed "the territorial argument" by pointing to the fact that Palestine's territory was occupied by Israel.[44]

Without referring to the criteria for statehood, Australia said that it did "not recognize the 'State of Palestine' because it believed that the establishment of such a State is an option which can only come in the context of an overall settlement of the Arab-Israeli dispute."[45] The German Democratic Republic, Turkey, and India said they would have voted to admit Palestine because they found it to be a state.[46] Zimbabwe said that it "recognizes the State of Palestine," and that "the State of Palestine's problems are those of the League of Nations, which must be addressed quietly and properly by the United Nations system."[47]

Nigeria abstained on the resolution. Its delegate explained that Nigeria had "recognized Palestine as a State and therefore believes that it has the right to be a Member of WHO," but that "its membership has to be accommodated in such a way that it does not upset the main functions of our Organization," an obvious reference to the U.S. threat to withdraw funding.[48]

Cuba responded to Secretary Baker's charge that the PLO was politicizing the WHO, saying that it was those who threatened to withdraw funds who were politicizing the issue. Explaining why Cuba had voted against the resolution to postpone, Cuba's delegate said:

> We voted against the blackmail reflected in the arrogant declarations to withdraw funds when we are speaking about health, and about the right of a people to be in a health-oriented organization.[49]

PALESTINE AND UNESCO

The Palestine membership application to UNESCO, filed on April 27, 1989, would suffer a similar fate.[50] As with WHO, membership in UNESCO is open only to states.[51] A memorandum of law was submitted by Algeria, Indonesia, Mauritania, Niger, Senegal and Yemen in support of the Palestine application. The memorandum asserted that Palestine qualified as a state under the criteria for statehood. Israel filed in response, arguing that Palestine did not meet those criteria. The six states filed a counter-response. They recited that since the onset of the *intifadah*, departments operating under the auspices of the PLO Executive Committee "play an important role in organizing and serving the population of the towns, villages and refugee camps in the occupied territory." The six states asserted that "full jurisdiction is for the time being in abeyance, owing to the Israeli occupation, which in itself, cannot negate the sovereignty of the State of Palestine." They recounted the situation of Palestine during the mandate, arguing that under League of Nations Covenant Article 22, the Class A mandates, including Palestine, were states. They said that recognition is not required for statehood, but gave the figure 98 as the number of states that had recognized Palestine.[52]

As in the WHO, political considerations were at the fore as the Palestine application was considered. The United States had been a UNESCO member and had withdrawn, but was considering re-joining. It sent a message to UNESCO, saying that it would not re-join if Palestine were admitted as a member state.[53] The message read:

> The question of an enhanced status in UNESCO of PLO "rights and privileges" would create a highly undesirable precedent within the U.N.

system and disturb the delicate ongoing process of negotiations aimed at securing peace in the Middle East.

The message said that the admission of Palestine as a member state would "virtually foreclose any consideration of U.S. re-entry into UNESCO."[54] Voice of Palestine Radio condemned the US action:

> the United States, as is its wont, issued unabashed, public threats against specialised UN agencies like UNESCO and WHO. It warned them against raising the level of Palestinian representation in these agencies to the status of a state and then to full-fledged membership. The spokeswoman for the US State Department declared that her administration would cut off financial contributions to these world organisations if they did so.[55]

The UNESCO Executive Board decided to defer consideration of Palestine's application, but to implement a series of programs beneficial to Palestine in Gaza and the West Bank.[56]

RATIFICATION OF GENEVA CONVENTIONS

In June 1989, the PLO submitted to the Government of Switzerland ratification documents for the four Geneva conventions of 1949. These conventions provide rules for the conduct of warfare and apply, importantly for Palestine, to belligerent occupation. Ratification of the Geneva Conventions is open only to states.[57] Switzerland is the depositary agency for these conventions, which means that it receives ratification documents.[58] Three months after receiving the Palestine ratification documents, the Swiss Government replied to the PLO with the following note:

> Due to the uncertainty within the international community as to the existence or the non-existence of a State of Palestine and as long as the issue has not been settled in an appropriate framework, the Swiss Government, in its capacity as depositary of the Geneva Conventions and their additional Protocols, is not in a position to decide whether this communication can be considered as an instrument of accession in the sense of the relevant provisions of the Conventions and their additional Protocols.[59]

Switzerland was saying that it did not regard it as proper for it, as a single state, to make a determination that would have implications for the international community.

MORE ACTION ON PALESTINE AT THE UNITED NATIONS

The matter of Palestine's status was being addressed in various ways at the international level. Several additional initiatives surfaced at the United Nations. In November 1989, the General Assembly's Committee on the Exercise of the Inalienable Rights of the Palestinian People responded to the Palestine Declaration by calling for Palestine to be admitted to UN membership, a position premised on Palestine being a state. Noting the widespread recognition of Palestine by states, the Committee said:

> Accordingly, the Committee considers that the State of Palestine should be accorded its rightful place within the international community and the United Nations Organization.[60]

No steps were taken in the Security Council or General Assembly, however, to admit Palestine as a member state. Admission to the United Nations requires a favorable vote in each of these two organs.

The UN Food and Agriculture Organization (FAO), another specialized agency of the UN, entertained a proposal to collaborate with the PLO to help teach food-growing techniques in Gaza and the West Bank. The United States threatened to withhold funding for the FAO if the FAO approved. The PLO was not applying for FAO membership, but the U.S. objected even to FAO collaboration with the PLO as action that would acknowledge its status. Despite the threats, the FAO approved the proposal on November 30, 1989.[61] From the standpoint of the PLO's status, the FAO resolution did acknowledge that the PLO was playing a role in governance in Gaza and the West Bank, as it in fact was.

In December 1989, a group of eighteen states, mostly Arab, proposed in the UN General Assembly a resolution that would have stipulated that the designation "Palestine" as used at the UN to refer to the observer mission meant "state." The draft resolution referenced "the increased number of States Members of the United Nations that have recognized the State of Palestine," and recited that the General Assembly "[d]ecides that the designation Palestine shall be construed, within the United Nations, as the State of Palestine."[62] The United States threatened to stop paying UN dues if the resolution were adopted.

In the face of this threat, the proponents withdrew the draft resolution.[63] The Chair of the Group of Arab States said it would "not insist at present on that draft resolution being put to the vote." He expressed "our deep regret at the steps taken by the United States and at its threats."[64] The Chair of the Non-Aligned Movement noted that Palestine was a full member of that organization and called the draft resolution a "justifiable request by Palestine that the present realities be adequately reflected." He criticized "the pressures that were used in connection with the consideration of this request, which at one point threatened to throw the world Organization into crisis."[65] The Arab grouping similarly "deplored using threats to withhold financial obligation to the United Nations to achieve political ends."[66]

Shortly, however, the US threats were made even more strongly when they were written into statutory law. On February 16, 1990, the U.S. Congress adopted the Foreign Relations Authorization Act, which provided for expenditures related to foreign affairs. In one provision, the Act recited:

> (a) PROHIBITION. – No funds authorized to be appropriated by this Act or any other Act shall be available for the United Nations or any specialized agency thereof which accords the Palestine Liberation Organization the same standing as member states.[67]

PALESTINE AGAIN IN THE WORLD HEALTH ORGANIZATION

In April 1990 Palestine asked that the World Health Assembly follow through on its 1989 commitment to reconsider the Palestine application for membership in the WHO. In a letter to Director General Nakajima, Palestine's representative as permanent observer to the WHO, Nabil Ramlawi, urged that the Organization not succumb to "pressure and political blackmail." "[O]therwise," Ramlawi wrote, "it will produce negative effects on the organization's credibility and humanitarian role in the world."[68]

Still concerned over the effects of a withdrawal of US funding, Nakajima urged the World Health Assembly to vote again to postpone action on the Palestine application.[69] On May 11, 1990, the Assembly voted to ask Nakajima to "continue his studies" on the Palestine application and to report back "at the appropriate time."[70] Again, the Assembly mandated special health programs to benefit Palestinians in Gaza and the West Bank. Whatever may have been meant by "the appropriate time," no further action was taken on the matter.

Crawford states, in regard to the WHO and UNESCO postponement actions: "The continuing reservations held about the status of Palestine were reflected in the practice of international organizations."[71]

Such reservations were, as indicated, expressed by some states in debate about the Palestine applications. However, the overriding factor was the threat of a funding cutoff. As reflected most clearly in the pleas of WHO Director General Nakajima to the World Health Assembly, these organizations feared for their existence if they admitted Palestine.

14

Palestine in the Peace Process

In the 1990s, the acceptance of Palestine as a state became evident in a new way, as a result of efforts toward a territorial settlement with Israel. In 1991, the United States and the USSR initiated an Israeli-Palestinian dialogue, starting with a Middle East Peace Conference in Madrid.[1] The PNC, meeting in Algeria, approved Palestinian involvement in bilateral talks with Israel, to be held in Washington DC. Participation on the Palestinian side was by Palestinian individuals who were part of a joint Palestinian-Jordanian delegation, as Israel was not willing to talk with the PLO.[2] One of the issues to be resolved was the future of the Israeli settlements in Gaza and the West Bank. The Palestinian negotiators were concerned that Israel was continuing to build new settlement housing and insisted that construction stop before issues of substance were addressed in the talks. Israel was unwilling to comply, and as a result these talks, though they continued, never addressed matters of substance.[3]

In 1993, despite Israel's public position that it would not talk with the PLO, confidential PLO-Israel discussions took place in Oslo, Norway. The PLO did not insist on cessation of settlement construction as a pre-condition. The Norway discussions focused on setting up a temporary Palestinian administration in Gaza and the West Bank, to lead after a period of time to negotiations for a final settlement between the two parties. As secrecy on these talks was lifted, Israeli Prime Minister Yitzhak Rabin publicly recognized the PLO "as the representative of the Palestinian people."[4] Rabin demanded that the PLO recognize Israel, and in response Arafat wrote him a letter, stating that "[t]he PLO recognizes the right of the State of Israel to exist in peace and security."[5]

On September 13, 1993, a bilateral agreement was signed to implement temporary Palestinian administration and to provide for eventual negotiations. Termed the Declaration of Principles on Interim

Self-Government Arrangements, this document was communicated to the United Nations by the United States and the Russian Federation, co-organizers of the Madrid conference.[6] The United States and the Russian Federation signed the Declaration as witnesses. The Declaration provided that Israel would cede some, but not all, of the control it exercised as a belligerent occupant. And it called for transitional Palestinian administration to be accompanied by negotiations.

> The aim of the Israeli-Palestinian negotiations within the current Middle East peace process is, among other things, to establish a Palestinian Interim Self-Government Authority, the elected Council (the "Council"), for the Palestinian people in the West Bank and the Gaza Strip, for a transitional period not exceeding five years, leading to a permanent settlement based on Security Council resolutions 242 (1967) and 338 (1973). It is understood that the interim arrangements are an integral part of the whole peace process and that the negotiations on the permanent status will lead to the implementation of Security Council resolutions 242 (1967) and 338 (1973).[7]

Specifying the modalities of this process, the Declaration provided that

> The five-year transitional period will begin upon the withdrawal from the Gaza Strip and Jericho area. Permanent status negotiations will commence as soon as possible, but not later than the beginning of the third year of the interim period, between the Government of Israel and the Palestinian people's representatives. It is understood that these negotiations shall cover remaining issues, including: Jerusalem, refugees, settlements, security arrangements, borders, relations and cooperation with other neighbours, and other issues of common interest. The two parties agree that the outcome of the permanent status negotiations should not be prejudiced or preempted by agreements reached for the interim period.[8]

Arafat suggested that Palestine might eventually seek confederation with Jordan, in keeping with the PNC's 1988 statement.[9]

PALESTINE STATEHOOD IN THE DECLARATION
OF PRINCIPLES

The Declaration identified the Israeli party as "the Government of the State of Israel." It identified the Palestinian party by reference to its mode of representation at the Madrid meeting as "the PLO team (in the Jordanian-Palestinian delegation to the Middle East Peace Conference)."[10] Prime Minister Rabin denied that Israel had recognized Palestine, but

Benjamin Netanyahu, leader of the opposition Likud party, understood that Israel had done precisely that. Addressing Rabin from the floor of the Knesset, Netanyahu declared:

> Despite its denials, the government has accepted the creation of a Palestinian state. I will start at the beginning, in the introduction to the agreement which says it all, or almost everything, and I quote: The government of the State of Israel and the Palestinian team representing the Palestinian people agree to recognize their mutual legitimate and political rights. Mr Prime Minister, what are the legitimate and political rights of any nation? A state. What are the legitimate political rights of the Israeli nation? A state. What are mutual legitimate political rights with the Palestinians? A state for them too. And you gave this away not as a beginning of an agreement, but even before the negotiations on the permanent arrangements have started.

Netanyahu explained that the text of the Declaration

> presents the structure of a state. A state and any government is made up of three arms: judiciary, executive and naturally, above all, the legislative arm, which is the most distinct mark of sovereignty. The three are mentioned in the agreement. The authority of the legislative and executive arms applies to the entire territory, including state-owned lands. When you make an agreement which gives away the territory, the legislative power over it, and – I add – the powers of security in the territory, you are creating the structure of a state.

Netanyahu said that it mattered little that the Declaration of Principles did not use the term "state" to refer to Palestine.

> I believe that everyone here has been to a zoo once. When you walk into the zoo and see an animal that looks like a horse and has black and white stripes, you do not need a sign to tell you this is a zebra. It is a zebra. When you read this agreement, even if the words a Palestinian state are not mentioned there, you do not need a sign; this is a Palestinian state.[11]

Former U.S. Secretary of State Henry Kissinger focused on the election of a legislative council, as called for in the Declaration, and said, "the elected government will, in effect, be a legitimate government."[12]

Antonio Cassese read the Declaration of Principles as being premised on what he termed independent international status for Palestine. Cassese pointed to the Declaration's call for a permanent status consistent with UN Security Council Resolution 242. That resolution, he noted, was based on several objectives.

(i) the "establishment of a just and lasting peace in the Middle East"; (ii) the "withdrawal of Israel armed forces" from occupied territories as a consequence of the "inadmissibility of the acquisition of territory by war"; (iii) "respect for and acknowledgment of the sovereignty, territorial integrity and political independence of every State in the area"; (iv) "a just settlement of the refugee problem".

Cassese said:

> The attainment of all these objectives logically presupposes not only the establishment of an autonomous Palestinian authority in the occupied territories, but also the acquisition, by this authority and the territories which it shall control, of some sort of independent international status.[13]

Resolution 242 did not specify in whose favor Israel would withdraw. By the Declaration of Principles, Israel agreed that the PLO would be the party negotiating Israel's withdrawal. Negotiation of borders, mentioned in Article 5, meant that the two parties would determine a territorial division between them. The PLO would agree that certain territory fell to Israel, and Israel would agree that certain territory fell to Palestine. Israel's willingness to negotiate borders presumed Palestine's capacity to reach an agreement that would be valid at the international level as a definitive determination of the borders of both Israel and Palestine. An agreement over territory and borders can be concluded only by a state. Israel's agreement in the Declaration to negotiate borders with the PLO meant that Israel considered the PLO to possess legal capacity to act on behalf of a state.

Israel's acknowledgment of Palestine statehood was also implicit in the demand by Prime Minister Rabin that the PLO recognize Israel. Recognition is an act done by governments of states.[14] Entities that purport to be states gain acceptance in the international community by recognition by states. If Israel had not regarded Palestine as a state, there would have been no point in asking for recognition. Both the Declaration and the process leading to its conclusion reflected a tacit acceptance by Israel of Palestine as an existing state, and not simply as an entity that might one day become a state.

The recognition of Palestine's status extended beyond Israel. By encouraging the parties to issue their Declaration of Principles, the United States and the Russian Federation were also acknowledging Palestine's status as a state. The Russian Federation, of course, had already done so, but for the United States the promotion of the Declaration of Principles represented a change of policy.

ADMINISTRATION OF TERRITORY BY PALESTINE

On the basis of Israel's consent to cede partial control, the PLO Central Council set up a Palestinian National Authority.[15] The UN General Assembly welcomed this arrangement and the anticipated negotiations.[16] By endorsing the Declaration of Principles, the member states of the General Assembly were reiterating their previously stated understanding that Palestine was a state.

Bilateral agreements were concluded to define and extend interim administration. The first was an agreement on the Gaza Strip and the Jericho area (1994) that provided for Israeli redeployment out of Gaza and the environs of the city of Jericho in the West Bank.[17] In 1995, the more comprehensive Interim Agreement on the West Bank and the Gaza Strip replaced the 1994 instrument, extending the area of Palestinian control in the West Bank.[18] It provided for Palestinian control of the main urban centers of the West Bank, which were designated as "Area A." Israel retained control of most of the rural area, designated as "Area C." The two parties had joint control in what was designated "Area B."[19] The 1994 and 1995 agreements used the terminology "Palestinian Authority" to refer to the Palestinian administration, whereas the PLO used the name "Palestinian National Authority," and that is how the authority would refer to itself.[20]

The international community had encouraged the parties to conclude both the 1994 and 1995 agreements. The United States and the Russian Federation signed the 1994 agreement as witnesses, as they had done on the 1993 Declaration of Principles, and they were joined by Egypt. When the 1995 agreement was signed, again the United States, the Russian Federation, and Egypt signed as witnesses, and this time they were joined by Norway and the European Union.

POSSIBLE REASSERTION OF STATEHOOD IN 1996

By 1996, the Palestinian National Authority (PNA) was exercising governmental functions in much of the West Bank and Gaza. Little progress had been made, however, toward starting negotiations on the final status issues. Blaming Israel for this impasse, Arafat indicated that he planned to declare statehood anew in 1999, when the five-year period contemplated in the 1993 Declaration of Principles would expire.[21] Arafat's aim in saying he would re-declare statehood was to put pressure on Israel to negotiate the final status issues.

The 1993 Declaration of Principles provided that the "transitional period" would begin upon Israel's withdrawal from Gaza and the Jericho Area.[22] The agreement for that withdrawal was signed on May 4, 1994,[23] putting the end of the "transitional period" at May 4, 1999. The PLO regarded the Interim Agreement as needing to be implemented by a peace agreement on or before May 4, 1999.[24]

The American lawyer John Whitbeck saw the utility of a new statement of Palestine statehood, viewing it as a confirmation of the 1988 declaration and regarding it as legally justified. Whitbeck thought that Palestine satisfied the criteria for statehood. He pointed out that Palestine's claim to the portion of Palestine occupied by Israel in 1967 was uncontested. Israel had not asserted sovereignty there, other than in Jerusalem. Israel's position was that of an occupying power only. [25]

In London, the editors of the *Economist* also viewed a new statement of Palestine statehood as useful and justified. In an editorial that was exceedingly prescient in light of the later failure of the peace negotiations, they explained their reasons.

> The settlements grow, the talks stagnate and the prospect of Palestinian frustration leading to endless violence grows apace. Is there a way for Yasser Arafat to avert the coming explosion and make Israelis once again take the "peace process" seriously?

> Mr Arafat has few instruments at his command other than gestures, and gestures can often prove empty. Even so, this could be the moment to take a risk – and proclaim Palestine independent.

The editors posed the question,

> What would all this achieve? It would pre-empt time-wasting argument about what the Palestinian "entity" should eventually be. More important, it would raise the sights of the peace process. Instead of an indeterminate crowd of former guerrillas and exiles begging for "concessions" from the all-powerful state that defeated them, the negotiations would be between two states, equal under international law even if far from equal in brute power, and the talks would be about borders, security and perhaps a shared capital....

Continuing, the editors advocated UN membership for Palestine.

> By giving Palestine international standing, membership of the UN could help cement that foundation. Palestine already has observer status. Were it to gain full membership, it would be no more curious than some other UN members. Its alphabetical neighbour, Palau, for instance, is a fully

sovereign and independent state of 15,000 people on 340 Pacific islands with its own American zip code. It makes no pretence of being responsible for its own defence.

As to whether Palestine satisfied the criteria for statehood, the editors thought it might.

> Is Palestine a defined territory over which sovereignty is not seriously contested? And has it effective control over territory and population? A fuzzy yes can be given to both questions. Israel has not claimed sovereignty over the Palestinian land it conquered in 1967, East Jerusalem apart (admittedly, a crucial exception). Egypt administered Gaza but never asserted sovereignty over it. Jordan renounced all claims to the West Bank in 1988. And the Palestinian Authority, with its sometimes brutal security forces, does control most of the people in the territory, if not most of the land itself. [26]

The statehood criteria to which Whitbeck and the *Economist* editors referred will be examined in Chapter 16.

Israel's reaction to the PLO plan was negative. Uzi Landau, chair of the Knesset Foreign Affairs and Defense Committee, threatened retaliation.

> When he [Arafat] declares a state, we must immediately impose Israeli law and the Israeli administration on Judaea and Samaria. It is absolutely clear that the Oslo accord would then no longer exist in its present form and that everything would have to start from scratch. But then, we would be sovereign in Areas B and C. We must start demanding a price from Arafat. There are no free lunches. [27]

By saying that if statehood were declared Israel would be sovereign in Areas B and C, Landau was apparently assuming that Palestine statehood would apply only to the territory over which the PNA exercised control under the Interim Agreement. This was clearly not what the PLO intended.

Benjamin Netanyahu, who by then was Prime Minister of Israel, reinforced Landau's threat. Netanyahu said that a declaration of statehood would be a breach of the agreement to settle issues by negotiation.

> This would contravene the Oslo accords. If he [Arafat] does so, an Israeli response should be expected. Believe me, this would be a very grave mistake on his part. [28]

Then events took a curious turn. Israel turned the town of Hebron over to PNA control, and Netanyahu aide David Bar-Ilan, citing enhanced

Palestinian control in the West Bank and Arafat's stated intention of reasserting statehood, declared, "We are probably closer to an entity that will probably call itself a state, because developments point in that direction." Bar-Ilan said, "There's very little doubt that the Palestinian entity will call itself a state, and that the world will recognize it[ ] as such."[29]

Was Netanyahu prepared to concede the inevitable, that Palestine was a state? When a reporter confronted Netanyahu with Bar-Ilan's statement, Netanyahu replied that Bar-Ilan "was misquoted."[30] Whether Bar-Ilan was misquoted or misspoke, or whether this was a trial balloon was never clarified. In any event, Arafat perceived prospects for a start of negotiations improving, and backed off the issue. Still the PLO said it would reassert after May 4, 1999, if no agreement were reached by then with Israel. Ahmed Qurei, speaker of the Palestinian Legislative Council, explained (translation from Arabic):

> If we reach agreement, then this is good. If we do not reach agreement we would have shown the entire world that we have good intentions and did our best to reach an agreement with the Israeli government. If we fail to reach an agreement on the morning of 5th May [1999], then we are supposed to declare the establishment of our independent Palestinian state, delineate its borders, designate its capital, and define the relations I will have with other countries.[31]

Qurei was saying that not only statehood would be asserted but also independence, although he did not explain how this would be accomplished if it were opposed by Israel.

PALESTINE AND EUROPE

While this Israeli-Palestinian sparring over Palestine statehood continued, Europe was dealing with Palestine on the basis of its being a state. In 1997, the European Union concluded a tariff agreement with the PLO, applicable to Gaza and the West Bank. Part of an EU initiative with many of the states surrounding the Mediterranean, this treaty carried a cumbersome title: Euro-Mediterranean Interim Association Agreement on trade and cooperation between the European Community, of the one part, and the Palestine Liberation Organization (PLO) for the benefit of the Palestinian Authority of the West Bank and the Gaza Strip, of the other part.[32] The title indicates that the treaty was being concluded with the PLO on the understanding that the Palestinian Authority was the entity actually in a position to deal with export and import.

The EU concluded the treaty with the PLO on the evident assumption that the PLO represented the Palestine state because the EU concludes such treaties only with states. Article 133 of the treaty establishing the European Community provides that such bilateral treaties are concluded only with states or with organizations of states:

> Where agreements with one or more States or international organisations need to be negotiated, the Commission shall make recommendations to the Council, which shall authorize the Commission to open the necessary negotiations.[33]

The European Council decision to conclude the treaty with the PLO notes that the basis in community law for the treaty was the identical prior version of Article 133, which had been numbered Article 113.[34] Thus, the European Community understood that it was entering into a treaty with a state.

Protocol 3 to the treaty calls for an invoice declaration certifying the territorial origin of goods, to be executed by an exporter approved by the "customs authorities of the exporting country."[35] For goods originating in the West Bank or Gaza, the "country" hence is Palestine. Protocol 3 thus reflected an understanding of Palestine as a state.

The European Court of Justice had occasion to construe the term "country" as used in Protocol 3 when litigation arose over efforts by Israel to gain tariff preference for goods produced in Israeli settlements in the West Bank. Exporters approved by Israel were issuing invoice declarations for goods produced in the West Bank. The European Court of Justice found this practice to violate the European treaty with the PLO.[36] The Court said that under Protocol 3, an invoice declaration is to be executed by an exporter approved by the "customs authorities of the exporting [State]." For "country," the term used in Protocol 3, the Court substituted "state." The European Court of Justice thus understood that the entity whose customs authorities must approve the exporter is a state.[37]

This Euro-Mediterranean treaty was concluded in the implementation of a plan for a free-trade area comprising Europe and Mediterranean littoral states, developed at the Euro-Mediterranean Conference held in Barcelona in 1995. This conference was attended by Yassir Arafat for the Palestinian National Authority and by Ehud Barak for Israel, along with the representatives of twenty-five other European and Mediterranean states, plus the European Union. They collectively adopted a Declaration setting forth the aim of a free-trade area.[38] The invitation to the PNA reflected Palestine's status as a state. In the mentioned litigation over goods originating in the West Bank, Advocate-General Yves Bot of the European Court of Justice referred to the PNA as one of the "non–member States" that attended the Barcelona conference.³⁹

ENHANCEMENT OF PALESTINE'S UN STATUS

In the years following the Oslo agreements, the UN General Assembly strengthened Palestine's position by further enhancing its status within the organization. In July 1998, the General Assembly accorded Palestine privileges that ever more clearly reflected an understanding that Palestine was a state.⁴⁰ The Assembly's July 1998 resolution, Participation of Palestine in the Work of the United Nations, began by mentioning, by way of precedents, actions by which other international organizations had recognized Palestine as a state. One preamble clause "recall[ed]" that "Palestine enjoys full membership in the Group of Asian States and the Economic and Social Commission for Western Asia."⁴¹ Another preamble clause recited that the Assembly was "[a]ware that Palestine is a full member of the League of Arab States, the Movement of Non-Aligned Countries, the Organization of the Islamic Conference, and the Group of 77 and China."⁴² The apparent reason for reciting these organizational memberships was to show that Palestine was being accepted as a state in the world community.

The Participation resolution then accorded Palestine a series of parliamentary privileges that reflected that understanding. It gave Palestine "the right to participate in the general debate of the General Assembly." That meant debate on any topic, whether or not relating to Palestine. The right of participation attached only to member states. So Palestine was being treated as a state.

The resolution gave Palestine the right to be inscribed on the list of speakers "after the last Member State inscribed on the list," thus allowing Palestine to speak before any other observer. This stipulation distinguished Palestine from the other observer missions, reflecting its higher status.

The resolution gave Palestine the right of reply. As was seen in Chapter 11, this right was given only to states and had been accorded to Palestine on a particular occasion. Now the resolution made it general policy that Palestine should always have the right of reply.

The resolution gave Palestine "the right to raise points of order related to the proceedings on Palestinian and Middle East issues." It gave Palestine "the right to co-sponsor draft resolutions and decisions on Palestinian and Middle East issues." These two were rights normally reserved for member states.

The resolution further provided that there would be no need for the chair of a General Assembly meeting to explain each time Palestine might seek to make a statement that it had the right to do so. Instead, it would be announced "only once by the President of the General Assembly at the start of each session of the Assembly." This procedure was subsequently followed at both regular[43] and special sessions[44] of the General Assembly.

The resolution also provided for a new seating arrangement for Palestine that reflected statehood status. Palestine was to be seated "immediately after non-member States and before the other observers." Like the provision on inscription on the list of speakers, this stipulation recognized Palestine as having a higher status than the Assembly's other observers. The resolution finally dealt with the number of seats to which Palestine would be entitled. It provided for "the allocation of six seats in the General Assembly Hall," the number accorded to member states. Previously, Palestine had had only two.

The fact that the General Assembly elevated Palestine in these ways in its parliamentary practice reflected the importance the Assembly attached to Palestine being regarded as a state. Never before had an observer been accorded such privileges.

The General Assembly, in the text of the Participation resolution, asked the Secretary-General to ensure implementation of the new privileges. The Secretary-General did so by issuing a note titled, "Participation of Palestine in the work of the United Nations." Importantly, the Secretary-General indicated that the privileges in question would apply not only in the General Assembly, but as well "in the other organs of the United Nations."[45]

In 1999, the European Union took another action that implied that Europe considered Palestine a state. In a resolution that was communicated to the UN General Assembly, the EU spoke of Palestine as follows:

> The Heads of State and Governments reaffirmed the continuing and unqualified Palestinian right to self-determination including the option of a State and looked forward to the early fulfilment of this right. They appealed to the parties to strive in good faith for a negotiated solution on the basis of the existing agreements, without prejudice to this right, which is not subject to any veto. They expressed the conviction that the

creation of a democratic, viable and peaceful sovereign Palestinian State on the basis of existing agreements and through negotiations would be the best guarantee of Israel's security and Israel's acceptance as an equal partner in the region. They stated the readiness of the Union to consider the recognition of a Palestinian State in due course in accordance with these principles.[46]

Fully aware that Palestine statehood had already been declared, the EU was saying that the right of self-determination was not subject to "any veto," meaning veto by Israel. Although the EU had called for negotiations, it said that Israel could not deny Palestine statehood. The EU was suggesting that its member states were ready to recognize the Palestine state but were waiting for an Israel-Palestine agreement as the appropriate time to do so.

POSSIBLE REASSERTION OF STATEHOOD IN 1999

As May 4, 1999, the end of the "transitional period" and the date before which Palestine had said it would not assert statehood, approached, the PLO considered whether to declare with no prospect of an agreement on the final status issues. By 1999, the Palestinian National Authority had established itself and was exercising many governmental functions, albeit within a limited territory. Some Palestinian political figures feared that an assertion of statehood in that situation would be taken as an affirmance that Palestine's territory was limited to what it controlled, even if it were to state otherwise.[47] Hisham Sharabi, a Palestinian political analyst, posed the question by asking,

> Would declaring the state on May 4 really bring about an independent Palestinian state or, on the contrary, would it only make it easier for Israel to have the Palestinians themselves embrace the updated Bantustan system it has fashioned for them in parts of the West Bank and Gaza?[48]

As the debate within the Palestine government became a matter of public knowledge, Israel's government weighed in and said that Palestine statehood could come only at the end of the negotiation process. Israel regarded an assertion of statehood prior to that time as a repudiation of further negotiation. It viewed the five-year period as one in which it was hoped that negotiations could be completed, but it did not regard May 4, 1999 as the date on which the negotiation process would terminate.

Israel argued, moreover, that a Palestinian assertion of statehood would be unlawful. In a statement, the Foreign Ministry said that a unilateral declaration by the Palestinian Authority on the establishment of a Palestinian state, prior to the achievement of a Final Status Agreement, would constitute a substantive and fundamental violation of the Interim Agreement. In the event of such a violation, the Government would consider itself entitled to take all necessary steps, including the application of Israeli rule, law and administration to settlement areas and security areas in Judea, Samaria and Gaza, as it sees fit. Israel reiterates its position, in accordance with the agreement of the PA, that the Final Status must be the result of free negotiations between the parties without the implementation of unilateral steps which will change the status of the area.[49]

In another memorandum that it made public, the Foreign Ministry explained more fully its position that it would be unlawful for Palestine statehood to be declared "unilaterally" after May 4, 1999. The Ministry cited the Interim Agreement of 1995, Article 31(7), which prohibited "any step that will change the status of the West Bank and the Gaza Strip pending the outcome of the permanent status negotiations."[50] The Ministry regarded an assertion of statehood as a change in status.

The Foreign Ministry also regarded as an undertaking not to declare statehood a statement in Arafat's letter to Rabin of September 9, 1993, in which Arafat said that "all outstanding issues relating to permanent status will be resolved through negotiations." The Ministry argued that a declaration would be unlawful on the additional ground that Palestine did not satisfy the criteria for statehood. On that point, it recited:

International law has established a number of criteria for the existence of a state: effective and independent governmental control, possession of defined territory; the capacity to freely engage in foreign relations; and control over a permanent population. In order to be recognized as a state, an entity must satisfy all four criteria; the Palestinian entity, however, cannot actually be said to satisfy any of them: Palestinian governmental control is far from independent – it is partial, temporary, and reliant on Israeli assistance and cooperation; the territory is not defined – it is non-contiguous and indeterminate – nor do the Palestinians hold sovereign title to it; the interim agreements explicitly prohibit the exercise of foreign relations by the Palestinian Council; and its control over its population is neither independent or comprehensive. Additionally, over recent years new additional criteria have been established by the international community for recognition as a state. These include the principle that a state cannot arise as a result of illegality. It follows that, even if the Palestinian entity were to satisfy the criteria for statehood, the unlawfulness of a unilateral declaration of statehood would invalidate any Palestinian claim to recognition.[51]

The Palestinian position was precisely the contrary on the question of whether a new assertion of Palestine statehood would be illegal. Palestine's Permanent Representative at the United Nations, Nasser al-Kidwa, explained:

> The Israel-PLO Declaration of Principles and subsequent interim agreements do not and cannot negate, substitute for, or supersede relevant instruments of international law. Until a final Israeli-Palestinian settlement is reached, final status issues remain subject to international law. The right of the Palestinian people to establish their own state emanates from their national right to self-determination, consistent with international law, the Charter of the United Nations, and relevant UN resolutions. Because the Palestinian people are a long-established and indigenous people, this right is not dependent on and does not emanate from the existing Oslo agreements.[52]

Al-Kidwa was challenging the Israeli position that whatever Palestine entity that might exist was a creature of the agreements with Israel.

World leaders became concerned about the fate of the Oslo process as the two parties sparred over a possible reassertion of Palestine statehood. They worried further that a new assertion of Palestine statehood would help Prime Minister Netanyahu in the upcoming Israeli elections and that his retention of power would reduce the chances for an Israel-Palestine settlement.[53] U.S. President Bill Clinton sent Arafat a letter asking him to postpone any new statement on statehood. At the same time, Clinton wrote, "We support the aspirations of the Palestinian people to determine their own future on their own land."[54] In the event, the PLO decided to forego a new declaration of statehood.[55] A few days before May 4, 1999, the Palestine National Council issued a statement that it would continue to work toward independence:

> Our rights can only be achieved through a courageous national decision to exercise our natural right to establish our independent state on our homeland with Jerusalem as its capital. This is in accordance with the overwhelming international acceptance of a Palestinian state as a Palestinian decision not subject to negotiations and not connected to any veto power from any party.[56]

LEGALITY OF A REASSERTION OF PALESTINE STATEHOOD

Israel's argument that a declaration would have been unlawful proceeded on two prongs. The first was that it would violate the bilateral agreement of 1993 and other agreements that followed from it. The second was that it would violate general international law. The Israeli argument under general international law related to the effectiveness of the control exercised by Palestine, an issue that will be considered in Chapter 16. The argument under the bilateral agreements had the most immediate consequences, because Israel drew from it the proposition that a declaration of Palestine statehood would allow Israel to end the peace process, terminate the bilateral agreements, and reassert its prior level of control in Gaza and the West Bank.

Israel's reference to the agreements that came after the 1993 Declaration of Principles was, most centrally, to the Interim Agreement of September 28, 1995, and specifically to its Article 31(7), which read:

> Neither side shall initiate or take any step that will change the status of the West Bank and the Gaza Strip pending the outcome of the permanent status negotiations.[57]

Israel argued that a reassertion, or declaration, of statehood would "change the status." Mala Tabory agreed with Israel's view that the PNA derived whatever powers it had solely from the agreements with Israel.[58] Crawford said that while the PLO was not dependent on Israel for its positions, the PNA was, because PNA powers derived from the arrangements between Israel and the PLO, and further, that the PLO had pledged not to alter the situation unilaterally during the interim period.[59]

Israel's reliance on Article 31(7) of the Interim Agreement was, however, questionable. It was not clear that a reassertion of Palestine statehood would "change the status of the West Bank and the Gaza Strip." The PLO had made known its position on statehood in 1988, and arguably even earlier, in any event well before the onset of the Oslo process. Moreover, the Interim Agreement of September 28, 1995 contained a kind of savings clause in regard to the parties' claims and positions. Article 31(6), which immediately preceded Article 31(7), read:

> 6. Nothing in this Agreement shall prejudice or preempt the outcome of the negotiations on the permanent status to be conducted pursuant to the DOP. Neither Party shall be deemed, by virtue of having entered into this Agreement, to have renounced or waived any of its existing rights, claims or positions.

Thus, the Interim Agreement preserved to each side whatever "claims or positions" it held as of that time. Palestine statehood was a "claim" or a "position" held at that time on the Palestinian side.

Crawford made the related argument, also made by Israel, that the PLO had accepted "an important agenda of issues" to be resolved through permanent status negotiations, and that a statehood declaration would violate that commitment.[60] Writing in 1999, he said that

> a process of negotiation toward identifiable and acceptable ends is still, however precariously, in place. It misrepresents the reality of the situation, in my view, to claim that one party already has that for which it is striving (if so, why strive?).[61]

That argument is based on an assumption that statehood was something for which the Palestinian party was "striving." However, the agenda of issues as specified in the 1993 Declaration of Principles did not include statehood. That agenda included "Jerusalem, refugees, settlements, security arrangements, borders."[62] Statehood was not mentioned as an item to be negotiated. There was no basis for Israel's position that a statehood declaration would violate any of the bilateral agreements connected with the Oslo process.

REQUEST FOR A UNITED NATIONS PRESENCE

In June 1999, the United Nations took action relating to Kosovo that involved a role for the world body that was more extensive than what it had ever done in regard to Palestine. The UN took over the administration of Kosovo, a province of Serbia inhabited predominantly by Albanians. The Security Council authorized the Secretary-General to set up an "interim administration for Kosovo," to function as an "international civil presence," to protect the population and to enforce autonomy for the Kosovo Albanians within Serbia.[63] Arafat was quoted as saying at a Palestinian cabinet meeting that the international community should act in the West Bank as it was doing in Kosovo.[64] The UN General Assembly in Resolution 43/176 in December 1988, quoted in Chapter 13, had noted the desire of the PNC, as expressed in connection with its Declaration of Independence, to "place the Palestinian territory occupied since 1967, including Jerusalem, under the supervision of the United Nations for a limited period, as part of the peace process."[65]

POSSIBLE REASSERTION OF STATEHOOD IN 2000

In early 2000, the PLO again considered whether to reassert Palestine statehood. On February 11, 2000, the PLO Central Council voted to declare Palestine an independent state on September 13, 2000. Arafat and Ehud Barak, who was now Prime Minister of Israel, had focused on September 13 as a date by which to achieve agreement on the final status issues. Again, the apparent reason for a new assertion of statehood was to inject urgency into the bilateral negotiations.[66] On June 25, 2000, President Arafat said, "The next few weeks are the most important and difficult, because at the end of these weeks we will declare the Palestinian state."[67] The PLO Central Council, meeting in Gaza on July 4, 2000, resolved to declare statehood on September 13, 2000, if agreement was not reached with Israel by that date.[68]

Barak reacted as Netanyahu had before him. Barak told the Knesset's Foreign Affairs and Defense Committee that if the PLO were to carry through, Israel might retaliate by extending its law to Israeli settlement blocks in Gaza and the West Bank, a measure that would be a major step toward annexation of the territory occupied by the settlements. Justice Minister Yossi Beilin proclaimed that a Palestine state could be declared only with Israel's approval. Beilin told Israel Radio, "There will be no Palestinian state as long as Israel doesn't recognize it." Beilin said that even if the entire world were to recognize a unilaterally declared Palestinian state, "as long as we are here we shall not let them exist as an independent entity. Beilin said that the Palestinians would have no open crossing points to the outside world, and they could not travel between the West Bank and the Gaza Strip "without our agreement."[69]

After the failed Camp David negotiations of July 2000, Arafat reiterated the September 13, 2000 date for a new assertion of statehood. A new declaration continued to be perceived by Israel as a hostile act that would lead it to break off negotiations.[70] In early September 2000, however, the PLO Central Council decided again to postpone action on a reassertion of statehood, but said that it would do so in the near term. According to the Council's statement,

> Based on the Palestinian people's absolute right to an independent state with holy Jerusalem as its capital and with its sovereignty implemented on the ground as the natural and historic right of our people in establishing their state; in accordance with UN General Assembly Resolution 181, which acknowledged the existence of two states in Palestine within its mandate boundaries, and embodying the declaration of independence of 15th November 1988; the PCC [Palestine Central Council] assigns the PLO Executive Committee and the speakers of the PNC and PLC [Palestinian Legislative Council] with taking the necessary measures to establish the state of Palestine and enforce its sovereignty on occupied Palestine with holy Jerusalem as its capital over the next period.
>
> This shall include the issuance of the constitutional declaration, the finalization of the general elections law for the presidency of the state

and the Palestinian parliament, and the submission of a UN membership request for the state of Palestine. It stresses the need for the PLO
Executive Committee to submit a detailed report on these measures to a
PCC special session that shall be held before 15th November 2000, the
anniversary of the declaration of independence in the PNC's 19th round
in Algeria in 1988.[71]

The concern again was that, given partial Palestinian control in
Gaza and the West Bank, a declaration might be taken, regardless of
the PLO's intent, as being limited to areas in which Israel had ceded
administration.[72] By 2001, the conflict turned violent, and no plan to
reassert statehood was discussed publicly.

15

Palestine in the New Century

With Israel and Palestine in a stalemate over a new assertion of Palestine statehood and with negotiations at a standstill, the international community looked for ways to get the parties to come to terms. In so doing, the international community made proposals that, once again, demonstrated acknowledgment of Palestine statehood.

PALESTINE IN THE 2003 ROAD MAP

Independence for Palestine was anticipated in a document drawn up by the United States, Russia, the European Union, and the United Nations on April 30, 2003, titled the Performance-based Road Map to a Permanent Two-State Solution to the Israeli-Palestinian Conflict. This four-entity grouping had constituted itself as the "Quartet" in an effort to move the parties toward agreement. Its Road Map charted three "phases," each calling for certain action by a certain time. The third and last phase was to involve a resolution of outstanding issues and was to be completed by 2005. As envisaged for Phase Three,

> Parties reach final and comprehensive permanent status agreement that ends the Israel-Palestinian conflict in 2005, through a settlement negotiated between the parties based on UNSCR 242, 338, and 1397,[1] that ends the occupation that began in 1967, and includes an agreed, just, fair, and realistic solution to the refugee issue, and a negotiated resolution on the status of Jerusalem that takes into account the political and religious concerns of both sides, and protects the religious interests of Jews, Christians, and Muslims worldwide, and fulfills the vision of two states, Israel and sovereign, independent, democratic and viable Palestine, living side-by-side in peace and security.[2]

"Phase One" was to involve a build-up of Palestinian institutions over a period of only a few weeks, to be followed by "Phase Two," which was to begin only a few weeks later, in June 2003. "Phase Two" was to bring

> [c]reation of an independent Palestinian state with provisional borders through a process of Israeli-Palestinian engagement, launched by the international conference. As part of this process, implementation of prior agreements, to enhance maximum territorial contiguity, including further action on settlements in conjunction with establishment of a Palestinian state with provisional borders.[3]

The Road Map thus contemplated that provisional borders would be worked out within a short time. "Phase Two" called for the creation not of a Palestinian state but of an "independent Palestinian state." The Road Map thus mirrored the League Covenant's distinction between a state and an independent state.

Moreover, the major powers anticipated diplomatic recognition of Palestine within this short time frame. Recognition was foreseen in another "Phase Two" clause providing that

> [q]uartet members promote international recognition of Palestinian state, including possible UN membership.

By saying on April 30, 2003 that they would promote recognition beginning in June 2003, the members of the Quartet must have conceived Palestine to be a state as of April 30, 2003. Provisional borders were to be the subject of "engagement," but negotiation over Palestine's status was not contemplated. Nothing that might change how Palestine met the criteria for statehood was anticipated to occur during the few weeks that remained before June 2003.

Not all analysts read the Road Map as reflecting an assumption of Palestine statehood. Crawford relied on the Road Map to say that the "parties have agreed that unilateral action must not be taken in the meantime to change the status quo."[4] The Road Map does contemplate action in tandem by Palestine and Israel, but not as regards Palestine statehood. Any reassertion of Palestine statehood would not be inconsistent with the Road Map. Rather, it would promote the goals of the Road Map, which foresaw the early independence and early recognition (2003) that were to precede a Palestine-Israel agreement (2005).

The short timetable set by the Road Map was not, in the event, achieved. But in November 2003, it was endorsed by the UN Security Council, which evidently shared its view of Palestine as a state.[5] In 2004, the UN General Assembly adopted a resolution that again reflected its view of Palestine as a state. The Assembly recited "that the Palestinian people have the right to self-determination and to sovereignty over their territory."[6] If the territory were "theirs," it had to be the territory of their state.

The 2004 General Assembly resolution also addressed the status of Palestine indirectly when a question arose over whether Palestine's representatives should present credentials to the General Assembly's credentials committee. Representatives of member states are required to do so before the opening of each session.[7] Because of the fact that Palestine was not a member state, the resolution said "that Palestine, in its capacity as observer and pending its attainment of full membership in the United Nations, does not present credentials to the General Assembly." The reference to an eventual full membership for Palestine implied that its attainment was only a matter of time, hence that Palestine was qualified for membership. Statehood is a requirement for membership.

PALESTINE IN THE INTERNATIONAL COURT OF JUSTICE

The issue of Palestine statehood came up in two different ways albeit only in passing, in a 2004 case in the International Court of Justice, the judicial arm of the United Nations. The UN General Assembly, concerned over Israel's construction of a physical barrier extending through much of the West Bank, asked the Court to give an advisory opinion on the structure's legality.[8] Out of concern that the structure might impede the implementation of Palestine statehood by prejudging the border issue, the Court addressed self-determination, a right that it viewed as applying to the Palestinian people in the territory of the West Bank.[9] Regarding self-determination, the Court said,

> It is also for States, while respecting the United Nations Charter and international law, to see to it that any impediment, resulting from the construction of the wall, to the exercise by the Palestinian people of its right to self-determination is brought to an end.[10]

By "impediment," the Court was referring to the possibility that the wall's location would become a border. The Court was concerned lest the barrier be used to cut into the territory of Palestine. It regarded all states as being under an obligation under international law to keep Israel from using the barrier to prevent effectuation of Palestinian self-determination. The Court noted Israel's assurances of the structure's temporary character but said that it nevertheless cannot remain indifferent to certain fears expressed to it that the route of the wall will prejudge the future frontier between Israel and Palestine, and the fear that Israel may integrate the settlements and their means of access. The Court considers that the construction of the wall and its associated régime create a "fait accompli" on the ground that could well become permanent, in which case, and notwithstanding the formal characterization of the wall by Israel, it would be tantamount to *de facto* annexation.[11]

The Court noted that the structure was being built in such a fashion that most of Israel's West Bank settlers were on the Israeli side of it.[12] The Court did not elaborate on its statement about the "future frontier," but it makes little sense to address the question of a border between two territorial entities unless each of them is a state. The question of a border remained, to be sure, in the future, but in speaking about the "frontier between Israel and Palestine," the Court referred to Palestine in the present tense.

Crawford found support for his view that a Palestine statehood assertion would be unlawful in a statement the Court made that the parties must not take "unilateral action" that might "change the status quo."[13] In the relevant passage, the Court said:

> The Court would emphasize that both Israel and Palestine are under an obligation scrupulously to observe the rules of international humanitarian law, one of the paramount purposes of which is to protect civilian life. Illegal actions and unilateral decisions have been taken on all sides, whereas, in the Court's view, this tragic situation can be brought to an end only through implementation in good faith of all relevant Security Council resolutions, in particular resolutions 242 (1967) and 338 (1973).[14]

The Court did not specify what "unilateral decisions" it had in mind, but, as the quoted language indicates, the Court was referring to decisions relating to the implementation of humanitarian law, not to decisions relating to territorial status. The Court said nothing to suggest that an assertion of Palestine statehood would be unlawful.

Palestine statehood came up in one other way in the 2004 case. The Court treated Palestine as a state in the way it allowed Palestine to participate in the proceedings. The International Court of Justice is a court strictly for states. Under the Court's Statute, when it is presented with a request for an advisory opinion, the Court invites "any state entitled to appear before the Court" to submit a statement in the nature of a legal brief and to argue before the Court in the oral proceedings.[15] There is no provision in the Court's Statute for inviting a non-state entity. When the UN General Assembly sent its request to the Court for an advisory opinion, the Court issued an order to let Palestine submit a written statement and to participate in the oral proceedings.[16] Palestine did submit a written statement to the court and did make oral argument.[17] By letting Palestine participate, the Court treated it as a state. Judge Higgins, in a separate opinion she wrote in the case, so confirmed. Judge Higgins found Palestine's status to be relevant on one aspect of the case, namely, on the issue of whether violence attributable to it could be deemed an act of aggression. To demonstrate the status that the Court had found Palestine to enjoy, Judge Higgins averted to the fact that the Court had invited Palestine to participate by filing a written statement and by participating in oral argument. She said that the Court regarded Palestine as being "sufficiently an international entity to be invited to these proceedings."[18] As indicated, the only kind of "international entity" that can be invited under the Court's Statute is a state.

PALESTINE AND THE UN SECRETARIAT

The issue of Palestine's statehood came before the United Nations Secretariat when Palestine filed documents to adhere to three transportation treaties for which the UN Secretary-General is the depositary agency. The three treaties were concluded under the auspices of the Economic and Social Commission for Western Asia and were open only to states that were members of the Commission. As mentioned in Chapter 11, Palestine is a member state.

In 2005, Palestine filed a signature to become a party to a treaty titled Memorandum of Understanding on Maritime Transport Cooperation in the Arab Mashreq.[19] "Mashreq" is Arabic for "East." "Arab Mashreq" refers to the Arab states eastward of the Mediterranean Ocean. Palestine deposited with the UN Secretary-General a "definitive signature." The UN Secretary-General was identified in the treaty as the depositary agency, meaning that instruments of adherence were to be filed with him.[20] "Definitive signature" was one of the methods specified in the treaty as a means of adherence.[21] A state would become a party by filing a signature without a need for subsequent ratification.[22] The Secretary-General accepted the Palestine "definitive signature" and notified the other parties that Palestine had become a party to the treaty.[23]

In 2006, Palestine filed to adhere to the Agreement on International Roads in the Arab Mashreq.[24] In this treaty as well, the UN Secretary-General was designated as the depositary agency.[25] Palestine signed on

May 10, 2001, the date on which the text of the treaty was adopted by the parties. One means of adherence specified in this treaty was signature subject to ratification.[26] Palestine deposited with the Secretary-General an instrument of ratification in 2006, and the Secretary-General notified the other parties that Palestine had become a party.[27]

Also in 2006, Palestine filed to adhere to a third transport treaty, the Agreement on International Railways in the Arab Mashreq.[28] By the terms of this treaty as well, the UN Secretary-General is the depositary,[29] and this treaty too calls for a signature subject to ratification.[30] Palestine in 2003 deposited with the Secretary-General its signature and in 2006 an instrument of ratification. As with the other two treaties, the Secretary-General notified the other parties that Palestine had become a party.[31]

The Secretary-General provided an explanation for accepting Palestine's documents of adherence to the three treaties. Palestine's adherence to the three treaties is noted in *Multilateral Treaties Deposited with the Secretary General*, the annual UN publication in which the Secretary-General records adherences to the treaties for which he is depositary. All three of these treaties have entered into force. With respect to all three, the Secretary-General explained his acceptance of the Palestine adherences in a note under the heading "historical information," reading as follows:

> Agreements adopted under the auspices of the Economic and Social Commission for Western Asia (ESCWA) are open for signature by the members of ESCWA. Palestine was admitted to membership in ESCWA pursuant to ECOSOC resolution 2089 (LXIII) dated 22 July 1977, which amended paragraph 2 of the terms of reference of the Commission. Full powers for the signature of the Agreements were issued by the Chairman of the Executive Council of the Palestine Liberation Organization and the President of the Palestinian National Authority.[32]

The Secretary-General was saying that Palestine was a state based on its membership in ESCWA. The Secretary-General's practice, as the Secretariat has previously explained, is to decline instruments of adherence to multilateral treaties from entities that the Secretary-General determines not to be states.[33] In situations of doubt, but where the decision is made to accept an instrument, the Secretary-General may append to his notification of receipt a note explaining the decision that the entity is a state. The Secretary-General did so, as will be seen in Chapter 19, when presented with a ratification instrument for a multilateral treaty from Niue. In the case of Palestine's deposit of instruments of adherence to the three transportation treaties, the Secretary-General merely indicated in the "historical note" that Palestine was a member state of

ECSWA because that fact signified that Palestine was a state, and therefore that the adherences should be accepted.

TALKS WITH ISRAEL TOUCHING STATEHOOD

In 2007, Israel gave indications that it accepted Palestine statehood as
long as it applied only to the territory that was already under PNA control. The matter was raised in talks arranged by the United States at
Annapolis in November 2007. Following those talks, PNA President
Mahmoud Abbas recounted what was discussed, saying,

> There was debate about the statehood with provisional boundaries and
> we have rejected this idea at all because the temporary borders will turn
> into lasting frontiers.[34]

Abbas expressed concern that such an agreement on statehood might
also preclude satisfaction of Palestine's demands on other key issues:

> We also want a solution to the problem of the refugees in accordance with
> the Arab peace initiative and United Nations resolution 194.[35]

Abbas' reference to an Arab Peace Initiative was to a March 2002 declaration at an Arab-state summit in Beirut, proposing normalization of
relations with Israel in exchange for Israel's withdrawal from Gaza and
the West Bank, plus repatriation of Arabs displaced from Palestine in
1948. His reference to Resolution 194 was to the General Assembly of
1948, mentioned in Chapter 9, which called for the same repatriation.

Israel was ready to acknowledge statehood for Palestine if that statehood applied to a reduced territory. That willingness bespoke Israel's
acknowledgment that Palestine was a state. The only issue for Israel was
its borders. Israel was prepared to recognize Palestine if the territory it
claimed were sufficiently small.

SECURITY COUNCIL AND THE GOVERNMENT
OF PALESTINE

The following year, in December 2008, the UN Security Council adopted
Resolution 1850, which dealt with the peace process. In one clause, the
Security Council called on

> all States and international organizations to contribute to an atmosphere
> conducive to negotiations and to support the Palestinian government that
> is committed to the Quartet principles and the Arab Peace Initiative and

respects the commitments of the Palestinian Liberation Organization, to assist in the development of the Palestinian economy, to maximize the resources available to the Palestinian Authority, and to contribute to the Palestinian institution-building programme in preparation for statehood.[36]

The reference to "preparation for statehood" might imply that statehood was yet to be achieved, although what the resolution's drafters may have had in mind was independent statehood. Institution-building would seem to relate to Palestine's ability to prosper once independent. The reference in the resolution to "the Palestinian government" strongly implied Palestine statehood. Only a state has a government. If the Security Council thinks that Palestine has a government, it must regard Palestine as a state.

In another resolution a few weeks later, the Security Council again referred to Palestine in a way that suggested present statehood. The resolution addressed Israel's military action in Gaza at the end of the year 2008. After calling for a ceasefire and a withdrawal of Israeli forces, the Security Council

> [c]all[ed] for renewed and urgent efforts by the parties and the international community to achieve a comprehensive peace based on the vision of a region where two democratic States, Israel and Palestine, live side by side in peace with secure and recognized borders, as envisaged in Security Council resolution 1850 (2008) ...

Again, it was not clear whether the Security Council's language meant that a Palestine state that did not presently exist would emerge, or whether it meant that Palestine, presently a state, would be implemented on the ground, in the sense of coming to independence. In any event, the Security Council's phrasing seemed to place Israel and Palestine in a parity of status.

PALESTINE IN THE INTERNATIONAL CRIMINAL COURT

A quite practical consequence of Palestine statehood became an issue in early 2009. In the wake of Israel's military incursion into Gaza, which continued into the early weeks of 2009, allegations of war crimes violations were levelled against Israel by nongovernmental organizations.

These allegations reached the Office of the Prosecutor of the International Criminal Court, with a suggestion that he investigate and prosecute individuals who might be responsible. The governing instrument for the Court is its Statute. The Statute, which despite its title is a treaty, defines the war crimes over which the Court has jurisdiction.[37] The Court has jurisdiction only in situations specified in the Statute. It may try persons involved in a situation that the UN Security Council refers to the Court for prosecution.[38] Just as the Gaza hostilities were ending, Bolivia asked the UN Security Council to refer the Gaza situation to the Court,[39] but the Security Council did not act. Even absent a Security Council referral, the Court may try persons who are nationals of a state that is party to the Statute.[40] But Israel is not a party to the Statute,[41] hence Israeli officials could not be prosecuted based on Israeli nationality. The Court also has jurisdiction over a person who commits an act in the territory of a state that is party to the Statute.[42] But Palestine had not ratified, hence the Court had no jurisdiction based on the territory in which acts, by either Israelis or Palestinians, were committed.

The Statute allows for jurisdiction in one other circumstance, however. By Article 12(3), a state that is not a party to the Statute may confer jurisdiction for acts in its territory by lodging a declaration accepting the Court's jurisdiction with respect to particular offenses.

On January 21, 2009, a declaration in the name of Palestine was lodged in the Court. A letter was sent to the Court's Registrar on the letterhead of the Palestinian National Authority, Ministry of Justice, Office of Minister.

Declaration recognizing the Jurisdiction of the International Criminal Court

In conformity with Article 12, paragraph 3 of the Statute of the International Criminal Court, the Government of Palestine hereby recognizes the jurisdiction of the Court for the purpose of identifying, prosecuting and judging the authors and accomplices of acts committed on the territory of Palestine since 1 July 2002.[43]

As a consequence, the Government of Palestine will cooperate with the Court without delay or exception, in conformity with Chapter IX of the Statute.[44]

This declaration, made for an indeterminate duration, will enter into force upon its signature.

Material supplementary to and supporting this declaration will be provided shortly in a separate communication.

Signed in The Hague, the Netherlands, 21 January 2009

For the Government of Palestine

Minister of Justice s/Ali Khashan[45]

The Court's prosecutor, Luis Moreno-Ocampo, received the Minister of Justice and issued a press statement, saying that the letter would be taken under advisement:

> Since 27 December 2008, the OTP [Office of the Prosecutor] has also received 213 communications under Article 15[46] by individuals and NGOs, related to the situation context of Israel and the Palestinian Territories; some of them were made public by the senders. As per normal practice, the Office is considering all information, including open sources.

> The Office will carefully examine all relevant issues related to the jurisdiction of the Court, including whether the declaration by the Palestinian National Authority accepting the exercise of jurisdiction by the ICC meets statutory requirements; whether the alleged crimes fall within the category of crimes defined in the Statute, and whether there are national proceedings in relation to those crimes.[47]

On September 15, 2009, the United Nations Fact-Finding Mission on the Gaza Conflict identified war crimes that it thought had been committed in Gaza and, referencing the Palestine filing, said that

> accountability for victims and the interests of peace and justice in the region require that the legal determination should be made by the Prosecutor as expeditiously as possible.[48]

On September 17, 2009, in its annual report to the United Nations, the International Criminal Court recounted its receipt of the Palestine declaration and stated:

> Owing to the uncertainties of the international community with respect to the existence or non-existence of a State of Palestine, the Registrar accepted the declaration without prejudice to a judicial determination of the applicability of article 12, paragraph 3.

The report continued:

> The Office [of the Prosecutor] began to examine all issues related to its jurisdiction, including whether the declaration by the Palestinian Authority accepting the exercise of jurisdiction by the Court meets statutory requirements, whether crimes within the Court's jurisdiction have been committed and whether there are national proceedings in relation to alleged crimes.[49]

The sensitivity of the issue of the Court's jurisdiction became clear in September 2009, when Israel was reported to be pressuring the PNA over the filing.[50] At the time, a single telecommunications company was operating in Palestine territory to provide mobile telephone service. The PNA sought to arrange for an additional company but required Israeli acquiescence for a frequency on which to operate.[51] A defense ministry official tied Israeli consent to an end to the Palestinian effort to have Israeli officials prosecuted over Gaza. The official referred to the "embarrassing charges" of war crimes violations as "incitement."[52]

The Palestine letter purported to give the Court jurisdiction not only over offenses committed during the Gaza hostilities, but over any offense committed in the entirety of the territory of Palestine, on either side of the conflict, since July 1, 2002. One provision in the Court's Statute defining acts that qualify as war crimes reads:

> The transfer, directly or indirectly, by the Occupying Power of parts of its own civilian population into the territory it occupies.[53]

Israel was an occupying power in the West Bank, and it promoted settlement there by members of its civilian population. If the Palestine declaration were valid, high Israeli officials might be subject to prosecution under a provision in the Statute that reads:

> This Statute shall apply equally to all persons without any distinction based on official capacity. In particular, official capacity as a Head of State or Government, a member of a Government or parliament, an elected representative or a government official shall in no case exempt a person from criminal responsibility under this Statute, nor shall it, in and of itself, constitute a ground for reduction of sentence.[54]

Israel had already criticized the inclusion in the Statute of civilian settlements as a war crime,[55] and this provision was a major reason for Israel's refusal to ratify the Court's Statute.[56]

Following a meeting with Palestine representatives on October 16, 2009, Moreno-Ocampo issued a press release saying, "We appreciate the efforts undertaken by the PNA and the extensive legal arguments presented on a highly complex area of law."[57] The validity of the Palestine filing turned on Palestine statehood, and on how strictly the Court might construe the concept of statehood for purposes of its Statute.[58] The statehood issue in any event suddenly had the potential of taking international action on the Israeli-Palestinian conflict in a new direction.

A EUROPEAN INITIATIVE

In July 2009, Palestine statehood was affirmed by the chief European minister for foreign affairs. Javier Solana, High Representative for the

Common Foreign and Security Policy of the European Union, called for Palestine's admission to the United Nations. Solana said that the UN Security Council should "accept the Palestinian state as a full member of the UN." Under the UN Charter, new members are admitted by the General Assembly, but on the recommendation of the Security Council. Since only a state may be admitted, Solana's call for Security Council action was premised on Palestine being a state. Solana also called on the Security Council to mandate the resolution of outstanding issues in a way that would permit the progression of Palestine to independence.[59]

AN ISRAELI ACKNOWLEDGMENT

In July 2009, the Government of Israel again impliedly acknowledged Palestine statehood. Prime Minister Netanyahu was pressing for Palestinian recognition of Israel as a state "of the Jewish people." The PLO had recognized Israel as a state in 1993, but Netanyahu sought recognition of Israel not only as a state, but as one of the Jewish people. Netanyahu framed his demand as follows, offering to recognize Palestine in the process:

> If we are asked, which we are, to recognize the Palestinian state as the nation-state of the Palestinian people – and we are willing to do so – it is only natural that we ask our Palestinian neighbors to recognize the State of Israel as the nation-state of the Jewish people.[60]

In international practice, recognition does not normally include any reference to the ethnicity of a state's inhabitants. There was reluctance on the Palestinian side to do what Netanyahu asked, because if Israel were understood to be the state "of the Jewish people," this might serve as a basis for refusing to repatriate the displaced Palestine Arabs and might jeopardize the situation of the Arabs living in Israel. Nonetheless, Netanyahu was expressing willingness, were there acceptance of his proposal on the other side, "to recognize the Palestinian state." If Israel was willing to recognize the Palestinian state, it must have understood such a state to exist.

A PALESTINIAN INITIATIVE

The PNA took steps to render Palestine capable of ruling its territory, hence to function as an independent state. The PNA set targets for "building

national institutions" that would bring into being "a *de facto* state appa-
ratus within the next two years." In a document issued in August 2009
that it called a Government Program, the PNA proclaimed:

> It is time now for the illegal occupation to end and for the Palestinian
> people to enjoy security, safety, freedom and independence.

The Program outlined steps to enhance both the quality and coverage
of PNA institutions. It recited that the "window of opportunity" for "a
viable two-state solution" was "mortally threatened by Israel's settlement
policy, the continuation of which will undermine the remaining opportunity of building an independent Palestinian State on the Palestinian
territory occupied in 1967."[61] Hence, the Program saw a need to move
expeditiously toward independence.

The Program recited that Palestine was a state, thereby reiterating the
position on statehood: "Palestine is an independent Arab state, with full
sovereignty over the West Bank and the Gaza Strip on the 1967 borders,
with Jerusalem as its capital."[62] Although the Program's main empha-
sis was on institutions of governance within Palestinian territory, it set
objectives for the Ministry of Foreign Affairs that included the building up of a professional diplomatic corps and the purchasing of more
embassy buildings in foreign capitals. The Program called for upgrading
relations with international organizations.[63]

A few months later, the PNA called on the major powers to secure a
UN Security Council resolution for an independent Palestine state. If the
Security Council were to decline to recognize Palestine as independent,
said the PNA leadership, the alternative would be a move toward independence for Palestine outside the context of bilateral negotiations. Israel
reacted, as it had to earlier moves at reasserting statehood, by saying that
this PNA initiative would violate the post-Oslo commitment that neither
side should take unilateral action affecting the status of territory.[64]

The United States reacted by reiterating its position that a Palestine
state should be brought into being through negotiations with Israel.[65]
The European Union too said it would not support a Security Council
resolution on Palestine independence, regarding it as "premature" for
Europe to recognize an independent Palestine before independence had
been brought about.[66] The EU appeared to be operating on the distinction between statehood and independence. The United States moved
closer in 2010 to an explicit recognition of Palestine statehood when it
upgraded the Palestine representation in Washington to the status of a
"general delegation."

PART FOUR

THE CONTOURS OF STATEHOOD

16

Palestine Meets Montevideo

The account given in Parts One, Two, and Three of Palestine's status has brought into play the concepts of sovereignty, recognition, and belligerent occupation, in addition to statehood itself. Palestine's situation cannot be analyzed without some understanding of what it takes to be a state, which involves these concepts and others. We have seen that Palestine's statehood has been challenged on the basis of criteria that are said to be required for statehood. We have seen that Palestine is recognized by some states but not by others. Palestine has been treated like a state by various UN organs, but it has not been admitted to the UN as a member state.

Part Four addresses these broader issues, as they relate to the status of Palestine. This chapter examines the criteria that are said to be relevant to determine whether a particular entity is a state, and whether Palestine meets them. Since, however, Palestine's territory is occupied, the relevance of these criteria is uncertain. The question of whether belligerent occupation affects the relevancy of the usual criteria is addressed in Chapter 17. Recognition by other states is sometimes said to be a prerequisite for statehood. The issue of recognition and its relevance to Palestine statehood is addressed in Chapter 18. One final, but key, issue is whether the criteria that are said to be required for statehood are applied with any rigor in the actual practice of the international community. That issue is addressed in Chapter 19.

ORIGIN OF THE MONTEVIDEO CRITERIA

As seen in Chapter 14, Israel's Foreign Ministry argued that Palestine was not a state because it lacked a population within a territory, control was not exercised by a government, and a capacity to engage in international relations was lacking. The Israeli Foreign Ministry did not invent these criteria. A body of practice has developed in the international community on what it takes to be a state.

The criteria for statehood that are customarily cited and that the Israeli Foreign Ministry referenced, are, however, of curious origin. They come not from any instrument drafted at the world level but from a Western Hemisphere treaty concluded in 1933 at Montevideo, Uruguay. That treaty, the Convention on the Rights and Duties of States, contained a single article – Article 1 – that referred to a state as follows as an entity possessing four characteristics:

> The state as a person of international law should possess the following qualifications: a) a permanent population; b) a defined territory; c) government; and d) capacity to enter into relations with the other states.[1]

These criteria were not formulated, however, as part of a project to ascertain standards for statehood. They were written in the context of a political struggle in the Western Hemisphere. The Convention on the Rights and Duties of States was concluded at the initiative of Latin American states that were seeking to end the role played by the United States in the hemisphere in the early years of the twentieth century, involving intervention and efforts by the United States to determine who would govern. The Latin states wanted a commitment by the United States to respect their territorial integrity.

A new administration in the United States under President Franklin Roosevelt promoted what it called a "good neighbor" policy toward Latin America. No longer, pledged Roosevelt, would the United States interfere in domestic affairs there. According to U.S. Secretary of State Cordell Hull, the Montevideo conference that led to the conclusion of the Convention was a product of the "good neighbor" policy.[2] The fact that the Convention's main issue was the Latin states' concern about U.S. intervention is clear from a reservation the United States felt compelled to enter in which it protested that it had no intention of interfering in the internal affairs of the Latin states.[3] This aim is also clear from the content of the Convention's articles. One article negated the significance of recognition, because the United States had sometimes withheld recognition as a way of keeping governmental authorities from gaining international legitimacy:

> The political existence of the state is independent of recognition by the other states. Even before recognition the state has the right to defend its integrity and independence, to provide for its conservation and

prosperity, and consequently to organize itself as it sees fit, to legislate upon its interests, administer its services, and to define the jurisdiction and competence of its courts.[4]

Another article posited the equal status of all states and said that an entity could be a state even if another state was preventing it from exercising its powers:

> States are juridically equal, enjoy the same rights, and have equal capacity in their exercise. The rights of each one do not depend upon the power which it possesses to assure its exercise, but upon the simple fact of its existence as a person under international law.[5]

Still another article sought to protect the rights of states from outside interference:

> The fundamental rights of states are not susceptible of being affected in any manner whatsoever.[6]

The criteria for statehood recited in Article 1 were drafted less to define statehood than to counter previous U.S. assertions of a right to intervene. The purpose of Article 1 was to make clear that any territorial entity with a population and a government capable of relating to other states should be free from intervention. In its official report about the Convention, the U.S. delegation that negotiated it said nothing about Article 1. Rather the delegation focused on the issues in contention between the United States and the Latin states.[7]

The lack of serious attention to Article 1 as the Convention was being adopted has left uncertainty as to whether the criteria it mentions are actually required for statehood. The criterion of a capacity to enter international relations has particularly been questioned. Crawford considers the capacity to enter into international relations to be, as a matter of logic, "a consequence of statehood, not a criterion for it."[8] Similarly, Stefan Talmon finds a capacity to enter into international relations "not a generally accepted element of statehood;" but rather "a condition for recognition."[9]

The context in which the Montevideo Convention was drafted lends credence to Talmon's conclusion. One aim was to make clear that a state could exist apart from recognition. Even if the United States refused to have relations with the entity, it could still be a state. It needed only the "capacity" for relations, not the actuality. So the reference to a capacity for relations was another way of negating a requirement of recognition.

One requirement that has sometimes been suggested as an add-on to the Montevideo criteria is "independence." An entity that meets the

Montevideo criteria nonetheless fails to qualify as a state, it is said, if it lacks independence.[10] But immediately, proponents of this criterion are forced to qualify. The occupation of a state's territory by a foreign army, as will be seen in the next chapter, is not taken to negate statehood. A state is hardly "independent" when its territory is controlled by a foreign army. "Independence of other States," writes Talmon, in analyzing the criteria for statehood, "refers to legal, not factual, independence; that is, the State must only be subject to international law, not to the laws of any other State."[11] If an entity can be a state when it is factually under the control of another state, perhaps because it ceded powers or had powers taken away by force, then "independence" does not mean what is ordinarily understood by the term.

More fundamentally, as seen in Part One, the practice in regard to mandates negates independence as a criterion for statehood. Class A mandate territories were states, even though they lacked independence. Palestine was administered by Great Britain but was regarded as a state. Hence, a criterion of "independence," even if narrowly construed, does not seem to be observed in international practice.

PALESTINE UNDER THE CRITERIA

Some analysts mistakenly focus on the PLO or the PNA when they address the question of whether Palestine satisfies the Montevideo criteria. Gilad Noam, for example, writes, "The PA is not a state."[12] That statement is accurate but misleading. The PNA is an institution of governance. It may be a government, or part of a government, but it is not a state. The same is true for the PLO.

In January 1997, Douglas Jehl, a writer for the *New York Times*, provided a snapshot of life as it was being experienced by the inhabitants of Gaza and the West Bank. Jehl emphasized, in the following terms, the extent of Palestinian control:

> With the withdrawal of Israeli troops from most of Hebron this week, three out of four Palestinians in the West Bank and Gaza are now policed by their fellow Palestinians, not by the Israeli Army.
>
> In terms of civil affairs, virtually every Palestinian in those areas already lives under Palestinian Authority control. There are Palestinian schools, Palestinian taxes, even Palestinian passports. The accord that added most of Hebron to the Palestinian archipelago may have resolved little about the region's final status. But more and more, the emerging Palestinian area is beginning to resemble a state....

Even now, by the barest measures, what is now controlled by the Palestinian Authority might constitute a state. There is a population of more than two million; there is territory in Gaza and the West Bank; and there is de facto international recognition, with Palestinian Embassies in several Arab capitals and Mr. Arafat, an elected President, treated by some governments as a head of state.

People arrested by the Palestinian police, which is equipped more like a paramilitary army, stand trial in Palestinian courts. By the end of this year, perhaps, there will be a Palestinian international airport and a telephone dialing code. And passing from Israel to Gaza or urban areas of the West Bank requires passing through a Palestinian checkpoint.

And even now, said Yosi Beilin, a top minister in the Labor Party Governments of Yitzhak Rabin and Shimon Peres and an advocate of a Palestinian state, "When I go to Ramallah, I now feel as if I am going to a foreign country."

"We have, let's say, an emerging state, but we don't have full control over the crossing points or freedom of movement over our land," Mrs. Ashrawi[13] said in ticking off what she described as vital prerequisites of statehood.[14]

Although since 1997 Israel has increased its control in the West Bank in certain ways, it has withdrawn from internal administration in Gaza. Jehl's point was that, at least in the areas in which it had control, the PNA was acting like the government of a state.

POPULATION

Palestine has a permanent population inhabiting its territory. This criterion does not demand that a population must be ethnically homogeneous, although Palestine's largely is. The population need not have inhabited the territory for many centuries, although the population of Palestine has. The criterion of population does not demand large numbers. Yet Palestine's population is larger than that of many other states. Examples of states with far smaller populations will be seen in Chapter 19.

TERRITORY

Palestine has a defined territory, even if its exact borders remain to be clarified. Under the mandate, Palestine's territory was clearly defined, bounded by Lebanon on the north, Syria and Transjordan on the east, Egypt on the south, and the Mediterranean Sea on the west. After 1948,

Israel cut into that territory. But territory of Palestine remained, and that is all that is required. As indicated in Chapter 12, the communiqué issued in conjunction with the 1988 declaration referred to Gaza and the West Bank as territory of Palestine.

To satisfy the territory criterion for statehood, borders need not be definitively settled. Many states have disputes with neighboring states over their borders. The territory of a state may change over time. The International Court of Justice has said that there is

> no rule that the land frontiers of a State must be fully delimited and defined, and often in various places and for long periods they are not ...[15]

The extent of Palestine's territory need not be resolved to say whether Palestine has a defined territory.

Gaza and the West Bank are not contiguous, but contiguity of territory is not necessary to statehood. Pakistan has two parts. A number of states are archipelagos, composed of a grouping of islands. Statehood can be questioned on the territory criterion if some other state has a plausible claim to the territory in question. It is on that basis that the Turkish Republic of Northern Cyprus has met with international resistance to its claim of statehood, since the territory in question is viewed as belonging to Cyprus. Regarding Palestine's claimed territory of Gaza and the West Bank, one finds no other state making a claim.

The criterion of a "defined territory" does not require a particular size. A Palestine state encompassing Gaza and the West Bank is smaller than many states, but larger than many others. One finds so-called microstates routinely being accepted as states, as will be seen in Chapter 19.

One analyst has questioned whether Palestine qualifies on the territory criterion on the basis of the extent of its control. Omar Dajani writes in regard to the territory criterion, "What is an impediment is the fact that a Palestinian government does not yet exercise independent authority over a defined territory."[16] That analysis is based on a conception that the territory criterion is a component of the governance criterion.[17] In other words, the entity needs not only territory, but a certain level of control over that territory. If one follows this line of reasoning, however, the territory criterion becomes irrelevant because it merges with the governance criterion. A U.S. court analyzed Palestine this way, similarly conflating territory with control. The court did not question that the relevant territory consisted of Gaza and the West Bank, but said nonetheless,

[T]he PLO has no defined territory.[18] To be sure, the PLO's November 15, 1988 Declaration of Statehood "contemplates" that the state's territory will consist of the West Bank, the Gaza Strip, and East Jerusalem. The fact that the PLO hopes to have a defined territory at some future date, however, does not establish that it has a defined territory now. Indeed, the Declaration's assertion that "the State of Palestine is the state of Palestinians wherever they may be" underscores the PLO's current lack of a territorial structure. In addition, because the PLO does not have a defined territory, it cannot have a permanent population.

The PLO is also unable to demonstrate that the State of Palestine is under the control of its own government. After all, without a defined territory, what, we ask, could the PLO possibly control? Moreover, even accepting the PLO's contention that the State of Palestine incorporates the West Bank, the Gaza Strip, and East Jerusalem, these areas are all under the control of the State of Israel, not the PLO.[19]

While this analysis found a deficiency both as to territory and as to population, its primary focus was on control. The territory criterion properly should be considered apart from the government criterion.

CAPACITY TO ENTER INTO INTERNATIONAL RELATIONS

If indeed a capacity to enter into relations with other states is a requirement for statehood, as opposed to a requirement for recognition, Palestine would seem to satisfy it. States have shown a willingness to engage with Palestine on the basis that it is a state.

By international practice, a state need not conduct its own foreign relations. Mandate Palestine, as was seen, had the capacity for international relations, even though its exercise was in the hands of Great Britain. A state is not required to maintain diplomatic missions or to receive ambassadors of other states. Examples will be seen in Chapter 19 of states existing today that do not conduct their own foreign relations. Palestine, however, does so. It has diplomatic or quasi-diplomatic relations with many states. It maintains representative offices in other states and, in turn, Palestine hosts representative offices of other states. Whether the Palestine offices abroad are designated as "embassies" or "general delegations," they perform the tasks that are typical of diplomatic missions, maintaining political contact with host states. Palestine is an active participant in international organizations, being a member or observer in at least twenty-six organizations of states.

The issuance of passports is an accepted function of government in the conduct of foreign relations. States normally do not honor passports issued by entities they do not recognize.[20] Since 1995, the PNA has issued Palestine passports, which are accepted by other states for entry into their territory.[21] In 2009, the PNA began issuing electronically scannable passports, thereby participating in a coordinated international system whereby states share data for instantaneous verification of the identity of travelers.[22] The U.S. Department of State, while noting that the United States did not recognize Palestine as a state, advised,

> The U.S. Department of State has determined that the Palestinian Authority Passport/Travel Document meets the requirements of a passport as defined in Section 101(a)(30) of the Immigration and Nationality Act (INA) and therefore is acceptable for visa issuing purposes and travel to the United States.[23]

The Department of State in fact admits persons holding Palestine passports.[24] The definition of a passport in Section 101(a)(30) reads:

> The term "passport" means any travel document issued by competent authority showing the bearer's origin, identity, and nationality if any, which is valid for the admission of the bearer into a foreign country.[25]

If a passport is a document issued by a "competent authority," and if a passport shows the bearer's "nationality," it would seem that the United States considers the PNA to be a "competent authority" and that the nationality it is recognizing is that of Palestine. The PNA issues the passports, of course, as passports of Palestine. The United States would seem, therefore, to be acknowledging the existence of a Palestine state, even though it does not accord Palestine diplomatic recognition. The general recognition accorded Palestine passports shows that the states of the international community consider Palestine to be a state.

Another aspect of relations between states is consular representation of a state's nationals. States perform a variety of services for their own nationals at consular posts, which are often attached to diplomatic missions. Palestine missions perform consular functions for Palestine nationals. They serve Palestine citizens by issuing passports and providing notarial services related to documents. In the territory of Palestine, the PNA honors the right of other states similarly to perform consular functions on behalf of their own nationals.

In particular, the PNA fulfills the consular notification obligations found in customary international law. States are required, upon arresting a foreign national, to notify the individual of the right to contact a home-state consul. Depending on arrangements with another particular state, the state that carries out the arrest may also be required to notify the consul.[26] As reported by the U.S. Department of State, if a U.S. national is arrested by PNA police or security units, the practice of the PNA is that it notifies the Consulate-General of the United States in Jerusalem.[27] When a British national was arrested in Gaza in 2010, the authorities acted as is expected of states, by allowing a consular officer from the British Consulate-General in Jerusalem to enter the detention facility to meet with the man.[28] In this sphere of activity, other states relate to Palestine as they relate to states, and Palestine carries out the obligations incumbent upon a state.

Numerous treaties have been concluded for Palestine.[29] Many of them relate to trade, investment, and commerce.[30] Palestine treaties are most frequently concluded in the name of the PLO, and occasionally in the name of Palestine or the PNA. The three multilateral transport treaties described in Chapter 15 were concluded in the name of Palestine. An agreement with the Organization of Petroleum Exporting Countries on investment was concluded in the name of the Palestinian Authority.[31] The tariff agreement with the European Union, also described in Chapter 15, was concluded in the name of the PLO "for the benefit of the Palestinian Authority." That same phrasing is found in a bilateral treaty on invest-ment concluded with the United States.[32] This phrasing appears to derive from the Interim Agreement of 1995, which contemplates agreements by the PLO "with states or international organizations for the benefit of the Council" on economic and certain other matters.[33] By whatever names agreements are concluded, Palestine has an extensive treaty prac-tice demonstrating a capacity to enter into relations with other states.

CONTROL BY GOVERNMENTAL INSTITUTIONS

It is on the criterion of control by a government that Palestine has most often been said not to qualify as a state.[34] Several U.S. courts that have needed to decide whether Palestine is immune from suit because of being a state have decided against Palestine statehood based on the criterion of control.[35]

Anis F. Kassim, addressing the element of PLO governance in the West Bank and Gaza in 1980, wrote, even then, that the PLO "exercises a wide range of governmental authority, and this has been universally recognized."[36] Crawford and Francis Boyle wrote companion pieces in

1990, assessing as of that date. Boyle found Palestine to satisfy the control criterion, whereas Crawford did not.[37] Boyle cited a variety of ways in which Palestinian authorities exercised control, even in the face of Israel's occupation. At the time, the PLO operated a number of aid programs in communities in the West Bank and Gaza. Boyle concluded that sufficient control was exercised to satisfy this criterion for statehood. Crawford, looking at the same evidence, said that the control exercised did not suffice.

With the peace process the PNA became a governing institution in Gaza and the West Bank. Its scope of control was limited by Israel, but a belligerent occupant need not necessarily displace existing institutions. Israel had not done so in Gaza or the West Bank. The PNA assumed control of those aspects of administration that had previously been under Palestinian administration, prominently, the judiciary and the civil service.[38] Provision was made for continuity of the law of Palestine. A decree issued May 20, 1994 recited that "the laws, regulations and orders in force before June 5, 1967 in the West Bank and the Gaza Strip shall remain in force until unified."[39]

The law in force in Gaza continued to be the law of mandate Palestine. For criminal law, the Penal Code (No. 74) of 1936 remained in force in Gaza. In the West Bank, the law in force continued to be the law of mandate Palestine as modified by the law of Jordan. For criminal law, the Jordan penal code of 1960 remained in force.[40] Islamic and traditional procedures continued to be used for certain categories of legal disputes.

Legislation and executive decrees began to be published in an Official Gazette, starting in 1994. Texts of all such enactments (in Arabic) are maintained by the Birzeit University Institute of Law.[41] New legislation was adopted on a variety of major issues.[42] The PNA established a military-court system based on a penal code that the PLO had used in exile.[43]

In addition to assuming, and expanding upon, functions already performed by Palestinian institutions, the PNA initiated other forms of governance. The Palestinian Legislative Council, whose members were first chosen in a general election held in January 1996, approved laws and confirmed the appointment of cabinet members. The Council also set up procedures to monitor the performance of the executive organs.[44] The executive branch oversaw a civil service whose size numbered in the tens of thousands.[45] A law on the civil service adopted in 1998 aimed at rationalizing its operations.[46] A post of president of the PNA was established, and in the general election of January 1996, Yassir Arafat was elected. Thus, both an elected legislative body and an elected presidency were established.

The Palestine Liberation Army moved into Gaza and the West Bank and largely merged into the security forces set up by the PNA.[47] The PNA assumed control of the police force. It set up a cabinet, including the ministries that are typical of many governments: finance, economic, planning and international cooperation, information, interior. A cabinet of twenty-two ministers was appointed in June 1996.

The Basic Law for the National Authority in the Transitional Period was adopted as a constitutional document by the Palestinian Legislative Council in 1997.[48] The Basic Law provided for the three traditional branches of government – executive, legislative, and judicial – and set out fundamental rights and freedoms. It characterized the political system as a parliamentary democracy. In March 2003 the PLC approved an amendment to create a position of prime minister.[49]

Citizenship was regulated by law. An Elections Law adopted in 1995 defined "Palestinian" for voting purposes as a person who "was born in Palestine, as defined by the territory covered by the British Mandate, or had the right to the Palestinian citizenship according to the laws in force during that period."[50] Continuity with the citizenship of the mandate period thus was maintained.

In both Gaza and the West Bank, the courts of first instance continued to function as before. In each area, an appellate court existed to hear appeals. Prosecuting authority rested in an attorney general appointed by the President. The legal system was overseen by a minister of justice, also appointed by the President.[51] In 2001, a Criminal Procedure Code was adopted.[52]

Legislation was adopted to govern the judicial system. A law was passed on the practice of law, to regulate the Palestinian bar.[53] The Law on the Formation of Regular Courts (2001) gave a central role to the Ministry of Justice in determining court jurisdiction.[54] The Judicial Authority Law (2002) regulated relations among the Ministry of Justice, the courts and the Attorney General's office.[55] A law was adopted in 2006 to create a constitutional court, although implementation was not immediately forthcoming.[56] The High Court functioned when necessary as a constitutional court.[57]

Prisons and pre-trial detention facilities were operated by the Ministry of the Interior. Like other governments, the PNA came to be scrutinized for its human rights practices. The U.S. Department of State, in its annual human rights reports on states receiving U.S. financial aid, included the PNA, assessing its conduct by the standards applicable to the governments of states on such matters as treatment of persons in police custody.[58] Thomas Giegerich argues that the PNA can be subject to international human rights standards without being the representative of a state, but this assertion is questionable, given that human rights law developed specifically to apply to states.[59] Not only states, but nongovernmental organizations that monitor human rights have urged PNA compliance with international human rights standards. Human Rights Watch, for example, published an assessment of the PNA's criminal justice system in which it rationalized holding the PNA to international standards by saying, "Although it is not yet an independent state, the PA aspires to be the government of a sovereign state."[60] The PNA accepts human rights obligations as required of governments of states. The Basic Law provides that "[b]asic human rights shall be binding and respected," and "The Palestinian National Authority shall work without delay to join regional and international declarations and covenants which protect human rights."[61] In 2007, Palestine ratified the Arab Charter on Human Rights, thereby subjecting itself to scrutiny of its practices.[62]

In 1996, at PNA request, the United Nations High Commissioner for Human Rights initiated a technical cooperation project in Palestine, implemented through the PNA Ministry of Planning and International Cooperation, to promote compliance with human rights obligations.[63] Such services, according to the UN General Assembly resolution creating the post of High Commissioner for Human Rights, are provided "at the request of the State concerned."[64] Palestine was evidently considered a state as the entity to which the services would be provided.

In 2005, Israel withdrew its administrative structure, as well as its troops, from Gaza. Thereafter, Israel retained control from the outside and on the borders, but Palestinian officials exercised control internally. In January 2006, Legislative Council elections were found as having been conducted consistent with international standards for fair elections.[65] A Hamas-sponsored party prevailed, entitling it to set up a government. The resulting situation led to Hamas assuming control in Gaza from June 2007. Palestinian control of the two sectors was divided between two different administrations. In Gaza the Hamas-led administration established effective internal control.[66] The fact that administrative authority became split created practical difficulties but is not relevant to the governance criterion for statehood. When state administration becomes split as a result of internal conflict, statehood is not negated. Examples of a split in administration are Korea and Vietnam. Korea divided into two zones of administration in 1950, and Vietnam in 1954. Yet in both Korea and Vietnam, each administration regarded the entire territory as a single state. Korea and Vietnam remained states.

The split in Palestine was less complete than in either Korea or Vietnam. With those two states, separate institutions purported to represent the state at the international level. With Palestine, following the split of administration, the Palestinian institutions in the West Bank continued to function for Palestine in international diplomacy. In March 2008, the leadership of the two sectors signed a declaration at Sana'a, Yemen, in which they affirmed the "unity of the Palestinian people, territory and authority."[67] Hamas regarded itself as falling under the umbrella of Palestinian representative bodies functioning at the international level. Diplomatic activity continued to be carried out by the PLO. Under the Basic Law amendments of 2003, a Ministry of Foreign Affairs was established within the PNA. To the extent that it engages in foreign affairs, it does so as a creature of the PLO.

The Fatah-Hamas contention raised questions about the legitimacy of the governing institutions under domestic Palestine law. The issue of domestic legitimacy, however, is not relevant to statehood.[68] A state does not cease to exist if its government is changed by unconstitutional means, for example, by a military coup. Nor does a state cease to exist if a government holds office in a fashion that, in one way or another, violates the domestic constitution.

Dajani, writing in 1997, prior to Israel's withdrawal from domestic administration in Gaza, concluded that the control criterion was not met, given the extensive powers still exercised by Israel as belligerent occupant.[69] However, even disregarding the fact of belligerent occupation, the level of control exercised by the PNA would not need to be total or near total, in order to satisfy the control criterion. One relevant factor, even beyond the fact of belligerent occupation, is that the requirement of effective control over territory is applied less strictly if no competing entity claims title.[70] With Gaza and the West Bank, there are no competing claimants. Gaza, as indicated, was not held by Egypt under a claim of sovereignty. The West Bank was held by Jordan under a claim of sovereignty, but a claim explicitly subject to an overriding claim by Palestine. Israel has never claimed Gaza or the West Bank as its territory.[71]

RELEVANCE OF THE MONTEVIDEO CRITERIA

Whitbeck, enumerating the Montevideo criteria for statehood, wrote in 1996 that "the state of Palestine is on at least as firm a legal footing as the state of Israel." The Palestinian executive, elected legislature, and security forces, he noted, exercised authority over the areas in which Israel had ceded control under the Gaza-Jericho agreement of 1994 and the Interim Agreement of 1995. The PNA controlled much governmental activity in Gaza under these agreements, even prior to the 2005 withdrawal. It also controlled the major towns in the West Bank. The permanence of the Palestinian population there was unquestioned, Whitbeck noted, and the PNA had demonstrated its ability to discharge international obligations.[72]

In 2007, Vaughan Lowe opined that Palestine met the criteria for statehood as of that date.[73] That assessment is consistent with the facts of administration by Palestinian governing institutions. As will be seen in Chapter 19, the control criterion does not require the total absence of control by outside states. Entities whose control is less than exclusive are routinely deemed to be states. Belligerent occupation, however, radically changes the calculus in applying the Montevideo criteria to Palestine. It is to the issue of belligerent occupation that we now turn.

17

Statehood under the Gun

Even to the extent the Montevideo criteria are actually observed in the international community, their relevance is questionable when applied to a putative state whose territory is held by a foreign army. In a situation of belligerent occupation, the sovereign may be limited, to a greater or lesser degree, in its ability to exercise control by what the belligerent occupant permits. Or the occupant may deprive the sovereign of any role in governance.

The territory of Gaza and the West Bank came under belligerent occupation by Israel in 1967. In the advisory case recounted in Chapter 15, the International Court of Justice found Israel's tenure in the West Bank to be one of belligerent occupancy.[1] The United Nations Security Council and General Assembly have both characterized the situation in Gaza and the West Bank from 1967 as one of belligerent occupation.[2] The Supreme Court of Israel has found Gaza and West Bank to be under Israel's belligerent occupation in cases involving challenges to acts by the Israeli authorities there.[3] Gaza, as will be indicated shortly, still falls under this regime, despite Israel's 2005 withdrawal.

EFFECT OF BELLIGERENT OCCUPATION ON STATEHOOD

The control criterion cannot be considered in the usual way when a territory is under belligerent occupation. Some writers, among them Geoffrey Watson, analyze the control criterion with respect to Palestine by saying simply that Israel controls what goes on in the West Bank; therefore, Palestine lacks control and cannot be considered a state.[4] However, belligerent occupation does not impair the title to territory,[5] regardless of whether the occupant entered the territory by aggression or in self-defense.[6] "[B]elligerent occupation," it has been rightly said, "does not affect the continuity of the State."[7]

The concept that occupation does not bring a territory under the sovereignty of the occupant developed in Europe and crystallized in the nineteenth century.[8] "The *de jure* sovereign is, during the period of occupancy, deprived of power to exercise its rights as such."[9] Despite loss of control, the sovereign retains sovereign rights, a point on which the authorities are in agreement. Upon the entry of a belligerent occupant, "[t]he legal (*de jure*) sovereignty still remains vested where it was before the territory was occupied, although obviously the legal sovereign is unable to exercise his ruling powers in the occupied territory."[10] "[T]he occupant does not in any way acquire sovereign rights in the occupied territory but exercises a temporary right of administration on a trustee basis."[11] "An entity does not necessarily cease to be a state even if all of its territory has been occupied by a foreign power or if it has otherwise lost control of its territory temporarily."[12] Kuwait, for example, was a state in 1990–1991, even though its territory was completely occupied by Iraq.[13] The Kuwaiti government fled Kuwait and exercised no control. During World War II, as Germany occupied, for example, the low countries, Denmark, and Poland, those states remained states, even though Germany controlled them. Israel's control as a belligerent occupant does not affect Palestine statehood.[14]

EMERGENCE OF A STATE DURING A PERIOD OF BELLIGERENT OCCUPATION

The situation of Palestine is, of course, different in one respect from that of Kuwait or the states occupied by Germany: There was no Palestine government controlling the territory just prior to the onset of belligerent occupation. But there is no reason in principle why the sovereign would have to have a government in control at the onset of belligerent occupation. At that point in time, the territory could, for example, be under the control of another belligerent occupant. Assume that State A occupied the territory of State B, whereupon State C, at war with State A, entered and occupied State B. The rights of State B still hold. Its statehood subsists. The situation is not unlike that of a thief who steals from another thief. If Thief A steals goods from Owner, and then Thief B steals them from Thief A, Thief B's obligation is to return the goods to Owner, not to Thief A.

It has been argued, however, that the rule that belligerent occupation does not negate the statehood does not benefit Palestine because that result only follows if the state itself existed prior to the onset of the occupation, and Palestine did not exist prior to 1967. Thus, Crawford, while acknowledging that belligerent occupation does not defeat statehood, says in regard to Palestine:

> we are not dealing with the situation of the suppression of states which were once incontestably established as such (the Baltic states between 1941 and 1990; Kuwait during Iraqi occupation in 1990). The question is rather the establishment of a new state on territory over which other states have claims of one kind or another.[15]

With Palestine, however, no other state has a claim to the territory. As Crawford elsewhere states, Israel has made no claim of sovereignty in Gaza or the West Bank.[16] Palestine, moreover, as explained in Chapter 10, was a state prior to Israel's occupation.

One U.S. court addressed the question of a possible transfer of sovereignty to Palestine during the time of the belligerent occupation of Gaza and the West Bank by Israel. Palestine was being sued, and the court needed to determine whether it was immune from suit by virtue of being a state. The court, like Crawford, assumed that Palestine was not a state prior to the onset of the occupation. It then said, in the following terms, that statehood could not be achieved during a time of occupation:

> Under international law, a state will maintain its statehood during a belligerent occupation, ... but it would be anomalous indeed to hold that a state may achieve sufficient independence and statehood in the first instance while subject to and laboring under the hostile military occupation of a separate sovereign.[17]

The court did not explain why it would be "anomalous" for statehood to be initiated during belligerent occupation. The court seemed to require "independence," which, by hypothesis, could not be achieved during belligerent occupation, even though the court posited that belligerent occupation is not otherwise a bar to statehood. The court omitted, moreover, a critical factual circumstance in Palestine's situation, namely, that the community bringing the new state into being was universally recognized as enjoying a right of self-determination, including territorial rights in the specific territory at issue.

There is no reason in principle why a state cannot be brought into being under such circumstances. Take, as a hypothetical example,

Mozambique when it was close to being liberated by Portugal, the colonizing power. Suppose that, just at the time when Portugal was about to agree to Mozambique's independence, South Africa had invaded Mozambique militarily and occupied it. Suppose further that Portugal had nonetheless gone ahead with its plan to recognize Mozambique's independence. No one would have argued that Mozambique was not a state because it was occupied at the time the act that brought it into being took place. Statehood clearly can be achieved during a time of belligerent occupation.

THE NAMIBIA PRECEDENT

In one highly visible case, the international community took the position that a state may emerge during an occupation, even assuming that there was no previous statehood. In the 1970s, Namibia was under occupation by South Africa. The issue of Namibia's statehood arose when an application was made for Namibia's admission to the International Labor Organization (ILO).

Namibia had been under a League of Nations mandate administered by South Africa, which had never withdrawn or brought the territory to independence. Membership in the ILO is open only to states.[18] In 1967, the UN General Assembly created an agency, called, after 1968, the United Nations Council for Namibia, to administer Namibia pending the achievement of independence.

The Council submitted an application to the ILO for the membership of Namibia. The ILO acted favorably on the application, explaining its decision as follows in its resolution granting admission:

Noting that Namibia is the only remaining case of a former mandate of the League of Nations where the former mandatory Power is still in occupation,

Considering that an application for membership in terms of article 1 is prevented only by the illegal occupation of Namibia by South Africa, the illegal nature of this occupation having been confirmed by the ICJ in its Advisory Opinion of 21 June 1971,

Affirming that the ILO is not prepared to allow the legitimate rights of the Namibian people to be frustrated by the illegal actions of South Africa,

Making it clear that in now granting the application for membership it does not overlook the wording of article 1 and believes that in the near future the illegal occupation of Namibia by South Africa will be terminated,

Decides to admit Namibia to membership in the Organisation it being agreed that, until the present illegal occupation of Namibia is terminated, the United Nations Council for Namibia, established by the United Nations as the legal administering authority for Namibia empowered, inter alia, to represent it in international organisations, will be regarded as the Government of Namibia for the purpose of the application of the Constitution of the Organisation.[19]

Like Namibia at the time, Palestine enjoys a status at the United Nations just short of membership. The ILO found occupied Namibia to be a state on the rationale that its legitimate rights should not be frustrated by occupation. In other words, the occupation was no bar to the achievement of statehood. Namibia was admitted as a member state to other UN-related organizations of states as well: the United Nations Economic and Social Organization (UNESCO), the Food and Agriculture Organization (FAO), the International Atomic Energy Agency (IAEA), the International Telecommunication Union (ITU), and the United Nations Industrial Development Organization (UNIDO).[20]

Like the occupation of Namibia, the occupation of Palestine is regarded as unlawful, though the essential fact is occupation, rather than its legality or illegality. The General Assembly has, in any event, said that the occupation of Gaza and the West Bank is "in violation of the Charter of the United Nations, the principles of international law and relevant resolutions of the United Nations," and it has called for "the immediate, unconditional and total and unconditional withdrawal of Israel from all the territories occupied since June 1967."[21]

Frederic Kirgis found Namibia's admission to the ILO to be a weak precedent for Palestine's admission to international organizations. Kirgis regarded Namibia's status as more solid than that of Palestine because Namibia was represented by the United Nations Council for Namibia, an entity that was set up, as indicated, by the United Nations itself to act in place of a government – that of South Africa – that the Security Council had found to have lost a legal basis for a role in Namibia. Kirgis said that this fact provided a legal ground that was unavailable to Palestine.[22] As indicated in Chapter 11, however, the Security Council entertained requests from both the PLO and the United Nations Council for Namibia to participate in Security Council debate, and it admitted the PLO on the basis on which it admits representatives of states, whereas it declined to admit the Council for Namibia on that basis. The Security Council, at least in that instance, placed Palestine in a higher status than Namibia. Moreover, Palestine's status per its establishment under the League of

Nations was as a Class A mandate, whereas the status of South-West Africa (later Namibia) was as a Class C mandate.

The ILO legal adviser, as Kirgis pointed out, had advised against Namibia's admission to the ILO and relied on an advisory opinion of the Permanent Court of International Justice as a precedent.[23] The advisory opinion was issued on the question of whether the Free City of Danzig was eligible to join the ILO. In 1930, the Danzig Senate asked the ILO to admit Danzig as a member.[24] The Treaty of Versailles had made Danzig a "free city," under the supervision of the League of Nations with Poland conducting its foreign relations.[25] The ILO asked the Council of the League of Nations to refer the matter to the Court for an advisory opinion, which the Council did.[26] The Court noted that Danzig's foreign relations were conducted by Poland and reasoned that in order to function as a member of the ILO, Danzig would need to make various decisions. Since it could not make such decisions without Poland's consent, the Court said, Danzig could not effectively participate in the activity of the ILO and could not become a member.[27]

The PLO, however, is not subject to another state in regard to foreign relations. Thus, the reasoning of the ILO legal adviser in opposing (unsuccessfully) the admission of Namibia to the ILO would not apply to Palestine. In 1989, the relevance to Palestine of Namibia's admission to the ILO was considered by another international organization. At the time, it appeared that Palestine might apply for membership in UNIDO. In the event, it did not, but the Legal Service of UNIDO was asked for, and issued, an opinion about a possible Palestine application. Statehood is required for admission to UNIDO.[28] The Legal Service said that the Namibia admission to UNIDO, and to other inter-state organizations, would be a favorable precedent for Palestine's admission to UNIDO. The staff of the Legal Service reasoned:

> As some members may hold the view that Palestine does not presently have all the attributes required by international law for an entity to constitute a sovereign State, it is relevant to recall the precedent set by the admission of Namibia, represented by the United Nations Council for Namibia, to membership in UNIDO even though several members held (and continue to hold) the view that "Namibia is not a State". Namibia, represented by the Council for Namibia, being already a full member of ILO, UNESCO, FAO, IAEA and ITU and an associate member of WHO, was admitted under article 3(a) of the UNIDO Constitution.[29]

The various UN-related organizations found Namibia to be a state even though it was controlled by South Africa and therefore lacked independence. They did not regard independence as a prerequisite for statehood.

PARTIAL CESSION OF CONTROL

A belligerent occupant may cede partial control to the sovereign.[30] Israel ceded partial control with the Gaza-Jericho Agreement of 1994, additional control in the Interim Agreement of 1995, and then in 2005 ended its administration in Gaza. Israel kept control of the borders and the maritime and airspace of Gaza, and to the extent an occupant retains control, it remains bound by the law of belligerent occupation.[31] An occupation continues so long as an occupant exercises control at any level.[32]

The partial cession of control bore significance as regards Israel's view on sovereignty in Gaza and the West Bank. Israel ceded in favor of the PLO, which Israel acknowledged to represent the Palestinian people. Israel thus yielded control to an entity that it regarded as being entitled to the territory. Israel did not yield control to authorities representing Bangladesh or Honduras. It yielded control to authorities representing Palestine. Where a state in belligerent occupation cedes partial control to authorities who claim sovereignty in the territory, the belligerent occupant, by the very act of partial cession, acknowledges their status.

18

Recognition and Statehood

The acceptance of Palestine by the states of the international community has been a key element in bringing Palestine to statehood, beginning in the mandate period. It is sometimes said that an entity must be recognized in order to be a state, but what this means is less than obvious. It could mean formal, sometimes termed "diplomatic," recognition. Or it may be that recognition can be effected less formally, by acts that imply the acceptance of an entity as a state in some other way.

It is not evident, moreover, that any type of recognition is necessary for an entity to be a state. "The existence in fact of a new state or a new government" writes Green Hackwood in analyzing U.S. practice on recognition, "is not dependent upon its recognition by other states."[1] There is not universal agreement on this point.[2] There is no treaty that would reflect international agreement about the significance of recognition.

Whether an entity is in fact a state is said to involve legal elements. Thus, an international organ, for example, the Secretary-General of the United Nations, when called upon by an entity purporting to be a state to accept a treaty ratification document, will refer to legal elements. In making that assessment, as will be seen in Chapter 19, the Secretary-General may refer to recognition or other indications of acceptance by states.

A related, and equally difficult, question is the relation between recognition and the Montevideo criteria. If the Montevideo criteria control, then recognition may not be of great import. An entity would be a state if it qualifies under the criteria. On the other hand, it may be that recognition trumps the Montevideo criteria, rendering them irrelevant, or at least putting them in a subsidiary position. If an entity is widely recognized as a state, it becomes difficult to argue that it is not a state by reference to the Montevideo criteria. States may be under an obligation to use the Montevideo criteria when deciding whether to consider an entity a state, but if they disregard one or another of the criteria, there is no procedure for second-guessing their judgment.

One possible route to reconciliation of the two is through the criterion of a capacity to enter into relations with states. One way of demonstrating such a capacity is to have received recognition from other states. To this extent, recognition may be helpful, perhaps even necessary, to demonstrate satisfaction of the Montevideo criteria.

Thorny questions relating to recognition abound. Can a state legitimately be criticized for refusing to recognize an entity that seems to qualify as a state by the accepted criteria? According to one view, an entity that meets the qualifications may have a legitimate claim to recognition of its statehood, meaning that other states must recognize.[3]

In international practice, states sometimes withhold recognition in order to pressure the entity to undertake certain actions. This phenomenon is more than academic as regards Palestine. Some states – particularly European states – appear ready to recognize Palestine but insist that it first negotiate a settlement with Israel. They seem to be holding out recognition as a carrot to encourage Palestine to reach an accommodation with Israel. Thus, as a matter of *realpolitik*, recognition may be more a political weapon, wielded for good or for ill, than an act that must conform to rules of law.

Recognition has on occasion been withheld from entities that easily meet the Montevideo criteria. If an entity that meets the criteria violates a population's perceived self-determination right, one finds instances in which recognition has been denied. Thus, Southern Rhodesia was not accepted as a state after the European minority population declared independence from Britain and excluded the territory's African majority from the political process.[4] When South Africa promoted the statehood of enclaves, referred to as Bantustans, within its territory, their statehood was not recognized because they were regarded as being established in order to deny majority rule to the bulk of South Africa's African population.[5]

Entities that meet the Montevideo criteria may be denied status as states on the rationale that their existence violates the territorial rights of some other state. The Turkish Republic of Northern Cyprus, as already mentioned, has not been accepted as a state, on the rationale that the territory in question is appropriately that of Cyprus. There is some ambiguity as to whether entities that are denied recognition for violating the rights of populations or other states are non-states or whether they are states but not entitled to recognition. In any event, a doctrine has even developed that in these situations states are under a legal obligation not to recognize such entities.[6]

An area of uncertainty is the role of admission to membership in international organizations in determinations of statehood. Statehood is typically a requirement for membership, so if a state is admitted, may one presume that at least some of the states members of the organization regard the entity as a state? The UN Secretariat has taken the position that one may so presume. The UN Secretariat has referred to states joining UN specialized agencies (organizations of states) and has said that "those States became members of specialized agencies, and as such were in essence recognized as States by the international community."[7]

On the other hand, a denial of membership may not necessarily mean that an entity is not regarded as a state. The United Nations requires not only that an entity be a state but also that it be a "peace-loving" state. If an entity is denied admission, it may be on a rationale that it is not peace-loving. Or an international organization may decline to act on a membership application for reasons wholly apart from considerations of its status as a state. As seen in Chapter 13, Palestine's applications to the WHO and UNESCO resulted in no action being taken for reasons that may have had nothing to do with Palestine's statehood.

If recognition is necessary, or even relevant, it is not certain how general that recognition must be. How many states must recognize an entity before it is a state? If there is a minimum, is it simply the number of states? Does it matter whether the more influential states are among those that recognize? There is little consensus on these matters. Resolving the controversial issues related to recognition is beyond the scope of this book. But as already seen, recognition is frequently thrown into the mix in argumentation about Palestine's status.

IMPLIED RECOGNITION

As a technical matter, it is not clear how one determines whether one state has recognized another. A state may issue a formal statement recognizing an entity as state, particularly when the entity is asserting anew a claim to statehood. The Russian Federation, for example, issued a decree in 2008 to recognize South Ossetia as a state in the midst of Russia's military conflict with Georgia over South Ossetia.[8]

Often, however, documents of this kind are not issued; instead, states begin interacting with an entity in a way that seems to presume that it is a state. They may exchange diplomats, or consular officers. They may conclude treaties to deal with issues of common concern. If one asks how many states recognize a particular state, the answer may depend on what forms of interaction by particular states one considers sufficient to show recognition. Formal recognition, however, is probably not essential.

"[R]ecognition," writes Nii Lante Wallace-Bruce, "need not necessarily be express; it may be implied from the circumstances."[9] The Montevideo Convention provided a characterization of different modes of recognition. Recognition was defined to include nonexplicit acts. According to Article 7,

> The recognition of a state may be express or tacit. The latter results from any act which implies the intention of recognizing the new state.[10]

On the other hand, not every interaction with a putative state implies recognition. For example, attending an international conference of states at which an entity claiming statehood is present does not, it is said, imply recognition of that entity as a state.[11]

The rationale for implied recognition is that states often undertake interaction with an entity in ways that suggest that the entity is a state, but without making a formal statement to that effect. If enough activity of that sort occurs, the entity is deemed to be a state for such purposes as joining an international organization of states or for adhering to multilateral treaties that are open to states. Implied recognition thus avoids potentially negative consequences when an entity is not deemed to be a state. A non-state cannot be drawn into international interaction that would be beneficial to itself or other states, or to its citizens. Non-recognition makes it harder to hold an entity responsible for adverse actions affecting the citizens of other states.

Implied recognition – "tacit" recognition in the terms of the Montevideo Convention – raises difficult issues. Even if states interact with an entity like, let us say, Palestine, are they doing so in a way that suggests they regard Palestine as a state? Or are they interacting on the basis that the agency involved on the Palestinian side – the PLO, the PNA, or the Hamas party – represents the Palestinian people but does not constitute the basis of statehood?

Implied recognition can more readily be found where there is no competing claim, as is the case in Palestine as regards Gaza and the West Bank. If, hypothetically, two entities with pretensions to the same piece of territory claim to be states, other states may interact with both in ways that might imply recognition, but it is hazardous to draw inferences from the interaction since other states could not, logically, recognize both.

ACTS GIVING RISE TO IMPLIED RECOGNITION

In 1949, when Britain was deciding whether to recognize Israel, the British Cabinet discussed Egypt's attitude toward Israel and decided that Egypt had recognized Israel by entering into armistice talks held at Rhodes.

> The willingness of the Egyptian Government to enter into discussions with the Government of Israel at Rhodes was also significant, since by this the Egyptian Government were in effect recognizing the Government of Israel.[12]

The Cabinet took the act of entering into discussions about an armistice, not even a peace, as evidencing recognition. Concluding an agreement with a putative state does not necessarily imply recognition of it.[13] Whether the Cabinet was reading Egypt's action correctly could be debated. In a situation of hostilities, an armistice may be necessary, but it may not indicate how one party regards the other.

Palestine, however, has interacted with states in much more substantial ways in regard to territory. Israel has entered into discussions about a permanent arrangement with Palestine regarding territory, an act that implies that each party has the capacity to dispose of territory. Other states as well have encouraged Palestine to negotiate with Israel, thereby implying that they, too, regard Palestine as an entity with the capacity to dispose of territory.

"[I]nformal relations, without intent to recognize in the political sense, especially if these persist," writes Ian Brownlie, "have probative value on the issue of statehood."[14] Brownlie's point was made without regard to any particular situation, but it is telling in regard to Palestine. The states of the international community have acted in regard to Palestine, especially since 1993, in ways that are explicable only if they consider Palestine to be a state. Their "informal relations" with Palestine have "persisted."

RECOGNITION AND ADMISSION TO INTERNATIONAL ORGANIZATIONS

In any particular state's attitude toward a putative state, diplomatic recognition and a view as to its statehood are not necessarily one and the same. A state may well regard the putative state as a state but with-hold diplomatic recognition for a variety of reasons. An example is the admission of Macedonia to the United Nations in 1993.[15] Many states voted for Macedonia's admission even though they had not recognized Macedonia.[16] By their votes for admission, they took the position that Macedonia was a state. Thus, at the time of Macedonia's admission, if one had to answer the question of whether Macedonia was a state, one would probably have answered in the affirmative based on the view of the states that voted for its admission. Israel similarly was not recognized by many of the member states of the United Nations when the UN General Assembly voted its admission.

UN Secretary-General Trygve Lie, referring to the U.S. decision to grant de facto recognition to Israel in 1948 upon the proclamation of an Israeli state, highlighted the political character of recognition.

> The recognition of a new State, or of a new government of an existing State is a unilateral act which the recognizing government can grant or withhold. It may be true that some legal writers have argued forcibly that when a new government, which comes into power through revolutionary means, enjoys, with a reasonable prospect of permanency, the habitual obedience of the bulk of the population, other States are under a legal duty to recognize it. However, while States may regard it as desirable to follow certain legal principles in according or withholding recognition, the practice of States shows that the act of recognition is still regarded as essentially a political decision, which each State decides in accordance with its own free appreciation of the situation.[17]

The context of Lie's statement was the recognition issue that arose in 1950 over the question of which of the two competing governments in China should be seated at the United Nations as the representative of China. The Secretary-General explained:

> Various legal scholars have argued that this rule of individual recognition through the free choice of States should be replaced by collective recognition through an international organization such as the United Nations (e.g. Lauterpacht, *Recognition in International Law*). If this were now the rule then the present impasse would not exist, since there would be no individual recognition of the new Chinese Government,[18] but only action by the appropriate United Nations organ. The fact remains, however, that the States have refused to accept any such rule and the United Nations does not possess any authority to recognize either a new State or a new government of an existing State. To establish the rule of collective recognition by the United Nations would require either an amendment of the Charter or a treaty to which all Members would adhere.

On the other hand *membership* of a State in the United Nations and *representation* of a State in the organs is clearly determined by a collective act of the appropriate organs; in the case of membership, by vote of the General Assembly on recommendation of the Security Council, in the case of representation, by vote of each competent organ on the credentials of the purported representatives. *Since*, therefore, recognition of either State or government is an individual act, and either admission to membership or acceptance of representation in the Organization are collective acts, it would appear to be legally inadmissible to condition the latter acts by a requirement that they be preceded by individual recognition.

Lie found support for this view in the way both the League of Nations and the United Nations had handled admissions decisions. He said,

This conclusion is clearly born out by the practice in the case of admission to membership in both the League of Nations and in the United Nations.

In the practice of the League of Nations, there were a number of cases in which Members of the League stated expressly that the admission of another State to membership did not mean that they recognized such new Member as a State (e.g. Great Britain in the case of Lithuania; Belgium and Switzerland in the case of the Soviet Union; Colombia in the case of Panama).

In the practice of the United Nations there are, of course, several instances of admission to membership of States which had not been recognized by all other Members, and other instances of States for whose admission votes were cast by Members which had not recognized the candidates as States. For example, Yemen and Burma were admitted by a unanimous vote of the General Assembly at a time they had been recognized by only a minority of Members. A number of the Members, who, in the Security Council, voted for the admission of Transjordan (Jordan) [or] Nepal, had not recognized these candidates as States. Indeed, the declarations made by the delegation of the Soviet Union and its neighbors that they would not vote for the admission of certain States (e.g. Ireland, Portugal and Transjordan (Jordan), because they were not in diplomatic relations with the applicants, were vigorously disputed by most other Members, and led to the request for an advisory opinion of the International Court of Justice by the General Assembly.[19]

Recognition in the diplomatic sense and acknowledgment of the fact that a given entity is a state are thus regarded in international practice as two different matters. For admission to the United Nations, only the latter is required. Article 4 of the UN Charter requires statehood as a condition of membership; it does not require diplomatic recognition. In the International Court of Justice advisory opinion to which Lie referred, the Court said that the Article 4 requirement as to statehood is simply that and no more – a requirement that the applicant entity be a state.[20]

Lie referenced the practice of the League of Nations. There, too, entities that had not received extensive diplomatic recognition might be admitted as members on the rationale that they were states nonetheless. Lie mentioned Lithuania as an example. Lithuania was admitted to the League before being recognized by the major powers.[21]

In relation to Palestine, Lie's analysis is relevant to states that have not recognized Palestine but that have, by their actions, manifested their understanding that Palestine is a state. Such a state may be counted as one that regards Palestine as a state, even if it has not recognized Palestine.

A MINIMUM NUMBER OR PERCENTAGE?

Trygve Lie's analysis of international practice thus was that a decision can be made that an entity is a state even if it is not widely recognized. It has been suggested in relation to Palestine, however, that it would be a state only when it is recognized by nearly all states. Thus, Crawford writes that although Palestine has been recognized by over a hundred states, "it has never commanded anything like the level of quasi-unanimous support that would be required to establish a particular rule of international law to the effect that Palestine is a State."[22]

Why the issue should involve a "rule of international law" is not obvious. Recognition of a particular state is not a rule of law. It is rather an application of whatever rules may exist. Crawford does not make clear whether "support" means formal recognition only. The only source Crawford cites for a requirement of "quasi-unanimous" recognition is an advisory opinion of the International Court of Justice in which the Court used not that precise wording but the phrase "the vast majority of the members of the international community." The case was titled *Reparation for Injuries Suffered in the Service of the United Nations.*[23]

In that advisory opinion, however, the recognition of states was not at issue. Rather, the issue was the international personhood of the United Nations. The General Assembly asked the Court whether the United Nations was a legal person, such that it might possess the legal capacity to bring a legal claim for an injury suffered by one of its functionaries. The UN mediator for Palestine, Count Folke Bernadotte, had been assassinated in Jerusalem, and the United Nations wanted to bring a claim of responsibility against Israel.

The Court used the phrase "the vast majority of the members of the international community" as it examined the question of whether the United Nations was a legal person. The Court said that the United Nations was brought into being by "the vast majority of the members of the international community." The relevant passage reads:

> Accordingly, the question is whether the Organization[24] has capacity to bring a claim against the defendant State[25] to recover reparation in respect of that damage or whether, on the contrary, the defendant State, not being a member,[26] is justified in raising the objection that the Organization lacks the capacity to bring an international claim. On this point, the Court's opinion is that fifty states, representing the vast majority of the members of the international community, had the power, in conformity with international law, to bring into being an entity possessing objective legal personality, and not merely personality recognized by them alone, together with capacity to bring international claims.[27]

The Court's use of the phrase "vast majority" thus was in relation to the number that formed the United Nations, not in relation to the recognition of a state. One might think that if the Court requires a "vast majority" to create an international organization enjoying legal personality, then the same may be true for states. But the Court did not actually say that for the purposes of creating an international organization that would be a legal person, the "vast majority" of states is required. That was factually true for the United Nations, but it is not true for many other international organizations. The United States acknowledges as legal persons approximately eighty "public international organizations," many of which have only a few states as members.[28] The same is true for regional organizations of states, which have a limited membership.[29]

Membership in the United Nations, as already indicated, may be taken as evidence of statehood, since admission to membership involves a judgment that the entity is a state. However, near-unanimity is not required for admission to the United Nations. UN admission requires a favorable vote in both the Security Council and the General Assembly: nine votes out of fifteen in the Security Council,[30] and a two-thirds vote in the General Assembly.[31] Israel, for example, was admitted in 1949 into the UN General Assembly by thirty-seven states out of fifty-eight voting. Twelve voted against, while nine abstained.[32]

If recognition plays a role in determining whether a particular entity is a state, it is not clear how general that recognition must be. Whatever the rule may be, in the case of Palestine, one finds the generality of states acting in ways that suggest that they regard it as a state. That is true even for those that have not formally recognized. It is true even for the United States, which explicitly affirmed, in its legislation regarding Palestine passports, that it does not recognize Palestine in the formal sense.

19

When Is a State?

The issue of Palestine statehood can only be analyzed against the background of the generally applied standards for statehood. The Montevideo criteria are said to provide those standards, but even if they are relevant to Palestine under occupation, they have not, in fact, been applied rigorously by the international community in making determinations about statehood. As three noted authorities on international law have written, "In practice, global elites have interpreted these criteria quite flexibly."[1] This statement, if anything, understates the reality. Entities whose conformity to the Montevideo criteria is highly questionable are routinely accepted as states.

MONTEVIDEO MEETS REALITY

Entities that lack substantial control over their own affairs have been accepted as states. Ukraine and Belorussia during the Soviet period are two often-noted examples. Ukraine and Belorussia were admitted as original member states of the United Nations in 1945.[2] As already noted, admission to the United Nations is open only to states.[3] At the time of their admission, Ukraine and Belorussia were constituent republics of the USSR, itself a state. Around the same time, Ukraine and Belorussia were also admitted as member states to UN specialized agencies and other organizations of states.[4] The relationship of Ukraine and Belorussia with the USSR had been defined by the Soviet Constitution of 1936. That constitution used the term "sovereignty" in relation to the constituent republics, including Belorussia and Ukraine.[5]

The 1936 constitution, however, left little power in the hands of the constituent republics. The USSR enjoyed broad legislative power. It held authority in particular for war and peace, defense, foreign trade, state security, economic planning, taxation, banking, transportation, communications, and insurance.[6] As a result, Ukraine and Belorussia were seriously constrained in their control of their own foreign relations and domestic policy.

The 1936 constitution was amended in 1944 to allow constituent republics to make their own treaties with foreign states and to maintain diplomatic and consular relations with them,[7] and Ukraine and Belorussia did ratify a number of multilateral treaties in the following decades.[8] But since the USSR was typically also a party to these treaties, ratification by Belorussia and Ukraine had little practical significance.[9] Belorussia and Ukraine, moreover, were not free to conclude treaties at their own discretion. Internal rules required federal sanction for treaty activity by the constituent republics.[10]

The admission of Ukraine and Belorussia to the United Nations was sometimes viewed as an anomaly, required by political expediency. But Ukraine and Belorussia are not the only entities that have been accepted as states even though control of their affairs rested elsewhere. Bosnia, in the wake of the peace agreement of 1995 (the Dayton Agreement), came under international control to ensure cooperation among the groups that had been in conflict. The post of "high representative" was created to implement the peace agreement, with the authority to make decisions that would be binding on local officials. The parties to the Dayton Agreement agreed to the appointment of the "high representative." The Dayton Agreement provided:

> 2. In view of the complexities facing them, the Parties request the designation of a High Representative, to be appointed consistent with relevant United Nations Security Council resolutions, to facilitate the Parties' own efforts and to mobilize and, as appropriate, coordinate the activities of the organizations and agencies involved in the civilian aspects of the peace settlement.[11]

The "high representative" was to "monitor the implementation of the peace settlement."[12] In case of a disagreement with Bosnian officials, the opinion of the high representative was to prevail:

> The High Representative is the final authority in theater regarding interpretation of this Agreement on the civilian implementation of the peace settlement.[13]

Bosnia's status under this arrangement was characterized by one journalist as an "international protectorate." The high representatives made decisions, for example, about Bosnia's currency and about its national flag.[14] Bosnia's government was not free to make decisions on basic issues. Despite these restrictions, Bosnia's status as a state was not questioned.

"FAILED STATES"

Some states are deficient on the Montevideo effective government criterion as a result of a breakdown in public order. As indicated in Chapter 10, a state may continue to exist even if, for a time, it lacks an effective government. The term "failed state" has emerged in recent decades to describe such states.[15] Some retain control in parts of their territory, but not in others. The Democratic Republic of the Congo is an example of a state in which, as of 2010, the writ of the central government does not run far. In the DRC, persistent war with groups entering from outside has driven governmental institutions from some sectors. "[T]he eastern regions of the country," as related by the Human Rights Committee when it had to assess DRC compliance with human rights, "are not under the effective control of the Government."[16]

In Somalia in the 1990s, the government ceased to function. Somalia "failed" in the sense that its government collapsed, leaving no central administration. Local clan-based militias asserted themselves as de facto instruments of order. The UN Security Council found the breakdown of order in Somalia to be so serious as to constitute a threat to the peace.[17] At the Security Council meeting at which a resolution to this effect was adopted, member states expressed concern that basic needs of the Somali population were not being met.[18] No member state suggested that Somalia had ceased to be a state, however,[19] and even though the situation lasted into the next decade, Somalia continued to be regarded as a state.[20] The international practice in this situation is clear: A breakdown in governance does not negate statehood.[21]

ENTITIES DEEMED ENTITLED

Entities that have yet to establish firm control of territory have been treated as states because they were deemed entitled to statehood. Entities, like Palestine, that are regarded as enjoying a right to self-determination in a territory have been considered to be states, even while they remained under the control of an outside state. Legitimacy as endorsed by the international community plays an important role in the acknowledgment of statehood and sometimes overrides an ineffectiveness of control.

Philippines was admitted as an original member of the United Nations on October 24, 1945, even though it did not gain independence until the following year. India, too, was admitted to the United Nations as an original member on October 24, 1945, even though the country did not become independent until 1947. As Africa was being decolonized, recognition of the colonies as states became an issue as the colonial power remained in control but planned to withdraw. The Republic of the Congo was admitted as a UN member state after Belgium had granted the colony independence but remained in control.[22] Congolese authorities were in no sense the effective government, yet Congo was regarded as a state.[23] Similarly, Portugal remained in control for a time in its colony of Guinea-Bissau after it agreed to grant independence.[24] Nonetheless, Guinea-Bissau was admitted as a UN member state during that time.[25]

Bosnia was admitted as a UN member state less than three months after it declared independence from Yugoslavia, at a time when Yugoslavia still claimed it and was engaged in hostilities aimed at retaining control. Bosnia applied for UN membership on March 6, 1992, just days following a referendum vote that went in favor of independence from Yugoslavia but was boycotted by a substantial sector of Bosnia's population that opposed independence, and at a time when Yugoslavia was engaged in hostilities to retain control.[26] The European Community and United States recognized Bosnia as a state on April 7, 1992.[27] Bosnia was admitted to UN membership on May 22, 1992.[28] Bosnia was accepted as a state despite its lack of effective control, on a rationale that it was entitled to statehood.[29]

MONACO

Numerically, the most significant examples of states whose compliance with the Montevideo criteria raise questions are the so-called microstates. Small in population and in territory, microstates often exist under a formal agreement with a larger state, whereby the latter exercises considerable control. Monaco has a population of 30,000 people, of which only 5000 hold its nationality. The territory of Monaco is 1.95 square kilometers.[30] Despite its small population and physical size, Monaco is a state and has long been recognized as such by other states.[31] Monaco was admitted to the International Telecommunication Union in 1908. It was admitted to the WHO in 1948, to UNESCO in 1949, and to the International Atomic Energy Agency in 1957. It was admitted to the United Nations in 1993. At the time of its admission to these international organizations (with the exception of the ITU), Monaco's status was determined by two treaties with France, one dating from 1918, and the other from 1930. In 2002, these earlier treaties were replaced by the Treaty Designed to Adapt and Uphold the Friendly and Cooperative Relations between the French Republic and the Principality of Monaco.[32]

Under Monaco's 1930 treaty with France, key public posts were filled by seconded French civil servants: Minister of State, Director of Judicial Services, Government Counsellor for the Interior, Director of Public Security, Procurator-General of the Court of Appeal, Director of the Registry Office, Inspector of the Registry Office, chiefs of police, Director of the Labor Office, Head of Fiscal Services, Director of the Harbor.[33] Under Monaco's 1918 treaty with France, France became responsible for the defense of Monaco "as if that territory were part of France." In return, Monaco was committed "to exercise its rights of sovereignty in complete conformity with the political, military, naval and economic interests of France."[34] As for relations with foreign states, Monaco was required to gain the prior agreement of France.[35] Monaco was precluded by the treaty from affiliating with any state other than France.[36]

Monaco thus had few citizens, little territory, and little control of domestic or foreign policy. Reciting these serious limitations, David Raič argues that Monaco is not a state.[37] Yet its acceptance as a state by other states, as reflected in its admission to international organizations, is clear.

FORMER UNITED STATES TRUST TERRITORIES

Another series of states whose exercise of control is constricted is states that were formerly administered as trust territories. Several island archipelago states in the Pacific Ocean are former United Nations trust territories. As trust territories, they were administered by the United States, and they retain a connection with the United States. Two of these are the Republic of the Marshall Islands and the Federated States of Micronesia (FSM). Each has been accepted as a member state by the United Nations and other international organizations.[38]

The Republic and the FSM control much of their internal policy, and the inhabitants are their citizens. Neither the Republic nor the FSM, however, sets its own policies in certain key spheres.[39] The status of each is based on a tripartite Compact of Free Association, concluded between the two of them and the United States in 1986.[40] The Compact gives the United States "full authority and responsibility for security and defense matters in or relating to the Marshall Islands and the Federated States of Micronesia."[41] In the exercise of that authority, the United States is given "the option to establish and use military areas and facilities in the Marshall Islands and the Federated States of Micronesia."[42] Without any need for consent by the local governments, "the Government of the United States may conduct within the lands, waters and airspace of the Marshall Islands and the Federated States of Micronesia the activities and operations necessary for the exercise of its authority and responsibility."[43]

That authority of the United States includes "the option to foreclose access to or use of the Marshall Islands and the Federated States of Micronesia by military personnel or for the military purposes of any third country."[44] In the following terms, the United States is given a veto over any action by the local governments that it finds to interfere with its authority:

> The Governments of the Marshall Islands and the Federated States of Micronesia shall refrain from actions which the Government of the United States determines, after appropriate consultation with those Governments, to be incompatible with its authority and responsibility for security and defense matters in or relating to the Marshall Islands and the Federated States of Micronesia.[45]

Hence, the United States may act within the territory of these two states without their consent and may prevent them from allowing entrance by military units of other states. Moreover, if there is disagreement over these matters, the United States has the final say.

In foreign affairs, the two states in principle make their own decisions. However, "the Governments of the Marshall Islands and the Federated States of Micronesia shall consult, in the conduct of their foreign affairs, with the Government of the United States."[46]

The Compact of Free Association was concluded as a treaty, yet it was apparently not registered with the United Nations, in violation of the obligation of UN member states to register their treaties.[47] Concern over whether the Republic and the FSM control their own affairs led the USSR to raise questions in the 1980s, when they sought admission to the United Nations. The USSR said that the United States pursued a goal of "appropriating this Pacific Territory and permanently depriving the Micronesians of their independence." The USSR characterized the Compact as giving the United States "the exclusive right to control the external relations, defence and finances of the Micronesian territory."[48] Nonetheless, on the strength of the Compact, the United Nations admitted both the Republic and the FSM as member states.[49]

Another former Pacific island trust territory that had been administered by the United States is the Republic of Palau. Palau has its own Compact of Free Association with the United States.[50] Palau was admitted to UN membership in 1994.[51] Under its Compact, which is similar to that of the Republic of the Marshall Islands and the Federated States of Micronesia, the United States is responsible for the defense of Palau and may conduct in the territory of Palau any activities it deems necessary for that purpose. The United States may invite armed forces of other states to use military facilities in Palau, without Palau's consent,[52] while Palau is forbidden to extend a similar invitation.[53] Palau must refrain from actions that are determined by the United States to be incompatible with the U.S. authority over security and defense.[54] The U.S. defense authority may, moreover, be exercised to serve U.S. purposes. The Compact provides that the United States is to act "for the mutual security and benefit of Palau and the United States."[55] In the conduct of its foreign affairs, Palau is required to consult with the United States.[56]

In foreign affairs, all three of these Pacific island states formerly administered by the United States have generally adopted the policy positions of the United States. In the UN General Assembly, they have typically voted with the United States, even on resolutions in which the United States is in a tiny minority, such as resolutions critical of Israel.[57]

FORMER NEW ZEALAND TRUST TERRITORIES

New Zealand also held as trust territories certain Pacific islands that have since emerged as states. The Cook Islands (population 18,000) and Niue (population 1600) are in a relationship with New Zealand characterized as one of association. The relationship is similar to the relationship of the Republic of Palau, the Federated States of Micronesia, and the Republic of the Marshall Islands with the United States, with perhaps two key differences. One is that neither the Cook Islands nor Niue has any citizens. A second is that the relationship of the Cook Islands and of Niue with

New Zealand is fixed not by a treaty but by internal legislation of New Zealand. Neither has applied for UN membership, but each has been accepted as a member by UNESCO, WHO, and FAO, and Cook Islands additionally by the International Civil Aviation Organization.

The New Zealand Ministry of Foreign Affairs and Trade summarizes the key features of New Zealand's relationship the Cook Islands as found in a piece of New Zealand legislation, the Cook Islands Constitution Act 1965:[58]

- The Cook Islands has the power to make its own laws. New Zealand cannot make laws for the Cook Islands except as provided by Act of the Cook Islands Parliament. In practice this never happens;
- The Cook Islands Government has full executive powers;
- The Cook Islands remains part of the Realm of New Zealand (albeit a separate part), and the Queen in Right of New Zealand remains the Head of State of the Cook Islands;
- Cook Islanders retain New Zealand citizenship (and do not have additional Cook Islands citizenship);
- New Zealand retains responsibilities for the external affairs and defence of the Cook Islands. These responsibilities, however, confer no rights of control to the New Zealand Government and can only be acted on at the request of and on behalf of the Government of the Cook Islands.

The Cook Islands maintains diplomatic relations with approximately twenty states.

Similarly, Niue's status is set not by treaty but by New Zealand legislation, namely, the Niue Constitution Act of 1974.[59] Niue maintains no diplomatic relations with other states. Like the Cook Islands, Niue has no citizenship of its own; its inhabitants are citizens of New Zealand. New Zealand is responsible for Niue's foreign affairs and defense.[60]

The Cook Islands and Niue have each deposited with the UN Secretary-General ratification instruments for various multilateral treaties for which the UN Secretary-General is depositary and which are open only to states. The UN Secretary-General found both entities to be states but only after some consideration that led him to compose a lengthy notation on the point in *Multilateral Treaties Deposited with the Secretary-General*, a notation that reads as follows:

> Formerly administered by New Zealand, the Cook Islands and Niue currently have the status of self-governing States in free association with New Zealand.

The responsibility of the Cook Islands and Niue to conduct their own international relations and particularly to conclude treaties has evolved substantially over the years. For a period of time it was considered that, in view of the fact that the Cook Islands and Niue, though self-governing, had entered into special relationships with New Zealand, which discharged the responsibilities for the external relations and defence of the Cook Islands and Niue at their request, it followed that the Cook Islands and Niue did not have their own treaty making capacity.

However, in 1984 an application by the Cook Islands for membership in the World Health Organization was approved by the World Health Assembly in accordance with its article 6, and the Cook Islands, in accordance with article 79, became a member upon deposit of an instrument of acceptance with the Secretary-General. In the circumstances, the Secretary-General felt that the question of the status, as a State, of the Cook Islands, had been duly decided in the affirmative by the World Heath Assembly, whose membership was fully representative of the international community.

On the basis of the Cook Islands' membership in the World Health Organization, and of its subsequent admittance to other specialized agencies (Food and Agriculture Organization in 1985, United Nations Educational, Scientific and Cultural Organization in 1985 and the International Civil Aviation Organization in 1986) as a full member without any specifications or limitations, the Secretary-General considered that the Cook Islands could participate in a treaty in its own right as a State. Consequently, the Cook Islands signed the United Nations Framework Convention on Climate Change and the Convention on Biological Diversity in 1992.

The same solution was adopted by the Secretary General following the approval of Niue's application for membership in the United Nations Educational, Scientific and Cultural Organization UNESCO in 1993 and of the World Health Organization in 1994.

As a result of these developments, the Secretary-General, as depositary of multilateral treaties, recognized the full treaty-making capacity of the Cook Islands in 1992 and of Niue in 1994.[61]

The Secretary-General thus accepted the ratifications as emanating from representatives of states. The Secretary-General evidently did not read the criterion of having a population to mean that the members of the population must be citizens of the entity. Nor did he read the criterion of a capacity to enter into foreign relations to require the actual exercise of foreign relations.

ACTUAL STANDARD OF STATEHOOD
AS APPLIED TO PALESTINE

This brief survey – other examples could be related – suggests that an entity with only a handful of inhabitants can be a state, even if it has no citizenship for them. An entity can be a state with next to no territory. An entity can be a state even if another state controls it in significant ways. This result hardly seems compatible with the Montevideo criteria. Yet it must be taken into account if one is seeking to determine how statehood is defined at the international level. The criteria that states purport to follow are less significant than the criteria they actually follow.

By the standards actually followed in the international community, Palestine would seem to meet the criteria for statehood, even considering the powers exercised by Israel as belligerent occupant. Palestine's population and its territory are both large in comparison to those of the microstates. Palestine has a citizenship. Palestine exercises considerable control over domestic and foreign policy, despite the constraints imposed on it.

The USSR, which, as has been seen, had denounced the United States' Compacts of Free Association, ultimately voted in favor of the admission of the Federated States of Micronesia and the Marshall Islands to the United States, despite its reservations about their subjection to the United States. The Soviet representative, Valentin Lozinsky, was quoted at the time as saying of the Soviet vote that "there were no states with unlimited sovereignty in the world now."[62]

What Lozinsky apparently had in mind was that, beyond microstates and failed states, all states face serious limitations on their freedom of action. Avoiding economic crisis and keeping the planet habitable have emerged in recent decades as issues that states are unable to handle in isolation. States have formed themselves into economic units at the international level. They have agreed on standards for domestic industry. They have limited themselves in ways that would have been unimaginable to government leaders of earlier times.

One can say, of course, that states limit themselves by an act of free will, that they choose to cede elements of their power in order to obtain a greater advantage. That model of international interaction is increasingly out-of-date, however. In today's world, states are not in a position to stand aloof and maintain total control over their affairs. They cannot exist without ceding significant areas of control to regional groupings or to universal organizations of states. As Elihu Lauterpacht has written,

No longer is it possible to suggest that such limitations are marginal or incidental. And because these limitations affect states in their most vital interests, the notion of sovereignty – in the comprehensive sense of a plenitude of power remaining within the uncontrolled discretion of states – has been significantly eroded.[63]

The states of Europe are no longer free to decide what unit of measure they will use or whether to employ capital punishment. All states are constrained by international human rights standards to treat individuals in certain ways.[64]

Lauterpacht notes that the serious inroads on the autonomy of states does not derogate from their status as states. He says that "these limitations, extensive though they may be, operate without diminishing the legal quality of statehood of the states involved."[65] The Montevideo criteria must be read in light of the realities of the modern age, and in light of the actual practice of states.

Implications of Palestine Statehood

Palestine presents one of the more curious episodes in state formation. Although it is an ancient land, its modern statehood was devised around a conference table far from its shores.

The Ottoman territories had a particular claim to status because their populations had cooperated with France and Britain during the Great War. They had formed armies that bore the burdens of war, attacking from within. Britain and France would not keep the Ottoman lands as colonies, but neither would they be forced to grant them immediate independence. They would not reap the customary spoils of war, but neither would they sail off emptyhanded into the sunset.

The refusal of immediate freedom was tempered by a promise that it would come soon. Europe would be in control but only for a time. Oversight of the mandatories would be provided by the League of Nations, even if the overseers – the members of the Permanent Mandates Commission – were drawn from Europe rather than from the protected populations.

The mandate system was the uneasy compromise. The Versailles conferees decreed that the peoples of the Ottoman territories were "not yet able to stand by themselves." The populations of these territories did not necessarily share that view. They fought the mandate system with both the pen and the sword.

For the population of Palestine – at least for its majority population – the mandate system was particularly intolerable. Not only would a European state administer in Palestine, but it would promote a Jewish national home there. That project would take the administration of Palestine in a direction that differed from that of the other Class A mandates.

For all its peculiarities, the immediate status devised for the Class A mandates was statehood, albeit without independence. The League of Nations established a type of state with specific features that had not previously been seen. Yet, it was a type of state not wholly outside the concept of statehood as it was then conceived. The European powers had exercised control in non-European areas in a variety of legal forms, often involving a duty to benefit the local population. Indeed, what the British called the "white man's burden" and the French called their *"mission civiliatrise"* informed the stated rationale for colonialism as it developed in the nineteenth century. The mandate system took the rationale one step farther.

Palestine, under "tutelage," had the capacities of a state, even as the exercise of those capacities rested with Great Britain as the mandatory power. As Britain withdrew from Palestine after World War II, the international community, through Article 80 of the UN Charter, preserved rights that had been accorded under mandate, including the statehood of Palestine. Palestine statehood was not renounced, nor was it extinguished. Egypt and Jordan protected sectors of Palestine. The League of Arab States assumed an ancillary role in preserving Palestine statehood.

The international community continued to regard Palestine as a state, as it had during the mandate period. The United Nations dealt with the "Question of Palestine" as the issue to be resolved. When a movement formed in the 1960s to put administration back into Palestinian hands, the international community welcomed it with open arms. It recognized the organization that sought independence for Palestine. It promoted a multilateral process for resolving the situation between Israel and Palestine. When a bilateral process was urged by the United States in the 1990s, and negotiations between Palestine and Israel became a possibility, the international community urged an accommodation in ways that presumed that Palestine was a state.

IMPLICATIONS FOR PEACE NEGOTIATIONS

Palestine statehood has important implications for Palestine's future and for the course of peace efforts. On May 11, 2009, Bruno Stagno Ugarte, Foreign Minister of Costa Rica, spoke at a Security Council session at which the Palestine-Israel conflict was under discussion. Stagno Ugarte referred to the fact that Costa Rica had recognized Palestine on February 5, 2008. He called on states that had not already done so to do likewise.

He explained why he thought recognition mattered: "It is time for the international community ... to recognize the existence of two States," he said, "and to support a final, peaceful solution to a situation that has already generated far too much intolerance and violence and which urgently requires closure in keeping with the best interests of the parties." The recognitions he was urging would, he said, place Palestine "in a position of greater symmetry vis-à-vis other parties to the conflict."[1]

The Dominican Republic made a similar point when it announced on July 14, 2009 that it was establishing diplomatic relations with Palestine. President Leonel Fernandez said that Dominican Republic relations with Palestine would strike a "diplomatic balance," since the Dominican Republic had previously opened relations with Israel.[2] As these diplomats of Costa Rica and the Dominican Republic made clear, the issue of Palestine statehood has consequences for possible routes to a resolution of the Israel-Palestine conflict. Palestine statehood puts Palestine in a status equal to that of Israel.

Palestine statehood removes the leverage Israel seeks to exercise over Palestine in negotiations. Israel has set parameters for a negotiated settlement that fall far below the minimum that the international community has regarded as permissible. Israel seeks to reserve for itself the right to grant Palestine statehood in order to gain concessions from the Palestinian side.

THE UNITED NATIONS

Further enhancement of Palestine's status, in particular, admission to the United Nations, would position it even better to navigate the tortuous terrain of diplomacy. As a state, Palestine qualifies for membership in the United Nations. The reason it has been denied membership to date is unrelated to its satisfaction of the statehood criterion. Were the United States to change its position on Palestine admission, the remaining holdout states would likely fall in line.

Membership in the United Nations would bring Palestine more fully into the international system. As a UN member state, it could put itself forward as a candidate for membership on the Security Council or the Human Rights Council.

UN membership would not only afford greater opportunity to engage diplomatically. It would also entail greater accountability. The Human Rights Council conducts a review every four years of the human rights practices of each UN member state.[3] Palestine would become subject to this procedure. At present, Israel is subject to it, but Palestine is not. Palestine would be required to present a self-study report on human rights and would be cross-examined about it in Geneva. Other states, as well as human rights organizations, could present negative information, which Palestine would then have to address.

As a UN member state, Palestine would automatically become party to the Statute of the International Court of Justice. Here, too, Palestine would be afforded opportunities to gain enforcement of its rights by bringing claims against other states but might at the same time face suits brought by other states for violating international obligations.[4]

TREATIES AND SPECIALIZED UN AGENCIES

Multilateral treaties provide another mechanism whereby states more fully integrate themselves into the international system. Palestine to date has been allowed to ratify only a very few multilateral treaties. It has a coast on the eastern Mediterranean, but Palestine is one of the few coastal states that is not party to the United Nations Convention on the Law of the Sea. The Convention helps these states protect their off-shore areas for fisheries, for mining, and for protection of the environment.

Palestine, as indicated, attempted in 1989 to ratify the four Geneva conventions of 1949 on warfare. Given the volatility of Palestine's situation, particularly in its relations with Israel, participation in these conventions would enhance its ability to secure rights for combatants and for civilians affected by the hostilities. At the same time, these conventions would impose on Palestine greater accountability in its own treatment of both combatants and civilians.

Beyond maritime and military matters, a broad array of issues could usefully be addressed by Palestine's participation in multilateral treaties. The World Heritage Convention provides mechanisms for the protection of cultural property. Given its historical origins, Palestine is rich in ancient sites, many of which are deteriorating. Yet such sites qualify for international protection only if the state in whose territory they are found is a party to the World Heritage Convention.[5] The World Heritage Convention falls under the auspices of UNESCO, which engages in a spectrum of activities relating to educational, scientific, and cultural matters. Palestine is an observer at UNESCO. Under the terms of the World Heritage Convention, UNESCO membership qualifies a state to adhere to the Convention.[6] Palestine, it will be recalled, applied unsuccessfully for UNESCO membership in 1989.

Similarly, the World Health Organization, to which Palestine also applied unsuccessfully in 1989, promotes public health initiatives. Palestine is in dire need on the health front. Participation as a member state of the UN Food and Agriculture Organization would bring greater international attention to the dismal state of Palestine's agriculture, devastated after years of loss of agricultural land to Israeli settlements and road construction. As the twentieth century turned into the twenty-first, the international community treated Palestine in many contexts as a state, but without accepting it into international organizations as one would expect if it were on a par with the states enjoying independence.

CONSEQUENCES FOR PALESTINE

For Palestine, one feature of its statehood is that the statehood need not be converted into independence if some other path is freely chosen. Association with another state is one option. A state is free to merge with another state so long as the other consents. The UN General Assembly posed "free association" with another state as one way in which self-determination can be realized.[7] Palestine statehood therefore does not prejudice any particular final status arrangement. Palestine could affiliate with Jordan or with Israel, or it could remain on its own. In the early years of the present century, a possible affiliation with Israel was proposed by many Palestinian political analysts. They were concerned that Israel's terms for an independent Palestine state were so onerous as to render independence ephemeral, and that therefore a single state in the territory of mandate-era Palestine was preferable. Even the lead PLO negotiator, Saeb Erekat, opened the possibility in 2009 that the PLO might advocate merger with Israel. Erekat said that Israel's continued expansion of settlements in the West Bank might make it impossible to gain an acceptable independent Palestine state.[8]

One factor inclining Palestinian analysts toward "one state" was a belief that it would undercut an Israeli objection to repatriating the Palestine Arabs displaced in 1948. Israeli officials argued that if an independent Palestine state were established, the displaced should go there, rather than to their home areas in Israel. If, instead, "one state" were set up, this objection would lose its force. Even if an independent Palestine were to come into being, however, the matter of repatriation relates to a right to return to home areas; hence, it is not negated by an independent Palestine. The international position that Israel must repatriate the displaced Palestine Arabs is unrelated to territorial arrangements.

An objection is sometimes raised in the discussion of Palestine statehood that a Palestine state in Gaza and the West Bank is not economically viable. That issue, too, is irrelevant to whether or not Palestine is a state. While economic viability needs to be assured, statehood does not depend on it.

PALESTINE STATEHOOD AND THE WAY FORWARD

States cannot, over a period of years, proclaim that they will recognize Palestine when and if it comes to terms with Israel without creating the inference that they regard Palestine as a state. Those states that say that Palestine should become a state only by negotiations with Israel at the same time ask Palestine to negotiate borders. Their position is self-contradictory. Their aim of pressuring Palestine to make concessions prompts them to decline to recognize it as a state absent agreement with Israel, yet their demand that Palestine negotiate borders implies Palestine statehood. Moreover, these same states, in a myriad of ways, deal with Palestine as a state when it comes to practical issues. They make agreements with it, either explicitly on the basis of Palestine statehood or under verbal formulas aimed at disguising their acknowledgment of Palestine statehood. Within the context of the United Nations, they grant it privileges that attach only to states because Palestine's status logically requires such privileges.

The view that Palestine is not a state suffers from four errors. It disregards historical facts that show Palestine statehood dating from the mandate period. It applies criteria for Palestine statehood that are more stringent than those actually followed in the international community. It fails to account for the fact that Palestine's territory is under belligerent occupation. It fails to account for facts showing the implied recognition of Palestine.

Palestine should be brought into the community of nations as a full-fledged citizen. Given that microstates are admitted as members of interstate organizations, it is anomalous that Palestine is not similarly admitted. The international community purports to operate on the basis of principle, but the differential treatment that international organizations accord Palestine shows that they are constrained by other considerations. The very aims of peace and stability that the international community poses as its objectives would be served by following through on the logical implications of Palestine's statehood.

Notes

CHAPTER 1

Where works are cited in abbreviated form, full citations will be found earlier, in the notes to the given chapter.

1 James Crawford, Israel (1948–1949) and Palestine (1998–1999): Two Studies in the Creation of States, in Guy S. Goodwin-Gill and Stefan Talmon, eds., *The Reality of International Law: Essays in Honour of Ian Brownlie* (Oxford: Clarendon Press 1999), 95.

2 David Raič, *Statehood and the Law of Self-Determination* (Hague: Kluwer 2002), at 21–25.

3 Stephen D. Krasner, Rethinking the Sovereign State Model, in Michael Cox, Ken Booth and Tim Dunne, eds., *Empires, Systems, and States: Great Transformations in International Politics* (Cambridge: Cambridge University Press 2001), at 17.

4 Jean Bodin, *De la République, traité de Jean Bodin, ou traité de gouvernement* (Paris: Quillau 1756, orig. pub'd 1583), at 266.

5 Krasner, at 18.

6 United Nations Convention on the Law of the Sea, Art. 56, 10 December 1982, 1833 UNTS 3.

7 Ruth Lapidoth, Autonomy and Sovereignty – Are They Mutually Exclusive, in Amos Shapira and Mala Tabory, eds., *New Political Entities in Public and Private International Law: With Special Reference to the Palestinian Entity* (Hague: Kluwer Law International 1999), 3, at 11.

8 United Nations Convention on the Law of the Sea, Art. 62.

9 James Crawford, *The Creation of States in International Law* (Oxford: Clarendon Press 2006), at 33.

10 John Quigley, *Palestine and Israel: A Challenge to Justice* (Durham: Duke University Press 1990).

11 John Quigley, *The Case for Palestine: An International Law Perspective* (Durham: Duke University Press 2005).

CHAPTER 2

1 Division of Near Eastern Affairs, Department of State, *Mandate for Palestine* (Washington: U.S. Government Printing Office 1927), at 3–4.
2 Correspondence between Sir Henry McMahon and the Sherif Hussein of Mecca July 1915–March 1916, Cmd. 5957, at 8.
3 UN Doc. A/C.1/PV.52, 9 May 1947, at 191 (statement of Henry Cattan, Arab Higher Committee).
4 Michael J. Cohen, *The Origins and Evolution of the Arab-Zionist Conflict* (Berkeley: University of California Press 1987), at 20–22.
5 Light on Britain's Palestine promise, *Times* (London), 17 April 1964, at 15.
6 Palestine: Memorandum by Middle East Department, Colonial Office, para. 5, C.P. 21 (24), 12 February 1924, Secret, CAB/24/165.
7 White Paper: British Policy in Palestine, 3 June 1922, Cmd. 1700. Cohen, at 20.
8 Victor Kattan, *From Coexistence to Conquest: International Law and the Origins of the Arab-Israeli Conflict, 1891–1949* (New York: Pluto Press 2009), at 46–47.
9 Ameen Rihani, Palestine and the Proposed Arab Federation, *Annals of the American Academy of Political and Social Science*, vol. 164, 62, at 66 (1932).
10 *Mandate for Palestine*, at 5.
11 Sykes-Picot Treaty, available on the United Nations "Unispal" site: http://domino.un.org/unispal.NSF/0145a8233e14d2b585256cbf005af141/232358bacbeb7b55852571100078477c!OpenDocument
12 Sir Edward Grey to Count Benckendorff, Russian Ambassador in London, 23 May 1916, *Documents on British Foreign Policy 1919–1939*, First Series, vol. 4 (London: Her Majesty's Stationery Office 1952), at 247.
13 United Nations, Division of Palestinian Rights, *The Origins and Evolution of the Palestine Problem: 1917–1988* (New York: United Nations 1990), at 4.
14 Palestine and the Balfour Declaration: History of the Negotiations leading up to the Balfour Declaration of November 2, 1917, at 2, C.P. 60 (23), 23 January 1923, Secret, CAB 24/158. Esco Foundation for Palestine, *Palestine: A Study of Jewish, Arab, and British Policies* (New Haven: Yale University Press 1947), at 83–84. Doreen Ingrams, *Palestine Papers 1917–1922: Seeds of Conflict* (London: John Murray 1970), at 7.
15 Palestine and the Balfour Declaration: History of the Negotiations leading up to the Balfour Declaration of November 2, 1917, at 2, C.P. 60 (23), 23 January 1923, Secret, CAB 24/158.
16 Ingrams, at 173.
17 Palestine: Memorandum by Middle East Department, Colonial Office, para. 3, C.P. 21 (24), 12 February 1924, Secret, CAB/24/165.
18 Aharon Cohen, *Israel and the Arab World* (New York: Funk and Wagnalls 1970), at 124.
19 *Mandate for Palestine*, at 5.
20 V.I. Lenin, Imperialism the Highest Stage of Capitalism, in Robert C. Tucker, ed., *The Lenin Anthology* (New York: Norton 1975).

21 Robert J.C. Young, *Postcolonialism: An Historical Introduction* (Oxford: Blackwell 2001), at 125.

22 Decree on Peace, *Collected Laws of the Russian Soviet Federated Socialist Republic*, no. 1, item 2 (1917).

23 Jane Degras, ed., *Soviet Documents on Foreign Policy* (London: Oxford University Press 1951), vol. 1, at 8–9. F. Seymour Cocks, *The Secret Treaties and Understandings: Text of the Available Documents* (London: Union of Democratic Control 1918), at 11.

24 Cocks, at 47.

25 Antony Anghie, *Imperialism, Sovereignty and the Making of International Law* (Cambridge: Cambridge University Press 2004), at 139. Hersch Lauterpacht, The Mandate under International Law in the Covenant of the League of Nations, in Elihu Lauterpacht, ed., *International Law: Being the Collected Papers of Hersch Lauterpacht* (Cambridge: Cambridge University Press 1977), vol. 3, 29, at 32.

26 *President Wilson's State Papers and Addresses* (New York: Review of Reviews Co. 1918), at 468–470.

27 David Hunter Miller, *The Drafting of the Covenant* (New York: Putnam 1928), vol. 1, at 104.

28 J.A. Hobson, *Imperialism: A Study* (London: James Nisbet 1902).

29 Antony Anghie, Colonialism and the Birth of International Institutions: Sovereignty, Economy, and the Mandate System of the League of Nations, *New York University Journal of International Law and Politics*, vol. 34, 513, at 551–553 (2002).

30 Ingrams, at 24.

31 George Antonius, *The Arab Awakening: The Story of the Arab National Movement* (Beirut: Khayats 1938), at 433–434. John Norton Moore, *The Arab-Israeli Conflict: Readings and Documents* (Princeton: Princeton University Press 1974), vol. 3, at 36.

32 Parliamentary Debates, House of Commons, 5th Series, vol. 145, at 36 (1921).

33 Note, *Documents on British Foreign Policy 1919–1939*, First Series, vol. 4 (London: Her Majesty's Stationery Office 1952), at 251.

34 Muhammad Y. Muslih, *The Origins of Palestinian Nationalism* (New York: Columbia University Press 1988), at 178–190.

CHAPTER 3

1 *The League of Nations: A Practical Suggestion* (Smuts Plan), 16 December 1918, in David Hunter Miller, *The Drafting of the Covenant* (New York: Putnam 1928), vol. 2, at 27.

2 Ibid. at 28.

3 Ibid. at 27.

4 Ibid. at 29.

5 Ibid. at 29.

6 Ibid. at 31.

7 Ibid. at 32.

8 Ibid. at 32.

9 Pitman B. Potter, Origin of the System of Mandates under the League of Nations, *American Political Science Review*, vol. 16, 563 (1922).

10 J.A. Hobson, The Open Door, in C.R. Buxton, ed., *Toward a Lasting Settlement* (New York: Macmillan 1916), 87, at 106. See also J.A. Hobson, *Toward International Government* (London: George Allen & Unwin 1915), at 138–141.

11 Hersch Lauterpacht, The Mandate under International Law in the Covenant of the League of Nations, in Elihu Lauterpacht, ed., *International Law: Being the Collected Papers of Hersch Lauterpacht* (Cambridge: Cambridge University Press 1977), vol. 3, 29, at 40. Lauterpacht wrote this dissertation in German. The English in the quoted passages is not Lauterpacht's, but a translator's.

12 Smuts Plan at 34.

13 David Hunter Miller, *The Drafting of the Covenant* (New York: Putnam 1928), vol. 1, at 106–107. League of Nations, Secretariat, *The Mandates System: Origin, Principles, Application* (Geneva: League of Nations 1945), at 18.

14 Miller, vol. 1, at 106.

15 *Foreign Relations of the United States: Paris Peace Conference 1919* (Washington: U.S. Government Printing Office 1943), vol. 3, at 795–796. See also Miller, vol. 1, at 109–110.

16 Miller, vol. 1, at 110.

17 Constitution of the International Labor Organization, in Treaty of Peace with Germany (Treaty of Versailles), 28 June 1919, part 13, U.S. Congress, Statutes at Large, vol. 49, at 2712.

18 League of Nations, Covenant, Art. 22.

19 League of Nations, Secretariat, *The Mandates System: Origin, Principles, Application* (Geneva: League of Nations 1945), at 20, 24.

20 Ibid. at 20. Division of Near Eastern Affairs, Department of State, *Mandate for Palestine* (Washington: U.S. Government Printing Office 1927), at 12.

21 Miller, vol. 1, at 116.

22 James Crawford, Israel (1948–1949) and Palestine (1998–1999): Two Studies in the Creation of States, in Guy S. Goodwin-Gill and Stefan Talmon, eds., *The Reality of International Law: Essays in Honour of Ian Brownlie* (Oxford: Clarendon Press 1999), 95, at 118.

23 Doreen Ingrams, *Palestine Papers 1917–1922: Seeds of Conflict* (London: John Murray 1970), at 73.

24 H. Duncan Hall, *Mandates, Dependencies and Trusteeship* (London: Stevens & Sons 1948), at 80.

25 D.P. O'Connell, *The Law of State Succession* (Cambridge: Cambridge University Press 1956), at 46.

26 UN Security Council, 301st meeting, UN Doc. S/PV.301, 22 May 1948, at 21.

27 Shabtai Rosenne, The Effect of Change of Sovereignty Upon Municipal Law, *British Year Book of International Law*, vol. 27, 267, at 271 (1950).

28 *Antoine Bey Sabbagh v. Mohamed Pacha Ahmed and Others*, Mixed Court of Mansura, Egypt, 15 November 1927, *Annual Digest of Public International Law Cases 1927–1928*, at 48–49.

29 *Ungar v. Palestine Liberation Organization*, 402 F.3d 274 (1st Cir. 2005).

30 Resolutions of the General Syrian Congress, Damascus, 2 July 1919, in Antonius, at 440; also (translation varies) in *Foreign Relations of the United States: Paris Peace Conference 1919*, vol. 12, Report of the King-Crane Commission, at 780–781 (1947).

31 *Foreign Relations of the United States: Paris Peace Conference 1919*, vol. 12, Report of the King-Crane Commission, at 794–796 (1947).

32 Ingrams, at 90. Anne-Lucie Chaigne-Oudin, *La France et les rivalités occidentales au Levant: Syrie-Liban 1918–1939* (Paris: L'Harmattan 2006), at 80.

33 Ingrams, at 95.

34 Letter from Mr. Samuel to Earl Curzon, 2 April 1920, Enclosure: Syria, Palestine, Mesopotamia and the Arabian States, *Documents on British Foreign Policy 1919–1939*, First Series, vol. 13 (London: Her Majesty's Stationery Office 1963), at 244–245.

35 British Secretary's Notes of a Meeting of the Supreme Council, held at the Villa Devachan, San Remo, on Sunday, April 25, 1920, at 11 a.m., *Documents on British Foreign Policy 1919–1939*, First Series, vol. 8 (London: Her Majesty's Stationery Office 1958), at 176–177. The final clause was rendered in French, but is here translated by the author.

36 Earl Curzon (San Remo) to Lord Hardinge, 26 April 1920, *Documents on British Foreign Policy 1919–1939*, First Series, vol. 13 (London: Her Majesty's Stationery Office 1963), at 251.

37 King George's Message to the People of Palestine, read by the High Commissioner at the government House on July 7, 1920, reprinted in Max M. Laserson, *On the Mandate: Documents, Statements, Law and Judgments Relating to and Arising from the Mandate for Palestine* (Tel Aviv: Igereth 1937), at 33.

38 *Mandate for Palestine*, at 21–22.

39 Albert M. Hyamson, *Palestine under the Mandate 1920–1948* (London: Methuen & Co. 1950), at 35.

40 Chaigne-Oudin, at 82.

CHAPTER 4

1 Treaty of Peace between the Allied Powers and Turkey, Sèvres, 10 August 1920, British Treaty Series No. 11 (1920), reprinted in *American Journal of International Law*, vol. 15 (Supplement), at 179 (1921).

2 Jacob Stoyanovsky, *The Mandate for Palestine* (London: Longmans, 1928), at 233.

3 Turkey, Law of Nationality, 19 January 1869, translated in Richard W. Flournoy, Jr., and Manley O. Hudson, eds., *A Collection of Nationality Laws of Various Countries as Contained in Constitutions, Statutes and Treaties* (New York: Oxford University Press 1929), at 568–569.

4 Constitution of the Permanent Mandates Commission, approved by the Council on November 29th, 1920, League of Nations, *Official Journal*, vol. 1, no. 8 (November-December 1920), at 87–88.

5 Convention between Great Britain and France for the settlement of certain points connected with the Mandates for Syria and the Lebanon, Palestine and Mesopotamia, Art. 1, 23 December 1920, 22 LNTS 354.

6 Mandates A: Memorandum by the Secretary of State for Foreign Affairs. Printed for the Cabinet, C.P. 2197, 30 November 1920, Secret, CAB/24/115.

7 Ibid.

8 Ibid.

9 *Draft Mandates for Mesopotamia and Palestine as Submitted for the Approval of the League of Nations*: Draft of the Mandate for Palestine as submitted by Mr. Balfour on December 7, 1920, to the Secretariat-General of the League of Nations for the approval of the Council of the League of Nations, Cmd. 1176. Text of Art. 1 is identical in *Final Drafts of the Mandates for Mesopotamia and Palestine for the Approval of the council of the League of Nations (presented to Parliament by Command of His Majesty, August, 1921)*: Final Draft of the Mandate for Palestine for the Approval of the Council of the League of Nations, Cmd. 1500.

10 Stoyanovsky, at 163.

11 Letter from the President of the Third Palestinian Arab Congress (Moussa Kazem El-Hussaini) to the President of the League of Nations, 1 April 1921. Annex: Report on the State of Palestine Presented to the Right Honourable Mr. Winston Churchill, P.C., M.P., by the Executive Committee of the Third Arab Palestine Congress 28 March 1921, League of Nations, *Official Journal*, vol. 2, no. 4, 331, at 333. See also Doreen Ingrams, *Palestine Papers 1917–1922: Seeds of Conflict* (London: John Murray 1970), at 118.

12 Ingrams, at 119–120.

13 Ibid. at 121–123.

14 Palestine: Memorandum by the Secretary of State for the Colonies, C.P. 3213, 11 August 1921, Secret, CAB 24/127.

15 Sahar Huneidi, *A Broken Trust: Herbert Samuel, Zionism, and the Palestinians 1920–1925* (London: I.B. Tauris 2001), at 149–155.

16 Ingrams, at 143–145.

17 Christopher Sykes, *Cross Roads to Israel* (London: Collins 1965), at 82.

18 Ingrams, at 148.

19 Ibid. at 170.

20 Rapport de M. Henri Rolin sur les mandats internationaux, *Annuaire de l'Institut de droit international*, vol. 34(1), 33, at 36 (1928).

21 Mandate for Palestine, League of Nations, *Official Journal*, vol. 3, no. 8, at 1007 (1922). Also in 22 LNTS 354, and in *Terms of League of Nations Mandates: Republished by the United Nations*, UN Doc. A/70 (1946).

22 Treaty of Peace, Lausanne, 24 July 1923, 28 LNTS 11.

23 James Crawford, Israel (1948–1949) and Palestine (1998–1999): Two Studies in the Creation of States, in Guy S. Goodwin-Gill and Stefan Talmon, eds., *The Reality of International Law: Essays in Honour of Ian Brownlie*

(Oxford: Clarendon Press 1999), 95, at 98. Shabtai Rosenne, The Effect of Change of Sovereignty Upon Municipal Law, *British Year Book of International Law*, vol. 27, 267, at 271 (1950).

24 Stoyanovsky, at 233. To the same effect, see S.D. Myres, Jr., Constitutional Aspects of the Mandate for Palestine, *Annals of the American Academy of Political and Social Science*, vol. 164, 1, at 4 (1932).

25 Ibid. at 264.

26 Albert Millot, *Les Mandats Internationaux: étude sur l'application de l'Article 22 du Pacte de la Société des Nations* (Paris: Larose 1924), at 92.

27 *Antoine Bey Sabbagh v. Mohamed Pacha Ahmed and Others*, Mixed Court of Mansura, Egypt, 15 November 1927, *Annual Digest of Public International Law Cases 1927–1928*, at 48–49.

28 *King v. Ketter*, [1940] 1 K.B. 787, at 789–790.

29 Georg Schwarzenberg, British and Palestinian Nationalities (Notes of Cases), *Modern Law Review*, vol. 3, 164 (1939).

CHAPTER 5

1 Jacob Stoyanovsky, *The Mandate for Palestine* (London: Longmans 1928), at 36.

2 Phebe Marr, *The Modern History of Iraq* (Cambridge MA: Westview 2004) at 25. Hubert Young, *The Independent Arab* (London: John Murray 1933) at 326.

3 Green Hackworth, *Digest of International Law* (Washington: U.S. Government Printing Office 1940), vol. 1, at 117. Aaron M. Margalith, *The International Mandates* (Baltimore: Johns Hopkins Press 1930), at 134.

4 Marr, at 26.

5 Treaty of Alliance, Baghdad, 10 October 1922, ratifications exchanged at Baghdad, 19 December 1924, 35 LNTS 14.

6 Norman Bentwich, *The Mandates System* (London: Longmans 1930), at 66.

7 British Mandate for Iraq: Adoption of the Draft Instrument submitted by the British Government, 27 September 1924, League of Nations, *Official Journal*, vol. 5, no. 10, at 1346–1347 (October 1924). Bentwich (*The Mandates System*), at 55–57.

8 Margalith, at 134. Bentwich (*The Mandates System*), at 59–65.

9 Syria Mandate, League of Nations, *Official Journal*, vol. 3, no. 8, at 1013 (1922). Also in 22 LNTS 354, and in *Terms of League of Nations Mandates: Republished by the United Nations*, UN Doc. A/70 (1946).

10 Margalith, at 136. Bentwich (*The Mandates System*), at 73.

11 Bentwich (*The Mandates System*), at 80 (quoting Constitution Art. 91).

12 Ibid. at 72.

13 Ibid. at 81.

14 *In re Caussèque and Cot*, Conseil d'Etat, 11 October 1929, *Annual Digest of Public International Law Cases 1929–1930*, at 30–31.

15 International Telecommunication Convention, 9 December 1932, 151 LNTS 5, ratified by Lebanon and by Syria, 22 May 1934.

16 *States of the Levant under French Mandate v. Egypt*, in *United Nations Reports of International Arbitral Awards*, vol. 3, at 1871 (reprint 1997), translated as Arbitral Decision, *American Journal of International Law*, vol. 37, 341 (1943).

17 *Shehadeh v. Commissioner of Prisons, Jerusalem*, in *International Law Reports 1947*, vol. 14, 42–43 (1951).

18 Mandate for Palestine, League of Nations, *Official Journal*, vol. 3, no. 8, at 1007 (1922). Also in 22 LNTS 354, and in *Terms of League of Nations Mandates: Republished by the United Nations*, UN Doc. A/70 (1946).

19 League of Nations, Council, 8th meeting, 16 September 1922, Minutes of the Twenty-first Session of the Council held at Geneva from Thursday, August 31st, to Wednesday, October 4th, 1922, *Official Journal*, vol. 3, at 1188–1189 (1922).

20 As written by Sir Herbert Samuel in his report on the administration of Palestine for 1920–1925, as reprinted in Division of Near Eastern Affairs, U.S. Department of State, *The Palestine Mandate: Collected United States documents relating to the League of Nations Mandate for Palestine, to the possible future independence of Palestine and to the need for the creation of a separate Jewish state* (Documentary Publications, Salisbury NC 1977) at 23–24 (orig. pub'd as *Mandate for Palestine*, U.S. Government Printing Office, Washington, DC 1927).

21 Philip Robins, *A History of Jordan* (New York: Cambridge University Press 2004), at 28–29.

22 Henri Rolin, La pratique des mandats internationaux, *Recueil des cours* (Hague Academy of International Law), vol. 19, 530 (1927-IV). The author is Henri A. Rolin (1891–1973).

23 Agreement between His Britannic Majesty and the Amir of Transjordan, 20 February 1928, Cmd. 3488. Also as Agreement: The United Kingdom and Transjordan, 20 February 1928, J.C. Hurewitz, *Diplomacy in the Near and Middle East: A Documentary Record: 1914–1956* (Princeton: Nostrand 1956), vol. 2, at 156. And as Agreement Between the United Kingdom and Trans-Jordan, 20 February 1928, in Ma'an Abu Nowar, *The History of the Hashemite Kingdom of Jordan* (Oxford: Ithaca Press 1989), vol. 1 at 285.

24 Ibid., Art. 2.

25 Ibid., Arts. 5, 6, 9, 17.

26 Ibid., Art. 7.

27 Ibid. Art. 8.

28 League of Nations, Council, 3rd meeting, 1 September 1928, Minutes of the Fifty-first Session of the Council held at Geneva from Thursday, August 30th, to Saturday, September 8th, 1928, *Official Journal*, vol. 9, at 1452 (1928).

29 Ibid. at 1453.

30 Quincy Wright, *Mandates under the League of Nations* (Chicago: University of Chicago Press 1930), at 409.

31 Max M. Laserson, *On the Mandate: Documents, Statements, Law and Judgments Relating to and Arising form the Mandate for* Palestine (Tel Aviv: Igereth 1937), at xxii.

32 Stoyanovsky, at 40–41.
33 *The League of Nations: A Practical Suggestion* (Smuts Plan), 16 December 1918, in David Hunter Miller, *The Drafting of the Covenant* (New York: Putnam 1928), vol. 2, at 27, at 29.
34 Rapport de M. Henri Rolin sur les mandats internationaux, *Annuaire de l'Institut de droit international*, vol. 34(1), 33, at 40–45 (1928). The rapporteur is Henri A. Rolin (1891–1973).
35 David Hunter Miller, *The Drafting of the Covenant* (New York: Putnam 1928), vol. 1, at 113.
36 League of Nations, 13th meeting, held at St. James's Palace, London, 24 July 1922, *Official Journal*, vol. 2, at 823 (1922).
37 Division of Near Eastern Affairs, U.S. Department of State, *The Palestine Mandate: Collected United States documents relating to the League of Nations Mandate for Palestine, to the possible future independence of Palestine and to the need for the creation of a separate Jewish state* (Documentary Publications, Salisbury NC 1977) at 12 (orig. pub'd as *Mandate for Palestine*, U.S. Government Printing Office, Washington, DC 1927).
38 Recognition of Successor States in Palestine, 13 May 1948, in Whiteman, *Digest of International Law*, vol. 1, at 225.
39 Hackworth, at 105.
40 Stoyanovsky, at 23.
41 League of Nations, Permanent Mandates Commission, Minutes of the Thirty-Second (Extraordinary) Session devoted to Palestine, held at Geneva from July 30th to August 18, 1937, including the Report of the Commission to the Council, 10th Meeting, 5 August 1937, 10 a.m., No. C.330.M.222.

CHAPTER 6

1 Palestine Order in Council, 1922 (10 August 1922), *Statutory Rules and Orders 1922, No. 1282*, Art. 46; also in Norman Bentwich, comp., *Legislation of Palestine 1918–1925* (Alexandria: Whitehead Morris Ltd. 1926), vol. 1, at 12.
2 Robert H. Eisenman, *Islamic Law in Palestine and Israel* (Leiden: E.J. Brill 1978), at 106–107.
3 Mogannam E. Mogannam, Palestine Legislation Under the British, *Annals of the American Academy of Political and Social Science*, vol. 164, 47, at 53 (1932). Anis F. Kassim. Legal Systems and Developments in Palestine, *Palestine Yearbook of International Law*, vol. 1, 19, at 23 (1984).
4 Edoardo Vitta, *The Conflict of Laws in Matters of Personal Status in Palestine* (Tel Aviv: S. Bursi 1947), at 11. Raja Shehadeh, *From Occupation to Interim Accords: Israel and the Palestinian Territories* (London: Kluwer 1997), at 76. Eisenman, at 106–151.
5 Kassim (Legal Systems and Developments in Palestine), at 24. *A Survey of Palestine: Prepared in December 1945 and January 1946 for the information of the Anglo-American Committee of Inquiry*, vol. 1, at 112 (Jerusalem: Government Printer 1946).

6 Lynn Welchman, *Beyond the Code: Muslim Family Law and the Shari'a Judiciary in the Palestinian West Bank* (Hague: Kluwer Law International 2000), at 16.

7 *Yearbook of the International Law Commission 1950*, vol. 2 (communication from Israel), at 208, UN Doc. A/CN.4/SER.A/1950/Add.1. Shabtai Rosenne, Israël et les traités internationaux de la Palestine, *Journal du droit international*, vol. 77, 1140, at 1147–1149 (1950). Mutaz Qafisheh, *The International Law Foundations of Palestinian Nationality: A Legal Examination of Nationality in Palestine under Britain's Rule* (Leiden: Martinus Nijhoff 2008), at 180.

8 Oliver Lissitzyn, Territorial Entities Other Than States in the Law of Treaties, *Recueil des Cours* (Hague Academy of International Law), vol. 125, 5, at 55–56 (1968-III).

9 International Agreement for the Establishment of an International Bureau of Intelligence on Locusts, 20 May 1926, 109 LNTS 121.

10 Parcel Post Agreement between Palestine and the United States of America, 10 May 1943 & 6 September 1944, 147 UNTS 109.

11 Agreement concerning the Exchange of Postal Parcels, 5 & 16 May 1929, 95 LNTS 395.

12 Agreement concerning the Exchange of Postal Parcels, 6 & 16 December 1931, 139 LNTS 59.

13 Agreement on the Exchange of Parcels by Parcel Post, 13 & 28 March 1936, 170 LNTS 145.

14 Agreement on the Exchange of Parcels by Parcel Post, 31 March & 19 June 1936, 172 LNTS 17.

15 Agreement with Egypt, 12 January 1929, 9 LNTS 96.

16 Provisional Agreement with regard to the Extradition of Fugitive Offenders (Egypt-Palestine), 7 August 1922, 36 LNTS 343.

17 Exchange of Notes constituting a Provisional Commercial Agreement (Egypt-Palestine), 6 & 21 June 1928, 80 LNTS 277.

18 Shabtai Rosenne, Israël et les traités internationaux de la Palestine, *Journal du droit international*, vol. 77, 1140, at 1147–1157 (1950).

19 Arnold McNair, *The Law of Treaties* (Oxford: Clarendon Press 1961), at 36.

20 Ibid. at 43.

21 13 LNTS 9.

22 Lassa Oppenheim, *International Law: A Treatise*, Arnold McNair, ed. (London: Longmans 1928), vol. 1, at 211.

23 P. Weis, *Nationality and Statelessness in International Law* (Alphen aan den Rijn: Sijthoff & Noordhoff 1979), at 3–5.

24 Palestinian Citizenship Order in Council, 1925, S.R. & O., no. 777, at 474; also in *Legislation of Palestine 1928–1925*, vol. 1, at 37. Norman Bentwich, Nationality in Mandated Territories Detached from Turkey, *British Year Book of International Law*, vol. 7, 97, at 102 (1926); and Mutaz Qafisheh, *The International Law Foundations of Palestinian Nationality: A Legal Examination of Nationality in Palestine under Britain's Rule* (Leiden: Martinus Nijhoff 2008), at 75–85. See also Shabtai Rosenne, The

Israel Nationality Law 5712–1952 and The Law of Return 5710–1950, *Journal du droit international*, vol. 81, 4, at 39 (1954).

25 Palestine, Passport Ordinance 1925, Ordinance No. 37 of 1925 (15 December 1925), in *Legislation of Palestine 1928–1925*, vol. 1, at 594. Qafisheh, at 146–153.

26 *Klausner v. Levy*, 83 F.Supp 599, 600 (U.S.Dist.Ct. E.D.Va. 1949). This court decided that Palestine was not a state, but only after indicating that it would consider as a state only an entity formally recognized as such by the United States.

27 League of Nations, Permanent Mandates Commission, Minutes of the Thirty-Second (Extraordinary) Session devoted to Palestine, held at Geneva from July 30th to August 18, 1937, including the Report of the Commission to the Council, Tenth Meeting, 5 August 1937, 10 a.m., No. C.330.M.222. Also quoted in Victor Kattan, *From Coexistence to Conquest: International Law and the Origins of the Arab-Israeli Conflict, 1891–1949* (New York: Pluto Press 2009), at 137.

28 Albert M. Hyamson, *Palestine under the Mandate 1920–1948* (London: Methuen & Co. 1950), at 73.

29 Palestinian Citizenship Order in Council, 1925, Art 7.

30 Norman Bentwich, Palestine Nationality and the Mandate, *Journal of Comparative Legislation and International Law*, vol. 21, 230, at 232 (1939).

31 Lassa Oppenheim, *International Law: A Treatise*, Hersch Lauterpacht, ed. (London: Longmans 1955), vol. 1, at 654.

32 Palestinian Citizenship Order in Council, 1925, Art 7.

33 Luke T. Lee and John Quigley, *Consular Law and Practice* (Oxford: Oxford University Press 2008), at 55–56.

34 Quincy Wright, *Mandates under the League of Nations* (Chicago: University of Chicago Press 1930).

35 *Re Ezra Goralshvili*, Supreme Court of Palestine, as quoted by Quincy Wright, Some Recent Cases on the Status of Mandated Areas, *American Journal of International Law*, vol. 20, at 771 (1926). Wright possessed the text of the decision. A summary, apparently based on a news report, was published in *Annual Digest of Public International Law Cases 1925–26*, at 47–48.

36 *Mills Music v. Cromwell Music*, 126 F.Supp. 54, 56 (U.S. Dist.Ct. S.D.N.Y. 1954).

37 *Saikaly v. Saikaly*, Mixed Court, Egypt, 15 December 1925, *Annual Digest of Public International Law Cases 1925–26*, at 48.

38 *Ismael L. Ghonnama v. Saleh J. Ibrahim*, in *Gazette des tribunaux mixtes*, December 1928, at 26; reprinted in *Journal du droit international*, vol. 57, 212 (1930).

39 Weis, at 21.

40 *King v. Ketter*, [1940] 1 K.B. 787, at 791.

41 Daniel C. Turack, *The Passport in International Law* (Lexington MA: D.C. Heath 1972), at 215.

42 *Annuaire de l'Institut de droit international,* vol. 36(2), at 48 (1931).

43 *Ottoman Public Debt Case* (1925), United Nations, *Reports of International Arbitral Awards,* vol. 1, at 609–610.

44 *Mavrommatis Jerusalem Concessions,* at 7, PCIJ, Series A, no. 5, 26 March 1925.

45 Ibid. at 31.

46 Ibid. at 32.

47 *Mavrommatis Palestine Concessions,* at 23, PCIJ, Series A, no. 2, 30 August 1924.

48 Wright (*Mandates under the League of Nations*), at 446.

49 *Mavrommatis Palestine Concessions,* at 32, PCIJ, Series A, no. 2, 30 August 1924.

50 Ibid. at 81 (Bustamante, J., dissenting).

51 United Kingdom, Import Duties Act, 1932, §1, 22 Geo. 5, c. 8.

52 Ibid., §5.

53 United Kingdom, Import Duties (Mandated Territories) Preference Order, 1932, No. 133, 17 March 1932, in *Statutory Rules and Orders and Statutory Instruments Revised to December 31, 1948* (London: His Majesty's Stationery Office 1950), vol. 5, at 490.

54 Meeting of the Cabinet to be held at No. 10, Downing Street, at 2, C.P. 25 (32), 27 April 1932, Secret, CAB/23/71.

55 Ibid. at 1.

56 Ibid. at 2.

57 Ibid. at 2.

58 House of Commons, Debates, 14 March 1932, vol. 263, c.13.

59 League of Nations, Permanent Mandates Commission, Minutes of the 22d session, held at Geneva, 11th meeting, 10 November 1922. League of Nations, Permanent Mandates Commission, Minutes of the 23d session, Geneva, 13th meeting, 27 June 1933.

60 A Convention to regulate the Commerce between the Territories of the United States and of his Britannick Majesty, Art. 2, 3 July 1815, U.S. Congress, Statutes at Large, vol. 8, at. 228.

61 British Tariff Hits 46% of Our Goods, *New York Times,* 6 February 1932, at 8.

62 New British Tariff Held a Blow to US, *New York Times,* 29 February 1932, at 2.

63 The British Ambassador (Lindsay) to the Secretary of State, Washington, 15 July 1932, Doc. 641.67n3/2, in *Foreign Relations of the United States 1932* (Washington: U.S. Government Printing Office 1947), vol. 2, at 29.

64 The Secretary of State to the British Chargé (Osborne), Washington, 27 August 1932, Doc. 641.67n3/11, ibid. at 32. Also in Imperial Preference for Palestine: Memorandum by the Secretary of State for the Colonies, C.P. 333 (32), 7 October 1932, Secret, CAB/24/233. Referenced in Green Hackworth, *Digest of International Law* (Washington: U.S. Government Printing Office 1940), vol. 1, 115.

65 Memorandum by the Secretary of State for the Colonies, Imperial Preference for Palestine, Annexure IV, C.P. 333 (32), 7 October 1932, Secret, CAB/24/33.

See also The Chargé in Great Britain (Atherton) to the Secretary of State, Doc. 641.67n3/9, *Foreign Relations of the United States 1932*, at 33, and The Chargé in Italy (Kirk) to the Secretary of State, Rome, 22 October 1932, Doc. 641.67n3/17, *Foreign Relations of the United States 1932*, vol. 2 at 35–36 (both reporting on Italy's reply to the UK).

66 Memorandum by the Secretary of State for the Colonies, Imperial Preference for Palestine, Annexure V, C.P. 333 (32), 7 October 1932, Secret, CAB/24/33. See also The Ambassador in Spain (Laughlin) to the Secretary of State, Madrid, 28 October 1932, Doc. 641.67n3/18, *Foreign Relations of the United States 1932*, vol. 2 at 36–37 (reporting on Spain's reply to the UK).

67 Memorandum by the Secretary of State for the Colonies, Imperial Preference for Palestine, Annexure VI, C.P. 333 (32), 7 October 1932, Secret, CAB/24/33.

68 Ibid., Annexure VII.

69 Ibid. at 1.

70 Foreign Office, Suggested Extension of Imperial Preference to Palestine, at 1, E 5478/606/31, C.P. 363 (32), 20 October 1932, Secret, CAB 24/234.

71 Ibid. at 2.

72 Ibid. at 2.

73 Ibid. at 1.

74 Committee on Imperial Preference for Palestine, Report, C.P. 367 (32), 28 October 1932, Secret, CAB/24/234.

75 Chargé in Britain, Dispatch No. 433, 15 January 1934, Doc. 641.67n3/20, *Foreign Relations of the United States 1932*, vol. 2, at 37.

CHAPTER 7

1 H. Duncan Hall, *Mandates, Dependencies and Trusteeship* (London: Stevens & Sons 1948), at 73.

2 Henri Rolin, La pratique des mandats internationaux, *Recueil des cours* (Hague Academy of International Law), vol. 19, 497, at 615 (1927-IV) (listing analysts who located sovereignty in the League of Nations).

3 Hersch Lauterpacht, The Mandate under International Law in the Covenant of the League of Nations, in Elihu Lauterpacht, ed., *International Law: Being the Collected Papers of Hersch Lauterpacht* (Cambridge: Cambridge University Press 1977), vol. 3, 29, at 68.

4 Rolin, La pratique des mandats internationaux, at 615 (listing analysts who located sovereignty in the Allies).

5 Frederick Pollock, *The League of Nations* (London: Stevens and Sons 1922), at 181.

6 Charles Henry Alexander, Israel in Fieri, *International Law Quarterly*, vol. 4, 423, at 423–424 (1951).

7 Rolin, La pratique des mandats internationaux, at 614.

8 J.L. Brierly, *The Law of Nations: An Introduction to the International Law of Peace* (Oxford: Clarendon Press 1928), at 102.

9 Lassa Oppenheim, *International Law: A Treatise*, Hersch Lauterpacht, ed. (London: Longmans 1955), vol. 1, at 213–214.

10 International Status of South-West Africa, Advisory Opinion, 1950 ICJ 128, at 132.

11 James Crawford, *The Creation of States in International Law* (Oxford: Clarendon Press 2006), at 566.

12 Aaron M. Margalith, *The International Mandates* (Baltimore: Johns Hopkins Press 1930), at 46.

13 Norman Bentwich, Mandated Territories: Palestine and Mesopotamia (Iraq), *British Year Book of International Law*, vol. 2, 48, at 56 (1921–22).

14 Extradition Treaty (Great Britain-Uruguay), Montevideo, 26 March 1884, Art. 10, *Consolidated Treaty Series*, vol. 163, at 408.

15 Report, High Court of Justice of Uruguay, 7 March 1928, *Annual Digest of Public International Law Cases 1927–1928*, at 47.

16 Charles Rousseau, *Droit international public* (Paris: Editions Sirey 1974), vol. 2, at 386.

17 Campbell L. Upthegrove, *Empire by Mandate: A History of the Relations of Great Britain with the Permanent Mandates Commission of the League of Nations* (New York: Bookman Associates 1954), at 143–163.

18 League of Nations, Permanent Mandates Commission, Minutes of the Thirty-Fourth Session held at Geneva from June 8th to 23rd, 1938.

19 League of Nations, Permanent Mandates Commission, *Petition, dated July 15th, 1936, from the Arab Higher Committee, Jerusalem*, Minutes of the Thirty-Second (Extraordinary) Session devoted to Palestine, held at Geneva from July 30th to August 18th, 1937 (meeting of 30 July 1937).

20 Rapport de M. Henri Rolin sur les mandats internationaux, *Annuaire de l'Institut de droit international*, vol. 34(1), 33, at 52–53 (1928).

21 International Status of South-West Africa, Advisory Opinion, 1950 ICJ 128, at 150 (McNair, J., separate opinion).

22 Quincy Wright, *Mandates under the League of Nations* (Chicago: University of Chicago Press 1930), at 530.

23 Legal Consequences for States of the Continued Presence of South Africa in Namibia (South West Africa) notwithstanding Security Council Resolution 276 (1970), Advisory Opinion, 1971 ICJ 16, at 69 (Ammoun, J., separate opinion).

24 Paul Pic, Le régime du mandat d'après le Traité de Versailles; son application dans le Proche Orient: mandats français en Syrie, anglais en Palestine et Mésopotamie, *Revue Générale de Droit International Public*, vol. 30, 321, at 342 (1923).

25 Ibid. at 334.

26 Henry Cattan, *Le partage de la Palestine du point de vue juridique: Conférence prononcée à l'Université de Berne le 30 novembre 1970 sous les auspices de l'Association Suisse-Arabe, et à Genève, le 1er décembre 1970, à la salle de l'Athénée sous les auspices du Group d'Etude sur le Moyen-Orient* (Geneva: Group d'Etude sur le Moyen-Orient 1971), at 15–16.

27 Legal Consequences for States of the Continued Presence of South Africa in Namibia (South West Africa) notwithstanding Security Council Resolution 276 (1970), Advisory Opinion, 1971 ICJ 16, at 69 (Ammoun, J., separate opinion).

28 Cattan (*Le partage de la Palestine du point de vue juridique*), at 17.
29 Howard Grief, *The Legal Foundation and Borders of Israel under International Law: A Treatise on Jewish Sovereignty over the Land of Israel* (Jerusalem: Mazo Publishers 2008), at 136–137.
30 Nathan Feinberg, On an Arab Jurist's Approach to Zionism and the State of Israel (Jerusalem: Magnes Press 1971), at 18–21.
31 See, e.g., Ralph Wilde, *International Territorial Administration: How Trusteeship and the Civilizing Mission Never Went Away* (Oxford: Oxford University Press 2008), at 167.
32 Paul Fauchille, *Traité de droit international public* (Paris: Rousseau 1922) vol. 1, part 1, at 298.
33 Traité pour l'organisation du protectorat français dans l'Empire chérifien, Fez, 30 March 1912, British and Foreign State Papers, vol. 106, at 1023. *Consolidated Treaty Series*, vol. 216, at 20.
34 Rights of Nationals of the United States of America in Morocco (*U.S.A. v. France*), 1952 ICJ 176, at 185, 188.
35 Isthmian Canal Convention, 18 November 1903, Art. 3, U.S. Congress, Statutes at Large, vol. 33, at 2234.
36 Panama Canal Treaty, September 7, 1977, 33 U.S.T. 39 (preamble).
37 Lauterpacht, The Mandate under International Law in the Covenant of the League of Nations, at 46.
38 Ibid. The quoted phrases were taken by Lauterpacht from Franz von Liszt's definition of a protectorate. See also ibid. at 45 note 3, where Lauterpacht points to ways in which Palestine differed from the other Class A mandates. He, however, did not avert to such differences in the quoted passages about the Class A mandates.
39 Brierly, at 99.
40 Henri Rolin, Le Système des mandats coloniaux, *Revue de droit international et de législation comparée*, series 3, vol. 1, 329, at 340 (1920).
41 Ibid. at 348.
42 Rolin (La pratique des mandats internationaux), at 623.
43 Ibid. at 610.
44 Giulio Diena, Les mandats internationaux, *Recueil des cours* (Hague Academy of International Law), vol. 5, 211, at 242 (1924-IV).
45 Ibid. at 243.
46 Ibid. at 243–244.
47 Doreen Ingrams, *Palestine Papers 1917–1922: Seeds of Conflict* (London: John Murray 1970), at 61.
48 Ingrams, at 73.
49 *Ungar v. Palestine Liberation Organization*, 402 F.3d 274, at 290 (1st Cir. 2005).
50 Malbone W. Graham, *The League of Nations and the Recognition of States* (Berkeley: University of California Press 1942), at 33.
51 Jacob Stoyanovsky, *The Mandate for Palestine* (London: Longmans 1928), at 262.
52 Henry Cattan, *The Palestine Question* (London: Croom Helm 1988), at 23.

53 Quincy Wright, Sovereignty of the Mandates, *American Journal of International Law*, vol. 17, 691, at 693 (1923).

54 Minquiers and Ecrehos (France v. U.K.), 1953 ICJ 47, at 67.

55 James Crawford, Israel (1948–1949) and Palestine (1998–1999): Two Studies in the Creation of States, in Guy S. Goodwin-Gill and Stefan Talmon, eds., *The Reality of International Law: Essays in Honour of Ian Brownlie* (Oxford: Clarendon Press 1999), 95, at 117.

56 Succession of States: Succession in Respect of Treaties: Third Report on Succession in Respect of Treaties, by Sir Humphrey Waldock, Special Rapporteur, *Yearbook of the International Law Commission 1970*, vol. 2, at 28, UN Doc. A/CN.4/224.

57 Norman Bentwich, *The Mandates System* (London: Longmans 1930), at 21.

58 Convention between the United States and Great Britain concerning Palestine, 3 December 1924, U.S. Congress, Statutes at Large, vol. 44, at 2184.

59 Rapport de M. Henri Rolin sur les mandats internationaux, at 35.

60 *Annuaire de l'Institut de droit international*, vol. 36(2), at 50 (1931).

CHAPTER 8

1 Palestine: A Statement of Policy, Art. 10, Cmd. 6019, May 1939.

2 Ibid., Art. 8.

3 Alexandria Protocol, 7 October 1944, in *Basic Documents of the League of Arab States* (New York: Arab Information Center 1955), at 5.

4 Pact of the League of Arab States, Cairo, 22 March 1945, 70 UNTS 237.

5 The Representation of Palestine on the Council of the League, Res. 17, 4 December 1945, in Muhammad Khalil, *The Arab States and the Arab League: A Documentary Record* (Beirut: Khayats 1962), vol. 2, at 161.

6 The Higher Arab Executive Committee, Res. 82, 12 June 1946, ibid. at 162.

7 Avi Shlaim, The Rise and Fall of the All-Palestine Government in Gaza, *Journal of Palestine Studies*, vol. 20 (no. 1), 37, at 38 (1990).

8 League of Nations, *Official Journal (Special supplement No. 194): Records of the 20th (conclusion) and 21st ordinary sessions of the Assembly* (1946), at 62.

9 Ibid. at 58–59.

10 Ibid. at 58–59.

11 The date of independence for Iraq is given as 1923, but, as indicated in Chapter 5, Britain had regarded Iraq as continuing to be under its mandate until 1932. "1923" may be a typographical error.

12 League of Nations, at 28.

13 International Status of South-West Africa, Advisory Opinion, 1950 ICJ 128, at 133–134, and 137–138.

14 UN Doc. A/364/Add.2 PV.19, UN Special Committee on Palestine, Verbatim Record of the Nineteenth Meeting (public), Held at the Y.M.C.A. Building, Jerusalem Palestine Monday, 7 July 1947, at 9 a.m.

15 Anglo-American Committee of Inquiry, *Report to the United States Government and His Majesty's Government of the United Kingdom* (Washington: U.S. Government Printing Office 1946), at 4–5. Also published as Cmd. 6808.

16 Proposals for the future of Palestine July, 1946 – February, 1947: Extract from the speech by the Right Hon. Herbert Morrison in the House of Commons on 31st July, 1946, describing the "Provincial Autonomy Plan" for Palestine (with explanatory map), Cmd. 7044, at 4–5.

17 Ibid. at 6–7.

18 Constitutional Proposals put forward by the Arab States Delegations to the Palestine Conference on 30th September, 1946, at 9–11, Cmd. 7044.

19 The Proposals submitted by the British Delegation to the Palestine Conference on 7th February, 1947, and also Communicated to Representatives of the Jewish Agency, Cmd. 7044, at 11–14.

20 Letter dated 2 April 1947 from the United Kingdom delegation to the Acting Secretary-General requesting a special session of the General Assembly on Palestine, UN Doc. A/286, 3 April 1947.

21 GA Res. 105, 7 May 1947.

22 UN Doc. A/C.1/PV.52, 9 May 1947, at 197.

23 UN Doc. A/287, 21 April 1947 (Egypt to Secretary-General); UN Doc. A/288, 21 April 1947 (Iraq to Secretary-General); UN Doc. A/289, 22 April 1947 (Syria to Secretary-General); UN Doc. A/290, 22 April 1947 (Lebanon to Secretary-General); UN Doc. A/291, 22 April 1947 (Saudi Arabia to Secretary-General).

24 UN Doc. A/294, 25 April 1947.

25 Special Committee on Palestine, Report of the First Committee, UN Doc. A/307, 13 May 1947 (referring as well to presentation by Henry Cattan before the First Committee at its 52d meeting on 9 May 1947 on behalf of the Arab Higher Committee).

26 GA Res. 106, 15 May 1947.

27 United Nations Special Committee on Palestine, Report to the General Assembly, 3 September 1947, UN Doc. A/364, 3 September 1947.

28 Ibid. at 41.

29 Palestine: Memorandum by the Secretary of State for Foreign Affairs, para. 8, C.P. 47 (259), 18 September 1947, Secret, CAB/129/21.

30 Ibid., para. 4(iii).

31 *Ad Hoc* Committee on the Palestinian Question, Summary Records of Meetings 25 September – 25 November 1947, at 223.

32 Plenary Meetings of the General Assembly, 16 September – 29 November 1947, vol. 2, UN Doc. A/PV.128, at 1424–1425.

33 Vienna Convention on Succession of States in respect of Treaties, Art. 34, 23 August 1978, 1946 UNTS 3.

34 Vienna Convention on Succession of States in respect of State Property, Archives, and Debts, Arts. 33–36, 8 April 1983, UN Doc. A/CONF.117/14 (1983) (not yet in force). Hubert Beemelmans, State Succession in International Law: Remarks on Recent Theory and State Praxis, *Boston University International Law Journal*, vol. 15, 17 (1997).

35 UN Security Council, 386th meeting, UN Doc. S/PV.386, 17 December 1948, at 24.

36 Kermit Roosevelt, The Partition of Palestine: A Lesson in Power Politics, *Middle East Journal*, vol. 2, 1, at 10 (1948).

37 Arnold Toynbee, Two Aspects of the Palestine Question, in Arnold Toynbee, *Importance of the Arab World* (Cairo: National Publications House 1962), at 57–59.

38 Earl Harrison, Report to the President of the United States, *New York Times*, September 30, 1945, at A38.

39 UN Security Council, 253rd meeting, UN Doc. S/PV.253, 24 February 1948, at 258–259.

40 UN Security Council, 271st meeting, 19 March 1948, UN Doc. S/PV.271, at 31. See also The Acting Secretary of State to Certain Diplomatic and Consular Offices, 6 April 1948, *Foreign Relations of the United States 1948*, vol. 5 (Washington: U.S. Government Printing Office 1976), at 801.

41 SC Res. 44, 1 April 1948.

42 Summoning of the second special session of the General Assembly: Note by the Secretary-General, 1 April 1948, UN Doc. A/530.

43 SC Res. 46, 17 April 1948.

44 UN Doc. A/C.1/SR.118, 20 April 1948.

45 Draft Trusteeship Agreement for Palestine: Working Paper Circulated by the United States Delegation, Art. 2, UN Doc. A/C.1/277, 20 April 1948.

46 Ibid., Art. 8.

47 Ibid., Art. 35(6).

48 Ibid., Art. 47(1).

49 Thomas J. Hamilton, Arabs Tell U.N. They Plan a State: El-Husseini Says Independent Palestine Will Be Set Up if There Is No Trusteeship, *New York Times*, 27 April 1948, at A1 and A3.

50 Ibid.

51 UN Doc. A/C.1/SR.126, 26 April 1948, at 97. Also in Hamilton, at A1 and A3.

52 Hamilton, at A1 and A3. In abbreviated form as UN Doc. A/C.1/SR/126, 26 April 1948, at 97.

53 UN General Assembly, First Committee, 137th mtg., Resolution: Further Consideration of the Question of the Future Government of Palestine, 4 May 1948, UN Doc. A/C.1/292, 5 May 1948.

54 David Hirst, *The Gun and the Olive Branch: The Roots of Violence in the Middle East* (1984), at 139. Netanel Lorch, *The Edge of the Sword: Israel's War of Independence, 1947–1949* (New York: Putnam 1961), at 87. Walid Khalidi, Plan Dalet: The Zionist Master Plan for the Conquest of Palestine, *Middle East Forum*, 22, at 27 (November 1961). Ilan Pappé, *The Ethnic Cleansing of Palestine* (Oxford: One World 2006), at 88.

55 Ilan Pappé, *The Ethnic Cleansing of Palestine* (Oxford: One World 2006), at 143. Lorch, at 118–120. Benny Morris, *The Birth of the Palestinian Refugee Problem, 1947–1949* (New York: Cambridge University Press 1987), at 96–97. Rosemarie M. Esber, *Under the Cover of War: The Zionist Expulsion of the Palestinians* (Alexandria VA: Arabicus 2008), at 227–366.

56 Benny Morris, The Causes and Character of the Arab Exodus from Palestine: the Israel Defence Forces Intelligence Branch Analysis of June 1948, *Middle Eastern Studies*, vol. 22, 5, at 6–7 (1986).

57 Esber, at 392.

58 Egyptian Editors Flay Arab League, Denounce Leaders' Inaction on Palestine 'Catastrophe' – Invasion Widely Urged, *New York Times*, 25 April 1948, at A7.

59 Rapport de M. Henri Rolin sur les mandats internationaux, *Annuaire de l'Institut de droit international*, vol. 34(1), 33, at 48 (1928).

60 Palestine (Revocations) Order in Council, sec. 2, 12 May 1948, Statutory Instrument No. 1004 (1948).

61 Marjorie Whiteman, *Digest of International Law* (Washington: U.S. Department of State 1963), vol. 1, at 224–225.

CHAPTER 9

1 Va'ad leumi (National Council), a political organization of Palestine Jews dating from 1920. See Benzion Eshel, How to Found a New State: The Case of Israel, in *Public Administration in Israel and Abroad 1967: An Annual Collection of Articles* (Jerusalem: Israel Institute of Public Administration 1968), at 181–183.

2 Victor Kattan, *From Coexistence to Conquest: International Law and the Origins of the Arab-Israeli Conflict, 1891–1949* (New York: Pluto Press 2009), at 233.

3 Historical Note, *Foreign Relations of the United States 1948*, vol. 5, at 993. Alfred M. Lilienthal, *What Price Israel?* (Beirut: Institute for Palestine Studies 1953), at 83–86.

4 UN General Assembly, 135th plenary meeting, UN Doc. A/PV.135, 14 May 1948.

5 Philip C. Jessup, *The Birth of Nations* (New York: Columbia University Press 1974), at 289.

6 GA Res. 186, 14 May 1948.

7 Tsiang Tingfu, China, in UN Security Council, 292nd meeting, UN Doc. S/PV.292, 15 May 1948, at 15.

8 A reference to Jews who had migrated to Palestine but had not become naturalized as Palestine citizens.

9 Isa Nakhleh, Arab Higher Committee, in UN Security Council, 292nd meeting, UN Doc. S/PV.292, 15 May 1948, at 8–9.

10 Mordechai Eliash, Jewish Agency for Palestine, ibid. at 7.

11 James Crawford, *The Creation of States in International Law* (Oxford: Clarendon Press 2006), at 427.

12 Ibid. at 432.

13 Ibid. at 388.

14 Lassa Oppenheim, *International Law: A Treatise*, Hersch Lauterpacht, ed. (London: Longmans 1955), at 579.

15 Crawford (*The Creation of States in International Law*), at 375.

16 Cablegram from the Secretary-General of the League of Arab States to the Secretary-General of the United Nations, 15 May 1948, para. 10(e), UN Doc. S/745.

17 Ibid.

18 Ibid.

19 A series of meetings organized by the British government at St. James Palace, London, February–March 1939, with Arab and Jewish representatives from Palestine, aimed at resolving the situation in Palestine.

20 Cablegram from the Secretary-General of the League of Arab States to the Secretary-General of the United Nations, 15 May 1948, para. 10(e), UN Doc. S/745.

21 James Crawford, Israel (1948–1949) and Palestine (1998–1999): Two Studies in the Creation of States, in Guy S. Goodwin-Gill and Stefan Talmon, eds., *The Reality of International Law: Essays in Honour of Ian Brownlie* (Oxford: Clarendon Press 1999), 95, at 102 (note 34), citing UN Doc. S/745.

22 Ibid. at 101–102.

23 Cablegram dated 18 July 1948 from the Secretary-General of the League of Arab States to the Secretary-General in reply to the resolution (S/902) adopted by the Security Council at the 338th meeting, 15 July 1948, UN Doc. S/908.

24 UN Doc. S/745, 15 May 1948, para. 10(b).

25 Memorandum from the Political Committee of the Arab League to the U.N. Mediator (Bernadotte), 8 July 1948, in Muhammad Khalil, *The Arab States and the Arab League* (Beirut: Khayats 1962), vol. 2, at 563.

26 Statement by the Secretary-General of the Arab League Concerning the Setting-Up of the All-Palestine Government, ibid. at 566.

27 SC Res. 54, 15 July 1948.

28 Benny Morris, Operation Dani and the Palestinian Exodus from Lydda and Ramle in 1948, *Middle East Journal*, vol. 40, 82, at 96 (1986). Edgar O'Ballance, *The Arab-Israeli War, 1948* (Westport CT: Hyperion Press 1981, orig. pub'd. London: Faber and Faber 1956), at 147.

29 Progress Report of the United Nations Mediator on Palestine, at 18, UN Doc. A/648, 16 September 1948.

30 Proclamation of the Independence of Palestine by the Higher Arab Committee and the Representatives of Palestine Meeting in Congress, 1 October 1948, in Khalil (Muhammad), at 579.

31 Cablegram dated 28 September 1948 from the Premier and Acting Foreign Secretary of the All-Palestine Government to the Secretary-General concerning constitution of the All-Palestine Government, UN Doc. A/C.1.300, 28 September 1948.

32 Note, *Foreign Relations of the United States 1948*, vol. 5, part 2, at 1447.

33 September 1 – November 30, 1948, *Middle East Journal*, vol. 3, 63, at 64 (1949).

34 Asem Khalil, *Which Constitution for the Palestinian Legal System?* (dissertation) (Rome: Pontificia Universitas Lateranensis Institutum Utriusque Iuris 2003), at 60.

35 Avi Shlaim, The Rise and Fall of the All-Palestine Government in Gaza, *Journal of Palestine Studies*, vol. 20 (no. 1), 37, at 48 (1990). Anis F. Kassim,

The Palestine Liberation Organization's Claim to Status: A Juridical Analysis under International Law, *Denver Journal of International Law and Policy*, vol. 9, 1, at 18 (1980).

36 Shlaim (Rise and Fall), at 42. Kamal Salibi, *The Modern History of Jordan* (London: I.B. Tauris 1998), at 160.

37 Note, *Foreign Relations of the United States 1948*, vol. 5, part 2, at 1447, note 1.

38 Mary C. Wilson, *King Abdullah, Britain and the Making of Jordan* (New York: Cambridge University Press 1987), at 181. Rashid Khalidi, *The Iron Cage: The Story of the Palestinian Struggle for Statehood* (Boston: Beacon Press 2007), at 135.

39 Wilson, at 179. Richard Locke and Antony Stewart, *Bantustan Gaza* (London: Zed 1985), at 5.

40 Ilan Pappé, *Britain and the Arab-Israeli Conflict, 1948–51* (Oxford: Macmillan Press 1988), at 90. Wilson, at 182.

41 Marjorie Whiteman, *Digest of International Law*, vol. 2 (Washington: U.S. Government Printing Office 1963), at 1163.

42 Philip Robins, *A History of Jordan* (New York: Cambridge University Press 2004), at 71–72.

43 Marjorie Whiteman, *Digest of International Law*, vol. 2 (Washington: U.S. Government Printing Office 1963), at 1164.

44 Ilan Pappé, *The Ethnic Cleansing of Palestine* (Oxford: One World 2006), at 191–192. Avi Shlaim, *Collusion Across the Jordan: King Abdullah, the Zionist Movement, and the Partition of Palestine* (Oxford: Clarendon Press 1988), at 308–311. Simha Flapan, *The Birth of Israel: Myths and Realities* (New York: Pantheon 1987), at 48. *Troubled Truce, Economist*, August 21, 1948, at 289–290.

45 Jon and David Kimche, *Both Sides of the Hill: Britain and the Palestine War* (London: Secker & Warburg 1960), at 267–268. Shlaim (*Collusion Across the Jordan*), at 406.

46 Shlaim (*Collusion Across the Jordan*), at 387. Robins, at 69.

47 Letter dated 29 November 1948 from Israel's Foreign Minister to the Secretary-General concerning Israel's application for admission to membership of the United Nations and declaration accepting obligations under the Charter, UN Doc. S/1093.

48 Continuation of the discussion on the progress report of the United Nations Mediator on Palestine (A/648), Continuation of the consideration of the consolidated tabulation prepared by the working group, 1 December 1948, UN Doc. A/C.1/403.

49 Yearbook of the United Nations 1948–1949, at 395.

50 GA Res. 194, 11 December 1948.

51 Draft resolution submitted by Syria at the 385th meeting on the application of Israel for admission to the United Nations, UN Doc. S/1125, in UN Security Council, 385th meeting, 17 December 1948, UN Doc. S/PV.385, at 10.

52 UN Security Council, 386th meeting, 17 December 1948, UN Doc. S/PV.386, at 36–37.

53 Conclusions of a Meeting of the Cabinet, 10 Downing Street, 17 January 1949, 11 a.m. Cabinet 3 (49), Secret, CAB 128/15, at 14–16.

54 Tom Segev, *1949: The First Israelis* (New York: Free Press 1986), at 3. James McDonald, *My Mission in Israel, 1948–1951* (New York: Simon & Schuster 1951), at 116–117. The Special Representative of the United States in Israel (McDonald) to the Acting Secretary of State, 31 December 1948, *Foreign Relations of the United States 1948*, vol. 5 (Washington: U.S. Government Printing Office 1976), at 1705.

55 Message from Acting Secretary of State to U.S. Representative (McDonald) in Israel, 30 December 1948, *Foreign Relations of the United States 1948*, vol. 5 (Washington: U.S. Government Printing Office 1976), at 1704. James McDonald, *My Mission in Israel, 1948–1951* (New York: Simon & Schuster 1951), at 107–108.

56 Abba Eban, *An Autobiography* (New York: Random House 1977), at 137. O'Ballance, at 201.

57 General Armistice Agreement (Israel-Egypt), Art. 3, 24 February 1949, 42 UNTS 251.

58 Ibid., Art. 1(4).

59 General Armistice Agreement (Israel-Jordan), Art. 1(4), 3 April 1949, 42 UNTS 303.

60 Ibid., Art. 5(1)(d).

61 Ibid., Art. 6(7).

62 SC Res. 69, 4 March 1949.

63 GA Res. 273, 11 May 1949.

CHAPTER 10

1 GA Res. 394, Art. 2, 14 December 1950.

2 Memorandum received on 17 June 1949 from Mr. Isa Nakhleh, Representative of the Arab Higher Committee for Palestine, UN Doc. A/AC.25/Org/20 (restricted).

3 *Sifri v. Attorney-General, Israel*, Supreme Court sitting as the High Court of Justice, 20 July 1950, *International Law Reports 1950*, vol. 17, 92 (1956). Ilan Pappé, *The Ethnic Cleansing of Palestine* (Oxford: One World 2006), at 200–203. Arthur Koestler, *Bricks to Babel* (New York: Random House 1980), at 286.

4 Cablegram dated 18 July 1948 from the Secretary-General of the League of Arab States to the Secretary-General in reply to the resolution (S/902) adopted by the Security Council at the 338th meeting, 15 July 1948, UN Doc. S/908.

5 Assistance to Palestine Refugees, GA Res. 302, 8 December 1949. Richard Locke and Antony Stewart, *Bantustan Gaza* (London: Zed 1985), at 52.

6 Annual Report of the Director of the United Nations Relief and Works Agency for Palestine Refugees in the Near East, para. 10, UN Doc. A/1905, 28 September 1951. Locke & Stewart, at 4. Usamah Shahwan, *Public Administration in Palestine Past and Present* (Lanham MD: University Press of America 2003), at 42.

7 Yuval Shany, Faraway, So Close: The Legal Status of Gaza after Israel's Disengagement, *Yearbook of International Humanitarian Law*, vol. 8, 369, at 371 (2006).

8 Anis F. Kassim, Legal Systems and Developments in Palestine, *Palestine Yearbook of International Law*, vol. 1, 19, at 28 (1984).
9 Raja Shehadeh, *From Occupation to Interim Accords: Israel and the Palestinian Territories* (London: Kluwer 1997), at 77.
10 Kassim (Legal Systems), at 29. Raja Shehadeh, *From Occupation to Interim Accords: Israel and the Palestinian Territories* (London: Kluwer 1997), at 77.
11 Kassim (Legal Systems), at 28.
12 Ibid. at 29. J.L., The International Status of Palestine, *Journal du droit international*, vol. 90, 964, at 984 (1963). Resumé of Pronouncements bearing on the Structure of the Egyptian State, etc., 1952–1954, *Revue Égyptienne de droit international*, vol. 10, at 133 (1954). Resumé of Pronouncements bearing on the Structure of the Egyptian State, etc., 1952–1955, *Revue Égyptienne de droit international*, vol. 11, at 174 and 181 (1955).
13 Kassim (Legal Systems), at 29. J.L., The International Status of Palestine, *Journal du droit international*, vol. 90, 964, at 984 (1963).
14 Radwan Alagha, The Legal System in the Gaza Strip 1948–1967 [Arabic], in: *Which Legal System for Palestine? Conference Proceedings* (Ramallah: Birzeit University Law Center 1996), at 21. Raji Sourani, The Legal System in Gaza Strip 1948–1967 [Arabic], ibid. at 27.
15 Ilana Feldman, *Governing Gaza: Bureaucracy, Authority, and the Work of Rule, 1917–1967* (Durham NC: Duke University Press 2008), at 19.
16 Avi Shlaim, *Collusion Across the Jordan: King Abdullah, the Zionist Movement, and the Partition of Palestine* (Oxford: Clarendon Press 1988), at 611–612.
17 UN Security Council, 693rd meeting, UN Doc. S/PV.693, 17 March 1955. Locke and Stewart, at 6.
18 SC Res. 106, 29 March 1955.
19 Law No. 285, 26 July 1956, in *Revue Égyptienne de droit international*, vol. 12(2), at 76.
20 Sèvres Protocol (UK, France, Israel), 24 October 1956, text in Jean Allain, *International Law in the Middle East: Closer to Power than Justice* (Aldershot: Ashgate 2004), at 285–286.
21 Homer Bigart, Israel Terms Gaza Strip an Integral Part of Nation, *New York Times*, 11 November 1956, at A1.
22 Secretary-General, Aide-mémoire on the Israeli Position on the Sharm-el-Sheikh Area and the Gaza Strip, at 5, in General Assembly Official Records, 11th Session, Doc. A/3511, 24 January 1957. Report by the Secretary-General in Pursuance of the Resolution of the General Assembly of 19 January 1957 (A/RES/453), part 2, para. 5(a), UN Doc. A/3512, 24 January 1957.
23 Aide-mémoire to Ambassador Abba Eban by Secretary John Foster Dulles, 11 February 1957, Department of State Bulletin, vol. 36, p. 392 (11 March 1957). Cheryl Rubenberg, *Israel and the American National Interest* (Urbana IL: University of Illinois Press 1986), at 80–87. Richard Locke and Antony Stewart, *Bantustan Gaza* (London: Zed 1985), at 6.
24 *Middle East Record*, vol. 1, at 136 (Tel Aviv: Israel Oriental Society 1960). *Middle East Record*, vol. 2, at 112 (Tel Aviv: Israel Oriental Society 1960). Carol Farhi, On the Legal Status of the Gaza Strip, in Meir Shamgar, ed.,

Military Government in the Territories Administered by Israel 1967–1980: The Legal Aspects (1982), vol. 1, 61, at 77.

25 As quoted in Feldman (*Governing Gaza*), at 9.
26 Marcel Colombe, Le problème de 'l'entité Palestinienne' dans les relations interarabes, *Orient* (Paris), vol. 8, 57, at 66–74 (1964).
27 Farhi, at 75.
28 Anis Al-Qasem, Commentary on Draft Basic Law for the Palestinian National Authority for the Transitional Period, in *Palestine Yearbook of International Law*, vol. 7, 187, at 190 (1992–94).
29 Constitution of Palestine, Art. 1, *Palestine Gazette*, 29 March 1962, reprinted as Republican Decree Announcing Constitutional System of Gaza Sector, March 9, 1962, *Middle East Journal*, vol. 17, at 156 (1963).
30 Ibid., Art. 54.
31 Ibid., Art. 18.
32 Ibid., Art. 30. Locke and Stewart, at 7.
33 Farhi, at 78–79. Nimrod Raphaeli, Gaza under Four Administrations, *Public Administration in Israel and Abroad*, vol. 9, 40, at 46–47 (1969).
34 Usamah Shahwan, *Public Administration in Palestine Past and Present* (Lanham MD: University Press of America 2003), at 40.
35 Feldman (*Governing Gaza*), at 11.
36 Farhi, at 80.
37 Constitution of Palestine, 29 March 1962, Art. 73.
38 Kassim (Legal Systems), at 27. Asem Khalil, *Which Constitution for the Palestinian Legal System?* (dissertation) (Rome: Pontificia Universitas Lateranensis Institutum Utriusque Iuris 2003), at 18.
39 Ron Pundik, *The Struggle for Sovereignty: Relations between Great Britain and Jordan, 1946–1951* (Oxford: Blackwell 1994), at 219.
40 Kassim (Legal Systems), at 27. Philip Robins, *A History of Jordan* (New York: Cambridge University Press 2004), at 72. Raja Shehadeh, *From Occupation to Interim Accords: Israel and the Palestinian Territories* (London: Kluwer 1997), at 77.
41 Philip Robins, *A History of Jordan* (New York: Cambridge University Press 2004), at 73.
42 Marjorie Whiteman, *Digest of International Law*, vol. 2 (Washington: U.S. Government Printing Office 1963), at 1166. Albion Ross, Amman Parliament Vote Unites Arab Palestine and Transjordan, *New York Times*, 25 April 1950, at A1. Decision of the Council of Representatives and the Council of Notables in Joint Session on April 24, 1950, concerning the Union of Eastern and Western Jordan (where English translation varies slightly), in Helen Miller Davis, *Constitutions, Electoral Laws, Treaties of States in the Near and Middle East* (Durham: Duke University Press 1953), at 265.
43 G. Feuer, Les Accords Passés par les Gouvernements Jordanien et Libanais Avec les Organisations Palestiniennes (1968–1970), *Annuaire Français de Droit International*, vol. 16, 177, at 189 (1970).
44 Allan Gerson, *Israel, The West Bank and International Law* (London: Frank Cass 1978), at 79.

45 Marjorie Whiteman, *Digest of International Law*, vol. 2 (Washington: U.S. Government Printing Office 1963), at 1168.

46 Peter Malanczuk, Israel: Status, Territory and Occupied Territories, *Encyclopedia of Public International Law* (Amsterdam: North Holland 1990), vol. 12, at 171.

47 *Arab Bank v. Ahmed Daoud Abou Ismail*, Tribunal of Port Said, Judgment of 26 November 1950, *International Law Reports 1950*, vol. 17, 312 (1956), also in *Revue Égyptienne de droit international*, vol. 7, 191 (1951).

48 Agreement as to the Execution of Judgments (Jordan, Syria, Iraq, Saudi Arabia, Lebanon, Egypt, Yemen), 14 September 1952, *Revue Égyptienne de droit international*, vol. 8, at 333 (1952), and in Ligue des Etats Arabes, *Texte des Traités et Conventions conclus entre les États Membres dans le cadre de la Ligue Arabe* (Cairo: Al-Sabah Magazine Press 1959), at 23.

49 Gerson, at 78.

50 Theodore Mogannam, Developments in the Legal System of Jordan, *Middle East Journal*, vol. 6, 196 (1952).

51 Law No. 28, 16 September 1950, Art. 2, in *Compilation of Jordan's Laws and Regulations*, vol. 3, at 12, as quoted in Kassim, at 28.

52 Khalil (Asem), at 19. Raja Shehadeh, *From Occupation to Interim Accords: Israel and the Palestinian Territories* (London: Kluwer 1997), at 78.

53 Raja Shehadeh, *Occupier's Law: Israel and the West Bank* (Washington DC: Institute for Palestine Studies 1985), at 23.

54 Kamal Salibi, *The Modern History of Jordan* (London: I.B. Tauris 1998), at 160.

55 Arabs in Accord over Palestine, *New York Times*, 28 August 1960, at A9.

56 John Quigley, *The Case for Palestine: An International Law Perspective* (London: Duke University Press 2005), at 73–81.

57 UN General Assembly, Ad hoc Political Committee, Summary Records of Meetings 6 April – 10 April 1949, at 282.

58 Ibid. at 286–287.

59 Law and Administration Ordinance, Art. 11, *Laws of the State of Israel*, vol. 1, at 7 (1948).

60 Shabtai Rosenne, Israël et les Traités Internationaux de la Palestine, *Journal du droit international*, vol. 77, 1140, at 1141 (1950).

61 *Ungar v. Palestine Liberation Organization*, 402 F.3d 274, at 290 (1st Cir. 2005).

62 UN Security Council, 383rd meeting, UN Doc. S/PV.383, 2 December 1948, at 14.

63 Letter dated 10 November 1969 from Afghanistan, Indonesia, Pakistan and Saudi Arabia to Chairman, Special Political Committee, UN Doc. A/SPC/131. Text of letter in UN Doc. A/SPC/PV.665, 17 November 1969, at 8.

64 Letter dated 18 October 1965 from the Chairman of the Palestine Arab Delegation to the Chairman of the Special Political Committee, UN Doc. A/SPC/105, 18 October 1965, referenced in UN Doc. A/6115, 23 November 1965 (Check List of Documents).

65 UN Doc. A/6115, 23 November 1965, para. 6.

66 Special Political Committee, Verbatim Record of the 435th Meeting, UN Doc. A/SPC/PV.435, 20 October 1965, referenced and followed, Verbatim Record of the 665th Meeting, UN Doc. A/SPC/PV.665, 17 November 1969, at 8.

67 147 UNTS 109 (notation by UN Secretary-General: "Filed and recorded at the request of the United States of America on 29 October 1952").

68 Text of Eden's Address Offering to Mediate in the Mideast, *New York Times*, 10 November 1955, at 8. Robert C. Doty, Mideast Strife Spurs West Big 3; U.S. Egypt Dam Aid Furthered, *New York Times*, 17 December 1955, at 3.

69 Israel Rejects Eden's Plan to Settle Dispute, *Chicago Daily Tribune*, 16 November 1955, at 13; Harry Gilroy, Ben-Gurion Says New Eden Offer Benefits Arabs: Israel Asked to Cede Land, Admit Refugees for Mere Recognition, He Asserts, *New York Times*, 26 November 1955, at 1; John J. Lindsay, Sharett Rejects British Plan, *Washington Post*, 30 November 1955, at 36; Harry Gilroy, Britain Assures Israel on Negev: Ben-Gurion Is Told London Has no Aim to Require Cession of Territory, *New York Times*, 12 December 1955, at 10.

70 Anthony D'Amato, The Legal Boundaries of Israel in International Law (2002), accessible at http://jurist.law.pitt.edu.

71 *Veffer v. Canada* (Minister of Foreign Affairs), Federal Court, 2006 FC 540, 1 May 2006, aff'd [2008] 1 F.C.R. 641, 25 June 2007.

72 Marcel Colombe, Le problème de 'l'entité Palestinienne' dans les relations interarabes, *Orient* (Paris), vol. 8, 57, at 78–87 (1964). Memorandum from the Assistant Secretary for Near Eastern and South Asian Affairs (Talbot) to Secretary of State Rusk, 1 May 1961, in *Foreign Relations of the United States 1961–1963* (Washington: U.S. Government Printing Office 1994), vol. 17, at 95.

73 Arabs in Accord over Palestine, *New York Times*, 28 August 1960, at A9.

74 Agreement for the settlement of financial matters outstanding as a result of the termination of the Mandate for Palestine (with exchange of letters) (UK-Israel), London, 30 March 1950, 86 UNTS 231. But see *Shimshon Palestine Portland Cement Factory Ltd. v. Attorney-General*, Supreme Court of Israel, 12 April 1950, *International Law Reports 1950*, vol. 17, 72 (1956) (holding that Israel was not liable generally on financial obligations of the mandate government).

75 Krystyna Marek, *Identity and Continuity of States in Public International Law* (Geneva: E. Droz 1954), at 89.

76 Crawford (*The Creation of States in International Law*), at 704.

77 *British Year Book of International Law*, vol. 62, 558 (1991).

78 Crawford (*The Creation of States in International Law*), at 97.

79 A.B. *v.* M.B., District Court of Tel Aviv (Zeltner, J.), 6 April 1951, *International Law Reports 1950*, vol. 17, 110–111 (1956), also quoted in M.D. Gouldman, *Israel Nationality Law* (Jerusalem: Hebrew University 1970), at 15.

80 Andreas Zimmermann, The Nationality of the Inhabitants of the Palestinian Autonomous Territories, in Amos Shapira and Mala Tabory, eds., *New Political Entities in Public and Private International Law With Special Reference to the Palestinian Entity* (Hague: Kluwer Law International 1999), 231, at 235–236. Lex Takkenberg, *The Status of Palestinian Refugees in International Law* (Oxford: Clarendon Press 1998), at 180.

81 *Yearbook of the International Law Commission 1950*, vol. 2, at 17, Nationality, including Statelessness, Report by Manley O. Hudson, Special Rapporteur, UN Doc. A/CN.4/50, 21 February 1952, Annex III: Statelessness.

82 United Nations, Department of Social Affairs, *A Study of Statelessness*, at 9, UN Doc. E/1112/Add.1, 19 May 1949.

83 Victor Kattan, The Nationality of Denationalized Palestinians, in Victor Kattan, ed., *The Palestine Question in International Law* (London: British Institute of International and Comparative Law 2008), 121, at 144.

84 Takkenberg, at 180 (citing to Bierwirth).

85 GA Res. 194, para. 11, 11 December 1948.

86 United Nations Conciliation Commission for Palestine, Definition of a "Refugee" under paragraph 11 of the General Assembly Resolution of 11 December 1948, UN Doc. A/AC.25/W/61, 9 April 1951.

87 Addendum to Definition of a "Refugee" under paragraph 11 of the General Assembly Resolution of 11 December 1948 (Prepared by the Legal Advisor), UN Doc. A/AC.25/W/61/Add.1, 29 May 1951.

88 Guy Goodwin-Gill and Jane McAdam, *The Refugee in International Law* (Oxford: Oxford University Press 2007), at 459.

89 D.P. O'Connell, *State Succession in Municipal Law and International Law* (Cambridge: Cambridge University Press 1967), vol. 1, at 129.

90 Goodwin-Gill and McAdam, at 461.

91 Ibid.

92 Law No. 160 of 1950 as amended by Law No. 194 of 1951 concerning Egyptian nationality, *Revue Égyptienne de droit international*, vol. 7, 343 (1951).

93 Zimmermann, at 237.

94 Eyal Benvenisti and Eyal Zamir, Private Claims to Property in the Future Israeli-Palestinian Settlement, *American Journal of International Law*, vol. 89, 295, at 304 (1995).

95 Ilana Feldman, Waiting for Palestine: Refracted Citizenship and Latent Sovereignty in Gaza, *Citizenship Studies*, vol. 12 (no. 5), 447, at 458 (2008).

96 *Abdelwahed v. Immigration and Naturalization Service*, 22 Federal Appendix 811, at 812 (U.S. Ct. Appeals 9th Cir. 2001).

97 Jordan, Law No. 6 on Nationality (1954), Art. 3(2).

98 Nationality Law, *Laws of the State of Israel*, vol. 6, at 50 (1952).

99 Joe Nuseibeh, Palestine Students (letter to the editor), *Washington Post*, 30 September 1949, at 22.

100 Sam Zagoria, Arab Student Denied Visa by Israel, *Washington Post*, 1 September 1950, at B1.
101 As quoted in the document Zur Staatsangehörigkeit von Palästina-Flüchtlingen. Namensführung [On the Nationality of Palestine Refugees: Instruction as to a Name], Expert Committee No. 3103, 29/30 April 1987, rapporteur Dietrich Marcks, City Council, Minden, *Das Standesamt* (Frankfurt am Main) No. 12 (December 1987), 354, at 355. Also referenced by Zimmermann, at 235. However, a German trial level court, without mentioning the 1984 statement, declined to apply Palestinian law as to age of majority, on the grounds that Germany did not recognize a Palestine state. District Court of Neumünster, Decision of 16 December 1986, *Die deutsche Rechtsprechung auf dem Gebiete des Internationalen Privatrechts im Jahre 1986*, at 246 (Item No. 108) (1988). The Decision of 16 December 1986 appears in French translation in *Revue critique de droit international privé*, vol. 77, 675 (1988), and see analysis of it by Joe Verhoeven, ibid., at 676–682.
102 Abbas Shiblak, Residency Status and Civil Rights of Palestinian Refugees in Arab Countries, in Abbas Shiblak and Uri Davis, *Civil and Citizenship Rights of Palestinian Refugees* (Ramallah: Palestinian Diaspora and Refugee Centre 1996), 4, at 13–14.
103 Law No. 1311 (1963), on which see Ghada Hashem Talhami, *Palestinian Refugees: Pawns to Political Actors* (New York: Nova Science Publishers 2003), at 108. On Lebanon, see Wadie Said, The Obligations of Host Countries to Refugees under International Law: The Case of Lebanon, in Naseer Aruri, *Palestinian Refugees: The Right of Return* (London: Pluto Press 2001), 123, at 135–139.
104 Protocol for the Treatment of Palestinians in Arab States ("Casablanca Protocol"), 11 September 1965, accessible at www.unhcr.org/refworld
105 *Aboushehata v. U.S. Attorney-General*, 130 Federal Appendix 336 (U.S. Ct. Appeals 11th Cir. 2005). *Al-Fara v. Gonzales*, 404 F.3d 733 (3d Cir. 2005).
106 *Abdelwahed v. Immigration and Naturalization Service*, 22 Federal Appendix 811, at 814 (U.S. Ct. Appeals 9th Cir. 2001).
107 *Szife v. Minister for Immigration and Citizenship*, 2007 FCA 745, Federal Court of Australia, New South Wales District Registry, BC200703673, 10 May 2007.
108 *NACQ v Minister for Immigration & Multicultural & Indigenous Affairs*, Federal Court of Australia, New South Wales District Registry, [2002] FCAFC 355, N 367 of 2002.
109 *R (on the application of YA) v Secretary of State for Health*, Court of Appeal, Civil Division, [2009] All England Reports (D) 300 (Mar), [2009] EWCA Civ 225, 30 March 2009.

CHAPTER 11

1 Michael R. Fischbach, Palestine Liberation Army, in Philip Mattar, ed., *Encyclopedia of the Palestinians* (New York: Facts on File 2000), at 286. Hillel Frisch, *The Palestinian Military: Between Militias and Armies* (London: Routledge 2008), at 52.

2 Arabs Create Organization for Recovery of Palestine, *New York Times*, 29 May 1964, at A5. Palestinians Set 'Liberation' Goal, *New York Times*, 31 May 1964, at A6. Helena Cobban, *The Palestinian Liberation Organisation: People, Power and Politics* (Cambridge: Cambridge University Press 1984), at 30.

3 Arabs Create Organization for Recovery of Palestine, *New York Times*, 29 May 1964, at A5.

4 Palestine National Covenant, 1964, accessible on website of Permanent Observer Mission of Palestine to the United Nations, http://www.un.int/palestine/PLO/PNA2.html.

5 The nationality provision as relates to Jews would be amended in a 1968 revision of the Covenant to read: "Article 6: The Jews who had normally resided in Palestine until the beginning of the Zionist invasion will be considered Palestinians." *New York University Journal of International Law and Politics*, vol. 3, at 227 (1970). The "Zionist invasion" was taken to date from the Balfour Declaration (1917), as the point separating Jews considered Zionist colonialists from those considered Palestinian. Philip Mishalani, The National Question and the PLO, in Fouzi El-Asmar, Uri Davis, and Naim Khader, eds., *Debate on Palestine* (London: Ithaca 1981), at 106.

6 Anis F. Kassim, The Palestine Liberation Organization's Claim to Status: A Juridical Analysis Under International Law, *Denver Journal of International Law and Policy*, vol. 9, 1, at 18 (1980).

7 Letter dated 15 October from the representatives of Algeria, Iraq, Jordan, Kuwait, Lebanon, Libya, Morocco, Saudi Arabia, Sudan, Syria, Tunisia, United Arab Republic and Yemen to the Chairman of the Special Political Committee, UN Doc. A/SPC/104, referenced in UN Doc. A/6115, 23 November 1965 (Check List of Documents).

8 UN Doc. A/6115, 23 November 1965, para. 5.

9 See e.g. Special Political Committee, Verbatim Record of the 665th Meeting, at 8, UN Doc. A/SPC/PV.665, 17 November 1969.

10 Kassim (Claim to Status), at 19.

11 Frisch (*The Palestinian Military*), at 57.

12 Communication of Permanent Representative of Israel to President of the Security Council, UN Security Council, 1347th meeting, UN Doc. S/PV.1347, 5 June 1967, at 1 (para. 4), and at 4 (para. 30).

13 Frisch (*The Palestinian Military*), at 57–58.

14 Henry Cattan, The Arab-Israeli Conflict and the Principles of Justice, *Revue Égyptienne de droit international*, vol. 28, 44, at 49 (1972).

15 Admission on Attack, *Times* (London), 8 July 1967, at 3.

16 Yoram Dinstein, *War, Aggression and Self-Defence* (Cambridge: Cambridge University Press 2005), at 192. Kenneth Lewan, Justifications for the Opening of Hostilities in the Middle East, *Revue Égyptienne de droit international*, vol. 26, 88 (1970).

17 John Quigley, The United Nations' Response to Israel's Seizure of the Gaza Strip and West Bank, *Palestine Yearbook of International Law*, vol. 12, 145, at 150–154 (2002–2003).

18 GA Res. 2253, 4 July 1967.

19 Proclamation No. 2, 7 June 1967, Collection of Proclamations and Orders (Judea and Samaria), at 3, reprinted in Meir Shamgar, ed., *Military Government in the Territories Administered by Israel 1967–1980: The Legal Aspects*, vol. 1, at 450 (1982).

20 Ibid. at 450.

21 SC Res. 237, 14 June 1967.

22 SC Res. 242, 22 November 1967.

23 GA Res. 2443, 19 December 1968.

24 SC Res. 465, 1 March 1980.

25 George E. Bisharat, *Palestinian Lawyers and Israeli Rule: Law and Disorder in the West Bank* (Austin: University of Texas Press 1989), at 146. *The Civilian Judicial System in the West Bank and Gaza: Present and Future* (Geneva: International Commission of Jurists 1994), at 34–38.

26 Bisharat, at 128.

27 Ibid. at 109–110. Meir Shamgar, Legal Concepts and Problems of the Israeli Military Government – The Initial Stage, in Meir Shamgar, ed., *Military Government in the Territories Administered by Israel 1967–1980: The Legal Aspects*, vol. 1, 13, at 54 (1982).

28 *The Civilian Judicial System in the West Bank and Gaza*, at 52–56.

29 Bisharat, at 119. Lynn Welchman, *Beyond the Code: Muslim Family Law and the Shari'a Judiciary in the Palestinian West Bank* (Hague: Kluwer Law International 2000), at 4.

30 Bisharat, at 141.

31 Ibid. at 40–43.

32 Usamah Shahwan, *Public Administration in Palestine Past and Present* (Lanham MD: University Press of America 2003), at 51.

33 Ismail Suny, *The Organization of the Islamic Conference* (Jakarta: Pustaka Sinar Harapan 2000), at 20.

34 GA Res. 2535B, 10 December 1969.

35 GA Res. 2562C, 8 December 1970.

36 GA Res. 2787, 6 December 1971.

37 W.T. Mallison and S.V. Mallison, An International Law Appraisal of the Juridical Characteristics of the Resistance of the People of Palestine: The Struggle for Human Rights, *Revue Égyptienne de droit international*, vol. 28, 1, at 15 (1972).

38 GA Res. 2799, 13 December 1971.

39 Mishalani, at 107. David Hirst, *The Gun and the Olive Branch: The Roots of Violence in the Middle East* (1984), at 294. Helena Cobban, *The Palestinian Liberation Organization: People, Power and Politics* (1984), at 16.

40 Muhammad Hallaj, Palestinian Statehood, in Winston A. Van Horne, ed., *Global Convulsions: Race, Ethnicity, and Nationalism at the End of the Twentieth Century* (Albany: State University of New York Press 1997), 189, at 192.

41 Arafat talking, *Economist*, 12 April 1975, at 51. David Hirst, at 325–326.

42 Hallaj, at 193–194.

43 GA Res. 3210, 14 October 1974.

44 UN Charter, Art. 9.

45 *Anti-Defamation League of B'nai B'rith v. Kissinger*, Civil Case 74 C 1545 (U.S. Dist. Ct. E.D.N.Y.) 1 November 1974, excerpted in U.S. Department of State, *Digest of United States Practice in International Law* 1974, 27, at 28.

46 Text of Arab Resolution at Rabat, *New York Times*, 30 October 1974, at A18. Arabs Hail Leaders' Declaration of Support for the Creation of a Palestinian State, *New York Times*, 30 October, 1974, at A18.

47 Kassim (Claim to Status), at 18.

48 *New York Times*, 22 November 1974, at 4. Welchman, at 11.

49 Hillel Frisch, *Countdown to Statehood: Palestinian State Formation in the West Bank and Gaza* (Albany: State University of New York Press 1998), at 41.

50 Leo Gross, Voting in the Security Council and the PLO, *American Journal of International Law*, vol. 70, 470 (1976).

51 Erik Suy, The Status of Observers in International Organizations, *Recueil des cours* (Hague Academy of International Law), vol. 160, 75, at 132–133 (1978-II).

52 Transcripts of Addresses to the U.N. Assembly by Arafat and Israeli Delegate, *New York Times*, 14 November 1974, at A22.

53 GA Res. 3236, 22 November 1974.

54 GA Res. 3237, 22 November 1974.

55 Suy, at 112.

56 Ibid. at 101.

57 Ibid. at 84.

58 Ibid. at 108.

59 Economic Commission for Western Asia Res. 12(II), 9 May 1975, in Suy, at 168 (note 59). Theodor Meron, The Composition of the UN Regional Economic Commissions and the PLO, *International and Comparative Law Quarterly*, vol. 28, 52, at 60 (1979).

60 GA Res. 3375, 10 November 1975.

61 GA Res. 3376, 10 November 1975.

62 UN Doc. S/11889, text quoted in UN Security Council, 1856th meeting, UN Doc. S/PV.1856, 30 November 1975, at 3. See also Kassim (Claim to Status), at 2; and Suy, at 110.

63 UN Security Council, 1859th meeting, UN Doc. S/PV.1859, 4 December 1975, at 1.

64 Ibid. at 6–7.

65 Ibid. at 8–9.

66 Ibid. at 9.

67 Ibid. at 16.

68 Gross, at 476–477.

69 UN Security Council, 1870th meeting, UN Doc. S/PV.1870, 12 January 1976, at 2–3. Suy, at 138–139.

70 UN Security Council, 1870th meeting, UN Doc. S/PV.1870, 12 January 1976, at 3.

71 Ibid. at 6.

72 Talmon (*Recognition of Governments*), at 17.

73 Ibid. at 157.
74 UN Security Council, 1870th meeting, UN Doc. S/PV.1870, 12 January 1976, at 12–13.
75 Ibid. at 16.
76 Patrick J. Travers, The Legal Effect of United Nations Action in Support of the Palestine Liberation Organization and the National Liberation Movements of Africa, *Harvard International Law Journal*, vol. 17, 561, at 572 (1976).
77 UN Security Council, 1672nd meeting, UN Doc. S/PV.1672, 15 November 1972, at 1, referring to Letter dated 13 November 1972 from the representatives of Somalia and the Sudan to the President of the Security Council (UN Doc. S/10830).
78 UN Security Council, 1679th meeting, UN Doc. S/PV.1679, 30 November 1972, at 1, referring to Letter dated 28 November 1972 from the representatives of Somalia and the Sudan to the President of the Security Council (UN Doc. S/10841).
79 UN Security Council, 1756th meeting, UN Doc. S/PV.1756, 10 December 1973, at 1. UN Security Council, 1758th meeting, UN Doc. S/PV.1758, 11 December 1973, at 1.
80 Malabika Banerjee, *The Nonaligned Movement* (Calcutta: Firma KLM 1982), at 20.
81 League of Arab States Doc. D3462/S.66/M.2–9/9/1976, cited in Kassim (Claim to Status), at 22.
82 Henry G. Schermers and Niels M. Blokker, *International Institutional Law: Unity within Diversity* (Boston: Martinus Nijhoff 2003), at 58.
83 Palestinians: It is the cause, my soul, *Economist*, 19 March 1977, at 66. Uri Avnery, *My Friend, the Enemy* (Westport CT: Lawrence Hill 1986), at 190.
84 Mishalani, at 121. Cobban, at 17.
85 Meron, at 61–63.
86 ECOSOC Resolution 2089, 22 July 1977.
87 Suy, at 168.
88 UN Charter, Art. 7.
89 Report: Expert Group Meeting on International Multimodal Transport in the ESCWA Region, Cairo, 4–6 September 2007, at 8, UN Doc. E/ESCWA/GRID/2007/7, 25 September 2007.
90 UN General Assembly, 32d session, 27th plenary meeting, at 513, UN Doc. A/32/PV.27, 10 October 1977.
91 Rules of Procedure of the General Assembly, Rule 73, UN Doc. A/520/Rev.15.
92 UN General Assembly, 32d session, 29th plenary meeting, at 571, UN Doc. A/32/PV.29, 11 October 1977.
93 Suy, at 141.
94 GA Res. 32/40, 2 December 1977.
95 Cyrus Vance, *Hard Choices: Critical Years in America's Foreign Policy* (New York: Simon & Schuster 1983), at 230.
96 Framework for Peace in the Middle East Agreed at Camp David (Israel-Egypt), 17 September 1978, 1138 UNTS 39.

97 Hazem Nuseibeh, Permanent Representative of Jordan to the United Nations, The West Bank Is Not Up for Grabs (Letter), *New York Times*, 1 June 1979, at A24.
98 GA Res. ES/7-2, 29 July 1980.
99 GA Res. 36/120C, 10 December 1981.
100 GA Res. 38/58C, 13 December 1983.
101 GA Res. 39/49D, 11 December 1984.

CHAPTER 12

1 Jonathan C. Randal, PLO's Armed-Struggle Rhetoric Muted by Pragmatic Politicking, *Washington Post*, 2 March 1980, at A1.
2 Anis F. Kassim, The Palestine Liberation Organization's Claim to Status: A Juridical Analysis Under International Law, *Denver Journal of International Law and Policy*, vol. 9, 1, at 19 (1980).
3 A.R. Norton and M.H. Greenberg, eds., *The International Relations of the Palestine Liberation Organization* (Carbondale IL: Southern Illinois University Press 1989), at 209–212.
4 *Re Arafat and Salah*, Court of Cassation, 28 June 1985, in *Italian Yearbook of International Law*, vol. 7, 295, at 296–297 (1988), from Corte di Cassazione, sezione I penale, sentenza 28 giugno 1985, Arafat e altro, *Il Foro Italiano*, vol. 109, 278, at 280 (1986).
5 William V. O'Brien, The PLO in International Law, *Boston University International Law Journal*, vol. 2, 349, at 379 (1984).
6 *Re Arafat and Salah*, Court of Cassation, 28 June 1985, in *Italian Yearbook of International Law*, vol. 7, 295, at 296 (1988), from Corte di Cassazione, sezione I penale, sentenza 28 giugno 1985, Arafat e altro, *Il Foro Italiano*, vol. 109, 278, at 280 (1986).
7 Stefan Talmon, *Recognition of Governments in International Law: With Particular Reference to Governments in Exile* (Oxford: Clarendon Press 1998), at 42.
8 Ibid. at 158, citing BBC Summary of World Broadcasts 2d series, ME/5995/A/4, 15 December 1978.
9 PLO diplomat in Vienna is granted official status, *Globe and Mail*, 14 March 1980.
10 Senegal reaffirms support for Palestinian people, Xinhua General News Service, 1 December 1981.
11 Henry Kamm, In Europe, P.L.O. comes under close watch, *New York Times*, 13 March 1986, at A18.
12 Official status for PLO in Spain, *Guardian*, 15 August 1986.
13 Eileen Denza, *Diplomatic Law: Commentary on the Vienna Convention on Diplomatic Relations* (Oxford: Oxford University Press 2008), at 256.
14 Francis A. Boyle, *Palestine, Palestinians and International Law* (Atlanta: Clarity Press 2003), at 26–42 (text of memorandum prepared by Francis A. Boyle).

15 John Kifner, Hussein Surrenders Claims on West Bank to the P.L.O., *New York Times*, 1 August 1988, at A1.

16 Excerpts from Hussein's address on abandoning claims to the West Bank, *New York Times*, 1 August 1988, at A4.

17 Jordan, Instruction, 20 August 1988, Art. 2, quoted in Jordan, High Court of Justice, Case No. 164/90, 24 January 1991, translated in *Palestine Yearbook of International Law*, vol. 6, 68 (1990–1991).

18 Ibid., Art. 6. Anis F. Kassim, The Palestinians: From Hyphenated to Integrated Citizenship, in Nils S. Butenschon, Uri Davis and Manuel Hassassian, *Citizenship and the State in the Middle East: Approaches and Applications* (New York: Syracuse University Press 2000), 201, at 213.

19 Palestine National Council, Declaration of Independence, 15 November 1988, UN Doc. A/43/827, S/20278, Annex III, 18 November 1988, reprinted in *International Legal Materials*, vol. 27, 1668 (1988).

20 Ibid., Annex II.

21 The Central Council, made up of the members of the Executive Committee plus representatives of various Palestinian organizations, functioned as an intermediary between the PNC and the Executive Committee.

22 The Executive Committee was an 18-member organ elected by the Palestine National Council as the executive agency of the PNC.

23 Letter dated 9 December 1988 from the Permanent Observer of the Palestine Liberation Organization to the United Nations addressed to the Secretary-General: Annex: Declaration of the formation of the provisional Government of the State of Palestine, 15 November 1988, U.N Doc. A/43/928, 9 December 1988.

24 Patrick E. Tyler, Geneva forum gives Arafat chance to clarify views, *Washington Post*, 4 December 1988, at A40.

25 Arafat demands corridor linking West Bank, Gaza, *Globe and Mail*, 26 December 1988.

26 Lynn Welchman, *Beyond the Code: Muslim Family Law and the Shari'a Judiciary in the Palestinian West Bank* (Hague: Kluwer Law International 2000), at 8. Adrien Wing, Legal Decision-Making During the Palestinian Intifada: Embryonic Self-Rule, *Yale Journal of International Law*, vol. 18, 95 (1993).

27 Glenn E. Robinson, *Building a Palestinian State: The Incomplete Revolution* (Bloomington: Indiana University Press 1997), at 95–105. Usamah Shahwan, *Public Administration in Palestine Past and Present* (Lanham MD: University Press of America 2003), at 53.

CHAPTER 13

1 Philip Taubman, Moscow Lauds P.L.O. State But Is Vague on Recognition, *New York Times*, 19 November 1988, at A4.

2 Paul Lewis, Arabs at U.N. relax stand on P.L.O., *New York Times*, 6 December 1989, at A3. Countries that have recognized the State of Palestine, *Palestine Yearbook of International Law*, vol. 5, 291 (1989) (listing 95 states with dates on which they recognized Palestine).

3 Stefan Talmon, *Recognition of Governments in International Law: With Particular Reference to Governments in Exile* (Oxford: Clarendon Press 1998), at 158.

4 David Remnick, Soviet, PLO Upgrade Relations, *Washington Post*, 11 January 1990, at A28.

5 BBC Summary of World Broadcasts, ME/0334/i, 14 December 1988.

6 Uzi Rabi, Oman, *Middle East Contemporary Survey*, vol. 12, at 452 (1988).

7 Talmon (*Recognition of Governments*), at 42.

8 Maurice Flory, La Naissance d'un État Palestinien, *Revue générale de droit international public*, vol. 93, 385, at 401 (1989).

9 Ibid. at 401.

10 Talmon (*Recognition of Governments*), at 156–157.

11 *Libération* (Paris), 23 November 1988. See also France recognizes right of Palestinians, Mitterrand says, Xinhua General Overseas News Service, 22 November 1988.

12 Jean-Pierre Filiu, François Mitterand and the Palestinians: 1956–95, *Journal of Palestine Studies*, vol. 38 (no. 2), 24, at 34 (2009).

13 Note (authored by N.H.), following Cour d'appel de Paris, 26 février 2004, Hani Al Hassan c. Nahila El Yafi, no. 2001/18887, *Revue Générale de Droit International Public*, vol. 108, 1066, at 1067 (2004).

14 13 Countries Back Palestinian Move, *New York Times*, 16 November 1988, at A10.

15 Robert Pear, U.S. won't oppose U.N. Geneva session, *New York Times*, 29 November 1988, at A3.

16 UN Doc. A/RES/43/177, 15 December 1988. Paul Lewis, U.N. ends its session in Geneva, approving 2 Mideast resolutions, *New York Times*, 16 December 1988, at A15.

17 Frederic L. Kirgis, Jr., Admission of "Palestine" as a Member of a Specialized Agency and Withholding the Payment of Assessments in Response, *American Journal of International Law*, vol. 84, 218, at 219 (1990).

18 James Crawford, *The Creation of States in International* Law (Oxford: Clarendon Press 2006), at 440–441.

19 John Dugard, *Recognition and the United Nations* (Cambridge: Grotius 1987), at 41–80. The Security Council plays a role as well, because under UN Charter, Art. 4, the General Assembly admits new members only on recommendation of the Security Council.

20 SC Res. 338, 22 October 1973, re-affirmed SC Res. 242.

21 GA Res. A/43/176, 15 December 1988.

22 SC Res. 541, 18 November 1983.

23 UN Security Council, 2841st mtg., UN Doc. S/PV.2841, 11 January 1989. See also Letter dated 21 May 2008 from the Permanent Observer of Palestine to the United Nations addressed to the President of the Security Council, UN Doc. S/2008/335 (2008) (referring to the Security Council's "past practice").

24 Security Council, Provisional Rules of Procedure, Rule 14, UN Doc. S/96/Rev.4 (1946).

25 PLO, Central Council, Decision of 3 April 1989, WAFA (Palestine News Agency), 4 April 1989, translated in *Palestine Yearbook of International Law*, vol. 5, 291 (1989).

26 UNESCO is not to be confused with the UN Economic and Social Council (ECOSOC), referenced earlier in the text, which is one of the main organs of the UN itself.

27 Robert Pear, Baker would ask cutoff of funds if U.N. agencies upgrade P.L.O., *New York Times*, 2 May 1989, at 12.

28 Constitution of the World Health Organization, Art. 3, 22 July 1946, 14 UNTS 185.

29 Adam Pertman, US Vows Cutoff in WHO Funds if PLO Joins, *Boston Globe*, 2 May 1989, at A1.

30 Paul Lewis, U.N. Health Agency Seeks Compromise on P.L.O., *New York Times*, 7 May 1989, at A5; U.S. Warns WHO on Admitting PLO, *Los Angeles Times*, 1 May 1989, at A1 (statement of State Dept. spokesperson Margaret Tutwiler).

31 Jonathan C. Randal, PLO Defeated in Bid to Join World Health Organization, *Washington Post*, 13 May 1989, at A1.

32 Norman Kempster, PLO Urged to Drop Bid to U.N. Unit; U.S. Warns It Would Withhold Money for Health Agency, *Los Angeles Times*, 3 May 1989, at A9.

33 *Hobart Mercury* (Nationwide News Australia), 5 May 1989.

34 Norman Kempster, PLO urged to drop bid to U.N. unit; U.S. warns it would withhold money for health agency, *Los Angeles Times*, 3 May 1989, at A9.

35 *Hobart Mercury* (Nationwide News Australia), 5 May 1989.

36 Robert Pear, Baker Would Ask Cutoff of Funds If U.N. Agencies Upgrade P.L.O, *New York Times*, 2 May 1989, at A12.

37 World Health Assembly, Provisional Verbatim Record of the Tenth Plenary Meeting, 12 May 1989, at 9, WHO Doc. A42/VR/10.

38 Jonathan C. Randal, PLO Defeated in Bid to Join World Health Organization, *Washington Post*, 13 May 1989, at A1. Burton Bollag, U.N. Health Agency Defers P.L.O. Application to 1990, *New York Times*, 13 May 1989, at A3.

39 Request of Palestine for admission as a Member of the World Health Organization, World Health Assembly Res. 42.1, preamble clause, Handbook of Resolutions, vol. 3 (1st ed.), 5.2 (tenth plenary meeting 12 May 1989).

40 Ibid., para. 1 & para. 2(1) and 2(2).

41 Ibid., para. 2(3) and 2(4).

42 World Health Assembly, Provisional Verbatim Record of the Tenth Plenary Meeting, 12 May 1989, at 7, WHO Doc. A42/VR/10.

43 Ibid. at 40.

44 Ibid. at 5.

45 Ibid. at 36.

46 Ibid. at 38 (G.D.R., Turkey), and 42 (India).

47 Ibid. at 39.

48 Ibid. at 34.

49 Ibid. at 40.

50 PLO launches bid to join UNESCO, *Toronto Star*, 10 May 1989, at A18.

51 UNESCO, Constitution, Art. 2, 16 November 1945, 4 UNTS 275.

52 *Palestine Yearbook of International Law*, vol. 5, 293–316 (1989).

53 U.S. Warns UNESCO on PLO Role, *Los Angeles Times*, 5 October 1989, at A2. UNESCO warned by U.S. against vote for PLO, *Globe and Mail* (Toronto), 6 October 1989.

54 Keep PLO out, U.N. group warned, *Toronto Star*, 6 October 1989, at A19.

55 PLO requests upgraded status at UN, commentaries condemn USA's 'relentless war, BBC Summary of World Broadcasts, 4 December 1989, ME/0630/A/1, quoting Voice of Palestine Radio, Baghdad, 1 December 1989.

56 UNESCO Doc. 132 EX/31, UNESCO, Decisions Adopted by the Executive Board at its 132nd Session (Paris, 28 September – 14 November 1989), UNESCO Doc. 132 EX/Decisions, 13 December 1989. Decision of Executive Board confirmed by Resolution 20 of General Conference, UNESCO Doc. 25 C/Res. 20 (1989).

57 Convention for the Amelioration of the Condition of the Wounded and Sick in Armed Forces in the Field, Art. 60, 12 August 1949, 75 UNTS 31; Convention for the Amelioration of the Condition of Wounded, Sick and Shipwrecked Members of Armed Forces at Sea, Art. 59, 12 August 1949, 75 UNTS 85; Convention Relative to the Treatment of Prisoners of War, Art. 139, 12 August 1949, 75 UNTS 135; Convention Relative to the Protection of Civilian Persons in Time of War, Art. 155, 12 August 1949, 75 UNTS 287.

58 Vienna Convention on the Law of Treaties, Art. 77, 23 May 1969, 1155 UNTS 331.

59 Government of Switzerland, Note of Information, Berne, 13 September 1989, reprinted in *Palestine Yearbook of International Law*, vol. 5, 322 (1989).

60 Report of the Committee on the Exercise of the Inalienable Rights of the Palestinian People, para. 112, UN Doc. A/44/35, 17 November 1989.

61 James Bone, Palestinian Win at UN Imperils Funding by US, *Times* (London), 30 November 1989.

62 UN Doc. A/44/L.50, 29 November 1989.

63 Paul Lewis, Arabs at U.N. relax stand on P.L.O., *New York Times*, 6 December 1989, at A3. Arabs defer plan to upgrade Palestine, Inter Press Service, 6 December 1989.

64 UN General Assembly, Provisional verbatim record of the seventy-sixth meeting, 6 December 1989, at 7, UN Doc. A/44/PV.76, 20 December 1989.

65 Ibid. at 11.

66 Arabs Defer Plan to Upgrade Palestine, Inter Press Service, 6 December 1989.

67 Foreign Relations Authorization Act, Fiscal Years 1990 and 1991, §414(a), U.S. Congress, Statutes at Large, vol. 104, at 15.

68 Palestine again applies for W.H.O. membership, Xinhua General Overseas News Service, 12 April 1990.

69 John A. Calcott, Resolution to postpone Palestinian debate, United Press International, 8 May 1990.

70 World Health Assembly Res. 43.1, 11 May 1990, *Handbook of Resolutions and Decisions of the World Health Assembly and the Executive Board*, vol. 3

(3rd ed.), item 5.2 (1993). UN health agency postpones vote on admitting Palestine, *Chicago Tribune*, 11 May 1990, at M4. U.N. Agency Rejects P.L.O. Role, *New York Times*, 11 May 1990, at A8.

71 Crawford (Israel (1948–1949) and Palestine (1998–1999)), at 116.

CHAPTER 14

1 The Peace Conference, *Palestine Yearbook of International Law*, vol. 6, 262–302 (1990–91).

2 U.S. applauds Palestinian vote, *Chicago Tribune*, 29 September 1991, at C3.

3 Edward Lucas, "Collision" stalls Mid-East talks, *Independent* (London), 16 January 1992, at 10.

4 Letter, Prime Minister Yitzhak Rabin to P.L.O. Chairman Arafat, 9 September 1993, *Palestine Yearbook of International Law*, vol. 7, 231 (1992–94).

5 Letter, PLO Chairman Arafat to Prime Minister Rabin, 9 September 1993, ibid. at 230.

6 Declaration of Principles on Interim Self-Government Arrangements (Israel-P.L.O.), 13 September 1993, UN Doc. A/48/486, S/26560 (Annex). The Russian Federation (a designation assumed upon the breakup of the USSR) was regarded as continuing the statehood of the USSR hence was the same state.

7 Ibid., Art. 1. SC Res. 338, 22 October 1973, called for implementation of Res. 242 but added nothing of substance.

8 Declaration of Principles on Interim Self-Government Arrangements, Art. 5.

9 Conor O'Clery, Arafat hopes to go to Gaza, Jericho, *Irish Times*, 14 September 1993, at 9. Mark Fineman, Jordan's King calls Palestinian ties premature, *Los Angeles Times*, 16 September 1993, at A1. Bob Hepburn, Syria blocking peace in Mideast, Rabin says, *Toronto Star*, 16 September 1993, at A18.

10 Declaration of Principles on Interim Self-Government Arrangements, preamble.

11 Opposition leader Netanyahu criticizes agreement with PLO during Knesset debate, BBC Summary of World Broadcasts, 23 September 1993, ME/1801/MED, from Voice of Israel, Jerusalem, in Hebrew 0947 gmt, 21 September 1993.

12 Douglas Davis, Kissinger: Peres is on an emotional binge, *Jerusalem Post*, 15 September 1993, at 2B.

13 Antonio Cassese, The Israel-PLO Agreement and Self-Determination, *European Journal of International Law*, vol. 4, 564, at 569 (1993).

14 Hersch Lauterpacht, *Recognition in International Law* (Cambridge: Cambridge University Press 1947), at 6.

15 Arafat is backed to head new authority, *Times* (London), 13 October 1993. PLO Central Council endorses PLO-Israel agreement, BBC Summary of World Broadcasts, 13 October 1993, ME/1818/MED.

16 GA Res. 48/58, 13 December 1993. See also GA Res. 49/62D, 14 December 1994, GA Res. 51/29, 2 November 1997.

17 Agreement on the Gaza Strip and the Jericho Area, 4 May 1994, in *Palestine Yearbook of International Law*, vol. 7, at 243 (1992–94), and as UN Doc. A/49/180, S/1994/727.
18 Interim Agreement on the West Bank and the Gaza Strip, 28 September 1995, in *Palestine Yearbook of International Law*, vol. 8, at 353 (1994–95), and as UN Doc. A/51/889, S/1997/357.
19 Ibid., Arts. 11, 13, and Annex 1.
20 Since "Palestinian National Authority" is the name used by the Authority itself, that name will be used in the text to refer to it. Many authors and governments use "Palestinian Authority" on the basis of that usage in the agreements.
21 Arafat sets two-year deadline for proclaiming Palestinian state, *Times* (London), 23 November 1996 (Overseas News section).
22 Declaration of Principles on Interim Self-Government Arrangements, Art. 5.
23 Agreement on the Gaza Strip and the Jericho Area.
24 Nasser Al-Kidwa, Re-Declaring Palestinian Statehood: Fears and Expectations, in *May 4, 1999: Implications of Declaring the State* (Washington DC: Center for Policy Analysis on Palestine 1999), at 11.
25 William Pfaff, Is Palestine ready to declare itself into being? *Baltimore Sun*, 5 December 1996, at 27A (quoting Whitbeck article in Jerusalem daily *Al Quds*).
26 Palestine by proclamation, *Economist*, 21 December 1996, at 13.
27 Israeli official says West Bank would be annexed if Palestinian state declared, Israel TV Channel 1, Jerusalem, in Hebrew 1800 gmt 26 November 1996, BBC Summary of World Broadcasts, 28 November 1996.
28 Netanyahu admits there is "international pressure" on Israel, IDF Radio, Tel Aviv, in Hebrew 1100 gmt 28 November 1996, BBC Summary of World Broadcasts, 29 November 1996.
29 Douglas Jehl, In Hebron accord, the future begins to take shape, *New York Times*, 19 January 1997, at A6.
30 Netanyahu optimistic about talks with Palestinians, Syria, BBC Summary of World Broadcasts, 24 January 1997, from Israel TV Channel 1, Jerusalem, 1845 gmt, 22 January 1997, ME/D2825/MED.
31 Palestinian Speaker says state to be declared at end of interim stage, BBC Summary of World Broadcasts, 14 May 1997, ME/D2918/MED, quoting Radio Monte Carlo in Arabic 1260 gmt, 12 May 1997.
32 Euro-Mediterranean Interim Association Agreement on trade and cooperation between the European Community, of the one part, and the Palestine Liberation Organization (PLO) for the benefit of the Palestinian Authority of the West Bank and the Gaza Strip, of the other part – Protocol 1 on the arrangements applying to imports into the Community of agricultural products originating in the West Bank and the Gaza Strip – Protocol 2 on the arrangements applying to imports into the West Bank and the Gaza Strip of agricultural products originating in the Community – Protocol 3 concerning the definition of the concept of 'originating products' and methods of administrative cooperation – Final Act – Joint Declarations – Declaration by the European Community, 24 February 1997, Council Decision 97/430/EC of 2 June 1997, *Official Journal* L 187, 16 July 1997, at 0003–0135.

33 Consolidated Version of the Treaty Establishing the European Community, Art. 133(3), *Official Journal* C325/33, 24 December 2002.

34 Council Decision 97/430/EC, 2 June 1997, *Official Journal* L 187, 16 July 1997, at 0001–0002. Andrea Ott and Ramses Wessel, The EU's External Relations Regime: Multilevel Complexity in an Expanding Union, in Steven Blockmans and Adam Łazowski, eds., *The European Union and its Neighbours: A Legal Appraisal of the EU's Policies of Stabilisation, Partnership and Integration* (Hague: TMC Asser Press 2006), 19, at 25 (note 25).

35 Euro-Mediterranean Interim Association Agreement, Protocol 3 concerning the definition of the concept of "originating products" and methods of administrative cooperation, Art. 20(5).

36 *Brita GmbH v. Hauptzollamt Hamburg-Hafen*, European Court of Justice, Case C-386/08, 25 February 2010, para. 58.

37 Ibid., para. 50. The brackets around "State," in the text above, are those of the Court.

38 Barcelona Declaration adopted at the Euro-Mediterranean Conference, 27–28 November 1995.

39 *Brita GmbH v. Hauptzollamt Hamburg-Hafen*, European Court of Justice, Case C-386/08, Opinion of Advocate General Bot, 29 October 2009, para. 9.

40 Participation of Palestine in the Work of the United Nations, GA Res. 52/250, 7 July 1998. On this resolution, see Robbie Sabel, *Procedure at International Conferences: A study of the rules of procedure at the UN and at inter-governmental conferences* (Cambridge: Cambridge University Press 2006), at 54–55.

41 In 1985, the name of the Economic Commission for Western Asia was changed to Economic and Social Commission for Western Asia.

42 China works closely with the Group of 77, hence the organization is sometimes referred to as Group of 77 and China. The number "77" is retained in the title, even though the membership has passed 130.

43 UN General Assembly, 56th Session, 3d plenary meeting, UN Doc. A/56/PV.3, at 12–13, 19 September 2001.

44 UN General Assembly, 25th Special Session, 1st meeting, UN Doc. A/S-25/PV.1, at 1, 6 June 2001.

45 Participation of Palestine in the work of the United Nations: Note by the Secretary-General, UN Doc. A/52/1002, 4 August 1998.

46 Commission of the European Communities, 26 March 1999, Presidency conclusions: Berlin European Council 24 and 25 March 1999. Memorandum circulated concurrently with the speech delivered at the General Assembly of the United Nations on September 21, 1999 by H.E. Ms Tarja Halonen, Minister for Foreign Affairs of Finland, on behalf of the European Union.

47 Azmi Bishara, 4 May 1999 and Palestinian Statehood: To Declare or Not to Declare, *Journal of Palestine Studies*, vol. 28 (no. 2), 5, at 11 (Winter 1999).

48 Hisham Sharabi, Declaring the State: Opening Remarks, in *May 4, 1999: Implications of Declaring the State* (Washington DC: Center for Policy Analysis on Palestine 1999), at 5.

49 Government Decision on the Wye River Memorandum, 11 November 1998, para. 8, www.mfa.gov.il.

50 *Palestinian declaration of statehood and May 4, 1999: frequently asked questions*, communicated by the Israeli Ministry of Foreign Affairs, 19 April 1999, www.mfa.gov.il. See, to same effect, Tal Becker, International Recognition of a Unilaterally Declared Palestinian State: Legal and Policy Dilemmas, Jerusalem Center for Public Affairs (electronic), www.jcpa.org/art/becker2.htm (circa 2000).

51 Ibid.

52 Herbert Hansell and Nicholas Rostow, *Legal Implications of May 4, 1999* (Washington DC: Washington Institute for Near East Policy 1999), at xi (transcription of remarks of Nasser al-Kidwa).

53 Graham Usher, After Oslo? *Middle East International*, 9 April 1999, at 7.

54 John M. Broder, Clinton Tells Palestinians To Go Slow on Statehood, *New York Times*, 27 April 1999, at A8.

55 Graham Usher, Arafat evades the issue, *Middle East International*, 7 May 1999, at 4.

56 Palestinian Council, Press release concerning 4 May 1999 and the declaration of statehood, Ramallah, 20 April 1999, in *Journal of Palestine Studies*, vol. 28 (no. 4), at 153 (Summer 1999).

57 Interim Agreement on the West Bank and the Gaza Strip.

58 Mala Tabory, The Legal Personality of the Palestinian Autonomy, in Amos Shapira and Mala Tabory, eds., *New Political Entities in Public and Private International Law With Special Reference to the Palestinian Entity* (Hague: Kluwer Law International 1999), 139, at 142.

59 James Crawford, Israel (1948–1949) and Palestine (1998–1999): Two Studies in the Creation of States, in *The Reality of International Law: Essays in Honour of Ian Brownlie* (Oxford: Clarendon Press 1999, Guy S. Goodwin-Gill and Stefan Talmon, editors), 95, at 121.

60 Ibid. at 124.

61 Ibid. at 122.

62 Declaration of Principles on Interim Self-Government Arrangements, Art. 5(3).

63 SC Res. 1244, 10 June 1999, para. 10.

64 Moshe Zak, Samaria is not Kosovo, *Jerusalem Post*, 18 June1999, at 8A.

65 GA Res. 43/176, 15 December 1988, para. 4.

66 Christopher Slaney, Palestinians Differ on Desirability of Statehood, But Not on Need for Independence From Israel, *Washington Report on Middle East Affairs*, October/November 2000, at 9–10.

67 Arafat says Palestinian state will be declared on 13th September, Voice of Palestine (radio), Ramallah, in Arabic 1105 gmt 25 June 2000, BBC Monitoring Middle East Political.

68 Deborah Sontag, P.L.O. decides on early statehood move, *New York Times*, 4 July 2000, at A5. Palestinian State This Year: Arafat, *Daily Telegraph* (Australia), 4 July 2000, at A27.

69 Israel: No Palestinian State without OK, United Press International, 4 July 2000.

70 Khalid Amaryeh, Statehood dilemma, *Middle East International*, 18 August 2000, at 6. Christopher Slaney, Palestinians Differ on Desirability of Statehood, But Not on Need for Independence From Israel, *Washington Report on Middle East Affairs*, October/November 2000, at 9–10.

71 PLO Central Council Issues Statement on Statehood, Further Talks, Palestinian Satellite Channel TV, Gaza, in Arabic 1822 gmt 10 September 2000, BBC Summary of World Broadcasts, 12 September 2000.

72 Israeli premier denies readiness to hand over land, uproot settlements, Israel TV Channel 1, Jerusalem, in Hebrew 1900 gmt 25 Mar 01, BBC Summary of World Broadcasts, 27 March 2001.

CHAPTER 15

1 SC Res. 1397, 12 March 2002, called for resumed negotiations based on SC Res. 242 and SC Res. 338.

2 UN Doc. S/2003/529, 7 May 2003.

3 Ibid.

4 James Crawford, *The Creation of States in International Law* (Oxford: Clarendon Press 2006), at 448.

5 SC Res. 1515, 19 November 2003.

6 Status of the Occupied Palestinian Territory, including East Jerusalem, GA Res. 58/292, 17 May 2004.

7 Rules of Procedure of the General Assembly, Rule 27, UN Doc. A/520/Rev.15.

8 GA Res. A/RES/ES-10/14, 8 December 2003.

9 Legal Consequences of the Construction of a Wall in the Occupied Palestinian Territory, Advisory Opinion, 2004 ICJ 136, at 183.

10 Ibid. at 200.

11 Ibid. at 184.

12 Ibid. at 184.

13 Crawford (*The Creation of States in International Law*), at 448.

14 Legal Consequences of the Construction of a Wall in the Occupied Palestinian Territory, Advisory Opinion, 2004 ICJ 136, at 200–201.

15 Statute of the International Court of Justice, Art. 66, para. 2.

16 Legal Consequences of the Construction of a Wall in the Occupied Palestinian Territory, Order of 19 December 2003, 2003 ICJ 428, at 429.

17 Legal Consequences of the Construction of a Wall in the Occupied Palestinian Territory, Advisory Opinion, 2004 ICJ 136, at 141.

18 Ibid. at 215 (Higgins, J., separate opinion).

19 Memorandum of Understanding on Maritime Transport Cooperation in the Arab Mashreq, text adopted by Economic and Social Commission for Western Asia, Res. 256 (XXIII), 9 May 2005, UN Doc. E/ESCWA/23/RES/L.254, also UN Doc. E/ESCWA/GRID/2005/11, 17 November 2005.

20 Ibid., Art. 22.

21 Ibid., Art. 18.

22 Vienna Convention on the Law of Treaties, Art. 12, 23 May 1969, 1155 UNTS 331.

23 Memorandum of Understanding on Maritime Transport Cooperation in the Arab Mashreq, Damascus, 9 May 2005, Palestine: Definitive Signature, Reference C.N.624.2005.TREATIES-10 (Depositary Notification), 9 August 2005 (stating, "The Secretary-General of the United Nations, acting in his capacity as depositary, communicates the following: The above action was effected on 9 May 2005.")

24 Agreement on International Roads in the Arab Mashreq, text adopted by Economic and Social Commission for Western Asia, 10 May 2001, UN Doc. E/ESCWA/TRANS/2001/3, 2228 UNTS 410.

25 Ibid., Art. 12.

26 Ibid., Art. 5.

27 Agreement on International Roads in the Arab Mashreq, Beirut, 10 May 2001, Palestine: Ratification, Reference C.N. 1275.2006.TREATIES-3 (Depositary Notification), 5 January 2007 (stating, "The Secretary-General of the United Nations, acting in his capacity as depositary, communicates the following: The above action was effected on 28 November 2006").

28 Agreement on International Railways in the Arab Mashreq, text adopted by Economic and Social Commission for Western Asia, 14 April 2003, UN Doc. E/ESCWA/TRANS/2002/1/Rev.2, 5 March 2003.

29 Ibid., Art. 11.

30 Ibid., Art. 4.

31 Agreement on International Railways in the Arab Mashreq, Beirut, 14 April 2003, Palestine: Ratification, Reference C.N. 1274.2006.TREATIES-2 (Depositary Notification, 5 January 2007 (stating, "The Secretary-General of the United Nations, acting in his capacity as depositary, communicates the following: The above action was effected on 28 November 2006").

32 *Multilateral Treaties Deposited with the Secretary-General*, see section "Historical Information," entry for "Palestine," www.un.org.

33 Summary of Practice of the Secretary-General as Depositary of Multilateral Treaties, at 24, UN Doc. ST/LEG/7/Rev.1 (1999).

34 Abbas: Palestinians Reject Temporary-Borders Statehood, Xinhua General News Service, 6 December 2007. World & Nation Update: Abroad, *Newsday*, 7 December 2007, at A42.

35 Khalid Abu Toameh, PA Bill Bans Concessions on Jerusalem, *Jerusalem Post*, 7 December 2007, at 5. Suzanne Goldenberg, Arabs Offer Peace Plan but the Killing Goes On: Recognition of Jewish State in Historic Move, *Guardian*, 29 March 2002, at 1.

36 SC Res. 1850, 16 December 2008.

37 Rome Statute of the International Criminal Court, 17 July 1998, 2187 UNTS 3, Arts. 6, 7, 8.

38 Ibid., Art. 13(b).

39 General Assembly Tenth Emergency Special Session 16 January 2009, States News Service, January 16, 2009 (statement of Javier Loayza Barea, Bolivia).

40 Rome Statute of the International Criminal Court, Art. 12(2)(b).

41 Israel signed the Statute on 31 December 2000 but advised the UN Secretary-General on 28 August 2002 that it did not intend to ratify. See *Multilateral Treaties Deposited with the Secretary-General*.

42 Rome Statute of the International Criminal Court, Art. 12(2)(a).
43 The Court has jurisdiction only over acts occurring after its Statute, as a treaty, came into force, which was 1 July 2002.
44 Chapter, actually "Part," IX of the Statute requires states party to cooperate with the Court in its investigations and prosecutions.
45 www.icc-cpi.int/NR/rdonlyres/74EEE201–0FED-4481–95D4-C807108710 2C/279777/20090122PalestinianDeclaration2.pdf.
46 Rome Statute of the International Criminal Court, Art. 15 (allowing the prosecutor to initiate investigations "on the basis of information on crimes within the jurisdiction of the Court").
47 www.icc-cpi.int/NR/rdonlyres/4F8D4963-EBE6–489D-9F6F-1-B3C1057EA0A/279794/ICCOTP20090122Palestine.pdf.
48 Human Rights Council, Report of the United Nations Fact-Finding Mission on the Gaza Conflict (Goldstone report), UN Doc. A/HRC/12/48, 15 September 2009, para. 1970.
49 Report of the International Criminal Court to the United Nations for 2008/09, para. 51, UN Doc. A/64/356, 17 September 2009.
50 BBC Summary of World Broadcasts, 30 September 2009, relaying report from Gaza by Huda Barud, Al-Mansi Denounces Israel's Obstruction of the Work of Wataniya Mobile, from Filastin website, Gaza, in Arabic 28 September 2009. Eli Lake, Israelis may stay home to avoid arrest, *Washington Times*, 13 October 2009, at 1.
51 Adam Gonn, PA Asks for International Help in Cellular Network Dispute with Israel. West Bank Firm Accuses Israel of Withholding Frequencies, *Jerusalem Post*, 9 October 2009, at 6.
52 Ben Lynfield, Palestinians Accuse Israel of Blackmail in Battle for Airwaves, *Independent* (London), 2, October 2009, at 26.
53 Rome Statute of the International Criminal Court, Art. 8(2)(b)(viii).
54 Ibid., Art. 27.
55 International Criminal Court – Press Briefing by Israel Foreign Ministry Legal Advisor Alan Baker Jerusalem, 3 January 2001http://www.mfa.gov.il/MFA/MFAArchive/2000_2009/2001/1/International+Criminal+Court+-+Press+Briefing+by+I.htm.
56 Orna Ben-Naftali, Aeyal M. Gross, and Keren Michaeli, Illegal Occupation: Framing the Occupied Palestinian Territory, *Berkeley Journal of International Law*, vol. 23, 551, at 581 (2005).
57 ICC Prosecutor receives Palestinian Minister of Justice, Arab League and Independent Fact-Finding Committee, International Criminal Court Doc. ICC-OTP-20091016-PR465, 16 October 2009.
58 John Dugard, Make a Case of It, *International Herald Tribune*, 23 July 2009, at 6. Al-Haq Position Paper on Issues Arising from the Palestinian Authority's Submission of a Declaration to the Prosecutor of the International Criminal Court under Article 12(3) of the Rome Statute, 14 December 2009 (Ramallah: Al-Haq) (Michael Kearney, Stijn Denayer), accessible at www.alhaq.org.
59 Assaf Uni, Solana to UN: Accept Palestinian State Even if Israel Does Not, *Haaretz*, 12 July 2009 (electronic).

60 Benjamin Netanyahu, Speech at the National Defense College Graduation Ceremony, 28 July 2009, http://www.pmo.gov.il/PMOEng/Communication/PMSpeaks/speechmabal280709.htm

61 Palestinian National Authority, *Palestine: Ending the Occupation, Establishing the State: Program of the Thirteenth Government*, August 2009, at 5 (electronic)

62 Ibid. at 6.

63 Ibid. at 18.

64 Donald Macintyre, Palestinian Push for an Independent State Causes Israeli Alarm: Netanyahu to Denounce Prime Minister's Drive to Sidestep Israel and Secure Support from UN Security Council, *Independent* (London), 16 November 2009, at 18.

65 Ian Kelly, Department Spokesman, Daily Press Briefing, U.S. Department of State, Washington DC, 16 November 2009, accessible at www.state.gov/r/pa/prs/dpb/2009/nov/131982.htm

66 EU rejects request to recognize independent Palestine, euobserver.com, 17 November 2009 (electronic).SC Res. 1850, 16 December 2008.

CHAPTER 16

1 Convention on Rights and Duties of States, Art. 1, Montevideo, 26 December 1933, 165 LNTS 19.

2 *Some of the Results of the Montevideo Conference: Address by the Honorable Cordell Hull, Secretary of State, before the National Press Club, Washington, February 10, 1934* (Washington: U.S. Government Printing Office 1934), at 4.

3 *Report of the Delegates of the United States of America to the Seventh International Conference of American States, Montevideo, Uruguay, December 3–26, 1933* (Washington: U.S. Government Printing Office 1934), at 170.

4 Convention on Rights and Duties of States, Art. 3.

5 Ibid., Art. 4.

6 Ibid., Art. 5.

7 *Report of the Delegates of the United States of America to the Seventh International Conference of American States*, at 18–21.

8 James Crawford, *The Creation of States in International Law* (Oxford: Clarendon Press 2006), at 61.

9 Stefan Talmon, Recognition of States and Governments in International Law, *Azerbaijan in the World*, vol. 1, no. 19 (1 November 2008) (electronic), http://ada.edu.az/biweekly/issues/158/20090328015413680.html

10 Crawford (*The Creation of States in International Law* [2006]), at 62.

11 Stefan Talmon, Recognition of States and Governments in International Law, *Azerbaijan in the World*, vol. 1, no. 19 (1 November 2008) (electronic), http://ada.edu.az/biweekly/issues/158/20090328015413680.html

12 Gilad Noam, Territorial Aspects of the Israeli-Palestinian Conflict: A Legal Perspective on Some Historical and Contemporary Issues, at 18, Hebrew

University International Law Research Paper No. 6–06 (2005), accessible at www.ssrn.com/abstract=902944.

13 Ashrawi at the time was Minister of Higher Education and Research in the Palestinian National Authority.

14 Douglas Jehl, In Hebron Accord, the Future Begins to Take Shape, *New York Times*, 19 January 1997, at A6.

15 North Sea Continental Shelf Cases (F.R.G./Denmark; F.R.G./Netherlands), 1969 ICJ 3, at 32.

16 Omar M. Dajani, Stalled Between Seasons: The International Legal Status of Palestine During the Interim Period, *Denver Journal of International Law and Policy*, vol. 26, 27, at 84 (1997).

17 Dajani, at 83, citing James Crawford, *The Creation of States in International Law* (Oxford: Clarendon Press 1979), at 40.

18 The court posed the question inaccurately by asking whether "the PLO" was a state. It should have asked whether "Palestine" was a state.

19 *Klinghoffer v. S.N.C. Achille Lauro*, 937 F.2d 44, at 47–48 (2nd Cir. 1991).

20 Daniel C. Turack, *The Passport in International Law* (Lexington MA: D.C. Heath 1972), at 237–241.

21 *Jaber v Minister for Immigration and Multicultural Affairs*, Federal Court of Australia, Western Australia District Registry [2001] FCA 1878, W 428 of 2001. And see http://www.ica.gov.sg/services_centre_overview. aspx?pageid=252&secid=165 (Singapore).

22 New Palestinian Passports Available Beginning Sunday, Ma'an News Agency, 29 March 2009.

23 United States Bureau of Citizenship and Immigration Services, *Palestine/ Occupied Territories: Information on Passports Issued by The Palestine National Authority*, 17 December 1998, PAL99001.ZCH.

24 *Majd v. Gonzales*, 446 F.3d 590, at 592 (5th Cir. 2006).

25 Codified as 8 U.S.C. §1101(a)(30).

26 Luke T. Lee and John Quigley, *Consular Law and Practice* (Oxford: Oxford University Press 2008), at 146–147.

27 U.S. Department of State, "Israel, the West Bank and Gaza," accessible at http://travel.state.gov/travel/cis_pa_tw/cis/cis_1064.html (posted 12 June 2009).

28 Isabel Kershner, Hamas arrest British journalist in Gaza, *New York Times*, 16 February 2010, at A9.

29 Al-Haq Position Paper on Issues Arising from the Palestinian Authority's Submission of a Declaration to the Prosecutor of the International Criminal Court under Article 12(3) of the Rome Statute, 14 December 2009 (Ramallah: Al-Haq) (Michael Kearney, Stijn Denayer), para. 26, accessible at www.alhaq.org.

30 Marshall J. Breger and Shelby R. Quast, International Commercial Arbitration: A Case Study of the Areas under Control of the Palestinian Authority, *Case Western Reserve Journal of International Law*, vol. 32, 185 (2000).

31 OPEC Fund and Palestine Sign Investment Encouragement and Protection Agreement, OPEC press release no. 28/2001, Vienna, 17 May 2001.

32 Agreement on Encouragement of Investment Between the United States of America and the Palestine Liberation Organization for the Benefit of the Palestinian Authority Pursuant to the Agreement on the Gaza Strip and the Jericho Area, 11 August and 12 September 1994, U.S. State Dept. No. 94-233, TIAS 12564.

33 Interim Agreement on the West Bank and the Gaza Strip, Art. 5(b), 28 September 1995, in *Palestine Yearbook of International Law*, vol. 8, at 353 (1994–95), and as UN Doc. A/51/889, S/1997/357. See also Geoffrey Watson, *The Oslo Accords: International Law and the Israeli-Palestinian Peace Agreements* (Oxford: Oxford University Press 2000), at 245.

34 Jean Allain, *On Achieving Palestinian Statehood: Concepts, Ends and Means from the Perspective of International Law* (Birzeit: Ibrahim Abu-Lughod Institute of International Studies 2002), at 14–15.

35 *Ungar v. Palestine Liberation Organization*, 402 F.3d 274, at 288–292 (1st Cir. 2005).

36 Anis F. Kassim, A Response to Dr. Evyatar Levine, *Denver Journal of International Law and Policy*, vol. 10, 259, at 261 (1980).

37 Francis A. Boyle, The Creation of the State of Palestine, *European Journal of International Law*, vol. 1, 301 (1990). James Crawford, The Creation of the State of Palestine: Too Much Too Soon? *European Journal of International Law*, vol. 1, 307 (1990).

38 Inge Amundsen and Basem Ezbidi, PNA Political Institutions and the Future of State Formation, in Mushtaq Husain Khan, ed., *State Formation in Palestine: Viability and Governance during a Social Transformation* (London: Routledge 2004), at 141.

39 Quoted and translated in Raja Shehadeh, Questions of Jurisdiction: A Legal Analysis of the Gaza-Jericho Agreement, *Journal of Palestine Studies*, vol. 23 (no. 4), 18, at 23 (1994).

40 Jordan, Law No. 16 (1960).

41 Birzeit University, Institute of Law, http://muqtafi2.birzeit.edu/en/pg/.

42 Usamah Shahwan, *Public Administration in Palestine Past and Present* (Lanham MD: University Press of America 2003), at 65.

43 Mona Rishmawi, The Actions of the Palestinian Authority Under the Gaza/Jericho Agreements, in *The Palestine National Authority: A Critical Appraisal* (Washington: Center for Policy Analysis on Palestine 2005), 3, at 7.

44 Shahwan, at 65.

45 Ibid. at 68. Hillel Frisch, *Countdown to Statehood: Palestinian State Formation in the West Bank and Gaza* (Albany: State University of New York Press 1998), at 133–134.

46 Shahwan, at 71.

47 Michael R. Fischbach, Palestine Liberation Army, in *Encyclopedia of the Palestinians* (Philip Mattar ed.), (New York: Facts on File 2000), at 286. Hillel Frisch, *The Palestinian Military: Between Militias and Armies* (London: Routledge 2008), at 75.

48 Basic Law, Palestine, *Official Gazette*, Special Issue, 7 July 2002, accessible at http://muqtafi.birzeit.edu/mainleg/14138.htm.
49 Palestine, *Official Gazette*, Special Issue No. 2, 19 March 2003, reprinted in *Palestine Year Book of International Law*, vol. 12, 377 (2002–2003).
50 Law No. 15 (1995), Elections Law, Art. 7(2)(a).
51 Human Rights Watch, *Justice Undermined: Balancing Security and Human Rights in the Palestinian Justice System* (New York: Human Rights Watch 2001), at 13–14.
52 Law No. 3 (2001).
53 Law No. 3 (1999) on Regulating Legal Practice, reprinted in *Palestine Year Book of International Law*, vol. 11, 298 (2000–2001).
54 Law No. 5 (2001), Art. 1.
55 Law No. 1 (2002).
56 Supreme Constitutional Court Law No. 3 (2006).
57 Constitutional Objection No. 1, High Court, Ramallah, Judgment (2006), 19 December 2006. Constitutional Objection No. 5, High Court, Gaza (2005), 27 November 2005. Both accessible in Birzeit University, Institute of Law, Palestinian Legal and Judicial System "al-muqtafi" at http://muqtafi. birzeit.edu/en/index.asp. The latter case also in *Palestine Yearbook of International Law*, vol. 14, 99 (2006–2007).
58 U.S. Department of State, *Country Reports on Human Rights Practices for 2007* (Washington: Government Printing Office 2008), at 1904.
59 Thomas Giegerich, The Palestinian Autonomy and International Human Rights Law: Perspectives on an Ongoing Process of Nation-Building, in Amos Shapira and Mala Tabory, eds., *New Political Entities in Public and Private International Law With Special Reference to the Palestinian Entity* (Hague: Kluwer Law International 1999), 183, at 206–230.
60 Human Rights Watch, Justice Undermined: Balancing Security and Human Rights in the Palestinian Justice System, at 3.
61 Basic Law, Art. 10.
62 Arab Charter on Human Rights, adopted by the League of Arab States, reprinted in *Human Rights Law Journal*, vol. 18, 151 (1997). Entered into force 16 March 2008. Ratification by Palestine 28 November 2007, noted at www.arableagueonline.org/lasimages/picture_gallery/human8–3-2010.PDF
63 http://www.ohchr.org/EN/Countries/MENARegion/Pages/PSSummary. aspx.
64 High commissioner for the promotion and protection of all human rights, GA Res. 48/141, para. 4(d), 7 January 1994.
65 U.S. Department of State, *Country Reports on Human Rights Practices for 2007* (Washington DC: Government Printing Office 2008), at 1900.
66 Nathan Brown, Palestine: The Schism Deepens, Carnegie Endowment for International Peace, Web Commentary, August 2009, www.carnegieendowment.org/files/palestine_schism1.pdf. Yezid Sayigh, Hamas rule in Gaza: three years on, Crown Center for Middle East Studies, Brandeis University, Middle East Brief 41, March 2010, http://www.brandeis.edu/ crown/publications/meb/meb41.html.
67 Michael Jansen, Fatah and Hamas agree on reconciliation plan, *Irish Times*, 24 March 2008, at 10.

68 Crawford (*The Creation of States in International Law* [2006]), at 69.

69 Dajani, at 89.

70 Crawford (*The Creation of States in International Law* [2006]), at 59.

71 James Crawford, Israel (1948–1949) and Palestine (1998–1999): Two Studies in the Creation of States, in Guy S. Goodwin-Gill and Stefan Talmon, eds., *The Reality of International Law: Essays in Honour of Ian Brownlie* (Oxford: Clarendon Press 1999), 95, at 114.

72 William Pfaff, Is Palestine ready to declare itself into being? *Baltimore Sun*, 5 December 1996, at 27A (quoting Whitbeck article in Jerusalem daily *Al Quds.*)

73 Vaughan Lowe, *International Law* (Oxford: Oxford University Press 2007), at 164.

CHAPTER 17

1 Legal Consequences of the Construction of a Wall in the Occupied Palestinian Territory, Advisory Opinion, 2004 ICJ 136, at 183.

2 See, e.g., GA Res. 61/184, 20 December 2006; SC Res. 1322, 7 October 2000.

3 *Tamimi v. Minister of Defence*, H.C. 507/85, 41(4) P.D. 57, excerpted in *Israel Yearbook on Human Rights*, vol. 18, 248, at 249 (1988).

4 Geoffrey Watson, *The Oslo Accords: International Law and the Israeli-Palestinian Peace Agreements* (Oxford: Oxford University Press 2000), at 62.

5 James Crawford, *The Creation of States in International Law* (Oxford: Clarendon Press 2006), at 73. R.Y. Jennings, *The Acquisition of Territory in International Law* (Manchester: University of Manchester Press 1963), at 5.

6 Jennings, at 55–56.

7 Crawford (*The Creation of States in International Law* [2006]), at 73.

8 Eyal Benvenisti, The Origins of the Concept of Belligerent Occupation, *Law and History Review*, vol. 26, 621, at 627–632 (2008).

9 Charles Hyde, *International Law Chiefly as Interpreted and Applied by the United States* (Boston: Little, Brown 1922), vol. 2, 362–363.

10 Morris Greenspan, *The Modern Law of Land Warfare* (Berkeley: University of California Press 1959), at 217.

11 Gerhard von Glahn, *The Occupation of Enemy Territory* (Minneapolis: University of Minnesota Press 1957), at 31.

12 *Restatement of the Foreign Relations Law of the United States* (St. Paul: American Law Institute 1987), vol. 1, §201, Comment b.

13 Eyal Benvenisti, *The International Law of Occupation* (Princeton: Princeton University Press 1993), at 151. Jeffrey L. Dunoff, Steven R. Ratner, and David Wippman, *International Law: Norms, Actors, Process* (New York: Aspen 2006), at 116.

14 Eugene Cotran, Some Legal Aspects of the Declaration of Principles: A Palestinian View, in Eugene Cotran and Chibli Mallat, eds., *The Arab-Israeli Accords: Legal Perspectives* (London: Kluwer 1996), 67, at 73.

15 James Crawford, Israel (1948–1949) and Palestine (1998–1999): Two Studies in the Creation of States, in Guy S. Goodwin-Gill and Stefan Talmon, eds., *The Reality of International Law: Essays in Honour of Ian Brownlie* (Oxford: Clarendon Press 1999), 95, at 115.

16 Ibid. at 114.

17 *Knox v. Palestine Liberation Organization*, 306 F.Supp.2d 424, at 437 (U.S. Dist.Ct. S.D.N.Y. 2004).

18 International Labor Organization, Constitution, Art. 1.

19 International Labor Conference, 64th session, Record of Proceedings, Resolution 5, at 50 (1978).

20 Membership in UNIDO – Possible Request by Palestine, Memorandum to the Director-General (Legal Opinion), *United Nations Juridical Yearbook*, at 373 (1989).

21 GA Res. 38/180D, para. 5, 19 December 1983.

22 Frederic L. Kirgis, Jr., Admission of "Palestine" as a Member of a Specialized Agency and Withholding the Payment of Assessments in Response, *American Journal of International Law*, vol. 84, 218, at 222 (1990).

23 Kirgis, at 221–222.

24 Free City of Danzig and International Labour Organization, Advisory Opinion, at 7, PCIJ, Series B, no. 18, 26 August 1930.

25 Treaty of Peace with Germany (Treaty of Versailles), 28 June 1919, Arts. 102, 106, U.S. Congress, Statutes at Large, vol. 49, at 2712.

26 Free City of Danzig and International Labour Organization, at 8–9.

27 Ibid. at 15–16. Kirgis, at 222.

28 Constitution, United Nations Industrial Development Organization, Art. 3, 8 April 1979, UN Doc. A/CONF.90/19, *International Legal Materials*, vol. 18, at 667 (1979).

29 Membership in UNIDO – Possible Request by Palestine, Memorandum to the Director-General (Legal Opinion), *United Nations Juridical Yearbook*, at 373 (1989).

30 Yoram Dinstein, *The International Law of Belligerent Occupation* (New York: Cambridge University Press 2009), at 275.

31 Dinstein, at 277–279. *Disengaged Occupiers: The Legal Status of Gaza* (Tel Aviv: Gisha Legal Center for Freedom of Movement 2007), at 75–82. Raja Shehadeh, The Gaza Occupation: Beginnings and Endings, *Palestine Yearbook of International Law*, vol. 14, 13, at 25 (2006–2007). Cf. Yuval Shany, Faraway, So Close: The Legal Status of Gaza after Israel's Disengagement, *Yearbook of International Humanitarian Law*, vol. 8, 369, at 380 (2006).

32 Convention Relative to the Treatment of Civilians in Time of War, 12 August 1949, Art. 6, 75 UNTS 287.

CHAPTER 18

1 Green Hackworth, *Digest of International Law* (Washington: U.S. Government Printing Office 1940), vol. 1, at 161.

2 Vaughan Lowe, *International Law* (Oxford: Oxford University Press 2007), at 161–166.

3 Hersch Lauterpacht, *Recognition in International Law* (Cambridge: Cambridge University Press 1947), at 26.

4 David Raič, *Statehood and the Law of Self-Determination* (Hague: Kluwer 2002), at 128–134.

5 Ibid. at 134–140.

6 John Dugard, *Recognition and the United Nations* (Cambridge: Grotius 1987), at 81–111. Stefan Talmon, The Duty Not to 'Recognize as Lawful' a Situation Created by the Illegal Use of Force or Other Serious Breaches of a *Jus Cogens* Obligation: An Obligation without Real Substance? in Christian Tomuschat and Jean-Marc Thouvenin, eds., *The Fundamental Rules of the International Legal Order*: Jus Cogens *and Obligations* Erga Omnes (Leiden: Martinus Nijhoff 2006), 99, at 117–118.

7 Summary of Practice of the Secretary-General as Depositary of Multilateral Treaties, UN Doc. ST/LEG/7/Rev.1 (1999).

8 President of Russia, Decree "On recognition of the Republic of South Ossetia," 26 August 2008 (electronic, in Russian), www.kremlin.ru/text/docs/2008/08/205758.shtml.

9 Nii Lante Wallace-Bruce, *Claims to Statehood in International Law* (New York: Carlton Press 1994), at 74.

10 Convention on Rights and Duties of States, Art. 7, Montevideo, 26 December 1933, 165 LNTS 19.

11 Lauterpacht, at 380.

12 Conclusions of a Meeting of the Cabinet, 10 Downing Street, 17 January 1949, 11 a.m., at 17, Cabinet 3 (49), Secret, CAB 128/15.

13 Lauterpacht, at 376.

14 Ian Brownlie, *Principles of Public International Law* (Oxford: Clarendon Press 1998), at 94.

15 Admission of the State whose application is contained in document A/47/876-S/25147 to membership in the United Nations, GA Res. 47/225, UN Doc. A/RES/47/225, 8 April 1993. SC Res. 817, 7 April 1993.

16 Crawford, (Israel (1948–1949) and Palestine (1998–1999)), at 114, note 92.

17 Letter dated 8 March 1950 from the Secretary-General to the President of the Security Council transmitting a memorandum on the legal aspects of the problem of representation in the United Nations, UN Doc. S/1466, 8 March 1950.

18 Lie was referring to the government that had established itself on the Chinese mainland in 1949 for what it called the People's Republic of China, forcing the prior government, which referred to the state as Republic of China, to flee to Taiwan.

19 Ibid.

20 Admission of a State to the United Nations (Charter, Art. 4), Advisory Opinion, 1948 ICJ 57, at 62.

21 Malbone W. Graham, *The League of Nations and the Recognition of States* (Berkeley: University of California Press 1942), at 31–33. Dugard, at 18–19.

22 James Crawford, *The Creation of States in International Law* (Oxford: Clarendon Press 2006), at 438, note 247.
23 Ibid. at 438, citing Reparation for Injuries Suffered in the Service of the United Nations, Advisory Opinion, 1949 ICJ 174, at 185.
24 A reference to the United Nations.
25 In the context of facts underlying the request for an advisory opinion, the "defendant State" would have been Israel.
26 As of the date of the incident, Israel was not yet a member state of the United Nations.
27 149 ICJ at 185.
28 22 U.S.C. §288, annotation (listing states designated pursuant to this statute by President as public international organizations).
29 Organization of American States, Charter, Art. 133 (giving the OAS legal capacity in the territory of member states). 22 U.S.C. §288 (acknowledging legal capacity of public international organizations in the territory of the United States by designation of the President, which took place for OAS in 1954).
30 UN Charter, Art. 27(3).
31 UN Charter, Art. 18(2).
32 UN General Assembly, 207th plenary meeting, UN Doc. A/PV.207, 11 May 1949.

CHAPTER 19

1 Jeffrey L. Dunoff, Steven R. Ratner, and David Wippman, *International Law: Norms, Actors, Process* (New York: Aspen 2006), at 115.
2 Ukraine and Belorussia became UN members on 24 October 1945.
3 UN Charter, Art. 4.
4 P.P. Kremnev, Autonomy of Soviet Socialist Republics in International Relations, *Russian Law: Theory and Practice* 218, at 228 (2009).
5 USSR Constitution, 5 December 1936, Art. 15.
6 Ibid., Art. 14.
7 Ibid., Art. 18(a), as amended Vedomosti Verkhovnogo Soveta SSSR [Gazette of the Supreme Soviet of the USSR], 1944, no. 8, item 303 (1 February 1944).
8 *Belorusskaia SSR v mezhdunarodnykh otnosheniiakh: mezhdunarodnye dogovory, konventsii i soglasheniia Belorusskoi SSR s inostrannymi gosudarstvami (1944–1959)* [Belorussian SSR in International Relations: International treaties, conventions and agreements of the Belorussian SSR with Foreign States (1944–1959)] (Minsk: Academy of Sciences of the Belorussian SSR 1960).
9 Kremnev, at 221.
10 Ibid. at 222–223.
11 General Framework Agreement for Peace in Bosnia and Herzegovina, Annex 10, Art. 1(2), 14 December 1995, UN Doc. A/50/790.
12 Ibid., Art. 2(1)(a).

13 Ibid., Art. 5.
14 Kevin Sullivan, Bosnia Runs Through Its Elections, But the Biggest Test Is for the West, *Christian Science Monitor*, 14 September 1998, at 8.
15 Rosa Ehrenreich Brooks, Failed States, or the State as Failure? *University of Chicago Law Review*, vol. 72, 1159 (2005).
16 Concluding observations of the Human Rights Committee: Democratic Republic of the Congo, para. 4, UN Doc. CCPR/C/COD/CO/3, 26 April 2006.
17 SC Res. 794, UN Doc. S/INF/48 (1992).
18 UN Security Council, 3145th meeting, UN Doc. S/PV.3145, 3 December 1992, at 27–28.
19 Dunoff, Ratner, and Wippman, at 116.
20 David Raič, *Statehood and the Law of Self-Determination* (Hague: Kluwer 2002), at 70.
21 James Crawford, *The Creation of States in International Law* (Oxford: Clarendon Press 2006), at 720–723.
22 GA Res. 1480, 20 September 1960. At the time of independence, the name of the DRC was Republic of the Congo.
23 Crawford (*The Creation of States in International Law* [2006]), at 57.
24 Joint Declaration (Guinea-Bissau, Portugal), Algiers, 26 August 1974, reprinted in *Revue générale de droit international public*, vol. 78, at 1252–53 (1974).
25 GA Res. 3205, 17 September 1974.
26 Yugoslav Region Tense after Vote on Separation, *Toronto Star*, 2 March 1992, at 10.
Tim Judah, Bosnia goes for all-out recognition, Times (London), 7 March 1992 (Overseas news).
27 Mary Curtius, US gives backing to 3 Yugoslav republics, *Boston Globe*, 8 April 1992, at 2.
28 GA Res. 46/237, 22 May 1992.
29 Raič, at 414–418.
30 Jorri Duursma, *Fragmentation and the International Relations of Micro-States: Self-Determination and Statehood* (Cambridge: Cambridge University Press 1996), at 261.
31 Ibid. at 305. Jeffrey L. Dunoff, Steven R. Ratner, and David Wippman, *International Law: Norms, Actors, Process* (New York: Aspen 2006), at 116. Georges Grinda, *The Principality of Monaco: State, International Status, Institutions* (Hague: Asser Press 2006) at 11–13.
32 Grinda, at 32.
33 Treaty on the Admission of Monegasque Nationals to Certain Public Positions in France and on the Recruitment of Certain Civil Servants of the Principality, Art. 5, 28 July 1930, 981 UNTS 369, as implemented by exchange of letters of 7 May 1973. See Duursma, at 283.
34 Treaty establishing the relations of France with the Principality of Monaco, Art. 1, 17 July 1918, 981 UNTS 359. See also Dunoff, Ratner, and Wippman, at 116 (noting that Monaco's defense is the responsibility of France).
35 Ibid., Art. 2. Duursma, at 307.

36 Treaty establishing the relations of France with the Principality of Monaco, Art. 3, 17 July 1918, 981 UNTS 359.
37 Raič, at 77.
38 Stanley K. Laughlin, *The Law of United States Territories and Affiliated Jurisdictions* (Danvers MA: Thomson Legal 1995), at 472–475.
39 Dunoff, Ratner, and Wippman, at 116.
40 Compact of Free Association (US-Marshall Islands-Federated States of Micronesia), 14 January 1986, U.S. Congress, Statutes at Large, vol. 99, at 1770.
41 Ibid., Sec. 311(a).
42 Ibid., Sec. 311(b)(3).
43 Ibid., Sec. 312.
44 Ibid., Sec. 311(b)(2).
45 Ibid., Sec. 313(a).
46 Ibid., Sec. 123(a).
47 UN Charter, Art. 102.
48 Letter dated 14 February 1986 from the representative of the Union of Soviet Socialist Republics to the Secretary-General, UN Doc. S/17838: Annex: Text of the statement, in Security Council Official Records, Supplement for January, February, and March 1986, at 76–77.
49 GA Res. 46/2, 17 September 1991. GA Res. 46/3, 17 September 1991.
50 Compact of Free Association (US-Palau), 10 January 1986, U.S. Congress, Statutes at Large, vol. 100, at 3672.
51 UN Doc. A/RES/49/63, 15 December 1994.
52 Ibid., Sec. 312.
53 Ibid., Sec. 311.
54 Ibid., Sec. 313.
55 Ibid., Sec. 352.
56 Ibid., Sec. 123.
57 Jerusalem, GA Res. 63/30, UN Doc. A/RES/63/30, 23 January 2009 (resolution criticizing Israel for applying its own laws to east Jerusalem adopted 163 to 6 (Israel, Marshall Islands, Micronesia, Nauru, Palau, United States).
58 An Act to make provision for self-government by the people of the Cook Islands (other than Niue) and to provide a constitution for those islands, Act 69 (NZ), 17 November 1964.
59 Niue Constitution Act, Act 42 (NZ), 19 October 1974.
60 Dunoff, Ratner, and Wippman, at 116.
61 *Multilateral Treaties Deposited with the Secretary-General (status as at 31 December 2006)*, at xxviii.
62 UN Security Council recommends admission of new members, TASS, 11 August 1991.
63 Elihu Lauterpacht, Sovereignty – Myth or Reality, *International Affairs* (Royal Institute of International Affairs), vol. 73, 137, at 141 (1997).
64 R. Y. Jennings, Sovereignty and International Law, in Gerard Kreijen, ed., *State, Sovereignty, and International Governance* (Oxford: Oxford University Press 2002), 27, at 33.
65 Lauterpacht, (Sovereignty – Myth or Reality), at 141.

CHAPTER 20

1 UN Security Council, 6123rd meeting, UN Doc. S/PV.6123, 11 May 2009, at 12.
2 Dominican Republic strikes "diplomatic balance" with Israel, Palestine, *Dominican Today*, 14 July 2009, www.dominicantoday.com
3 General Assembly Resolution 60/251. 5/1. Human Rights Council, Institution-building of the United Nations Human Rights Council, Res. 5/1, 18 June 2007.
4 Statute of the International Court of Justice, Art. 36(2).
5 Convention concerning the Protection of the World Cultural and Natural Heritage, 16 November 1972, 1037 UNTS 151.
6 Ibid., Art. 31.
7 GA Res. 2625, 24 October 1970, Annex: Declaration of Principles of International Law concerning Friendly Relations and Co-operation among States in accordance with the Charter of the Untied Nations, Principle 5, para. 4.
8 Palestinian state may have to be abandoned: Erakat, Reuters, 4 November 2009.

Bibliography

Alexander, Charles Henry. Israel in Fieri, *International Law Quarterly*, vol. 4, 423 (1951).

Al-Haq Position Paper on Issues Arising from the Palestinian Authority's Submission of a Declaration to the Prosecutor of the International Criminal Court under Article 12(3) of the Rome Statute, December 14, 2009 (Ramallah: Al-Haq) (Michael Kearney, Stijn Denayer), accessible at www. alhaq.org.

Al-Kidwa, Nasser. Re-declaring Palestinian Statehood: Fears and Expectations, in *May 4, 1999: Implications of Declaring the State* (Washington DC: Center for Policy Analysis on Palestine 1999).

Allain, Jean. *On Achieving Palestinian Statehood: Concepts, Ends and Means from the Perspective of International Law* (Birzeit: Ibrahim Abu-Lughod Institute of International Studies 2002).

International Law in the Middle East: Closer to Power Than Justice (Aldershot: Ashgate 2004).

Anghie, Antony. Colonialism and the Birth of International Institutions: Sovereignty, Economy, and the Mandate System of the League of Nations, *New York University Journal of International Law and Politics*, vol. 34, 513 (2002).

Imperialism, Sovereignty and the Making of International Law (Cambridge: Cambridge University Press 2004).

Antonius, George. *The Arab Awakening: The Story of the Arab National Movement* (Beirut: Khayats 1938).

Avnery, Uri. *My Friend, the Enemy* (Westport CT: Lawrence Hill 1986).

Banerjee, Malabika. *The Nonaligned Movement* (Calcutta: Firma KLM 1982).

Becker, Tal. International Recognition of a Unilaterally Declared Palestinian State: Legal and Policy Dilemmas, Jerusalem Center for Public Affairs (electronic), www.jcpa.org/art/becker2.htm (circa 2000).

Ben-Naftali, Orna, Aeyal M. Gross, and Keren Michaeli, Illegal Occupation: Framing the Occupied Palestinian Territory, *Berkeley Journal of International Law*, vol. 23, 551 (2005).

Bentwich, Norman. Mandated Territories: Palestine and Mesopotamia (Iraq), *British Year Book of International Law*, vol. 2, 48 (1921–22).

Nationality in Mandated Territories Detached from Turkey, *British Year Book of International Law*, vol. 7, 97 (1926).

Palestine Nationality and the Mandate, *Journal of Comparative Legislation and International Law*, vol. 21, 230 (1939).

The Mandates System (London: Longmans 1930).

Benvenisti, Eyal. *The International Law of Occupation* (Princeton: Princeton University Press 1993).

The Origins of the Concept of Belligerent Occupation, *Law and History Review*, vol. 26, 621 (2008).

Benvenisti, Eyal, and Eyal Zamir, Private Claims to Property in the Future Israeli-Palestinian Settlement, *American Journal of International Law*, vol. 89, 295 (1995).

Bishara, Azmi. 4 May 1999 and Palestinian Statehood: To Declare or Not to Declare, *Journal of Palestine Studies*, vol. 28 (no. 2), 5 (Winter 1999).

Bisharat, George E. *Palestinian Lawyers and Israeli Rule: Law and Disorder in the West Bank* (Austin: University of Texas Press 1989).

Bodin, Jean. *De la République, traité de Jean Bodin, ou traité de gouvernement* (Paris: Quillau 1756, orig. pub'd 1583).

Boyle, Francis A. *Palestine, Palestinians and International Law* (Atlanta: Clarity Press 2003).

The Creation of the State of Palestine, *European Journal of International Law*, vol. 1, 301 (1990).

Breger, Marshall J., and Shelby R. Quast. International Commercial Arbitration: A Case Study of the Areas under Control of the Palestinian Authority, *Case Western Reserve Journal of International Law*, vol. 32, 185 (2000).

Brierly, J.L. *The Law of Nations: An Introduction to the International Law of Peace* (Oxford: Clarendon Press 1928).

Brooks, Rosa Ehrenreich. Failed States, or the State as Failure?, *University of Chicago Law Review*, vol. 72, 1159 (2005).

Brownlie, Ian. *Principles of Public International Law* (Oxford: Clarendon Press 1998).

Cassese, Antonio. The Israel-PLO Agreement and Self-Determination, *European Journal of International Law*, vol. 4, 564 (1993).

Cattan, Henry. *Le partage de la Palestine du point de vue juridique: Conférence prononcée à l'Université de Berne le 30 novembre 1970 sous les auspices de l'Association Suisse-Arabe, et à Genève, le 1er décembre 1970, à la salle de l'Athénée sous les auspices du Group d'Etude sur le Moyen-Orient* (Geneva: Group d'Etude sur le Moyen-Orient 1971).

The Palestine Question (London: Croom Helm 1988).

The Arab-Israeli Conflict and the Principles of Justice, *Revue Égyptienne de droit international*, vol. 28, 44 (1972).

Chaigne-Oudin, Anne-Lucie. *La France et les rivalités occidentales au Levant: Syrie-Liban 1918–1939* (Paris: L'Harmattan 2006).

Cobban, Helena. *The Palestinian Liberation Organisation: People, Power and Politics* (Cambridge: Cambridge University Press 1984).

Cocks, F. Seymour. *The Secret Treaties and Understandings: Text of the Available Documents* (London: Union of Democratic Control 1918).

Cohen, Aharon. *Israel and the Arab World* (New York: Funk & Wagnalls 1970).

Cohen, Michael J. *The Origins and Evolution of the Arab-Zionist Conflict* (Berkeley: University of California Press 1987).

Colombe, Marcel. Le problème de 'l'entité Palestinienne' dans les relations inter-arabes, *Orient* (Paris), vol. 8, 57 (1964).

Cotran, Eugene. Some Legal Aspects of the Declaration of Principles: A Palestinian View, in Eugene Cotran and Chibli Mallat, eds., *The Arab-Israeli Accords: Legal Perspectives* (London: Kluwer 1996).

Crawford, James. *The Creation of States in International Law* (Oxford: Clarendon Press 1979).

The Creation of States in International Law (Oxford: Clarendon Press 2006).

Crawford, James. Israel (1948–1949) and Palestine (1998–1999): Two Studies in the Creation of States, in Guy S. Goodwin-Gill and Stefan Talmon, eds., *The Reality of International Law: Essays in Honour of Ian Brownlie* (Oxford: Clarendon Press 1999), 95.

Crawford, James. The Creation of the State of Palestine: Too Much Too Soon?, *European Journal of International Law*, vol. 1, 307 (1990).

Dajani, Omar M. Stalled Between Seasons: The International Legal Status of Palestine During the Interim Period, *Denver Journal of International Law and Policy*, vol. 26, 27 (1997).

Davis, Helen Miller. *Constitutions, Electoral Laws, Treaties of States in the Near and Middle East* (Durham: Duke University Press 1953).

Degras, Jane, ed. *Soviet Documents on Foreign Policy* (London: Oxford University Press 1951).

Denza, Eileen. *Diplomatic Law: Commentary on the Vienna Convention on Diplomatic Relations* (Oxford: Oxford University Press 2008).

Diena, Giulio. Les mandats internationaux, *Recueil des cours* (Hague Academy of International Law), vol. 5, 211 (1924-IV).

Dinstein, Yoram. *War, Aggression and Self-Defence* (Cambridge: Cambridge University Press 2005).

Dugard, John. *Recognition and the United Nations* (Cambridge: Grotius 1987).

Dunoff, Jeffrey L., Steven R. Ratner, and David Wippman. *International Law: Norms, Actors, Process* (New York: Aspen 2006).

Duursma, Jorri. *Fragmentation and the International Relations of Micro-States: Self-Determination and Statehood* (Cambridge: Cambridge University Press 1996).

Eban, Abba. *An Autobiography* (New York: Random House 1977).

Eisenman, Robert H. *Islamic Law in Palestine and Israel* (Leiden: E.J. Brill 1978).

Esber, Rosemarie M. *Under the Cover of War: The Zionist Expulsion of the Palestinians* (Alexandria VA: Arabicus 2008).

Eshel, Benzion. How to Found a New State: The Case of Israel, in *Public Administration in Israel and Abroad 1967: An Annual Collection of Articles* (Jerusalem: Israel Institute of Public Administration 1968).

Farhi, Carol. On the Legal Status of the Gaza Strip, in Meir Shamgar, ed., *Military Government in the Territories Administered by Israel 1967–1980: The Legal Aspects* (1982), vol. 1, 61.

Fauchille, Paul. *Traité de droit international public* (Paris: Rousseau 1922).

Feinberg, Nathan. *On an Arab Jurist's Approach to Zionism and the State of Israel* (Jerusalem: Magnes Press 1971).

Feldman, Ilana. *Governing Gaza: Bureaucracy, Authority, and the Work of Rule, 1917–1967* (Durham NC: Duke University Press 2008).

  Waiting for Palestine: Refracted Citizenship and Latent Sovereignty in Gaza, *Citizenship Studies*, vol. 12 (no. 5), 447 (2008).

Feuer, G. Les Accords Passés par les Gouvernements Jordanien et Libanais Avec les Organisations Palestiniennes (1968–1970), *Annuaire Français de Droit International*, vol. 16, 177 (1970).

Filiu, Jean-Pierre. François Mitterand and the Palestinians: 1956–95, *Journal of Palestine Studies*, vol. 38 (no. 2), 24 (2009).

Fischbach, Michael R. Palestine Liberation Army, in Philip Mattar, ed., *Encyclopedia of the Palestinians* (New York: Facts on File 2000).

Flapan, Simha. *The Birth of Israel: Myths and Realities* (New York: Pantheon 1987).

Flournoy, Richard W., Jr., and Manley O. Hudson, eds. *A Collection of Nationality Laws of Various Countries as Contained in Constitutions, Statutes and Treaties* (New York: Oxford University Press 1929).

Flory, Maurice. La Naissance d'un État Palestinien, *Revue générale de droit international public*, vol. 93, 385 (1989).

Frisch, Hillel. *Countdown to Statehood: Palestinian State Formation in the West Bank and Gaza* (Albany: State University of New York Press 1998).

  The Palestinian Military: Between Militias and Armies (London: Routledge 2008)

Gerson, Allan. *Israel, the West Bank and International Law* (London: Frank Cass 1978).

Goodwin-Gill, Guy, and Jane McAdam. *The Refugee in International Law* (Oxford: Oxford University Press 2007).

Graham, Malbone W. *The League of Nations and the Recognition of States* (Berkeley: University of California Press 1942).

Greenspan, Morris. *The Modern Law of Land Warfare* (Berkeley: University of California Press 1959).

Gresh, Alain, and Didier Billion, eds. *Actualités de l'État palestinien* (Brussels: Éditions complexe 2000).

Grief, Howard. *The Legal Foundation and Borders of Israel under International Law: A Treatise on Jewish Sovereignty over the Land of Israel* (Jerusalem: Mazo Publishers 2008).

Grinda, Georges. *The Principality of Monaco: State, International Status, Institutions* (Hague: Asser Press 2006).

Gross, Leo. Voting in the Security Council and the PLO, *American Journal of International Law*, vol. 70, 470 (1976).

Hackworth, Green. *Digest of International Law* (Washington: U.S. Government Printing Office 1940).

Hall, H. Duncan. *Mandates, Dependencies and Trusteeship* (London: Stevens & Sons 1948).

Hallaj, Muhammad. Palestinian Statehood, in Winston A. Van Horne, ed., *Global Convulsions: Race, Ethnicity, and Nationalism at the End of the Twentieth Century* (Albany: State University of New York Press 1997).

Hansell, Herbert and Nicholas Rostow. *Legal Implications of May 4, 1999* (Washington DC: Washington Institute for Near East Policy 1999).

Hirst, David. *The Gun and the Olive Branch: The Roots of Violence in the Middle East* (1984).

Hobson, J.A. The Open Door, in C.R. Buxton, ed., *Towards a Lasting Settlement* (New York: Macmillan 1916), 87.

Towards International Government (London: George Allen & Unwin 1915).

Huneidi, Sahar. *A Broken Trust: Herbert Samuel, Zionism, and the Palestinians 1920–1925* (London: I.B. Tauris 2001).

Hyamson, Albert M. *Palestine under the Mandate 1920–1948* (London: Methuen & Co. 1950).

Hyde, Charles. *International Law Chiefly as Interpreted and Applied by the United States* (Boston: Little, Brown 1922).

Ingrams, Doreen. *Palestine Papers 1917–1922: Seeds of Conflict* (London: John Murray 1970).

Jennings, R.Y. Sovereignty and International Law, in Gerard Kreijen, ed., *State, Sovereignty, and International Governance* (Oxford: Oxford University Press 2002), 27.

The Acquisition of Territory in International Law (Manchester: University of Manchester Press 1963).

Jessup, Philip C. *The Birth of Nations* (New York: Columbia University Press 1974).

Jiryis, Sabri. *The Arabs in Israel* (New York: Monthly Review Press 1976).

Kassim, Anis F. A Response to Dr. Evyatar Levine, *Denver Journal of International Law and Policy*, vol. 10, 259 (1980).

Legal Systems and Developments in Palestine, *Palestine Yearbook of International Law*, vol. 1, 19 (1984).

The Palestine Liberation Organization's Claim to Status: A Juridical Analysis under International Law, *Denver Journal of International Law and Policy*, vol. 9, at 18 (1980).

The Palestinians: From Hyphenated to Integrated Citizenship, in Nils S. Butenschon, Uri Davis and Manuel Hassassian, *Citizenship and the State in the Middle East: Approaches and Applications* (New York: Syracuse University Press 2000), 201.

Kattan, Victor. *From Coexistence to Conquest: International Law and the Origins of the Arab-Israeli Conflict, 1891–1949* (New York: Pluto Press 2009).

The Nationality of Denationalized Palestinians, in Victor Kattan, ed., *The Palestine Question in International Law* (London: British Institute of International and Comparative Law 2008), 121.

Khalidi, Rashid. *The Iron Cage: The Story of the Palestinian Struggle for Statehood* (Boston: Beacon Press 2007).

Khalidi, Walid. Plan Dalet: The Zionist Master Plan for the Conquest of Palestine, *Middle East Forum*, 22 (November 1961).

Khalil, Asem. *Which Constitution for the Palestinian Legal System?* (dissertation) (Rome: Pontificia Universitas Lateranensis Institutum Utriusque Iuris 2003).

Khalil, Muhammad. *The Arab States and the Arab League: A Documentary Record* (Beirut: Khayats 1962).

Kimche, Jon and David. *Both Sides of the Hill: Britain and the Palestine War* (London: Secker & Warburg 1960).

Kirgis, Frederic L., Jr. Admission of "Palestine" as a Member of a Specialized Agency and Withholding the Payment of Assessments in Response, *American Journal of International Law*, vol. 84, 218 (1990).

Koestler, Arthur. *Bricks to Babel* (New York: Random House 1980).

Krasner, Stephen D. Rethinking the Sovereign State Model, in Michael Cox, Ken Booth and Tim Dunne, eds., *Empires, Systems, and States: Great Transformations in International Politics* (Cambridge: Cambridge University Press 2001), 17.

Laserson, Max M. *On the Mandate: Documents, Statements, Law and Judgments Relating to and Arising form the Mandate for Palestine* (Tel Aviv: Igereth 1937).

Laughlin, Stanley K. *The Law of United States Territories and Affiliated Jurisdictions* (Danvers MA: Thomson Legal 1995).

Lauterpacht, Elihu. Sovereignty – Myth or Reality, *International Affairs* (Royal Institute of International Affairs), vol. 73, 137 (1997).

Lauterpacht, Hersch. *Recognition in International Law* (Cambridge: Cambridge University Press 1947).

The Mandate under International Law in the Covenant of the League of Nations, in Elihu Lauterpacht, ed., *International Law: Being the Collected Papers of Hersch Lauterpacht* (Cambridge: Cambridge University Press 1977), vol. 3, 29.

Lee, Luke T. and John Quigley, *Consular Law and Practice* (Oxford: Oxford University Press 2008).

Lenin, V.I. Imperialism the Highest Stage of Capitalism, in Robert C. Tucker, ed., *The Lenin Anthology* (New York: Norton, 1975).

Lesch, Ann Mosely. Gaza: History and Politics, in Ann Moseley Lesch and Mark Tesssler, *Israel, Egypt, and the Palestinians: From Camp David to Intifada* (Bloomington: Indiana University Press 1989).

Lewan, Kenneth. Justifications for the Opening of Hostilities in the Middle East, *Revue Égyptienne de droit international*, vol. 26, 88 (1970).

Lilienthal, Alfred M. *What Price Israel?* (Beirut: Institute for Palestine Studies 1953).

Lissitzyn, Oliver. Territorial Entities Other Than States in the Law of Treaties, *Recueil des Cours* (Hague Academy of International Law), vol. 125, 5 (1968-III).

Locke, Richard, and Antony Stewart, *Bantustan Gaza* (London: Zed 1985).

Lorch, Netanel. *The Edge of the Sword: Israel's War of Independence, 1947–1949* (New York: Putnam 1961).

Lowe, Vaughan. *International Law* (Oxford: Oxford University Press 2007).

Mallison, W.T. and S.V. Mallison. An International Law Appraisal of the Juridical Characteristics of the Resistance of the People of Palestine: The Struggle for Human Rights, *Revue Égyptienne de droit international*, vol. 28, 1 (1972).

Marek, Krystyna. *Identity and Continuity of States in Public International Law* (Geneva: E. Droz 1954).

Margalith, Aaron M. *The International Mandates* (Baltimore: Johns Hopkins Press 1930).

Marr, Phebe. *The Modern History of Iraq* (Cambridge MA: Westview 2004).

McDonald, James. *My Mission in Israel, 1948–1951* (New York: Simon & Schuster 1951).

McNair, Arnold. *The Law of Treaties* (Oxford: Clarendon Press 1961).

Meron, Theodor. The Composition of the UN Regional Economic Commissions and the PLO, *International and Comparative Law Quarterly*, vol. 28, 52 (1979).

Miller, David Hunter. *The Drafting of the Covenant* (New York: Putnam 1928).

Millot, Albert. *Les Mandats Internationaux: étude sur l'application de l'Article 22 du Pacte de la Société des Nations* (Paris: Larose 1924).

Mishalani, Philip. The National Question and the PLO, in Fouzi El-Asmar, Uri Davis, and Naim Khader, eds., *Debate on Palestine* (London: Ithaca 1981).

Mogannam, Mogannam E. Palestine Legislation Under the British, *Annals of the American Academy of Political and Social Science*, vol. 164, 47 (1932).

Mogannam, Theodore. Developments in the Legal System of Jordan, *Middle East Journal*, vol. 6, 196 (1952).

Moore, John Norton. *The Arab-Israeli Conflict, Documents* (Princeton: Princeton University Press 1974).

Morris, Benny. Operation Dani and the Palestinian Exodus from Lydda and Ramle in 1948, *Middle East Journal*, vol. 40, 82 (1986).

   The Birth of the Palestinian Refugee Problem, 1947–1949 (New York: Cambridge University Press 1987).

   The Causes and Character of the Arab Exodus from Palestine: the Israel Defence Forces Intelligence Branch Analysis of June 1948, *Middle Eastern Studies*, vol. 22, 5 (1986).

Muslih, Muhammad Y. *The Origins of Palestinian Nationalism* (New York: Columbia University Press 1988).

Myres, S.D., Jr. Constitutional Aspects of the Mandate for Palestine, *Annals of the American Academy of Political and Social Science*, vol. 164, 1 (1932).

Noam, Gilad. Territorial Aspects of the Israeli-Palestinian Conflict: A Legal Perspective on Some Historical and Contemporary Issues, Hebrew University International Law Research Paper No. 6–06 (2005), accessible at www.ssrn.com/abstract=902944.

O'Ballance, Edgar. *The Arab-Israeli War, 1948* (Westport CT: Hyperion Press 1981, orig. pub'd. London: Faber and Faber 1956).

O'Brien, William V. The PLO in International Law, *Boston University International Law Journal*, vol. 2, 349 (1984).

O'Connell, D.P. *State Succession in Municipal Law and International Law* (Cambridge: Cambridge University Press 1967).

The Law of State Succession (Cambridge: Cambridge University Press 1956).

Oppenheim, Lassa. *International Law: A Treatise*, Arnold McNair, ed. (London: Longmans 1928).

International Law: A Treatise, Hersch Lauterpacht, ed. (London: Longmans 1955).

Ott, Andrea, and Ramses Wessel, The EU's External Relations Regime: Multilevel Complexity in an Expanding Union, in Steven Blockmans and Adam Łazowski, eds., *The European Union and its Neighbours : A Legal Appraisal of the EU's Policies of Stabilisation, Partnership and Integration* (Hague: TMC Asser Press 2006), 19.

Pappé, Ilan. *Britain and the Arab-Israeli Conflict, 1948–51* (Oxford: Macmillan Press 1988).

The Ethnic Cleansing of Palestine (Oxford: One World 2006).

Pic, Paul. Le régime du mandat d'après le Traité de Versailles; son application dans le Proche Orient: mandats français en Syrie, anglais en Palestine et Mésopotamie, *Revue Générale de Droit International Public*, vol. 30, 321 (1923).

Pollock, Frederick. *The League of Nations* (London: Stevens and Sons 1922).

Potter, Pitman B. Origin of the System of Mandates under the League of Nations, *American Political Science Review*, vol. 16, 563 (1922).

Pundik, Ron. *The Struggle for Sovereignty: Relations between Great Britain and Jordan, 1946–1951* (Oxford: Blackwell 1994).

Qafisheh, Mutaz. *The International Law Foundations of Palestinian Nationality: A Legal Examination of Nationality in Palestine under Britain's Rule* (Leiden: Martinus Nijhoff 2008).

Quigley, John. *Palestine and Israel: A Challenge to Justice* (Durham: Duke University Press 1990).

The Case for Palestine: An International Law Perspective (Durham: Duke University Press 2005).

The United Nations' Response to Israel's Seizure of the Gaza Strip and West Bank, *Palestine Yearbook of International Law*, vol. 12, 145 (2002–2003).

Raič, David. *Statehood and the Law of Self-Determination* (Hague: Kluwer 2002).

Raphaeli, Nimrod. Gaza under Four Administrations, *Public Administration in Israel and Abroad*, vol. 9, 40 (1969).

Rapport de M. Henri Rolin sur les mandats internationaux, *Annuaire de l'Institut de droit international*, vol. 34(1), 33 (1928) (Rolin 1891–1973).

Rihani, Ameen. Palestine and the Proposed Arab Federation, *Annals of the American Academy of Political and Social Science*, vol. 164, 62 (1932).

Rishmawi, Mona. The Actions of the Palestinian Authority under the Gaza/ Jericho Agreements, in *The Palestine National Authority: A Critical Appraisal* (Washington: Center for Policy Analysis on Palestine 2005), 3.

Robins, Philip. *A History of Jordan* (New York: Cambridge University Press 2004).

Robinson, Glenn E. *Building a Palestinian State: The Incomplete Revolution* (Bloomington: Indiana University Press 1997).

Rolin, Henri (1874–1946). Le Système des mandats coloniaux, *Revue de droit international et de législation comparée*, series 3, vol. 1, 329 (1920).

Rolin, Henri A. (1891–1973). La pratique des mandats internationaux, *Recueil des cours* (Hague Academy of International Law), vol. 19, 530 (1927-IV).

Roosevelt, Kermit. The Partition of Palestine: A Lesson in Power Politics, *Middle East Journal*, vol. 2, 1 (1948).

Rosenne, Shabtai. Israël et les traités internationaux de la Palestine, *Journal du droit international*, vol. 77, 1140 (1950).

The Effect of Change of Sovereignty Upon Municipal Law, *British Year Book of International Law*, vol. 27, 267 (1950).

The Israel Nationality Law 5712–1952 and The Law of Return 5710–1950, *Journal du droit international*, vol. 81, 4 (1954).

Rubenberg, Cheryl. *Israel and the American National Interest* (Urbana IL: University of Illinois Press 1986).

Sabel, Robbie. *Procedure at International Conferences: A Study of the Rules of Procedure at the UN and at Inter-governmental Conferences* (Cambridge: Cambridge University Press 2006).

Said, Wadie. The Obligations of Host Countries to Refugees under International Law: The Case of Lebanon, in Naseer Aruri, *Palestinian Refugees: The Right of Return* (London: Pluto Press 2001), 123.

Salibi, Kamal. *The Modern History of Jordan* (London: I.B. Tauris 1998).

Schermers, Henry G., and Niels M. Blokker, *International Institutional Law: Unity within Diversity* (Boston: Martinus Nijhoff 2003).

Schwarzenberg, Georg. British and Palestinian Nationalities (Notes of Cases), *Modern Law Review*, vol. 3, 164 (1939).

Segev, Tom. *1949: The First Israelis* (New York: Free Press 1986).

Shahwan, Usamah. *Public Administration in Palestine Past and Present* (Lanham MD: University Press of America 2003).

Shamgar, Meir. Legal Concepts and Problems of the Israeli Military Government – The Initial Stage, in Meir Shamgar, ed., *Military Government in the Territories Administered by Israel 1967–1980: The Legal Aspects* (1982), vol. 1, 13.

Shany, Yuval. Faraway, So Close: The Legal Status of Gaza after Israel's Disengagement, *Yearbook of International Humanitarian Law*, vol. 8, 369 (2006).

Shapira, Amos, and Mala Tabory. *New Political Entities in Public and Private International Law With Special Reference to the Palestinian Entity* (Hague: Kluwer Law International 1999).

Sharabi, Hisham. Declaring the State: Opening Remarks, in *May 4, 1999: Implications of Declaring the State* (Washington DC: Center for Policy Analysis on Palestine 1999), 5.

Shehadeh, Raja. *From Occupation to Interim Accords: Israel and the Palestinian Territories* (London: Kluwer 1997).

Occupier's Law: Israel and the West Bank (Washington DC: Institute for Palestine Studies 1985).

Questions of Jurisdiction: A Legal Analysis of the Gaza-Jericho Agreement, *Journal of Palestine Studies*, vol. 23 (no. 4), 18 (1994).

Shiblak, Abbas, and Uri Davis. *Civil and Citizenship Rights of Palestinian Refugees* (Ramallah: Palestinian Diaspora and Refugee Centre 1996).

Shlaim, Avi. *Collusion Across the Jordan: King Abdullah, the Zionist Movement, and the Partition of Palestine* (Oxford: Clarendon Press 1988).

The Rise and Fall of the All-Palestine Government in Gaza, *Journal of Palestine Studies*, vol. 20 (no. 1), 37 (1990).

Stoyanovsky, Jacob. *The Mandate for Palestine* (London: Longmans 1928)

Suny, Ismail. *The Organization of the Islamic Conference* (Jakarta: Pustaka Sinar Harapan 2000).

Suy, Erik. The Status of Observers in International Organizations, *Recueil des cours* (Hague Academy of International Law), vol. 160, 75 (1978-II).

Sykes, Christopher. *Cross Roads to Israel* (London: Collins 1965).

Takkenberg, Lex. *The Status of Palestinian Refugees in International Law* (Oxford: Clarendon Press 1998).

Talhami, Ghada Hashem. *Palestinian Refugees: Pawns to Political Actors* (New York: Nova Science Publishers 2003).

Talmon, Stefan. *Recognition of Governments in International Law: With Particular Reference to Governments in Exile* (Oxford: Clarendon Press 1998).

Recognition of States and Governments in International Law, *Azerbaijan in the World*, vol. 1, no. 19 (1 November 2008) (electronic), http://ada.edu.az/biweekly/issues/158/20090328015413680.html

The Duty Not to "Recognize as Lawful" a Situation Created by the Illegal Use of Force or Other Serious Breaches of a *Jus Cogens* Obligation: An Obligation without Real Substance?, in Christian Tomuschat and Jean-Marc Thouvenin, eds., *The Fundamental Rules of the International Legal Order: Jus Cogens and Obligations Erga Omnes* (Leiden: Martinus Nijhoff 2006), 99.

Toynbee, Arnold. Two Aspects of the Palestine Question, in Arnold Toynbee, *Importance of the Arab World* (Cairo: National Publications House 1962).

Travers, Patrick J. The Legal Effect of United Nations Action in Support of the Palestine Liberation Organization and the National Liberation Movements of Africa, *Harvard International Law Journal*, vol. 17, 561 (1976).

Turack, Daniel C. *The Passport in International Law* (Lexington MA: D.C. Heath 1972).

Upthegrove, Campbell L. *Empire by Mandate: A History of the Relations of Great Britain with the Permanent Mandates Commission of the League of Nations* (New York: Bookman Associates 1954).

Vance, Cyrus. *Hard Choices: Critical Years in America's Foreign Policy* (New York: Simon & Schuster 1983).

Vita, Edoardo. *The Conflict of Laws in Matters of Personal Status in Palestine* (Tel Aviv: S. Bursi 1947).

von Glahn, Gerhard. *The Occupation of Enemy Territory* (Minneapolis: University of Minnesota Press 1957).

Wallace-Bruce, Nii Lante. *Claims to Statehood in International Law* (New York: Carlton Press 1994).

Watson, Geoffrey. *The Oslo Accords: International Law and the Israeli-Palestinian Peace Agreements* (Oxford: Oxford University Press 2000).

Weis, P. *Nationality and Statelessness in International Law* (Alphen aan den Rijn: Sijthoff & Noordhoff 1979).

Welchman, Lynn. *Beyond the Code: Muslim Family Law and the Shari'a Judiciary in the Palestinian West Bank* (Hague: Kluwer Law International 2000).

Wilson, Mary C. *King Abdullah, Britain and the Making of Jordan* (New York: Cambridge University Press 1987).

Wing, Adrien. Legal Decision-Making During the Palestinian Intifada: Embryonic Self-Rule, *Yale Journal of International Law*, vol. 18, 95 (1993).

Wilde, Ralph. *International Territorial Administration: How Trusteeship and the Civilizing Mission Never Went Away* (Oxford: Oxford University Press 2008).

Wright, Quincy. *Mandates under the League of Nations* (Chicago: University of Chicago Press 1930).

Sovereignty of the Mandates, *American Journal of International Law*, vol. 17, 691 (1923).

Young, Hubert. *The Independent Arab* (London: John Murray 1933).

Young, Robert J.C. *Postcolonialism: An Historical Introduction* (Oxford: Blackwell 2001).

Index

Made in United States
North Haven, CT
04 March 2024

49561681R00207